Challenged by C

Women's Colleges Since the 1960s

D1177102

Challenged by Coeducation

Women's Colleges Since the 1960s

Edited by Leslie Miller-Bernal
and Susan L. Poulson

Vanderbilt University Press / Nashville

© 2006 Vanderbilt University Press
All rights reserved
First Edition 2006

10 09 08 07 06   1 2 3 4 5

Printed on acid-free paper.
Manufactured in the United States of America

Library of Congress Cataloging-in-Publication Data

Challenged by coeducation : women's colleges since
    the 1960s / [edited by] Leslie Miller-Bernal,
    Susan L. Poulson.—1st ed.
        p. cm.
Includes index.
ISBN 0-8265-1542-8 (cloth : alk. paper)
ISBN 0-8265-1543-6 (pbk. : alk. paper)
1. Women's colleges—History.
2. Women—Education (Higher)—History.
I. Poulson, Susan L., 1959-
II. Miller-Bernal, Leslie, 1946-
LC1567.C483 2006
378.008209—dc22
    2006010321

To Lisa Marsh Ryerson, a courageous college president.

−Leslie Miller-Bernal

To my parents, Ellen Moore Poulson and Norval Poulson, with love and gratitude.

−Susan L. Poulson

Contents

Preface

Women's colleges are an endangered species. Over the past forty years, three-quarters of them have admitted men, merged with another institution, or closed. From about 230 women's colleges in 1960, there were fewer than 60 in 2005. Most of those that remain struggle to survive, creating educational programs for new populations—part-time, adult, or graduate students—thereby becoming fundamentally different institutions than they were in the 1950s. While researchers have studied the early history of women's colleges and their importance for women's access to higher education, little has been written about their recent transformations.

Challenged by Coeducation explores the recent history of women's colleges in the age of coeducation. It includes institutions that represent the variety among women's colleges: two Seven Sister colleges, three secular independent colleges, two Catholic colleges, a coordinate college, a vocationally based college, a state institution, a historically black college, and, for comparative purposes, two colleges in England's Cambridge University. The book's five sections partly reflect the fundamental outcomes for women's colleges since the 1960s: a brief history of women's colleges; a review of institutions that have adopted coeducation or have closed; studies of several women's colleges that are still single sex; a look at some coordinate women's colleges; and a conclusion that reflects upon the struggles women's colleges face either in maintaining their single-sex status or in striving for gender equity while adopting coeducation.

This decline in women's colleges mirrors a similar, even more drastic change in men's colleges—they have almost disappeared. During the 1960s and 1970s most men's colleges opened their doors to women for financial and social reasons. Since the large majority of male students preferred coeducation, men's colleges had to admit women in order to stay competitive. Many colleges found that coeducation enabled them to increase their revenue by expanding their enrollment and at the same time to become more academically competitive. Yet as we note in our previous work, *Going Coed: Women's Experiences in Formerly Men's Colleges and Universities, 1950–2000,* the admission of women to these institutions did not necessarily bring equity. Many campuses made little preparation for the presence of women, and many of the early women students had to maneuver in a difficult gender environment.

One might think that the transitions to coeducation at men's and women's colleges are parallel experiences. Yet they are not, for men and women have been unequal in society and the effects of coeducation have been very different. Because of the prestige of many formerly men's colleges and universities, academically talented women students have flocked to them, enhancing their competitiveness. In the initial years of coeducation at a women's college, however, men students have not shown a similar desire to attend formerly women's colleges, as Griffen and Daniels document in their chapter on the conversion of Vassar to a coeducational institution. Because women have been a lower-status group in society, men have little to gain by attending a formerly women's college. At some institutions bearing a woman's name, there has even been discussion of changing the name so that the association with a woman is unapparent. Some at Sarah Lawrence, for example, believe that the small proportion of men (26 percent) enrolled decades after men were first admitted is partly attributable to the female name.

The greater mixing of men and women in higher education was both a reflection of and a contributor to the dramatic changes in gender norms in the last half of the twentieth century. So long as women and men were seen as distinctly different in their appetites, ambitions, and talents, sex segregation seemed normal. When the most recent wave of feminism challenged these assumptions, and when the moral force of the civil rights movement confronted the social and legal boundaries that kept some social groups subordinate, Americans were primed to accept a reorganization of gender boundaries. Not only were women students subsequently admitted to formerly men's campuses, but the more sex-neutral environment often spurred further change in their ambitions and in the college campus. Women were freer to plan a future in which marriage and motherhood were optional or additional to a career.

Now that many more options are available to women, the question remains: Why are women's colleges desirable? In an era when women can attend formerly men's colleges, the military academies, and graduate and professional schools, what can women's colleges offer that other colleges cannot?

For many supporters of women's colleges, the answer is that they provide a unique environment with several advantages to women that are unavailable at a coeducational institution. They are filled with role models, a supportive culture and history, and in some institutions, an acceptance of alternative sexual norms. They may also act as a repository for ideas that are critical of the status quo. Women's colleges, in short, may offer a subculture that keeps the dominant culture at a distance. They can challenge the existing order by transforming what seems to be natural and offer alternative views of how society may be organized.

The reality of today's higher education, however, is that few women students want to attend a single-sex college. This means that many women's colleges must admit men to survive as institutions. Some, like Mills College, are successful in resisting this pressure by developing alternative sources of revenue, such as graduate programs. Others, like Wells College, resist coeducation for years only to face it as an inevitability. For those who cherish the subculture of women's colleges and the attention to gender equity that exists at many of them, the question becomes: How does the institution retain as much as possible those desirable qualities of a single-sex college? The case studies of Part Two attempt to answer this, as several institutions give special attention to gender equity at their formerly single-sex college.

Coeducation at formerly women's colleges reflects a common reaction to subordinate groups that suddenly gain access to institutions long controlled by dominant groups. In the beginning, there is unfettered enthusiasm for mixing. When the issue of coeducation appeared in the 1960s, it experienced tremendous momentum and general cultural approval. Many at women's colleges were eager for coeducation or affiliation with a men's college. Most Vassar students, for example, approved coeducation when the college admitted men in 1969. A few years later, St. Mary's College students were deeply disappointed when a potential merger with nearby University of Notre Dame fell through. During the 1970s, however, as a more sophisticated understanding of equity developed, enthusiasm for coeducation moderated. Many began to see the challenges for women in formerly male environments that had mostly male role models and where women were sometimes treated as sex objects. From this perspective, women's colleges seemed a supportive alternative. Many at women's colleges became more opposed to the possibility of coeducation. A similar pattern may be seen in the initial enthusiasm many blacks felt for racial integration in schools and the subsequent disenchantment when black students entered an institution that had few black role models and less sensitivity to race issues. Black students have a higher graduation rate from historically black colleges and universities than from other types of institutions. In short, students and educators began to see that in education, context can be as important as access.

Some would argue that affiliated women's colleges—those that are a part of a larger university but are still single sex—have the best of both worlds. In their studies of Barnard and of Girton and Newnham, Andrea Walton and Leslie Miller-Bernal show how the central location of the women's colleges affiliated with Columbia and Cambridge Universities can retain the positive aspects of a women's college.

The editors bring historical and sociological insights to this study. Leslie Miller-Bernal is a professor of sociology who has written extensively on gender in higher education. She first noticed the lack of scholarship on the recent history of women's colleges several years ago at a conference at Wilson College, a small women's college in southern Pennsylvania. As a faculty member at Wells College, she has been an integral part of the transition to coeducation there. Susan Poulson is a professor of history at the University of Scranton, a Jesuit institution in northeastern Pennsylvania. She, too, has written on gender and higher education, with a particular focus on Catholic institutions, where in recent decades the move toward coeducation has been the most dramatic.

We have several purposes for writing this book. The first is to describe in general terms what has happened to women's colleges since the 1960s. In doing so, we review the common pressures and incentives in U.S. higher education that push women's colleges toward coeducation. By looking at women's colleges that have survived, we hope to document how these institutions adapted in order to retain their single-sex status. The trend toward coeducation will continue. It is impossible to predict where it will stop and how many women's colleges will remain in the future. But by documenting how formerly women's colleges attempt to retain their focus on gender equity, we hope to give some guidance to institutions undergoing that process. Finally, we hope to convey the importance of gender as a factor in higher education, both in the past and in the present. It has been a central characteristic in the organization of U.S. colleges and universities, even at institutions that have long been coeducational. As we note in this book and in our previous book on women in formerly men's colleges and universities, the mere mixing of men and women in an institution does not bring equality; it is the nature of that mixing which determines whether the best climate for all students will prevail.

PART I

The Place of Women's Colleges in Higher Education

1

Introduction

Changes in the Status and Functions of Women's Colleges over Time

Leslie Miller-Bernal

People tend to associate women's colleges with the past, when women's and men's spheres were more separate than they are today. For this reason it may be surprising to learn that the first college in the United States that accepted women was coeducational—Oberlin College in Ohio, which admitted women in 1837. And yet the generalization still holds: Most of the few women who attended college in the mid-nineteenth century did go to women's colleges. Most colleges and universities were for men only, so women's colleges were important to women who wished to receive higher education.

This chapter traces the rise and fall of women's colleges from their beginnings in the mid–nineteenth century to their precarious position in the early twenty-first century. Not only has the number of women's colleges declined dramatically, from 233 as recently as 1960 to about 58 today (see Appendix 2), but the types of students and their reasons for attending single-sex institutions have also changed markedly. Today many people question whether women's colleges will continue to survive, despite the ardent belief of many of their students and alumnae that they provide the best education for women.

Origins of Women's Colleges

Scholars debate which was the first women's college. Some institutions described themselves as "colleges" even though that designation seems unwarranted given the age of their students and the curriculum they offered. Candidates for the earliest women's college include Mary Sharp in Tennessee, which awarded its first degrees in 1855, and Elmira in upstate New York, which opened in 1855.

Both these antebellum institutions required their students to study Greek, a hallmark of the curriculum of men's colleges of the time. Neither of these colleges fared well, however; Mary Sharp closed in 1896, and Elmira shut down for a while during the Civil War.[1]

Some women's colleges developed from seminaries, for example, Mills (see Chapter 7), Mount Holyoke, and Wheaton (see Chapter 3). Seminaries were not institutions for religious training but rather combined secondary education with some college work while they strictly regulated students' lives. Even if they were not first seminaries, early women's colleges often modeled themselves after seminaries. Vassar College, for example, opened in 1865 with one large seminary-like building in which all students and women faculty lived together (see Chapter 2). Such living arrangements enabled women teachers to monitor students closely to fulfill the colleges' claims that they provided a homelike atmosphere in which young women were trained to be "ladies." Students' posture and voice, for example, could be improved on a daily basis.

The heyday for women's colleges occurred at the end of the Civil War. Vassar, located in Poughkeepsie, New York, was the most famous women's college of that era because from its beginning, it had an endowment and a rigorous curriculum. Wells College in Aurora, New York, opened only three years later, in 1868 (see Chapter 6). Only for its first two years was Wells called a seminary, but its lack of endowment, its weak academic standards, and its large preparatory department for students not ready to do collegiate work meant that it functioned as a seminary for many more years. By 1885 such famous women's colleges as Smith, Wellesley, and Bryn Mawr had opened.

Opposition to Women's Higher Education

While today it is common to ask why women were prohibited from studying at most colleges in the nineteenth century, at the time people often asked: Why should women go to college? After all, women's "natural" place was in the home, looking after their husbands and children. Even if a woman did not marry and needed to support herself, most occupations, including such prestigious ones as medicine and law, did not require a college degree; many practitioners in these fields learned through apprenticeships. Also retarding the development of collegiate education for women was the widespread belief that women harmed their reproductive organs by too much study. In a book that was very popular at the time, *Sex in Education; or a Fair Chance for the Girls*, retired Harvard professor and doctor Edward Clarke claimed that women would experience dire effects if they failed to obey the "law of periodicity." He based his research mainly on seven women, including a student at Vassar who fainted during gym because, Clarke argued, she should have been quiet at that time of the month. Moreover, when she was examined, she was found to have "an arrest of the development of the reproductive apparatus" and, in place of developed breasts, "the milliner had supplied the organs Nature should have grown."[2]

Women researchers and organizations that favored women's higher education, such as the influential Association of Collegiate Alumnae (ACA), refuted Clarke's research. Yet his book resonated with popular beliefs and managed to frighten young women, including the later president of Bryn Mawr College and famous feminist M. Carey Thomas.[3] Opposition to educating women may have been overcome more by practical concerns than by rational argument. As more and more communities established public schools, they favored hiring women as teachers since they received half or less of men's salaries. Teachers, of course, needed to be educated. A few other occupations opening up to women, such as clerical work, also required education.[4]

Women's Educational Options by the Late Nineteenth and Early Twentieth Centuries

Women's colleges remained important for women's access to higher education throughout the nineteenth century. Many people saw them as more appropriate for women than were coeducational institutions, since their curricula could be modified in ways that were believed to fit women's talents and proclivities. The suspicion that women's colleges were thus not as intellectually challenging as men's colleges led most nineteenth-century women's rights advocates to favor coeducational institutions.[5] Yet women's colleges did improve academically in response to student and alumnae pressures, as well as to the exacting standards of the ACA, the forerunner of the American Association of University Women. They closed their preparatory departments and offered only collegiate-level education, all the time employing mainly women faculty, thus providing "critical entry points" for women wishing to enter academic life.[6] Nonetheless, even by 1880, a majority of women were being educated in coeducational institutions.[7]

Single-sex institutions for women and men were more prevalent in certain areas. Women's and men's colleges were mostly found in the Northeast, where many older colleges existed and which was a fairly wealthy region, and in the South, where people tended to adhere to traditional gender roles. In the Midwest and West, in contrast, frontier conditions often necessitated economizing through coeducation; gender roles were also more flexible and egalitarian, not as supportive of the separate-spheres ideology favored in more settled regions. Because of such practical and ideological factors, colleges like Oberlin (1833) and Antioch (1852) in Ohio, as well as some universities like Chicago (1892), opened as coeducational institutions.[8]

Significant differences in preferences for single-sex education also existed among segments of the population defined by religious and ethnic affiliation.

Catholic institutions, almost all single sex, were founded later than were the first secular or Protestant-affiliated women's colleges. They developed as the daughters of Catholic immigrant groups increasingly sought higher education and would have attended secular institutions in their absence. They also provided education for nuns or, more generally, the women religious. The earliest Catholic women's college to grant a bachelor's degree was College of Notre Dame in Maryland, which awarded its first college degrees in 1899 (see Chapter 10). The rate of founding of Catholic women's colleges increased over the first few decades of the twentieth century, with the greatest number, thirty-seven, opening between 1915 and 1925.[9]

Black colleges and universities, in contrast to Catholic institutions, were almost all coeducational, with a few notable exceptions. For about one hundred years, these separate institutions were virtually the only place African Americans could receive higher education. Two black women's colleges opened in the first two decades after the Civil War: Barber-Scotia in Concord, North Carolina (1867),[10] and Huston-Tillotson in Austin, Texas (1877),[11] but both later became coeducational. In contrast, Bennett College was founded in 1873 in Greensboro, North Carolina, as a coeducational institution, but it became a liberal arts college for women in 1926. The best-known historically black college for women is Spelman College in Atlanta, Georgia, which opened in 1881 and remains to this day a women's college (see Chapter 9).[12]

While most women's colleges were small and private, a few public institutions for women also existed. Some state women's colleges developed in the South and Southwest. The first state women's university was the Mississippi Industrial Institute and College (later called the Mississippi State University for Women), which opened in 1884. By 1908, state women's colleges had been also been established in Georgia, North Carolina, Alabama, Texas (see Chapter 5), Florida, and Oklahoma.[13] New York City supported a women's college for the training of teachers—Hunter College, which opened in 1870 as the Normal College of the City of New York.[14] Many states developed colleges for teacher training; these were usually referred to as "normal schools" and enrolled all or mostly women.

Founding dates influenced the nature of women's colleges. Women's colleges that began in the nineteenth century tended to stress liberal education for women's refinement. Simmons, in contrast, which opened during the Progressive Era, focused on career preparation for working- and lower-middle-class women (see Chapter 8). Mills, in Oakland, California, changed from a seminary to a college in the early twentieth century. Its curriculum changed over time, with more practical courses offered in the early part of the twentieth century and purely liberal arts later.

A Hybrid Form: Coordinate Colleges for Women

In addition to women's colleges and coeducational institutions, a third form of higher education developed in the late nineteenth century: coordinate colleges. Essentially, coordinate colleges were "sister" colleges of men's institutions, established in response to pressure to educate women. Educators could point to Girton and Newnham, two women's colleges of Cambridge University, as models of how prestigious men's institutions could incorporate women without admitting them outright (see Chapter 12).[15] Some of the most famous examples in the United States were Radcliffe, the coordinate of Harvard; Sophie Newcomb, the coordinate of Tulane; Barnard, Columbia's coordinate (see Chapter 11); and Pembroke, Brown's coordinate. Many lesser-known men's colleges or universities had coordinate colleges for women, for example, William Smith, the coordinate of the men's college, Hobart; Westhampton, associated with University of Richmond; and Saint Mary's, affiliated with University of Notre Dame. Still other universities had what were essentially coordinate colleges, but because they did not have a different name, they tended not to be widely recognized as such. This was true, for example, of Cornell University and the University of Pennsylvania.

Coordinate colleges represented a desire to keep women separate from men students to retain the prestige of men's institutions. Nonetheless, such separation had unanticipated benefits for women in terms of the support they received, as well as leadership opportunities.[16] Coordination was also one of the ways coeducational institutions sometimes considered dealing with the "threat" of women, whose attendance rates were increasing faster than men's and who were receiving disproportionate shares of academic awards. Middlebury College and the University of Rochester, for instance, created coordinate colleges for their women students, although Middlebury lacked sufficient funds to implement coordination fully. Other coeducational institutions responded differently to the fears of "feminization" that were particularly acute at the beginning of the twentieth century. Stanford was one of the universities that established quotas on the number of women admitted. Wesleyan ceased to admit women altogether, thereby reverting to its previous all-male status.

Women's Colleges: Paradoxical Roles and Images

Ambivalence about women's higher education did not cease as women's educational opportunities increased. In fact, the early twentieth century, when male dominance seemed less secure than it had earlier, was a period of backlash against women.[17] New arguments against educating women included the idea that educated women were less likely to get married or have children and hence caused "race suicide," a term popularized by Theodore Roosevelt in 1905.[18] Women's colleges were blamed in particular, although some commentators felt that coeducation caused greater damage, either by encouraging promiscuity or by contributing to the opposite problem—indifference to the opposite sex due to overfamiliarity.[19] In the early 1920s, Vice President Calvin Coolidge wrote that some of the eastern women's colleges fomented radicalism and Bolshevism.[20] The 1920s was also a decade when students experienced increased sexual freedom and when many Americans became familiar with Sigmund Freud's ideas. The "crushes" between women at women's colleges that had previously seemed innocent were now suspected of indicating lesbianism. Administrators at women's colleges felt compelled to take special measures to avoid such imputations.[21]

Another image of women's colleges was as "finishing schools" for privileged white Protestant women. Some researchers in the early twentieth century criticized them for not providing enough vocational guidance or training.[22] It was true that at many women's colleges, students received training in social graces, including how to be proper hostesses, how to talk in a refined manner, and how to develop good posture. While such training was not unknown in coeducational institutions, women's colleges generally gave more emphasis to the importance of women's refinement.[23]

Regardless of these conflicting images, women's colleges had a respectable place among institutions of higher education. By avoiding such applied subjects as home economics and keeping their student bodies homogeneous, many women's colleges retained or even enhanced their prestige. Women's colleges were known to be academically rigorous; some such as Wells College instituted demanding honor programs. By the late 1920s the most elite women's colleges—Barnard, Bryn Mawr, Mount Holyoke, Radcliffe, Smith, Vassar, and Wellesley—had come to be known as the Seven Sisters and were frequently seen as women's counterpart to what were later called the Ivy League colleges (Brown, Columbia, Cornell, Dartmouth, Harvard, Princeton, University of Pennsylvania, and Yale). In the 1920s some private women's colleges, including Wells, had many more applicants than they could admit. Wells considered expanding; since the president was concerned that this would mean the college would lose its "family" atmosphere, the college planned to open a "sister" college on the same grounds. This never happened, however, as the Great Depression intervened, affecting college enrollments and finances.[24]

Enrollment Trends over the Twentieth Century

Increasing numbers of women attended institutions of higher education throughout the twentieth century, from about 141,000 in 1909–10 to more than one million in the mid-1950s. At the same time, the percentage that enrolled in women's colleges decreased. Even as early as 1920, more than four-fifths of women attended coeducational colleges and universities. This proportion gradually grew, so that by the mid-1950s, nine of ten women attending institutions of higher education were enrolled in coeducational institutions.[25] These increases in enrollments at coeducational institutions affected women's colleges not only directly but also indirectly, as more and more faculty were likely to have received their education at coeducational institutions. Thus most people connected to higher education began to take coeducation for granted.

The rise of state universities affected women's colleges, since most women's colleges were and are private.[26] Particularly at times of economic hardship—for instance, during the Great Depression—students found the lower tuition of state institutions attractive. Traditional private liberal arts women's colleges responded to enrollment threats by offering more scholarships and becoming slightly more diverse, enrolling some Catholics and a small percentage of Jews.[27] Nonetheless, some new private women's colleges opened—many Catholic women's colleges but also some secular ones, notably Sarah Lawrence (1928) and Bennington (1932) in the Northeast, and Scripps (1926) in California.[28]

After World War II, many veterans took advantage of support from the Servicemen's Readjustment Act, frequently referred to as the G.I. Bill, to enter colleges and universities. While the number of women students also grew, the rate of growth for men was much greater, so the proportion of women in higher education decreased to about 30 percent. As women had been about 55 percent of college students at the end of the war, this drop was dramatic.[29] At the same time, marriage rates were high, and college women, as well as administrators and faculty, began to raise the familiar question of what women should learn if they were almost all going to become mothers. Some women's colleges, such as Vassar and Barnard, instituted programs to respond to women's interrupted lives and their return to college after marriage and childbearing.[30]

The buoyant economy of the 1960s, with increasing foundation and federal support for higher education, had positive effects on many institutions, including women's colleges. In this halcyon period, colleges could both expand and be more selective. Wells College, for example, had its highest-ever enrollments—more than six hundred students—for seven consecutive years, from 1966 to 1972, while admitting only about half its applicants. New colleges were founded to meet the increased demand for higher education. Of approximately seven hundred new institutions established between 1960 and 1969, three-quarters were public institutions, including community colleges; some were experimental, for example, Old Westbury; and some were women's colleges.[31] These categories overlapped, of course. Traditional all-male Hamilton College in upstate New York established Kirkland College in 1968, for instance, as an experimental coordinate women's college. Similarly, Pitzer College opened as an innovative women's college in the Claremont cluster of colleges. Neither of these colleges lasted in this form, however. Hamilton College absorbed Kirkland a decade after it opened, and in less than ten years, Pitzer admitted men students.[32]

Enrollees also diversified during the 1960s. At many colleges, including women's colleges, students and faculty, influenced by the national civil rights movement, pressured their institutions to recruit minority students, staff, and faculty. The civil rights movement's push for integration and, slightly later, the women's movement's demands for women to be admitted to male bastions meant that separate institutions of all kinds, including women's and men's colleges, began to be seen as old-fashioned or even anachronistic.[33]

Men's colleges were some of the first to respond to this new cultural mood. Beginning in the mid-1960s, many men's colleges, particularly prestigious ones like Princeton and Yale, started to consider ways to incorporate women undergraduates. They were not motivated only by a desire to extend their educational privileges to women, however. Demographic trends favored women's admission: Women's enrollments were increasing at a faster rate than men's. Moreover, women were known to be serious students. By the late 1960s, as inflation became a national economic issue, all colleges were anticipating financial problems. Some colleges that had borrowed money to expand during the 1960s began to be concerned about filling their campuses and paying back their loans during the high inflation period of the 1970s.[34] Men's colleges knew that by admitting women, they could increase enrollments, reduce debts, become more selective, and obtain hard-working students. And this, in short, is what happened. The admission of women to the remaining all-men Ivy League colleges, as well as to such prestigious men's colleges as Amherst and Williams, maintained or improved these institutions' finances and academic standings. By the 1990s, virtually no men's colleges remained, as almost all had become coeducational.[35]

Men's colleges' decision to become coeducational created problems for women's colleges. Given the sexism of society at large, anything male tends to be defined as superior to anything female.[36] Educators at women's colleges recognized that women students, particularly some of the academically strongest who previously would have attended their colleges, would now apply to formerly men's colleges. To avoid anticipated declines in enrollments and academic standards, some women's colleges decided to admit men. Vassar, which had been negotiating with Yale about developing a coordinate relationship, chose instead to become "coeducational."[37] Other women's colleges that made this transition in the late 1960s or early 1970s included Connecticut, Elmira, Sarah Lawrence, and Skidmore.

Justifying the Need for Women's Colleges

At the same time that the number of women's colleges declined—from 233 in 1960 to 90 in 1986—systematic research demonstrated their benefits to women.[38] For many years, journalists had noted the confidence of women who attended women's colleges and lauded the training for leadership these institutions provided.[39] The evidence was anecdotal, however. As the women's movement progressed, academics concerned with demonstrating how women fared under existing social arrangements began to conduct systematic studies of the relative advantages of single-sex education and coeducation.

Researchers coined the phrase the "chilly climate" to describe the many ways coeducational colleges discouraged women students' achievement and led to their loss of confidence. Studies found that professors called on men students more than on women students, were more likely to know men students' names, interrupted women more than men, asked women mundane questions but probed men students' answers for elaboration, and in general gave men students more of their time and attention.[40] Combined with information about women students' experiences of sexual harassment, date rape, lack of campus leadership positions, few female role models, and insufficient support for their sports, coeducational colleges and universities did indeed seem to be places where men consolidated their superior social position at the expense of women.

Women's colleges could correctly claim that they did not have "chilly climates." Moreover, a body of research, pioneered by M. Elizabeth Tidball in the early 1970s, began to accumulate that indicated that women who graduated from women's colleges were much more likely to succeed in later life than were women who graduated from coeducational institutions. Tidball's baccalaureate origin studies, which used listings in *Who's Who of American Women* and the *Doctorate Records File*, showed that graduates of women's colleges were two to three times more likely to become medical doctors, scientists, or recognized leaders in their fields.[41] These results fit with what some people already knew: Many women in Congress and successful women writers, for example, were graduates of women's colleges. And yet, other researchers criticized Tidball's methods—for her data sources (she used *Who's Who of American Women*, while some people argued *Who's Who in America* would be preferable), for not separating prestigious women's colleges (the Seven Sisters) from more ordinary women's colleges, and for confusing the benefits of attending a women's college with the advantages of having a privileged family background.[42] The latter—the so-called selection effect—would mean that women's colleges are successful not because of what they do for women but because of qualities that students bring to these colleges.[43]

The debate over the value of women's colleges continues. Some researchers report no benefits of single-sex education for women once sufficient controls for preexisting or social background differences are taken into account.[44] Even after they control for students' family backgrounds, however, other researchers continue to find that women who attend women's colleges experience advantages in later life.[45] Several researchers have used Tidball's "baccalaureate origin" research method for studying more recent cohorts of women graduates. Such studies have found generally positive results for women's colleges, although the differences between graduates of women's colleges and of coeducational colleges have not been as large as Tidball reported for earlier cohorts of women graduates.[46] Research on recent graduates is particularly interesting since, over time, the social characteristics of women who attend women's colleges have changed dramatically. While students at private women's colleges used to come from elite families, since the late 1970s and the use of extensive financial aid to attract students, they are more likely to come from families whose income and education level are lower than those of the families of women at comparable coeducational private liberal arts colleges.

Another argument made against the idea that women still need and benefit from single-sex education is that coeducational institutions have improved. Some analysts, noting that the original "chilly climate" studies were conducted during the 1980s, contend that their findings are no longer relevant.[47] While women's experiences in many coeducational colleges and universities have undoubtedly improved, equality does not yet exist. Women do not comprise half the faculty, for example, and the more prestigious the institution, generally the fewer the women faculty there are. Similarly, while more women are found among top administrators, they are still only about one-fifth of college presidents.[48] Women students' college experiences are different from and more likely to be negative than those of men students. Sex offenses on campuses throughout the country, most of them committed against women and many perpetrated by members of fraternities or athletic teams, have been documented, even though institutions report only some of these offenses to the federal government.[49]

While gender equality remains more a goal than an actuality, what is different from the past is that many institutions are concerned about how their women students are faring and implement policies to promote equal opportunities for women and men. A panel at Duke University, for example, recently did a study of gender issues on campus. The panel found that women undergraduates feel pressure to exhibit "effortless perfection," that they worry about the possibility of acquaintance rape, and that their campus leadership tracks are "somewhat separate" from men's. With knowledge of such difficulties faced by women, administrators at Duke are developing appropriate programs to help overcome them. These include, for instance, a "sustained leadership program" that will give undergraduate women who participate "some of the benefits of a single-sex educational experience embedded within their otherwise coeducational college life."[50]

Women's Colleges Today

Despite the evidence that women's colleges not only have played a key role in women's access to higher education but also have enhanced their postgraduation success, most young women no longer consider attending them. The Women's College Coalition, formed more than thirty years ago to publicize the benefits of women's colleges, has not succeeded in changing high school girls' minds. Nor have the articles that appear in the popular press about women students' attachment to and defense of their women's colleges. For more than two decades, a low percentage of girls, about 3 or 4 percent, says that they would "consider" a women's college, and a much lower percentage actually ends up attending one.[51] By 2006 only fifty-six women's colleges remained (see Appendix 2).

The persistent low interest in single-sex higher education continues to create enrollment and financial problems for women's colleges. Most women's colleges today no longer resemble people's images of a women's college—an isolated liberal arts college for women aged eighteen to twenty-two. Only a few very wealthy and prestigious women's colleges, such as Wellesley (whose endowment is over $1 billion), Smith, Mount Holyoke, and Agnes Scott, have been able to continue successfully in this mold.[52] The case studies of *Challenged by Coeducation* illustrate four major ways colleges typically have responded to the institutional problems created by the overwhelming coeducation trend:

- admit men, as the "first wave" of formerly women's colleges did, for example, as Vassar did (discussed in Chapter 2), as Wheaton (Chapter 3) and Wells (Chapter 6) have done more recently, and as Texas Women's University (Chapter 5) did as a result of court orders;
- develop close relationships with nearby men's or coeducational colleges and in that way be able to offer students both a single-sex and a coeducational environment (see Chapter 11 on Barnard, Chapter 9 on Spelman, and Chapter 12 on Girton and Newnham in Cambridge, England, for illustrations of this method);
- develop other programs to compensate for insufficient revenues from the traditional undergraduate program, for example, part-time and evening graduate programs (which by law must be open to men) or weekend colleges for mature students (Chapter 7 on Mills, Chapter 8 on Simmons, and Chapter 10 on College of Notre Dame exemplify this approach); or
- close, merge, or be taken over by another institution (Chapter 4 on Mundelein is an example of this).

The four types of responses to enrollment and financial difficulties are not equally desirable, nor equally possible, for all women's colleges. The first approach, admitting men, is often favored by those interested in improving the college's competitiveness and sustainability but is resisted by students and faculty who fear the "chilly climate" of coeducational institutions. In this book the chapters that illustrate the intense conflict that often erupts when a women's college considers admitting men are those on Mills, which, as a result of student protests, remained a women's college despite trustees' decision in 1990 to admit men; Wheaton, which did admit men in 1987; Texas Women's University, required in 1995 to admit men in order to receive state funds; and Wells, which in 2004 decided that men would be admitted beginning in 2005. And yet a comparison of formerly women's colleges with continuing women's colleges shows that as a result of making the transition to coeducation, enrollment applications (mostly of women) greatly increase, the college can become more selective, and as a result, finances improve.

Table 1.1, prepared by professor of mathematics A. Shilepsky at Wells College, compares two formerly women's colleges (Wheaton and Goucher) with three continuing women's colleges (Randolph-Macon, Sweet Briar, and Wells) using data from the *U.S. News and World Report* issues on colleges. It makes clear that when women's colleges open up to men, applications, selectivity, and enrollments improve dramatically.

Not all women's colleges can employ the second approach, developing close ties with another coeducational or a men's college. The institutions must be physically close enough that it is feasible for students at one institution to take courses and share college activities with students at the other. In addition to the examples in this book, some other women's colleges that benefit from close ties with coeducational or men's institutions include Bryn Mawr, linked to Haverford; Wellesley, associated with Massachusetts Institute of Technology (MIT); and College of St. Benedict in Minnesota, linked with St. John's. Stressing ties with another institution may create problems; in particular, the generally

Table 1.1. Admissions data, before and after coeducation

	Number of Applications		Percent Accepted		Number of First-year students enrolled	
	1985	2002	1985	2002	1985	2002
A. Women's colleges that became coeducational						
Goucher	696	2,596	87	68	189	365
Wheaton	1,000	3,534	85	44	339	412
B. Women's colleges that remained single-sex						
Randolph-Macon	1,100	723	48	85	240	206
Sweet Briar	608	415	82	86	222	151
Wells	313	404	86	86	114	109

Source: Prepared by A. Shilepsky, professor of mathematics, Wells College, from data from the *U.S. News and World Report* issues on colleges. Used with permission.

smaller women's college may find that its autonomy is compromised. And yet, all college constituencies generally favor this approach since it does not require the women's college to change, and it usually helps maintain enrollments. For reasons of efficiency, however, administrators and trustees sometimes recommend merging with the other college or university.

The third approach, changing the college and curriculum in dramatic ways to appeal to new constituencies, works best for institutions located in urban areas. By offering applied subjects at times of the day and week that are compatible with working people's schedules, and by giving more degrees than just bachelor's, women's colleges can often survive in the highly competitive higher education market. Simmons College was designed with the needs of working women in mind, and so this adaptation is actually part of its historical mission. The College of Notre Dame in Maryland, however, is a Catholic women's college that has changed from being a liberal arts college for traditional-aged women to a college that has more part-time than full-time students, many older than twenty-two. Mills College is another example. While Mills's undergraduate enrollment has declined or remained about the same in recent years, its graduate school enrollment has increased.

The degree to which college constituencies favor this third approach may well depend on how many curricular and programmatic changes are involved. Faculty often dislike changing from a liberal arts curriculum to less prestigious preprofessional or vocational programs, but they generally do not mind or even favor opening up graduate programs. If the alternative appears to be closing a college, opposition to even more dramatic curricular changes often fades, however.[53]

The fourth approach, closing a women's college or merging it with another institution, is undoubtedly the least desirable. Alumnae and students cease having an alma mater; faculty and administrators usually lose their jobs. Some women's colleges close without a trace, as Trinity in Burlington, Vermont, did in 2001. When colleges or universities take over a women's college, however, they sometimes establish an institute in the former women's college's name, frequently with a focus on gender. The most famous instance of this occurred when Harvard took over Radcliffe in 1999; today Radcliffe still has an endowment, and there is a Radcliffe Institute for Advanced Study, whose purpose, in part, is to further research on women, gender, and society. Similarly, when Hamilton College took over Kirkland, the coordinate women's college it had originally worked to establish, it set up the Kirkland Project, concerned with the intersections of gender, race, class, and sexual orientation.[54] Another takeover, George Washington University's acquisition of Mount Vernon College (MVC), was more hostile. Some faculty filed a suit, alleging breach of the 1996 affiliation agreement, which was "settled in confidence" about two and a half years later. Today the name Mount Vernon College is used only to describe a campus of George Washington University (GWU). From GWU's Web site, it is not possible to learn the history of MVC or to know why a part of the campus has this name.[55] A final example is Loyola University Chicago's takeover in 1991 of the Catholic women's college Mundelein. Although today the name Mundelein is not found on the campus, the Ann Ida Gannon, BVM, Center for Women and Leadership, which houses archives, the women's studies program, and the Institute for Women and Leadership, is named after a long-serving and important president of Mundelein.

Conclusions

Women's colleges appear to be a dying institutional form of higher education in the United States. Each year fewer remain, and most of those that do are struggling to survive. Forecasting the demise of women's colleges is not the same as arguing that they are not valuable, however. Indeed, the majority of studies of outcomes for women who were educated at women's colleges compared to those educated at coeducational colleges shows that women fare better in single-sex environments. And yet the overwhelming preference of young women today is for coeducational colleges. With fewer than 5 percent willing to consider women's colleges, these institutions' enrollment and associated financial problems remain severe.

The case studies in *Challenged by Coeducation* detail the diverse and innovative ways women's colleges have responded to the challenges of coeducation. Even colleges that seem to be the same today as they were before the recent upsurge in coeducation about thirty-five years ago have tried various methods to stem enrollment declines or to prevent being taken over by another institution. In many other instances the changes in the women's colleges have been dramatic and hence easily visible. Whether college adaptations have been subtle or major, a basic question we have kept in mind, and to which we will return in the concluding chapter, is whether the colleges seem to have been successful in meeting the challenges of an environment that increasingly favors coeducation. We are not interested solely in the question of whether each college will be able to survive, however. A major focus of this book, as well as of our previous *Going Coed* volume, is how women have fared as colleges have changed. We are particularly interested in whether formerly women's colleges have retained characteristics that help women students flourish (see Appendix 1 for a statement of six former presidents of formerly women's colleges about this issue). In other words, the key questions motivating this book have been: Are formerly women's colleges distinctly different from formerly male coeducational colleges? Have they been able to live up to the promise of coeducation by creating gender-equal environments?

Women's colleges have played an important role in the lives of thousands of women. They are defended passionately by many students and alumnae who see them as having a unique environment in which women's interests and needs are given priority. It behooves all of us who are committed to gender equity to study women's colleges so that we can better understand the particular ways in which they have benefited women and so that we can use them as models for the increasingly prevalent coeducational institutions. We hope the case studies in *Challenged by Coeducation* assist in this important endeavor.

Notes

1. Thomas Woody, *A History of Women's Education in the United States*, vol. 2 (New York: Science Press, 1929), 171–78.
2. Edward H. Clarke, *Sex in Education; or A Fair Chance for the Girls* (Boston: James R. Osgood, 1873/1972), 92–93.
3. See M. Carey Thomas's own assessment of her fears of Edward Clarke's conclusions: Refutations of Clarke can be found in Mary Putnam Jacobi, *The Question of Rest for Women during Menstruation* (London: Smith, Elder & Co., 1878); other refutations of Clarke's research are summarized in Sue Zschoche, "Dr. Clarke Revisited: Science, True Womanhood, and Female Collegiate Education," *History of Education Quarterly* 29 (1989): 545–69; and Rosalind Rosenberg, *Beyond Separate Spheres* (New Haven: Yale University Press, 1982), 20.
4. Barbara Sicherman, "Colleges and Careers: Historical Perspectives on the Lives and Work Patterns of Women College Graduates," in John Mack Faragher and Florence Howe, eds., *Women and Higher Education in American History* (New York: Norton, 1988).
5. Leslie Miller-Bernal, *Separate by Degree* (New York: Peter Lang, 2000), 203–5.
6. The role that the ACA played in strengthening women's colleges is discussed in ibid., 33–34. On the role of women faculty at women's colleges, see Mary Ann Dzuback, "Gender and the Politics of Knowledge," historycooperative.press.uiuc.edu/journals/heq/43.2/dzuback.html, accessed June 28, 2005. Also available in *History of Education Quarterly* 43, 2 (2003).
7. Mabel Newcomer, *A Century of Higher Education for Women* (New York: Harper and Row, 1959), 40.
8. Rosalind Rosenberg, "The Limits of Access: The History of Coeducation in America," in Faragher and Howe, *Women and Higher Education in American History*.
9. By 1955, there were 116 Catholic colleges for women. See Mary J. Oates ed., *Higher Education for Catholic Women: An Historical Anthology* (New York: Garland, 1987), 121. Other helpful discussions of Catholic women's colleges can be found in Susan L. Poulson and Leslie Miller-Bernal, "Two Unique Histories of Coeducation: Catholic and Historically Black Institutions," in Leslie Miller-Bernal and Susan L. Poulson, *Going Coed: Women's Experiences in Formerly Men's Colleges and Universities: 1950–2000* (Nashville: Vanderbilt University Press, 2004), as well as in Paula S. Fass, *Outside In: Minorities and the Transformation of American Education* (New York: Oxford University Press, 1989), chap. 6, "Imitation and Autonomy: Catholic Education in the Twentieth Century."

10. In 1867, this institution was called Scotia Seminary, dedicated to preparing black women for careers in teaching and social work. In 1916, it became Scotia Women's College; in 1930 it merged with Barber College and changed its name shortly thereafter. In 1954 it became coeducational. www.petersons.com/blackcolleges/profiles/barber-scotia.asp?sponsor=13, accessed July 4, 2005.

11. Tillotson opened in 1877 as a Collegiate and Normal Institute and went through various changes over time. In 1926 it was reorganized as a junior college and in 1926 as a women's college. In 1931 it became coeducational. In 1952 it merged with nearby Samuel Huston College. www.umcgiving.org/content/BCF/sc_huston.asp, accessed July 4, 2005.

12. A few black colleges for men were also established, probably the most famous being Morehouse, located adjacent to Spelman, and Lincoln University in Pennsylvania, which began admitting women in the 1950s. See Leslie Miller-Bernal and Susan Gunn Pevar, "A Historically Black Men's College Admits Women: The Case of Lincoln University," in Miller-Bernal and Poulson, *Going Coed.*

13. Archived Information Web site, Irene Harwarth, Mindi Maline, Elizabeth DeBra, "Women's Colleges in the United States: History, Issues, and Challenges," www.ed.gov/offices/OERI/PLLI/webreprt.html, accessed July 4, 2005.

14. www.hunter.cuny.edu/news/inbrief.shtml, accessed July 4, 2005.

15. Thomas M. Landy, "The Colleges in Context," in Tracy Schier and Cynthia Russett, eds., *Catholic Women's Colleges in America* (Baltimore: Johns Hopkins University Press, 2002), 61, cites an article written in 1898 that mentioned Girton as one of three prestigious institutions that women could attend.

16. Miller-Bernal, *Separate by Degree,* and Leslie Miller-Bernal "Conservative Intent, Liberating Outcomes: The History of Coordinate Colleges for Women," in Amanda Datnow and Lea Hubbard, eds., *Doing Gender in Policy and Practice: Perspectives on Single-Sex and Coeducational Schooling* (New York: Routledge/Falmer, 2002).

17. Woody, *History of Women's Education,* 2:251; Rosenberg, "The Limits of Access"; Miller-Bernal, *Separate by Degree,* 65–66.

18. Patricia A. Palmieri, "From Republican Motherhood to Race Suicide: Arguments on the Higher Education of Women in the United States, 1820–1920," in Carol Lasser, ed., *Educating Men and Women Together* (Urbana: University of Illinois Press, 1987), 57.

19. The first president of the American Psychological Association, G. Stanley Hall, argued in his famous book on adolescence that the easy association between the sexes in coeducational institutions caused men and women to lose interest in each other. "Familiar camaraderie brings a little disenchantment . . . [and] weakens the motivation to marriage." See Hall, *Adolescence,* vol. 2 (New York: D. Appleton, 1904), 620–21. At the same time, the then president of Stanford, David Starr Jordan, defended coeducational institutions because although they encouraged marriage, the unions were of the "best sort," based on "common interests and intellectual friendships." Jordan, "The Higher Education of Women," *Popular Science Monthly* 62 (1902): 107.

20. Calvin Coolidge, "Enemies of the Republic," *Delineator* 98 (1921): 4–5, 66–67.

21. Florence Howe, *Myths of Coeducation* (Bloomington: Indiana University Press, 1984), 277, 314; Dorothy Dunbar Bromley and Florence Haxton Britten, *Youth and Sex: A*

Study of 1300 College Students (New York: Harper and Brothers, 1938), 118; Katherine Bennett Davis, *Factors in the Sex Life of Twenty-Two Hundred Women* (New York: Harper and Brothers, 1929), 245.

22. Marguerite Witmer Kehr, "A Comparative Study of the Curricula for Men and Women in the Colleges and Universities of the United States." *Journal of the Association of Collegiate Alumnae* 14 (1920): 3–26.

23. Miller-Bernal, *Separate by Degree*, 104–6.

24. Ibid., 99–101.

25. Newcomer, *A Century*, 49.

26. Enrollment in public institutions was about half of total enrollment by 1929–30, a proportion that remained fairly constant until the 1950s. Then the proportion increased, so that by 1977, it was a little over three-quarters, a proportion that has remained fairly constant since. For the earlier part of the twentieth century, see Thomas D. Snyder, ed., "Years of American Education: A Statistical Portrait," National Center for Education Statistics, nces.ed.gov/pubs93/93442.pdf. Figures from 1947 on can also be obtained at nces.ed.gov/programs/digest/d02/tables/dt172.asp.

27. Miller-Bernal, *Separate by Degree*, 101–3. See also Lynn D. Gordon, *Gender and Higher Education in the Progressive Era* (New Haven: Yale University Press, 1990), 47–48, on the treatment of Jewish women at Wellesley during the first two decades of the twentieth century. Gordon notes that there were fewer non-Protestant women in southern institutions than in colleges in the North (49).

28. These years refer to when these women's colleges opened, not their official founding dates.

29. Snyder, "Years of American Education."

30. See Fass, *Outside In*, 157–75.

31. Verne A. Stadtman, *Academic Adaptations: Higher Education Prepares for the 1980s and 1990s* (San Francisco: Jossey-Bass, 1980), 4.

32. For more information about Kirkland, see Miller-Bernal, *Separate by Degree*.

33. Miller-Bernal and Poulson, *Going Coed*.

34. Earl F. Cheit, *The New Depression in Higher Education* (New York: McGraw-Hill, 1971).

35. Three men's liberal arts colleges remain: Wabash in Indiana, Morehouse in Georgia, and Hampden-Sydney in Virginia. Deep Springs is an elite all-men two-year college in California.

36. For social-psychological evidence of this general principle, see the famous study by Goldberg on women's perception that essays are inferior if women are believed to have written them: Philip Goldberg, "Are Women Prejudiced against Women?" in C. Safilios-Rothschild, ed., *Toward a Sociology of Women* (Lexington, Mass.: Xerox College Publications, 1968), 10–13.

37. Most people refer to women's colleges that have admitted men students as having become "coeducational." This is ironic, since "coed" is a term that really pertains to women, and that originally had derogatory connotations. And yet, since this terminology is widespread, we sometimes also use it.

38. These figures come from Irene Hawarth, Mindi Maline, and Elizabeth DeBra, *Women's Colleges in the United States* (Washington, D.C.: National Institute on Postsecondary

Education, Libraries, and Lifelong Learning, U.S. Department of Education, 1997), 28. Different researchers come up with somewhat different numbers, but they all show a dramatic decline in the number of women's colleges. For different estimates, see, for example, Erich Studer-Ellis, "Diverse Institutional Forces and Fundamental Organizational Change: Women's Colleges and the 'Coed or Dead' Question," paper presented at the annual meeting of the American Sociological Association, Washington, D.C., 1995.

39. Eunice Fuller Barnard, "Our Colleges for Women: Co-ed or Not?" *New York Times Magazine.* March 26, 1933, 4–5.

40. For overviews of this research, see Roberta M. Hall with Bernice R. Sandler, *The Classroom Climate: A Chilly One for Women?* (Washington, D. C.: Project on the Status and Education of Women, Association of American Colleges, 1982); Howe, *Myths of Coeducation;* Bernice Resnick Sandler, "The Classroom Climate: Still a Chilly One for Women," in Carol Lasser, ed., *Educating Men and Women Together* (Urbana: University of Illinois Press, 1987); and Myra Sadker and David Sadker, *Failing at Fairness* (New York: Simon and Schuster, 1994). For examples of specific empirical studies of women and men's behavior in classrooms, see David A. Karp and William C. Yoels, "The College Classroom: Some Observations on the Meanings of Student Participation," *Sociology and Social Research* 60 (1975): 421–39; and Sarah Hall Sternglanz and Shirley Lyberger-Ficek, "Sex Differences in Student-Teacher Interactions in the College Classroom," *Sex Roles* 3 (1977): 345–52.

41. Some of Tidball's studies are the following: M. Elizabeth Tidball, "Perspective on Academic Women and Affirmative Action," *Journal of Higher Education* 54 (1973): 130–35; M. Elizabeth Tidball and Vera Kistiakowsky, "Baccalaureate Origins of American Scientists and Scholars," *Science* 193 (1976): 646–52; M. Elizabeth Tidball, "Women's Colleges and Women Achievers Revisited," *Signs* (1980): 504–17; M. Elizabeth Tidball, "Baccalaureate Origins of Entrants into American Medical Schools," *Journal of Higher Education* 56 (1985): 385–402; M. Elizabeth Tidball, "Baccalaureate Origins of Recent Natural Science Doctorates," *Journal of Higher Education* 57 (1986): 606–20; M. Elizabeth Tidball, "Comment on 'Women's Colleges and Women's Career Attainments Revisited,'" *Journal of Higher Education* 62 (1991): 406–9.

42. Mary J. Oates and Susan Williamson, "Women's Colleges and Women Achievers," *Signs* 3 (1978): 795–806; and Mary J. Oates and Susan Williamson, "Comment on Tidball's 'Women's Colleges and Women Achievers Revisited,'" *Signs* 6 (1980): 342–45.

43. For more detailed summaries of this research and its criticisms, see Miller-Bernal, *Separate by Degree,* 212–16, and M. Elizabeth Tidball, Daryl G. Smith, Charles S. Tidball, and Lisa E. Wolf-Wendel, *Taking Women Seriously* (Phoenix: Oryx Press, 1999).

44. Judith Stoecker and Ernest Pascarella, "Women's Colleges and Women's Career Attainments Revisited," *Journal of Higher Education* 62 (1991): 394–406.

45. Riordan found that attending a women's college for just a year had a positive effect on women's postgraduate education; attendance for more years was required for women's colleges to have a positive effect on women's obtaining higher-status occupations and higher incomes. See Cornelius Riordan, "The Value of Attending a Women's College," *Journal of Higher Education* 65 (1994): 486–510.

46. Joy K. Rice and Annette Hemmings, "Women's Colleges and Women Achievers: An Update," *Signs* 13 (1988): 546–59; Lisa E. Wolf-Wendel, "Models of Excellence: The Baccalaureate Origins of Successful European American Women, African American Women, and Latinas," *Journal of Higher Education* 69 (1998): 141–87. There have also been many studies that have examined differences between women at women's colleges and at coeducational colleges in terms of such factors as their satisfaction with college life, their self-confidence, and their choices of major fields. Almost all these studies have found that women's colleges have more positive environments for women students. See for example, Sherrilyn M. Billger, "Admitting Men into a Women's College: A Natural Experiment," *Applied Economics Letters* 9 (2002): 479–83; Mikyong Kim and Rodolfo Alvarez, "Women-Only Colleges: Some Unanticipated Consequences," *Journal of Higher Education* 66 (1995): 641–68; and Daryl G. Smith, "Women's Colleges and Coed Colleges: Is There a Difference for Women?" *Journal of Higher Education* 61 (1990): 181–97.

47. An anonymous reviewer of Miller-Bernal and Poulson, *Going Coed,* made this comment, for instance, arguing that we were too negative about coeducational institutions.

48. Women's representation among the lowest faculty ranks is almost equal to men's, but women are much less likely to have tenure and to be full professors. Thus in 2001 45 percent of assistant professors were women, while only 20 percent of full professors were. At a prestigious institution like Princeton University, though, only 14 percent of full professors were women. See Karen W. Arenson, "More Women Taking Leadership Roles at Colleges," *New York Times,* July 4, 2002, www.nytimes.com/2002/07/04/education. Women are more likely to be presidents of two-year colleges than of doctoral universities, with their share being 22.4 percent of the former and 13.2 percent of the latter. See Kit Lively, "Diversity Increases among Presidents," *Chronicle of Higher Education,* September 15, 2000, chronicle.com/weekly/v47/i03/03a03101.htm.

49. For information about underreporting college and university sex offenses, see Sara Hebel, "U. of Calif. Failed to Report Crimes," *Chronicle of Higher Education,* April 18, 2003, chronicle.com/weekly/v49/i32/32a03203.htm, accessed July 19, 2004. A recent notorious example of sexual assaults involved seven rape charges brought against University of Colorado football players and recruits. The head football coach was placed on administrative leave after he made derogatory comments about one of the women who brought charges, and the governor of Colorado appointed a special prosecutor to investigate the situation. See Murray Sperber, "Sex and Booze: Two Steps to Winning Football," *Chronicle of Higher Education,* March 12, 2004, chronicle.com/weekly/v50,i27/27b02401.htm.

50. Women's Initiative Steering Committee, *Women's Initiative* (Durham, N.C.: Duke University, 2003), 15. A useful Web site that provides links to studies of women's status at more than thirty educational institutions is universitywomen.stanford.edu/reports.html#ureports. Most of the studies listed focus on issues concerning women faculty, however.

51. This figure is based on a 2000 College Board survey in which only 4 percent of college-bound high school girls said that they would "consider" a women's college. It is mentioned in an article about Hollins College: Andrew Brownstein, "Enrollment Falls, and a Small College Debates Its Future," *Chronicle of Higher Education,* May 4, 2001,

p. A39. Other smaller studies report similar figures. A study conducted by Hood College of five Frederick-area schools, for example, found that only 3.6 percent of 1,200 high school girls surveyed said that they would prefer a single-sex college. See www.hood.edu/news/articles/index.cfm?pid=_executive_summary.htm, accessed April 4, 2004.

52.   A few women's colleges that do not have very high endowments and are not as well known have attempted to stay essentially the same but have had a great deal of trouble attracting a sufficient number of students. Besides using extensive financial aid and intensive, expensive recruitment, some of these women's colleges have tried slashing tuition dramatically. Pine Manor College, outside Boston, reduced its tuition by 34 percent in 1998; Wells College reduced its tuition by 30 percent in 1999 (see Chapter 3).

53.   Wilson College, located in rural southern Pennsylvania, was forced to close in 1979 but an alumnae lawsuit forced it to reopen. Presumably that dramatic experience made faculty less opposed than they otherwise might have been to such changes in its traditional liberal arts curriculum as majors in business, veterinary technology, and exercise-sports science, as well as certificate programs and an evening adult-learning program. Today Wilson has fewer traditional undergraduates (391) than students in its other programs (400) and as many part-time students as full-time, and its most popular majors are veterinary science and animal-health technology and business administration and management. See Eric Hoover, "A College's Near-Death Experience," *Chronicle of Higher Education,* June 18, 2004, chronicle.com/weekly/v50/i41/41a03701.htm. See also information on Wilson College in *U.S. News and World Report,* www.usnews.com/usnews/edu/college/rankings/rankindex.php.

54.   Leslie Miller-Bernal, "Coeducation after a Decade of Coordination: The Case of Hamilton College," in Miller-Bernal and Poulson, *Going Coed.* Information on Radcliffe and Harvard can be found on either institution's Web site.

55.   www.gwu.edu. For information about Radcliffe, see www.radcliffe.edu. Significantly, information about the Radcliffe Institute can easily be found on the Harvard University Web site; see www.harvard.edu/academics/. Information about former Trinity College (Vermont) can be obtained at a Web page for Trinity College Association of Alumni and Friends, www.tcvt.org/default.htm. The Web site describes a reunion held not in college buildings but at a hotel in Burlington, Vermont.

Case Studies of Women's Colleges That Have Become Coeducational or Have Closed

In contrast to the end of single-sex education at formerly men's college and universities, which happened in a relatively brief period from about 1969 to 1983, the conversion of women's colleges to coeducation has occurred over the past four decades and continues into the present. The vast majority of men's colleges went coeducational in this period. A few institutions, however, did not, most notably Morehouse College in Georgia, Hampton-Sydney College in Virginia, and Wabash College in Indiana.

The five institutions discussed in this section, Vassar, Wheaton, Wells, Mundelein, and Texas Women's University, represent the variety found among women's colleges: a Seven Sisters college, two secular independent colleges, a Catholic institution, and a state university. Beginning with the Vassar decision to admit men in 1969 and ending with Wells enrolling men in 2005, these chapters review the struggles that these women's colleges engaged in as they faced the issue of coeducation. They also document a rising controversy over the admission of men, as many began to perceive the loss of a particularly supportive environment for women students. When women's colleges do adopt coeducation, however, many of them do so with increased attention to gender equity at their transformed institutions.

In Chapter 2 Clyde Griffen and Elizabeth A. Daniels review the transition to coeducation at Vassar College, one of the first women's colleges and the only Seven Sisters college to admit men. It had been negotiating with Yale to develop a coordinate relationship but rejected that idea when it recognized the loss of autonomy and its own campus that plan would have involved. While Vassar had a good academic standing and solid finances, trustees knew that many of the academically strongest women would choose to attend prestigious formerly all-male colleges such as Yale and Princeton. Thus with strong support from the administration, faculty, and students, Vassar trustees decided to adopt coeducation in 1969. Griffen and Daniels note that Vassar remains concerned with promoting good gender relations on campus. They believe that the transition has been successful in admitting significant numbers of men students while creating a positive environment for students of both genders.

When Wheaton College adopted coeducation in 1987, the ensuing controversy reflected the anxieties of a different era. Large numbers of students, faculty, and alumnae protested the decision. They expressed a concern that was nearly absent during Vassar's transition: that coeducation would destroy the unique environment that women's colleges offer for the development of the full potential of women students. Despite unhappiness about the coeducation decision, Susan Semel and Alan Sadovnik assert in Chapter 3, that in the twenty years since coeducation, Wheaton has maintained particular attention to gender equity through a policy of "conscious coeducation."

Prudence Moylan's study of Mundelein College, Chapter 4, represents the fate of some women's colleges in recent years: Mundelein has closed. Mundelein was founded and run for decades with the selfless efforts of women religious (also referred to as nuns) from the Sisters of the Blessed Virgin Mary. When more of the administrative and teaching responsibilities fell to laypeople as the numbers of women religious declined, the cost of running the institution rose considerably. By the 1980s Mundelein encountered deep financial trouble and declining enrollments. In 1991 its board of trustees agreed that after a brief period of affiliation, Mundelein would be absorbed by nearby coeducational Loyola University, a larger, wealthier, and better-known institution. In the wake of Mundelein's demise as a college for women, its spirit and its attention to women have been partly restored in the Ann Ida Gannon Center for Women and Leadership. The absorption of Mundelein College is also notable for its relative quiet, in an era when the closing or admission of men to a formerly women's college has usually prompted vehement protest.

Claire Sahlin's study of Texas Women's University, Chapter 5, indicates that in many ways TWU could be considered a women's college. Its students are overwhelmingly women, and it has a mission and culture that promote the empowerment of women. It is included in this section, however, because the board of regents voted to admit men to all programs in 1995. When court pressure forced state-sponsored men's institutions such as the Citadel and Virginia Military Institute to adopt coeducation, TWU felt a similar pressure. Strong protests erupted on campus, modeled on the successful protests at Mills College. However, they were ultimately unsuccessful, since TWU's status as a state institution made it particularly vulnerable to judicial and legislative pressure. Ironically, Sahlin finds that while TWU has admitted men, it has also strengthened its institutional culture in support of women's education.

In Chapter 6, Leslie Miller-Bernal reviews the enrollment and financial problems of Wells College since the 1970s and the various strategies that administrators used in an attempt to stem the decline. All were ultimately unsuccessful, however, and in 2004 the Wells College Board of Trustees voted to admit men in 2005. Tremendous protests erupted on campus. While the protests were similar in some ways to those at Mills College, Wheaton College, and TWU, they differed in the role played by students' parents and by assertions that women's colleges offer uniquely supportive places for lesbian, bisexual, and transgendered students. Miller-Bernal argues that in the current marketplace of higher education, where only a small fraction of women high school students even considers attending a women's college, the continuance of single-sex education at Wells College was hampered by its isolated rural location, which precluded the options of graduate and nontraditional education developed by some urban women's colleges.

Most authors in this section have insider status at the institution they study. This can mean a unique familiarity with the institution's culture, as well as a particular perspective on the transition to coeducation. Griffen and Daniels are faculty emeriti at Vassar; Semel was a student at Wheaton College when it was still single sex; Moylan is a member of the Loyola University faculty and a former member of the Mundelein faculty; Sahlin is the director of the women's studies program at TWU; and Miller-Bernal has been a faculty member at Wells College since 1975.

2

Vassar College

A Seven Sisters College Chooses Coeducation

Clyde Griffen and Elizabeth A. Daniels

Matthew Vassar believed that "almost everything which pertains to human progress and elevates the condition of human society, in the outset is an experiment."[1] The Poughkeepsie brewer chose a then-radical innovation in higher education as his chief legacy, telling his board that "it is my hope to be the instrument, in the hand of Providence, of founding and perpetuating an Institution which shall accomplish for young women what our colleges are accomplishing for young men."[2] So the Vassar community today has no difficulty in imagining that its founder could have approved, though he never anticipated, its experiment since 1970 in developing truly equal coeducation.

Now Vassar educates both women and men in an atmosphere that it believes remains true to the college's mission of providing equal opportunity for women. The school has achieved a coeducation that now attracts the largest applicant pool in its history with increasingly better-qualified students. An enrollment of about 60 percent women and 40 percent men is taught by a faculty nearing parity between the sexes, with women as frequent in its upper as in its lower ranks. When the college began coeducation in 1969, weighing the respective needs of the two sexes was important, but that no longer is a matter for concern. Vassar's name remains to remind the world of its earlier history as a women's college and its continuing commitment to equal opportunity for women and men.

The Early History

Matthew Vassar secured a charter in 1861 for Vassar Female College in the small city of Poughkeepsie, New York, in the Hudson River Valley. In 1866 Vassar asked for a deletion of "Female" from the title as the result of a successful campaign mounted by Sarah Josepha Hale. The editor of *Godey's Ladies' Book* persuaded the twenty-eight members of the college's board of trustees that the title was repugnant. Hale's concerns about the word "female" stemmed from the publication in 1859 of *The Origin of Species,* in which Darwin discussed males, females, and the sexual chase in animals. Hale did not find "female" a timely reference for Vassar women.

Twenty-eight charter male trustees joined the board, which met for the first time on February 26, 1861; several of them were Baptist clergymen, some educators, and businessmen, lawyers, and artists. Five of these trustees had served with Vassar on the board of the University of Rochester, which opened in 1855, and contributed their expertise to the board. The trustees elected Milo P. Jewett, a Dartmouth-educated advocate of women's education, first president of the college, and Matthew Vassar presented the board with his endowment of $408,000. Thus Vassar College was launched as the first endowed college for women in the United States.

To design a suitable residential and educational environment under one roof for faculty and students, the trustees engaged James Renwick, architect for the Smithsonian Institution.[3] Vassar's Main Building at its completion in 1865 had the greatest floor space of any building in the United States. That year the initial enrollment of 353 young women from many areas of the United States, including 6 women from Confederate states, moved into Main, which today remains the multipurpose center of the campus, housing administration, services, and students. By the 1890s male faculty began to move out of their Main apartments, preferring to live off campus. In 1893 the college built the first of eight residence halls constructed before 1969 to accommodate an enrollment that grew to about 1,550 young women by 1969, the year coeducational Vassar got under way.

All the students in Vassar's early years took entrance exams upon arrival. In the first years the college was unable to classify students because there were such disparities in their preparation. (In Poughkeepsie in 1865 there was no functioning high school for either young men or women.) Matthew Vassar had indeed taken a big leap forward in trusting that women would be sufficiently prepared to undertake college work, when many of them had not had the opportunity to attend either public or private schools. Consequently, until 1890 the college was forced to offer the equivalent of high school preparatory work, as well as college work. John Raymond, president of the college between 1864 (when Jewett resigned) and 1878, said in his *Life and Letters:* "Such were the multifarious elements I found thrown suddenly under my hand, and demanding organizing and arrangement into a working scheme which would meet their diversified wants and furnish the embryo of a regular system hereafter."[4]

For 105 years Vassar educated women only, with the exception of a program the college offered during World War II to men, who received their degrees from the State University of New York, not from Vassar.[5] How and why, then, did a liberal arts college that had pioneered higher education for women make the momentous decision in 1968 to become coeducational by integrating men fully into its undergraduate life? Vassar chose coeducation after a long, sometimes controversial consideration of a variety of alternatives for the college's future. Vassar had not suffered financially or experienced any obvious problem in number and academic qualification of its applicants. But by the late 1950s there were signs that Vassar's isolated single-sex environment was becoming less attractive to the most active and talented women.

Questioning Vassar's Single-Sex Status

In March 1961 President Sarah Blanding told an alumnae gathering that "there is now real uncertainty about the future of women's colleges despite their splendid achievements, present high social esteem, and the influence and loyalty of their alumnae."[6] She predicted that "of the hundred or more women's colleges now in existence no more than ten will be functioning in the year 2061." In twenty-five years, she believed, many would become coeducational, join a university as coordinate colleges, or even become public institutions.

Rethinking what the college should be doing was anything but new at Vassar, which had pioneered in creating faculty governance. As late as the 1940s women comprised three-fifths of the faculty. Most, remaining unmarried, had dedicated their lives to teaching and scholarship; they had taken up their profession at a time when few women combined a career with marriage and family. They prided themselves on their readiness to consider innovations in curriculum, teaching, and college arrangements that might advance opportunities for their students. Their male faculty colleagues shared that pride.

In 1948 faculty rethinking received an extraordinary stimulus from a donor's gift. Paul Mellon made an unusual grant to Vassar, in memory of his wife, to finance an intensive investigation by professional psychiatrists and psychologists into the consequences of college experience for normal development in current students and alumnae.[7] The Vassar faculty shared with the new investigators certain assumptions about educational growth, such as their emphasis upon the questioning of authority and learning to live with ambiguity. But some disliked methods of the study, including a survey questionnaire they found objectionable. And psychiatrist Carl Binger deeply angered women faculty when he commented in a 1951 report that "a more equable distribution of the faculty between the sexes is desirable and an inclusion of more married couples, now greatly in the minority. I do not believe that a matriarchy provides a wholesome atmosphere in which students are likely to develop satisfactorily."[8]

Binger resigned, but the Mellon investigation continued with a profound, if subtle, influence on the college. The board of trustees instituted a house-fellow system in 1952 that placed faculty residents in the dormitories in loco parentis; many of them were young married men with families. The national media's preoccupation in the 1950s with women building happy families reinforced Vassar students' expectations of early marriage. In June 1958 thirty seniors had already married and one-third of the class was engaged.

The Mellon study highlighted one feature of college life that became a major source of complaints during the 1960s. Students disliked the split between the weekday round of activities on campus and the weekend exodus for dates and mixers at all-male or coeducational campuses. The increasing proportion of Vassar women who came from coeducational public high schools intensified unhappiness with the inability to meet men casually during the week. In 1948 only 38 percent of entering first-year students came from public schools; by 1960, 55 percent did. By 1967, 62 percent of all students would be graduates of public coeducational secondary schools.

In 1966 questionnaires sent to students accepted by Vassar who chose other schools showed that they tended to prefer coeducational colleges or other Seven Sister colleges located closer to comparable male institutions, mostly in metropolitan regions. This decline in Vassar's relative attractiveness for applicants came at a time in the history of higher education when small liberal arts colleges of all descriptions worried about their futures. How could you attract and hold increasingly expensive faculty, especially in the sciences, in the face of the growing resources and influence of universities aided by government and corporate grants for research?

Vassar began confronting this challenge during the 1950s and 1960s when men received the larger share of junior faculty appointments. By 1970 men, many of them with coeducational backgrounds, had become a majority of the Vassar faculty and also of its tenured faculty. As early as 1962 the faculty, creating their own long-range planning committee, voted to investigate expanding graduate study for both sexes at Vassar and—more controversial—educating undergraduate men. But faculty planning had not resulted in any major proposals for change by 1964 when Alan Simpson became the college's new president, emphasizing Vassar's traditional commitment to expanding opportunities for women.

Two years later, however, Simpson had encountered enough problems with faculty recruitment, admissions, and student dissatisfaction to conclude that Vassar must rethink its future. In 1966 students focused on what they perceived as overly restrictive social and curricular regulations. Like students in other liberal arts colleges, they pressed for more flexibility, independent study, and off-campus experience. Those subjects became part of the varied agenda taken up by the trustees, administrators, and faculty appointed to a newly created presidential Committee on New Dimensions.

Exploring Affiliation with Yale

Then, in November 1966, an academic bombshell recast Vassar's consideration of its future. Simpson and President Kingman Brewster of Yale University announced that the Vassar board of trustees had accepted an invitation from the Yale Corporation: Under a grant from the Ford Foundation, the two schools would conduct a joint study of the feasibility and desirability of Vassar's relocating in New Haven as a coordinate college affiliated with Yale. The Vassar trustees, divided even then in relative enthusiasm for affiliation, agreed that the investigation would be a powerful catalyst for considering major changes in the college.

The opportunities for experimentation with coeducation in New Haven received some attention from the Vassar-Yale Study staff created for the investigation with equal representation from the two colleges. Opening or closing particular courses to cross-registration could show the advantages and disadvantages of coeducation in different kinds of classrooms and at different levels of instruction. But the study quickly came under fire from Vassar alumnae, a majority of whom before long would oppose relocation. Increasingly they demanded a comparable study of what Vassar might do if it remained in Poughkeepsie. A new Committee on Alternatives under Dean Elizabeth Daniels considered a wide array of possibilities, including revitalization of the curriculum, coeducational relationships, and a new graduate center. The difference in funding for the two studies distressed those concerned with alternatives. Ford Foundation and Carnegie Corporation grants provided more than $300,000 for the Vassar-Yale Study, whereas the Vassar board allocated $25,000 for Dean Daniels's investigation.

As part of its investigation, the Committee on Alternatives administered a questionnaire; the responses from the 1,455 students who filled out the questionnaire reveal widespread doubts about arguments often advanced in favor of women's colleges. Only 10 percent found "generally true" the claim that "women do better academic work when men are not in the same class," whereas 58 percent deemed it "generally false." Asked if "the absence of men in Vassar classes involves any important loss in perspective," 68 percent believed it did.

Response was more divided regarding the claim that with men absent, "women have a better opportunity to organize and direct extracurricular activities"; but the largest percentage answered "generally false." When asked what type of college they would choose, other than Vassar, only 17 percent preferred another liberal arts college for women, compared to 37 percent who would choose a coeducational college and 41 percent, perhaps with Yale in mind, a women's college affiliated with a major university.

Vassar's board never asked for a referendum on affiliation, but it had become clear by the fall of 1967 that a majority of alumnae and faculty opposed relocation. They advanced many reasons, not least that Vassar would lose its identity, becoming subordinate to Yale, and that the Vassar faculty mostly would have second-class status in New Haven. At the moment the board announced its decision not to relocate, President Simpson believed that 60 percent of the students still favored joining Yale, but no vote verified his opinion.

Well before the decision, the board concluded that, in turning down Yale, it needed to offer an ambitious program of improvements for Vassar in Poughkeepsie. Many of the projects proposed died aborning, like graduate institutes and a graduate center. But the board's promise of some form of coeducation did not. Many alumnae, some trustees, and older members of the faculty preferred creating a coordinate college for men. Some of them hoped that other institutions could be persuaded to relocate next to Vassar in a Claremont Colleges–type of consortium. But when the form of coeducation came up for a vote by the faculty in May 1968, they resoundingly endorsed—102 ayes to 3 nays—admission of men to Vassar itself. It was a striking turnabout from earlier divided views.

To help Vassar decide how it wished to educate men, President Simpson appointed two former members of the Vassar-Yale Study staff, Clyde Griffen and George Langdon, to identify alternatives in size, organization, programs, and facilities. Drawing upon the experience of other undergraduate institutions and of consultants like David Riesman, their "Report on the Education of Men at Vassar," presented in May 1968, emphasized both the need for a distinctive curriculum if Vassar chose to create a coordinate college for men and the burdens of coordination, together with ongoing pressure for more integration.[9] But the turning point for faculty who might have preferred a coordinate college probably came with their realization that Vassar's board of trustees, not the Vassar faculty, would shape the creation of any separately chartered institution. Making Vassar itself coeducational had the advantages of being less costly and requiring the participation of the entire college community. Success would depend upon Vassar's reputation and creativity rather than upon a cadre of newcomers fashioning a new college next door.

In June 1973 the alumna chair of the Vassar Board, Elizabeth Purcell '31, publicly addressed the question of how Vassar could justify its changed character. She said that the three questions most often asked in 1968 were: "Isn't a famous woman's college denying its historic mission [in becoming coeducational]?" "Isn't coeducation a backward step for women?" "Isn't coeducation a fad of the moment among the eastern single-sex colleges (as men seem to be taking over the colleges)?" "Vassar's answer to all of these questions is a decided no," she insisted, "because we are developing equal coeducation on this campus. . . . I believe that Vassar's commitment in this second century is every bit as new and exciting as it was in its original commitment in 1861."[10] The board of trustees had agreed at the outset to increase enrollment to facilitate coeducation and to develop a much more diversified student population. The board further committed itself to reexamine every aspect of residential and academic life.

In the summer of 1968 Dean of the Faculty Nell Eurich and members of a reconstituted Committee on New Dimensions drew up materials for a comprehensive plan for change in the curriculum and residential life. The aim was to encourage "constant adjustment" in Vassar's educational program, "with an increased number of options for both students and faculty." The flexible provisions of this plan, approved by the faculty after incorporation of further contributions, continue to be the basis of a Vassar education. Assuming the plan's value for a newly coeducational Vassar, the committee also commissioned papers by two members of the Psychology Department, which proposed further research on various styles of learning in both men and women.[11]

In 1968 the board began making decisions to implement coeducation, voting to explore the possibility of exchange programs with other colleges to ease the introduction of male students at the upper level. That idea had been considered first in 1966 by the Committee on New Dimensions. Now the trustees asked the dean of faculty to devise a time table for implementation, after deciding that enrollment should be increased from its then-current 1,550 to no more than 2,400 to retain the qualities of a small residential college. But three years later, having reached 2,250 and 40 percent males, the college reconsidered and then withdrew its previous tentative goal of parity between the sexes and of further increase in enrollment size.

Implementing Coeducation

By March 1969 Vassar's charter had been amended, without legal challenge, to include the education of men. In the previous decade, Vassar's Office of Admissions had made its decisions in tandem with the practices of the other Seven Sisters colleges (Barnard, Bryn Mawr, Mount Holyoke, Radcliffe, Smith, and Wellesley). Their representatives met periodically to discuss practices and problems of both student admissions and financial aid. Vassar's office continued to follow its traditional ways during the 1960s. Admission offices at other colleges shifted gears to respond to new needs; in particular, attention turned to the nation's inner cities to consider minority students who had not previously aspired to the top liberal arts colleges.

Once the decision to remain in Poughkeepsie had been made, the college reorganized its admission office under new leadership with an enlarged staff. The reorganization came with the appointment of John Duggan, formerly vice president of the College Entrance Examination Board, to the newly created office of vice president of student affairs; Duggan had responsibility for overseeing everything involved in the housing, recreation, and recruitment of men.

The next year, members of the admissions staff visited four hundred schools instead of the thirty-seven visited the year before. Since not all high schools and guidance counselors receive fresh college catalogues every year, the process of informing college-bound students of Vassar's becoming coeducational took some doing and some time.

In October 1968, negotiations began among Bowdoin, Amherst, Dartmouth, Williams, Colgate, Trinity, and Vassar to form an exchange program beginning in January 1969 as a way of attracting students, especially of the opposite sex, into their upper classes for a semester or a year's credited study. Credit would be transferred to the visiting student's record at his home college. A number of other colleges, including Connecticut, Wesleyan, Wheaton, Mount Holyoke, and Smith, were convened to discuss the possibility of other exchanges on a semester-by-semester basis. Following these discussions came explorations at the presidential level of institutional cooperation in a consortium, including various kinds of cooperative centers for dedicated purposes such as an urban center in New York City and joint training of college teachers.

A twelve-college exchange program soon evolved from these explorations. In the second semester of 1968–69, seventy-seven male exchange students came to Vassar, of whom over one-third applied to transfer to Vassar at the end of their semester. By the fall of 1969 Vassar accepted both exchange students and transfer students, allowing already matriculated students to take leaves for academic work elsewhere. The scene was set for active recruitment of men as well as women into the class entering in 1970. The college began to be coeducational, at first amidst some skepticism and confusion in the offices of guidance counselors at schools across the country. Conditions for Vassar's pioneering men sometimes left a good deal to be desired.

Never having had boarding male students before the years of exchange and transfer, the college had to decide many things quickly. One of the most important and dramatic changes, the abandoning of parietal regulations, came with a suddenness that surprised and frequently shocked parents of women students. Their daughters had long pressed for easing of social regulations. Now the Student Senate recommended to the president that collegewide regulations for visiting hours be dropped. When students on a dormitory corridor agreed on restrictions they wished to impose, they still could do so. President Simpson did not hesitate long, aware that if Vassar kept parietals for women but not for men it would be guilty of creating a double standard. For a college committed to equal opportunity for the sexes, that prospect was not appealing. So after consultation, which suggested everyone favored the student resolution, the president accepted it. Some unhappy parents brought lawsuits against the college charging breach of contract, but the suits were unsuccessful.

Housing was a big problem, and furniture and furnishings another; Vassar soon discovered that men take up a lot of space. But gradually over the next few years problems diminished and finally disappeared. The college constructed terrace apartments and townhouses arranged in suites. Dean of Residence Elizabeth Drouilhet, central to campus life since the 1930s, led a dormitory committee that successfully urged reviving a previously deferred fundamental change. It called for replacing the current system of separate dining halls in each dormitory with an all-campus student union–type dining facility. The new facility allows longer hours for mealtimes and has improved campus sociability by mixing students from different dormitories.

Coeducation in the First Ten Years: A Difficult Time

The decade between 1969 and 1979 saw Vassar's coeducation slowly become stabilized, with its enlarged enrollment limited to about 2,250 students. In 1979, 61 percent were women and 39 percent men. Like other colleges in those years, Vassar enrolled larger numbers of transfer students, returning students, and minority students, especially African Americans, than at any other period in its history. The departmental disciplines remained largely intact, but the college introduced new interdisciplinary majors such as biopsychology and four new multidisciplinary programs. A women's studies program was funded, and departments began to cross-list courses in the women's studies cluster. Vassar undertook new educational responsibilities in Poughkeepsie and the larger mid-Hudson region, including creation of an urban center for African American students and participation in a consortium of nine regional colleges. Cooperative programs were started with other colleges: Fisk, Morehouse, Spelman, and York University, England.

In 1979 Vassar's self-study report, prepared for the Middle States Association in conjunction with the college's ten-year renewal of accreditation, discussed its progress in establishing coeducation. The concept of parity between the sexes had been questioned almost as soon as it had been announced as a goal, since Vassar's decision to educate men coincided with the peaking of the feminist movement, on campus and off. Although the poll taken during the Yale-Vassar Study showed a clear preference for coeducation, a "minor backlash" occurred soon thereafter. The trustees established a Committee on Women at Vassar in 1971 to investigate the situation and thereafter dropped the issue of parity. But by 1979 the gap between numbers of male and female students had decreased, and with that improvement came a greater ease and reduction in tensions with respect to a precise sex ratio.[12] The college was on unexplored ground on this issue, as on some others. As the self-study stated, there were many theories about how a nonsexist ambience could best be facilitated and few examples to follow. President Virginia B. Smith emphasized recruitment of women faculty to correct the then-current gender imbalance, and she gave the newcomers warm support.

Alumnae/i, Trustees, Administration, and Faculty

During the Yale-Vassar Study the college's alumnae voiced opinions on all sides of the issue of coeducation. Some threatened to remove their financial support if Vassar joined with Yale or became coeducational; others saw one or the other alternative as promising. Truly remarkable then was the rallying of alumnae over time to Vassar's new experiment of embarking on coeducation on its own, working in the light of its own traditions, keeping equality alive in its own fashion. Alumnae financial support for the college continued and strengthened again. In 2004 under the leadership of President Frances Fergusson, annual giving brought in well over $7 million, and the college endowment exceeded $600 million. President Fergusson, an architectural historian, has also been responsible for restoring the physical beauty of the Vassar landscape, delighting alumnae/i as well as students and parents.

Vassar graduates had organized the Alumnae Association in 1871, supporting the college in multiple ways. Soon thereafter it petitioned the all-male board of trustees, consisting of fourteen Baptist clergymen and fourteen educators and businessmen, for alumnae representation on the board. Not until 1886, however, would the trustees invite the alumnae to elect three to serve on the board. Over the years that number increased. By 1960, 10 women and 12 men served on the board. In 1965 the distribution was 12 women and 11 men, and by 1980 the board was composed of 7 men and 18 women. In 2000, with the board enlarged to 30 trustees, 12 men and 18 women served, all alumnae/i of Vassar. For some years now one representative of the faculty and one of the students, as well as the head of the alumnae/i organization, have attended board meetings as observers.

Similar gender balances have prevailed among the officers and staff of the college during the transition to coeducation. In 1960–61 the women's college numbered 7 males and 21 females in educational administration, 6 males and 5 females in business administration, 2 male and 14 female librarians, 10 male and 7 female house fellows, and 87 male and 122 female faculty members. By 1979, in good part as a result of appointments made before 1970, the enlarged faculty included a dramatic increase to 136 men, whereas the number of women remained the same as in 1960–61: 122. Since 1979, the proportion of women in the upper as well as lower ranks of the faculty has increased, as has the frequency with which women chair and serve on the most important committees, notably the Faculty Appointments and Salary Committee and the Faculty Planning and Conference Committee. The structure of the college to which students come, its administration as well as faculty, shapes their perception of the roles both sexes have and the authority they exercise. Relative equality in gender balance has been important in advancing a nonsexist atmosphere for Vassar's coeducation.

Athletics and Sports for Women and Men

Important in the development of coeducation at Vassar has been the history and current structure of athletics and sports. Athletics has been an integral part of the college's mission since its opening in 1865. Some commentators then thought higher education deleterious to the development of women, especially to their roles as bearers and nurturers of children. Theories ranged wildly, including the idea that the human body had only limited energy, so use of the brain drained it from the reproductive system. Not so, said Matthew Vassar. In 1861 he wrote one trustee: "I go for mental stimulus of some sort and for daily exposure to the pure air in joyous unrestrained activity."[13]

The Vassar prospectus of 1865 advertised that light gymnastics would be mandatory from the beginning in the college's curriculum. In 1933 the Physical Education Department defined its mission as helping the woman student "develop her maximum vitality and physical efficiency, mental and emotional balance through physical well-being." This definition emphasized "acquisition of skills and knowledge and enjoyment of individual and group recreational activities" through highly personalized programs focused on individual needs, tastes, and aptitude.

With the college's decision to become coeducational, the Vassar Physical Education Department recommended its own continuance as a single department for both sexes. It would continue to emphasize lifelong sports, but also would organize and coach varsity teams for both sexes. Intramural sports with in-campus competition, already in effect for women, would be enlarged as funding and personnel became available. Men's and women's teams would be funded equally.

In 1967 the entirely female department had no separate coaches or trainers and urgently needed new athletic fields. The college moved ahead with new plans for athletics under coeducation, augmenting both athletic facilities and teaching staff. But a 1978 report found Vassar still gravely inadequate in the physical education opportunities it provided its students.[14] During the 1980s the college began to implement varsity sports for both sexes. By 1990 much had improved. Vassar sponsored 18 varsity teams, 9 for men and 9 for women. In 2003 the college's varsity teams numbered 23, 11 men's and 12 women's.

Vassar is a member of the National Collegiate Athletic Association Division III and the Upstate College Athletic Association. It also belongs to the Eastern College Athletic Conference and the New York State Women's Collegiate Athletics Association and still competes in the Seven Sisters championships.

In 1998 further expansion of Vassar's Walker Fieldhouse included a five-thousand-square-foot weight-training center. In 2002 the college built an athletic and fitness center, attaching it to the Walker Fieldhouse. The new fitness center follows in the tradition of the college's emphasis on individual self-development in athletics. It has become a socializing influence in the

Vassar community, much used by young and old, both sexes, professors and students. In 2003 the college added another fieldhouse so visiting teams would have shower and changing rooms adjacent to the playing fields.

An additional community-integrating feature of the new physical education program is the repertory theatre dance program, which offers workshops throughout the academic year. For the last twenty years it has culminated in a spring weekend of performances for the general public at the Bardavon Theatre

Sports at Vassar College today include teams for men as well as women students. *Special Collections, Vassar College Libraries.*

in Poughkeepsie. Currently Kenyon, one of the early gymnasia, is being remod-
eled to include more classrooms and a dance theater.

Students' Perceptions

A widespread perception among Vassar faculty and administration is that preselection influenced many men who applied to Vassar in the early years.[15] In this
view, men did not see Vassar as just one among many good colleges but were
specially drawn to it because it offered a less macho environment, or because
they saw the beginning of its transformation as an exciting adventure, or because
they had relatives who had attended Vassar. Such preselection among male applicants in the 1970s and 1980s can't be quantified, nor can the sense among
some faculty that it is less frequent now. That seems probable, since Vassar's
coeducation no longer is a novelty. Its male graduates now spread across the
country, where prospective applicants meet them, and Vassar now attracts a
much larger, more competitive pool of male applicants. The college atmosphere
has changed; Vassar women today are less militant in their feminism than they
were in the 1970s, and the increasing gender gap in undergraduate education as
a whole has made Vassar's gender balance no longer unusual (see Table 2.1).

Those looking at Vassar from the outside in the 1970s feared the college
would attract less-masculine men. Some early publicity fanned that fear. *Esquire*
used the flamboyant "Jackie St. James" (a.k.a. Sheldon Weiss '74) to suggest a
gay Vassar, a suggestion enhanced by students' election, on a lark, of Jackie as

Table 2.1. Vassar College enrollment, 1965–2004

Year	Total enrollment	Percent Women	Percent Men
1965	1,601	100	
1969	1,550	100	
1971	2,250	60	40
1979	2,250	61	39
1987	2,267	60	40
1995	2,164	61	39
1999	2,285	62	38
2004	2,411	61	39

Sources: 1965 and 1979: James Cass and Max Birnbaum, *Comparative Guide to
American Colleges* (New York: Harper & Row); 1987: *American Universities and
Colleges,* 13th ed., (Washington, D.C.: American Council on Education); 1995,
1999, 2004: *America's Best Colleges* (Washington, D.C.: *U.S. News & World Report*);
1969, 1971: Vassar College Registrar.

their president. One alumnus recalled that St. James "did some damage, but in general the gays blended in." *Esquire* ignored the diversity of the first men, who included the bodybuilder who just wanted to be left alone with his weights and his philosophy books, and a soon-to-be New Orleans policeman. Influenced by the respect he had acquired for Vassar women, that alumnus would persuade his police force that pairing a woman with a man was smarter community relations than was pairing two men.[16]

Changes in the Selectivity of Students

Perhaps because of lingering doubts about coeducation, Vassar's acceptance rate for applicants for admission did not improve significantly until the 1990s. As a women's college between 1950 and 1962, Vassar had accepted 60 percent or more of its applicants. The acceptance rate dropped to between 50 and 60 percent in the mid-1960s, rose briefly to 60 percent or more with coeducation until 1977, and then hovered around 50 percent during the 1980s. In the 1990s the rate began dropping, first below 50 percent. In the last four years the acceptance rate has fallen to the lower 30 percent range, and in 2003 to less than 29 percent.[17] The great recent increase in the size of Vassar's applicant pool reflects a change in the perceived desirability of admission to Vassar. The best students at Vassar today have better records than ever before. Some faculty say that the academic ability of the bottom third of first-year students especially has improved dramatically in the last few years.

From the beginning, Vassar was determined to maintain the same standards of admission for men as for women. Judged by credentials like College Board scores and class rank, it succeeded, avoiding any significant gaps in achievement between the sexes. But the smaller applicant pool for men meant they enjoyed a higher acceptance rate in the early years of coeducation. And while the level of SAT verbal and math scores remained similar for men and women, Vassar's entering classes as a whole experienced some temporary decline in scores after the 1960s. In Vassar's last years as a women's college, 1960–72, the combined SAT scores of first-year students were mostly above 1,250. As the male contingent grew in the early 1970s, the combined scores, in the years 1973–84, ranged between 1,140 and 1,191, rising into the low 1200s from 1984 through 1994. But by 1995, the combined scores of Vassar first-year students had risen to 1,260, back to their previous highest level in the 1960s. Since then Vassar's scores have risen steadily from 1,310 in 1996 to 1,380 in 2003.

Gender balance in honors at graduation has varied over time. The first class of men (1974) set a high standard, 24 percent of them earning general honors and 41 percent departmental honors, compared to 20 percent and 29 percent respectively for women graduates. But in 2003, 23 percent of the women graduates earned general honors and 31 percent departmental honors, compared to

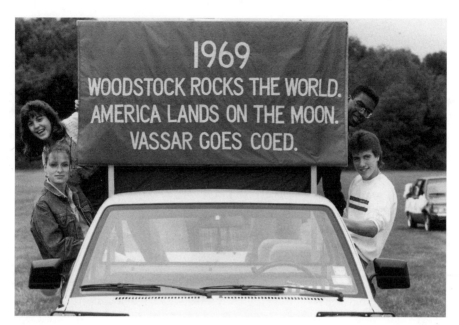

Riding in a float for the three-hundredth anniversary of the City of Poughkeepsie, Vassar students demonstrate their positive feelings about the 1969 decision to admit men students. *Special Collections, Vassar College Libraries.*

19 percent and 26 percent respectively of the men. Among the students who won both kinds of honors, 17 percent of the women did so and 14 percent of the men.[18] Vassar remains a college where women, and now men, flourish academically.

Racial, Ethnic, and Geographic Diversity among Students

Vassar's enrollment also has become more diverse racially, ethnically, and geographically. In attracting African American applicants, it quickly became apparent that gender balance would be a problem. Black males did not come to Vassar and comparable liberal arts colleges as frequently as did black women.[19] White ethnic diversity for both sexes showed up by the 1970s in the new frequency of ethnic surnames from the southern, central, and eastern European immigration of the early twentieth century. Vassar's percentage of foreign students has doubled in recent years, from 3 percent in both 1969 and 1984 to 5 percent in 1991 and 6 percent in 2002.

Distribution of Vassar students by U.S. region shifted somewhat between 1969 and 2003, with an increase from the West and New England and a decrease in the Midwest and South. But the most striking change occurred in the proportion from the Middle Atlantic States. Between 1969 and 1984, the early years of coeducation, that percentage rose from 54 to 60 percent of all students. This may have reflected greater comfort among students and their parents in the New York metropolitan region because of greater familiarity with Vassar and its changing enrollment. Young men in that adjacent region were likely to know more about the college and its academic strengths than males from other parts of the nation. Any concerns that Vassar might become more a regional than a national college, however, were dispelled in the next few years, as the percentage from the Middle Atlantic States dropped from 60 to 46 percent in 1991 and to 45 percent in 2002.[20] The college now has a wider geographic distribution of students than it had as a women's college in 1969.

Coeducation in the Classroom

Diversity of perspective in the classroom based on gender was perhaps the most important expected gain for Vassar in choosing coeducation. But many wondered at the time whether men would dominate discussion as they so often did in other coeducational settings. Despite their history of speaking up, encouraged by their faculty, would Vassar women be intimidated and marginalized by men in their classrooms? Would they shrink from raising questions or speaking out unless called upon by the instructor?

Three members of Vassar's Department of Psychology sought to find answers to these questions with two systematic studies, in 1984 and in 1986, of student participation in class discussion at Vassar. The second study included comparative investigations conducted at Trinity College, Hartford, and at Central Connecticut State University. The student observers who provided the data looked for particular behaviors in the classroom, notably volunteering information, making follow-up comments, and responding to what another student had said.[21]

To the central question, "Do men speak more in class than women?" the study provided mixed answers. Gender had a small and inconsistent effect on class participation at the three schools. The major exception: Men asked more questions of the instructor, especially in the social and natural sciences. The larger the class, the less often women took the initiative in interacting with the instructor by asking a question and the more often they withdrew from class participation. Class size made an important difference.

Two other keys to gendered differences in classroom behavior were the division of the curriculum and the sex of the instructor. The highest level of participation by both sexes occurred in the arts, where texts read by everyone focused discussion. In the social sciences, by contrast, men tended to speak up more frequently, whether or not they had done much reading. The studies found no evidence that teachers of either sex treated women or men in their

Men have been absorbed into some Vassar traditions: daisy chains at Vassar, 1963 and 1984. John Lane Studio [1963 photo] and Ben Rayfield [1984 photo] *Special Collections, Vassar College Libraries.*

classes differently. They did find that women instructors tended to begin asking questions of their classes earlier, seeming to invite discussion. Only in the arts at Trinity and in the natural sciences at Vassar and Connecticut State did male instructors have higher levels of class participation. Generally, the studies found that women teachers had more active classrooms, especially in the social sciences.

Students of either sex expect women faculty to be good listeners and more nurturing than male faculty. This can be a problem for some young women teachers who insist on tough standards and demand a great deal of their students. In 2003 some senior women faculty who had team taught with male colleagues observed that women students still tend to see male faculty as authorities whose views they should not challenge.[22] On the other hand, although students initially find arguments between teachers uncomfortable, seeing team teachers disagree with each other without taking their differences personally can change student participation. That example encourages both men and women to question authority and come to their own conclusions, a primary aim of a liberal education. The new multidisciplinary programs where team teachers make evident how their approaches to subjects are shaped by their differing disciplines can further reinforce that critical independence.

Male students still tend to offer unsupported opinions more readily. But faculty of both sexes have found effective ways to limit this tendency and to draw out the more reluctant but often better-prepared women in their classes. While there is some disagreement among senior women faculty about whether Vassar students may be becoming more competitive with each other, preselection in admissions so far seems to have maintained a cooperative atmosphere in the classroom and on campus. One of the psychologists who organized the three-college study, Anne Constantinople, believes that Vassar men and women become more like each other by graduation in both values and behavior.

Choices of Academic Majors

Female and male curricular choices do not conform nicely to gender stereotypes, although there is some of the traditional tendency for women to be overrepresented in the arts and languages, and for men, in the natural sciences. The ratios of women to men majoring in English, history, international studies, music, political science, religion, and Russian come close to the student ratio of 60 percent women to 40 percent men. Women in 2003 were overrepresented in anthropology, art, biology, drama, environmental studies, psychology, sociology, and most languages, and in the Science, Technology, and Society Program. Men are overrepresented in chemistry, economics, geology, mathematics, philosophy, and physics.[23] But even in economics, which has a largely male faculty, 44 percent of the majors are women. Male students sometimes enroll in courses in women's studies, but rarely major in the program. It currently has nineteen majors and a very strong faculty including some men, two of them participating in 2002–3. Besides cross-listed courses with departments, the program offers its own multidisciplinary introductory course and a variety of intermediate and advanced offerings: Issues in Feminism: Bodies and Texts, Construction of Gender, Twentieth-Century Feminist Performance, Queer Theory, and a senior seminar, Brave New Families: Politics and Private Lives.[24]

Gender balance in a department's faculty makes no consistent difference in a major's attractiveness to female or male students. Women comprised only 36 percent of the biology faculty in 2002, but 75 percent of biology majors were women. In the last decade the History Department faculty changed from three-quarters male to two-thirds female, yet men recently comprised 47 percent of the majors. One of the most important benefits of coeducation has been the exposure of male students to and resulting respect for the expertise and teaching skills of women faculty. That is good preparation for cooperation and possible reform in the work worlds they will inhabit subsequently. Ever since the beginning of Vassar's coeducation, male alumni have observed how profoundly that exposure changed their perspective on the sexes and their relations.

Student Government and Leadership

If there is some mixed evidence on how far coeducation enhances opportunities for both sexes in the classroom, dormitory life and leadership in extracurricular activities seem unambiguously favorable in this respect. The ease and flexibility in adaptation among Vassar women augurs well for their futures. In the early years of coeducation, there was some tendency for men more often to be elected presidents of student government, classes, and dormitories. But by now frequent gender rotation in all student offices seems taken for granted. In 2002–3 the officers of the Vassar Student Association (VSA) numbered 8 women and 5 men, of the executive board 3 women and 2 men, and of the council 6 women and 4 men, ratios almost identical to that of total students. The president of VSA for the year was male, but his successor female; 8 women and 3 men served as elected class officers—all three class presidents were women, however. Only in the dormitories were male officers more numerous: 17 men and 13 women. But the dormitory presidents split equally, 4 women and 4 men. Managing editors of the *Miscellany News* often have been women. One alumnus remembers serving under four successive women.[25]

A recent student directory lists eighty student organizations, fifty-one of which name a woman as their contact person, with twenty-nine organizations listing a man. They range from a singing group, the Accidentals, to a Zen Meditation Group. They include a wide variety of musical, sporting, performance, religious, service, outreach, and political groups like—the Renaissance Singers, sailing team, ski team, Men's and Women's Ultimate Frisbee, Patchwork Players, Emergency Medical Services, Poder Latino, Habitat for Humanity, Catholic Community, Feminist Majority Leadership Alliance, Philosopher's Holiday, Film League, Queer Coalition, and three organizations beginning with the label Vassar College: Entertainment, Television, and Think Tank.

Extracurricular and Residential Life

Social life on campus has been one of the greatest beneficiaries of coeducation. No longer does a large proportion of the students leave on weekends for other campuses. Instead, Vassar is lively all week long. Informal coeducational games and sporting activity occur near dormitories throughout the campus. The college also has facilitated an open and positive acceptance in extracurricular life of differences in race, ethnicity, religion, and sexual orientation. It provides places for groups who have distinctive cultural, culinary, or other needs to come together when they wish without any detraction from their participation in the general social life. The ALANA center on campus serves African American, Latino, Asian, and Native American students. The college has provided Bayit House for Jewish students and Blegen House for gay, lesbian, and bisexual students.

By now, coeducational dormitories and diversity in options in residential life are taken for granted. Women may request Strong House, the one remaining single-sex dormitory. But the number requesting Strong often is insufficient to fill its rooms, so first-year women who might have preferred coed dorms may be assigned there. In the coed dorms, individual rooms remain single sex, but since 1975, corridors have not.[26] Bathrooms, with individual shower and toilet facilities for privacy, became coed. That soon ceased to cause much surprise or discomfort. As one alumnus of '75 recalled: "Shorts and T-shirts and towels were OK garb there." Brushing teeth side by side made the sexes more like siblings than like sexual objects, paralleling a tendency by both sexes to hang out in groups more than in pairs. Much in demand at Vassar now are two residential complexes organized into suites with four or five bedrooms. Groups of students, single sex or coed, apply together to share a suite. The ratio of the sexes at Vassar can make that difficult for some women who would prefer a coed suite. Men have more choice in finding women housing partners, just as they do in pursuing romantic heterosexual relationships.

Vassar and the Future of Education

Overall, Vassar's experience in making its transition to coeducation shows how the sexes may benefit from interaction before they enter their worlds of work beyond college. That the gender differences in opportunity are lessening now, and the gender gap in higher education increasing, makes Vassar even more exemplary for our collective future.[27] In particular, it has much to teach coeducational colleges that now generally have a preponderance of female students but have not experienced the women's colleges historic preoccupation with equal opportunity for the sexes. That mission from the past remains at Vassar, even as its distance in time from the inception of coeducation increases.

Despite the prevalence of historical amnesia among even well-educated Americans, faculty as well as students, the Vassar community continues to think about the relationship between its past, present, and future. Institutions always have unfinished business. Currently Vassar is addressing issues of diversity. The discussion has moved beyond general access to "creating an environment of inclusiveness," as stated by retiring dean of the college, Colton Johnson, in the summer 2004 *Vassar Alumnae/i Quarterly.*

As Vassar faces the future with confidence, it benefits from the wisdom of the founder. Matthew Vassar had both a clear sense of mission for his college and a profound understanding of how that mission might require new measures as the college's circumstances changed. He told his board of trustees in 1864 that a "college should rise in power" by a process similar to the development of a tree.

> Much may be done by giving it a favorable planting, lopping off its redundant branches, and inserting fruit-bearing scions. So much may be done to plant and prune, and aid a college to absorb in itself the forces of society; but it will never become what we desire till those forces have produced their results. The old limbs will die and new ones will shoot up in their places, and perhaps give it a better form than anticipated. You cannot make a plantation to-day as it will appear half a century hence. It is a necessary condition of success to have a large margin for changes.[28]

The college has always worked on new branches shooting up to replace the old limbs. In a real way the current coeducational Vassar still resembles the single-sex college of the nineteenth and early twentieth centuries whose aim was to provide young women with a curriculum and an education equivalent to those at Harvard and Yale.

Notes

1. Matthew Vassar quoted in Daniel Klein and John Majewski, "Plank Road Fever in Antebellum America: New York State Origins," *New York History* 75 (1994): 57–58.
2. Matthew Vassar, *Communications to the Vassar Board of Trustees by Its Founder* (New York: Standard Printing, 1869), 6.
3. Elizabeth A. Daniels, *Main to Mudd, and More* (Poughkeepsie, N.Y.: Vassar College, 1996), 12–15.

4. In the *Life and Letters of John Howard Raymond Late President of Vassar College* edited by his eldest daughter (New York: Fords, Howard, and Hulbert, 1881).

5. Folders on veterans at Vassar in the Catherine Pelton Durrell '25 Archives and Special Collections, Thompson Library, Vassar College, Poughkeepsie, N.Y. (hereafter Special Collections). . Constance Ellis, ed., *The Magnificent Enterprise: A Chronicle of Vassar College* (Poughkeepsie, N.Y.: Vassar College, 1961), 100–101.

6. The summary in the text of the history of Vassar's decision to become coeducational is drawn from Clyde Griffen, "How Vassar Chose Coeducation," in Elizabeth A. Daniels and Clyde Griffen, eds., *Full Steam Ahead in Poughkeepsie: The Story of Coeducation at Vassar, 1966–1974* (Poughkeepsie, N.Y.: Vassar College, 2000).

7. Thanks to Professor Anne Constantinople for directing us to the materials from the Mellon program archives in Special Collections, Vassar College Libraries, for her analysis of the program's influence, and for other suggestions.

8. A report presented to the Vassar College Alumnae Council, on the Mary Conover Mellon Foundation for the Advancement of Education, by Florence Wislocki.

9. Clyde Griffen and George Langdon, "A Report on the Education of Men at Vassar" May 1968, 94–97. Special Collections, Vassar College Libraries.

10. This summary of the early history of Vassar's implementation of coeducation is drawn from Elizabeth A. Daniels, "After the Decision: How Vassar Coeducation Began," in Daniels and Griffen, *Full Steam Ahead.*

11. Dwight Chapman, "Known Sex Differences and Their Implications for Higher Education," and Malcolm Westcott, "Educational Practices and Individual Differences," in *Report of the Comprehensive Planning Committee,* Vassar College, September1968, 109–41. Special Collections, Vassar College Libraries.

12. After the preschool conference for incoming first-year students in 1978, college chaplain George Williamson observed that new students no longer joked about coeducation, apparently taking it for granted. Oral communication to Clyde Griffen, September 1978.

13. In the Matthew Vassar papers, Special Collections, Vassar College Library.

14. Data on athletics from Vassar College's 1979 self-study for the Middle States Association accreditation. Special Collections, Vassar College Libraries.

15. Seven senior women faculty, interviews by Clyde Griffen: Professors Miriam Cohen, Anne Constantinople, Lucy Johnson, Rachel Kitzinger, and Patricia Wallace, all of whom generously shared their perspectives on the past and current state of coeducation at Vassar and their concerns about potential challenges in the future. Elizabeth Daniels interviewed Professors Ann Imbrie and Molly Shanley; they discussed the relationship of male and female students to female teachers.

16. "Two Trustees of the Class of '74 and One of '76" and "An Alumnus in the Class of '74," in Daniels and Griffen, *Full Steam Ahead,* 110–11, 119.

17. Data supplied by the Vassar College Office of Admission, courtesy Nancy Rubsam, associate director. Also her "Update: A Newsletter for Alumni Admission Chairs, April, 2003."

18. Data on honors by sex supplied by the Vassar College Office of the Registrar, courtesy Colleen Mallett, associate registrar.

19. "A Trustee of the Class of '74," 113–14.

20. Data on geographic distribution of students supplied by the Vassar College Office of the Registrar.

21. Anne Constantinople, Randolph Cornelius, and Janet Gray, "The Chilly Climate: Fact or Artifact?" *Journal of Higher Education* 59 (1988): 527–50; Janet Gray, Randolph Cornelius, and Anne Constantinople, "Coeducation and the Vassar Classroom," *Vassar Quarterly* (Summer 1988): 25–27, 33; Randolph Cornelius, Janet Gray, and Anne Constantinople, "Student-Faculty Interaction in the College Classroom," *Journal of Research and Development in Education* 23 (1990): 189–97.

22. Seven senior women faculty interviews.

23. Data on student majors supplied by the Vassar College Office of the Registrar.

24. Data on gender balance in the faculty of individual departments and on Women's Studies courses derived from the Vassar College catalogue for 2002–3.

25. Annual listings of student officers (VSA, class, and dormitory) and of contact persons for extracurricular organizations are given in Vassar student directories.

26. David B. Brown, dean of students, interview by Clyde Griffen, April 11, 2003.

27. Andrew Hacker, "How the B.A. Gap Widens the Chasm between Men and Women," *Chronicle of Higher Education,* June 20, 2003. p. B10. Mark Clayton, "The Gender Equation, Part One: The Role Gender Plays in College Admissions and Campus Life," *Christian Science Monitor* Web site, www.csmonitor.com, May 22, 2001; and Mark Clayton, "The Gender Equation, Part Two: The Case of Former Women's Colleges: The K-12 Roots of the Gender Gap," *Christian Science Monitor* Web site, www.csmonitor.com, May 29, 2001.

28. Vassar, *Communications to the Board of Trustees,* 26.

3

Coeducation at Wheaton College

From Conscious Coeducation to Distinctive Coeducation?

Susan F. Semel and Alan R. Sadovnik

For more than 150 years Wheaton College, located in the small city of Norton, Massachusetts, dedicated itself to the higher education of women. Then in September 1988 this private liberal arts college admitted its first men undergraduates. Given its historical commitment to the education of women, Wheaton College pursued coeducation within a framework dedicated to ensuring that its commitment to women would be preserved in the transition to coeducation. Through its philosophy of "conscious coeducation," or what is also called "differently coeducational," Wheaton has attempted to create a coeducational institution that links its strengths as a formerly women's college to the education of both men and women. Such an education is grounded in the view that coeducation should help young men and women create a more just world, with men and women equal partners in this quest. The difficult task in this endeavor has been for Wheaton to expand its mission and yet not lose the historical commitment to women characteristic of women's colleges.

Wheaton College: 1812–1975

Judge Laban Wheaton founded Wheaton Female Seminary in 1834 with the assistance of Mary Lyon, who three years later established Mount Holyoke.[1] In the early years, Wheaton Female Seminary was similar to the other seminaries for women of the mid–nineteenth century, as it was part of a larger movement for women's education initiated by reformers such as Mary Lyon, Emma Willard, Catherine Beecher, and Zilpah Grant.[2] In the nineteenth and early twentieth centuries it reflected the changes since charted by Patricia Palmieri—from the Romantic Era (1820–60), concerned with "Republican motherhood," to the Reform Era (1860–90), with its debates about higher education for women, to the Progressive Era (1890–1920), with the entrance of women into the professions and the conservative reaction to women's higher education.[3] Like those of many women's seminaries founded before the Civil War, Wheaton's early mission did not stress education for the professions, but rather for republican motherhood through liberal learning.

During the Reform Era, after the Civil War, Wheaton provided for women the same type of rigorous liberal arts curriculum as the men's liberal arts colleges. By the time Wheaton was incorporated as a college in 1912, it was an important alternative to the prestigious group of women's colleges later called the Seven Sisters. Wheaton's location between Providence and Boston and its upper-middle-class students made it a desirable women's college. In line with the general expansion of higher education that began in the post–World War II period, Wheaton College doubled its enrollment between 1958 and the early 1970s to 1,200 women.[4] Wheaton was more likely than many of its Seven Sisters counterparts, however, to provide an education for an "MRS" along with an AB degree. When Susan Semel attended Wheaton in the early 1960s, the hidden curriculum was threefold: pinned by junior year, engaged by senior year, and married shortly after graduation.

As many of the Ivy League colleges and men's liberal arts colleges in New England became coeducational in the late 1960s and early 1970s, and as a number of women's colleges, including Vassar, Skidmore, and Connecticut College also became coeducational, Wheaton College began to consider its future as a women's college. Wheaton had started to have considerable difficulty attracting high-quality women applicants. Many women who formerly would have gone to women's colleges began to choose coeducational colleges, viewing women's colleges as quaint anachronisms. In 1970 the Wheaton College faculty voted by an almost four-to-one margin, 47 to 12, with two abstentions, to consider becoming a coeducational institution. President William Prentice recommended against this to the board of trustees, however, and the trustees decided not to make the change at that time.

The Balanced Curriculum Project

During the 1980s Wheaton moved in two contradictory directions. Under the leadership of Alice F. Emerson, who in 1975 became Wheaton's first woman president, the college first strengthened its position as a women's college and then became a coeducational institution. Although, before 1980, individual faculty such as Frinde Maher and Kirste Yllo had been implementing feminist curricula and pedagogy in their classrooms, in 1980 the effort became more systematic. Affected by the feminist movement in the larger culture, Wheaton began a four-year Balanced Curriculum Project, funded by a Fund for the Improvement of Post Secondary Education (FIPSE) grant. This initiative energized the Wheaton faculty in an institutional effort to infuse gender issues into all facets of the curriculum and campus life. Faculty committees worked at integrating readings and discussions related to women into many of the college's courses, including but not limited to its women's studies minor. For example, themes and concepts related to women were included in literature, social sciences, and some natural sciences courses. According to Bonnie Spanier, the director of the Balanced Curriculum Project, the "three key elements" to Wheaton's approach to incorporating women's studies throughout the college curriculum were to change departments' introductory-level courses, to encourage all faculty to participate, and to provide strong administrative leadership from the president and the provost.[5] Another important consequence of the Balanced Curriculum Project was that faculty became aware of the "neglect" of "race and class concerns along with gender issues." They realized that "gender issues cannot be understood without taking race and class into account."[6]

Through the Balanced Curriculum Project, Wheaton faculty and administration were making a concerted effort to change the institution from a college without men to a women's college, that is, a college with an explicit mission to provide women with a feminist curriculum. The project culminated in a conference on gender and curriculum and the publication of its proceedings as a model of women's education. As the college celebrated its sesquicentennial, it seemed to have defined its place as a college committed to the distinctive education of women.[7]

Reasons for Considering Coeducation

During President Emerson's tenure, Wheaton began to experience the effects of the larger culture's move toward coeducation. Enrollment at Wheaton declined from 1,319 women in 1975, Emerson's first year as president, to 1,039 students in 1987, the school's last year as a women's college. The quality of the applicant pool and of enrolled students declined as well.[8] Given these institutional problems, President Emerson announced to the faculty and students that the board of trustees was considering transforming Wheaton into a coeducational college. She explained that the college community would explore options in the spring 1987 semester and make a final decision by the end of the semester for implementation in fall 1988.

Several factors led Wheaton's trustees and president to favor coeducation. Although a declining applicant pool, in both numbers and admissions profiles, is cited most often, President Emerson and the board of trustee chair, MIT president Paul Gray, also stressed changes in the culture at large. Gray argued that since formerly men's liberal arts colleges had moved to coeducation in the 1970s, Wheaton could not compete with the other coeducational colleges, nor even with the women's colleges—Wellesley, Smith, and Mount Holyoke—in its New England twelve-college peer group. He pointed to successes of former women's colleges, Vassar and Connecticut College, as evidence of the need for coeducation at Wheaton and argued that only the well-endowed Wellesley, Smith, and Holyoke could possibly survive as women's colleges. Whereas in the 1960s Wheaton could choose among a large number of qualified women who did not get into these three Seven Sisters colleges, once all the men's colleges admitted women in the 1970s, there were fewer women applicants remaining after the Seven Sisters made their selections. President Emerson believed that since feminism had dramatically increased women's opportunities, some of the original reasons for separate colleges for women had become less important. Further, as women were making significant gains in the labor market, Emerson argued, women and men had to learn to work together as equals. Therefore, what was needed was a conscious coeducational philosophy that would enable college men and women to begin to create a more just and gender-balanced world. Educating men and women separately would not provide them with this opportunity. Providing men with a feminist curriculum and gender-balanced environment in a formerly women's college would also help socialize them toward gender equity. Thus, President Emerson argued, what was needed for both men and women was a different type of coeducation.

Faculty Reactions to the Announcement about Coeducation

At an all-community meeting in Cole Chapel in January 1987, President Emerson announced that the college was considering becoming coeducational in September 1988. The college community reacted with shock and dismay—even outrage. Community members later referred to this moment as the "red-letter day," because President Emerson was wearing a red dress when she made this upsetting announcement, and it was also the moment when the official notification was placed in faculty and student mailboxes. In contrast to 1970, when the faculty overwhelmingly voted in favor of coeducation, by 1987 at least a small majority of faculty wanted to maintain Wheaton as a women's college. Even those who believed that coeducation might improve student recruitment were upset with the proposed change. Virtually all faculty were upset by the failure of the administration and board to include them in the decision-making process, as they believed that, in fact, the decision to become coeducational had already been made. At the April 3, 1987, faculty meeting, the faculty passed the following resolution:

> Be it resolved that the faculty objects, in the strongest possible terms, to the process by which the Board of Trustees, in the absence of consultation with the faculty, decided in principle to admit men to Wheaton College in the fall of 1988, and to the violation of trust and mutual and respectful cooperation be-

tween faculty and the Board of Trustees and Administration that this decision in principle represents.[9]

Some faculty referred to the "feelings of betrayal" that the "unilateral" decision created. Paul Helmreich, for example, who had been a professor of history since 1958 and who wrote a history of Wheaton College from 1834–1957, was angry that the faculty had first been told they would be "part of the process to look at coeducation" and then were not consulted. On the other hand, he recognized some of the problems that a longer decision-making process might have created. "If the faculty had been given a year to decide," he later reasoned, "I think the faculty would have been bitterly split and in ways that would have taken a long time to heal."[10]

Even faculty who did not object to the move to coeducation saw problems with the process. Such faculty included Frinde Maher, who was active in the Balanced Curriculum Project, author of numerous works on feminist pedagogy, and herself a product of an all-girl's secondary school and women's college. While Maher saw advantages to Wheaton's becoming a coeducational college, including the "great chance . . . to look at classroom dynamics," she confessed that she had been "really upset by the process." Nonetheless, she was not "surprised" that Wheaton did it this way, "given the way colleges work." Maher recalled the day in January when the announcement was made:

> I had no inkling it was going to happen. January 1987 was the first year that Intro to Women's Studies was being offered and I was teaching it. I had met . . . [the students] once. I had assigned a short story about a utopian women's community and what happens when three men arrive. . . . Tish [President Emerson] announced that the decision was made to become coed and we went back to class and discussed the story and the decision. The students were very upset.[11]

Darlene Baroviak, former dean of faculty and one of the faculty members most active in the Balanced Curriculum Project, epitomized a majority of faculty who, despite being critical of the process, became immediately committed to making coeducation work. She described learning about the decision the evening before the announcement, when Provost Goldberg came to her house to inform her:

> I must say I was quite surprised and stunned by it. I said, "Oh no, how did we get here?" We were told the faculty was going to be involved in the decision. I remember saying that there probably [will] be many who are going to be upset because we think there is still a role for women's education. There are a number of faculty who are supportive of coeducation. For them, I don't think the substance will be the problem, but the process of making the decision. It's just incredible that no one has been involved in it.

I understood probably that there were reasons to make the decision. I was shocked by it, but the process was terribly flawed. . . . I was upset on both counts and was one of those faculty who cried at that first faculty meeting, but I quickly got over it. . . . It was quite clear that the decision was made and we needed to get to it.

. . . I met with alumnae in the weeks following the decision and made it clear that I was not going to work against coeducation in any public or private way because the decision was made and in order for Wheaton to survive we could not be an institution that was hostile to men. We could not be a faculty hostile to the students we would be teaching. And so I let them cry on my shoulder and advised them to make their views known in as wide a way as possible, but I would not join in protest.[12]

President Emerson realized that the administration's and trustees' decision about coeducation had damaged the relationship between faculty and administration. Even nine months after the coeducation announcement, faculty were still letting it be known that their input had not been "considered in the decision-making process and that the 'imbalance' that appeared then . . . [was] still continuing to appear."[13]

Student Reactions to the Announcement of the Coeducation Decision

Many students reacted angrily to the announcement that Wheaton would become coeducational in the fall of 1988. Some had come to Wheaton primarily because it was a women's college; others had become transformed by its feminist pedagogy and gender-balanced curriculum. Writing in the student newspaper, the *Wheaton Wire,* one student called the day of the announcement a "'red letter day' in the annals of Wheaton history. The shock, the distress—it was all there. The bomb had been dropped with four words: 'Wheaton is going Co-ed.'" A student who became a leader of a student opposition group, Save our School (SOS), argued that Wheaton had taught students "not to accept statistics alone" and so should use this lesson to "preserve" the college "for our future and the future of our daughters and all women." She noted that it was not only Wheaton that she was concerned about: "The loss of women's colleges, not just Wheaton, will have a tremendous effect on the education of women in this country."[14]

The SOS student opposition group organized demonstrations during the semester after the coeducation announcement. At a celebration of Eliza F. Wheaton Strong's birthday in April, students wore black clothes and armbands. One student carried a towel with the slogan, "Don't let Wheaton throw in the towel on 153 years of history." Senior Sara Bradshaw gave a speech in which she told assembled students: "It's up to us. We can accomplish a great deal. . . . We are not anti-male and we are not reacting out of emotion—we are not shedding tears."[15]

Years later, a student who had entered Wheaton in 1986 reflected on what had made attending Wheaton as a single-sex institution a positive experience and how she felt about the change to coeducation. When Wheaton was a women's college, traditions played an important role in creating an "affinity among the classes," she said. In combination with "the endless support of the faculty," such customs as "only seniors [being] granted the privilege to sit on the library steps or enter Cole Chapel through the front door . . . had a lasting impact on the incoming students and upperclasswomen." By "transmitting the culture," she noted, upper-classwomen "acted as great role models for underclasswomen." Not surprisingly, this woman found it "heart wrenching" when President Emerson announced the coeducation decision, believing that the change "would eliminate the benefits and uniqueness of a single-sex institution. The administration that once advocated single-sex education said that integration was the wave of the future. The students and alumnae felt betrayed and deserted."[16]

Alumnae Reactions to the Announcement of the Coeducation Decision

Alumnae may have been the college constituency most outraged by the co-education decision. They felt that they had been misled by the just-completed sesquicentennial fund-raising drive, which had been connected to preserving Wheaton as a women's college. Not all generations of alumnae reacted the same, however. Although each group had some who supported and some who opposed the decision, graduates from the late 1970s through the mid-1980s were most vocal in their opposition. Thus, the women who were the products of Emerson's feminist vision, those who had experienced the gender-balanced curriculum and feminist pedagogy, were the ones who most vocally and viscerally attacked the coeducation decision.

Alumnae wrote passionate, long letters to both President Emerson and board of trustees chair Gray in opposition to coeducation. Many described the benefits they felt they had received from attending a women's college. Some said that if Wheaton were to admit men, the college would never hear from them again, since as far as they were concerned, their college had "died" and they no longer had an alma mater. The two letters excerpted here provide examples of alumnae sentiment:

Dear President Emerson:
. . . I am a woman who spent three years in a girls' boarding school and three and a half years in a women's college. I am a much stronger person as a result of this experience. I never saw any field as off-limits to me due to my sex. My life and career choices were never defined due to my sex. I was always recognized in the classroom and on the athletic field and in the dorms as strong mentally,

physically, and emotionally as anyone else there. This was not the case for women that I know who attended coed colleges.

I spent one semester in a small coed university where girls (and they were *girls*) were totally overshadowed by the presence of boys. I was astounded by the fact that they would not go to class if they had a pimple that couldn't be hidden by several layers of Revlon cosmetics. (God forbid a woman should appear flawed.) I was appalled at the fact that they actually tried to get lower grades than that of the boy on whom they had a crush. This is not the kind of woman that I can be proud of as a person.

Other schools have gone coed in recent years. Soon one is never really aware that there are women on campus. The women, whose field hockey games were the big event on autumn Saturday afternoons, will become cheerleaders for the football games where admission can be charged and a profit made. The women will become the girls. The boys will become the men . . .

You are the last of a dying breed. If at all possible, give women a chance to enter the world as strong individuals who see the world as *their own place,* a place where choices are limitless, options are open, and where they *create* the shadow, not stand in it.[17]

Dear Sir [Paul Gray]:

I have received my copy of your most recent letter (announcing the Trustee's final vote), and it appears that the deed is finally done. Wheaton has failed. Wheaton has died. Yes, I cried when I read your letter, for you see, I have lost my alma mater. . . .

Many were shocked that I was considering, in 1972, a women's college. . . . But, to me, the decision was natural. My goal was the best college education I could obtain, and I believed it took a women's college to do that for a woman. I still believe that. . . . The most successful women today are graduates of women's colleges, where women are not relegated to cheerleader and home-coming queen status. If I knew that as a high school student in 1972, then I fail to believe that today's women are incapable of recognizing that, if they are made aware of those facts. . . .

So I have lost my alma mater. And women will suffer as a result. . . . My biggest fear, however, is that young women today don't even recognize or believe that there are still obstacles ahead of us, that women are still disadvantaged and discriminated against in the real world. . . .

How will I sweep up the damage. First, I will recognize that one doesn't give gifts or donations to dead institutions. . . . I respectfully request the college to return the $1,500 three-year pledge you collected from me just prior to your announcement. The gift didn't say "To Wheaton, so long as she remains a women's college," but that was because I didn't think it had to. Implicit in my gift was that it was a gift toward the education of women. I trusted you. You defrauded me of my very hard-earned money, and I think you should honor my request to return it. You took it under false pretenses.

. . . And so I, too, have made my decision. . . . With your vote I have decided to disassociate myself from what the college has become. I can't even muster up the good graces to wish you luck. You have forsaken Wheaton's commitment to women. Putting aside the disaster that I think will be Wheaton's future as a coeducation school, I really can't even bring myself to care. The future of Wheaton is meaningless to me. Wheaton is no longer my Wheaton. My Wheaton is dead.[18]

Alumnae also formed an organization, The Opportunity for Women's Education Is Our Legacy (TOWEL), which challenged trustees to review evidence that would cast doubt on the wisdom of the coeducation decision. Alumnae did not believe that proper studies had been conducted to determine whether admitting men would broaden the pool of qualified applicants or whether coeducation was indeed a "top priority" for students selecting a college. Members of TOWEL questioned what kind of men would come to Wheaton and whether Wheaton would be forced to lower its academic standards. They also expressed fears that a coeducational environment would not provide a "supportive intellectual environment for women" or "foster a sense of self and promote leadership." Their conclusion was that "a decision that so fundamentally changes the character of an institution such as Wheaton should not be made out of the sense of a need for change, nor should it be made without ample time to consider contrary data, information and opinions."[19]

After the trustees voted in June 1987 to finalize their decision to admit men beginning in the fall of 1988, the college began the painful process of trying to win over alumnae, some of whom were actively pursuing legal avenues to challenge the college's right to admit men. These interveners sued the college, saying that it had raised funds for its sesquicentennial under false pretenses by indicating the money would be used for the maintenance of Wheaton as a women's college; they also argued that coeducation violated Wheaton's charter. TOWEL organized a public campaign to reverse the coeducation decision. It was not until spring 1988 that the college reached an out-of-court settlement with those suing over its planned admission of men students. The settlement allowed alumnae to ask for refunds of their gifts and permitted Wheaton to proceed with coeducation. Ultimately only about $150,000 of a $25 million campaign was refunded.

The Transition to Coeducation: 1988–92

In fall 1988, 83 men students entered Wheaton College, making them about 20 percent of the 412 entering students and 7 percent of the enrollment of 1,148 students. During the first few years of coeducation, there was significant conflict between women and men students, and among women students

Predictably, given the opposition of a majority of women students who came to Wheaton as a women's college, many upperclasswomen resented the new men students. An alumna, looking back at the first year of coeducation, wrote about a dramatic incident:

> The first coeducational class showed little if any respect for the history, traditions, or values of the institution. As far as they were concerned, Wheaton was coed, thus it was a new college. They were on a mission to conquer the "old" Wheaton in order to create the "new." The first-year class isolated itself from the upper classes. We were reluctant to change and they were unwilling to follow the footsteps of the alumnae.
>
> After experiencing the first few months of coeducation, several of my friends and I decided to make a statement about what Wheaton once encouraged us to take pride in. About the history that was lost. We wanted to say, "Be proud of being a woman and remember the bonds of sisterhood that Wheaton once fostered."
>
> We copied 4,000 women's symbols and set out to cover the campus with the symbol of Wheaton's heritage. We also drew a 50-foot woman's symbol in the center of the central campus area.
>
> In the wee hours of Wednesday morning, a team of buildings and grounds workers were called in to clear the campus of the women's symbols. The administration had found them offensive. The symbol of the history was now seen as offensive.
>
> The following night some of the first-year men desecrated the 50-foot symbol in the center of the campus by transforming the symbol into a stick figure and drawing a penis in the mouth. Their way of putting the upper-class women in their place was to take a political issue and turn it into a sexually degrading situation.[20]

The new women students generally did not support such actions of upperclasswomen who had been at Wheaton when it was all women. After all, they had come to Wheaton because it was coeducational or, at the very least, with full knowledge that it was coeducational. These women, especially from the class of 1993, tended to bond with the men and felt alienated from their more overtly feminist classmates who preceded them at Wheaton. The women in the 1989–91 classes, the last all-female graduating classes, were sometimes angry at the younger women for their apparent lack of female solidarity and feminist consciousness. In our first visit to Wheaton in April 1991, we met a group of the last all-women's graduating class in a dormitory room. They all expressed anger at the underclasswomen's support of coeducation and their failure to support the protests of those upperclasswomen who opposed coeducation. Their statements confirm what a faculty member later noted: "There was a huge demarcation among the different classes. The last all-women's graduating class looked down at the women in the first coed class. How could they choose to come to a college with men?"[21] One student in the class of 1991 described to us her bitterness as follows:

> I understand the men's failure to understand our history and our concerns. They were recruited to a coeducational college and were met with our belligerence. However, I cannot understand the women, many of whom have made little or no effort to understand Wheaton's history. They, too, are saying, "We came here because it was coed, so get over it."

Another complained:

> It seems that many of the men and even some women go out of their way to violate Wheaton's customs. Underclassmen and -women take pleasure in sitting on the library steps and walking in the front door of Cole.

The college spent very little time examining curriculum reform for co-education. According to the provost of the time, Hannah Goldberg, the college believed that the gender-balanced curriculum developed in the early 1980s was an outstanding curriculum for both women and men, and therefore little curriculum reform was necessary. It is ironic, Goldberg observed in an interview, that many alumnae she met during the year before coeducation asked how the college was going to change its curriculum in light of the admission of men. "Did Dartmouth explore how to change its curriculum when it admitted women?" Goldberg asked. "If not, why should Wheaton have discussed curriculum change for men? We believed that if our curriculum was good for women, it was equally appropriate for men."[22]

Despite the faculty's feeling of betrayal, especially about how the decision to become coeducational was reached, most became committed to translating the balanced curriculum into a "differently coeducational curriculum." They were determined not to allow coeducation to destroy Wheaton's historical commitment to the education of women. Rather, the college would attempt to develop a program committed to gender equity for both men and women. The first groups of men students apparently shared this vision. At the spring 1991 graduation of the last all-women's class at Wheaton, men students presented the graduates with buttons saying, "The legacy will not be lost."[23]

In 1991 President Emerson announced her resignation, stating that she had guided Wheaton to coeducation, and it was now time for a new president to oversee the complete transition. Emerson thought that, given the continued faculty distrust emanating from her and the board's nonconsultative decision, a new leader was necessary to finish the transition to coeducation.[24] She continued to believe that the decision to go coed was the right one and that broad faculty, student, and alumnae consultation beforehand would have taken far too long.

A dorm scene at Wheaton College in the 1950s shows greater formality than the more casual relations between men and women evident in the 1990s photo of a residence hall. *1950s photo by William M Rittasi; 1990s photo by Richard A. Chase.*

At the 1992 inauguration ceremony of the next president, Dale Marshall, trustees urged her to "heed the proud history of Wheaton College, recognizing the promise of the future in the strengths of the past."[25] By the time she took office in 1992, the new president said in a later interview, the transition to coeducation appeared to be over.[26] She realized that there still was much to be done to ensure that the legacy of women's education remained and that the culture of gender equity would be improved, however. And yet she strongly believed that only by increasing enrollments, building the endowment, and creating fiscal stability could Wheaton successfully move to the next level: becoming a first-tier liberal arts college, albeit one with a different climate than that of most coeducational colleges.

Tensions between Wheaton's Past and Present

Although Wheaton's past as a women's college has continued to be recognized, the tension between past and present remains evident. In the years immediately following coeducation, there was a conscious and explicit attempt to honor the past. Today, however, less attention seems to be paid to it on a daily basis. As the college has moved into its fully coeducational period, it has to walk a fine line between reverence for the past and the reality of the present. Students come to Wheaton today because it is coeducational, and although most of them are aware, certainly by the end of the first year, of Wheaton's heritage as a women's college, their commitment is to coeducation. Nonetheless, the college is solidly committed to not letting the legacy of the past die. At an alumnae/i-weekend panel discussion in 1996, "Women's Lives, Men's Lives," an alumnus from the second coeducational class, commenting on Wheaton today and current students' apparent lack of awareness of the struggles over coeducation, stated: "My Wheaton is dead." In response, two alumnae from the early 1980s, asked: "What do you mean, your Wheaton? How do you think we feel?" In response, President Marshall stated: "We will never forget our past as a women's college, even as we continue to move successfully into a coeducational college."[27]

For many Wheaton men, the college's history remained important, as the following statement from the mid-1990s indicates:

As a current male student attending Wheaton College and a member of the class of 1996, . . . I assure you that Wheaton has not lost sight of this mission [to empower and educate women]. . . . As part of Wheaton's First Year student orientation staff for the past two years as well as from my own experience, I report that a respect for Wheaton's rich history can be seen the moment a new student arrives on campus. In continuing with Wheaton's traditions, the first night of orientation the incoming class is summoned to Cole Memorial Chapel by ringing the chapel bells the number of that graduating class's graduating year. Once gathered in front of the chapel, the incoming class is then escorted into the building via the side door (only the seniors are allowed to enter the front doors of the chapel). . . . During the vigil ceremony, the first year class is told of Wheaton's history, traditions, not to mention senior privileges (i.e. only seniors being allowed to enter the front doors of the chapel or to sit on the library steps).[28]

Wheaton appears to have made the transition to coeducation in such a way that the conflicts that marked the first years are not central to the routine activities on the campus. As the college becomes more comfortable as a coeducational institution, however, its relationship to its past becomes more ambiguous and at times tenuous. Yet the college has maintained its commitment to preserving the past and is struggling with how to best accomplish this. However, recent issues of the Wheaton alumna/i magazine have suggested that conscious coeducation and Wheaton's past as a women's college are becoming less salient. Up to 1996, most issues had a number of articles on both; more recent issues have few if any and appear to be playing down Wheaton's past and presenting a view of the college as another good liberal arts college, stressing its work and learning requirements (through the Filene Center for Work and Learning) as an important feature. President Marshall admitted that there has been pressure from some trustees to forget the past and to market the present. Although she indicated that it has been necessary to focus on the college's coeducational present and future, she has always ensured that its commitment to its past is, at the very least, implicit.

College leaders stress the importance of remembering Wheaton's history. They are concerned with the loss of institutional memory as people retire who were associated with the transition from a women's college to a "consciously" coeducational one. Former provost Goldberg, one of the architects of this philosophy, retired at the end of the 1997–98 academic year, and she had been a driving force for maintaining institutional memory. Before her retirement, Provost Goldberg worked diligently to impress on all new faculty the importance of Wheaton's past and its commitment to a different form of coeducation. A core of veteran faculty continues to attempt to socialize new faculty, formally and informally, to Wheaton's philosophy and practices. When asked her reactions if, in 2010, Wheaton were to be described as an excellent coeducational liberal arts college, with no mention of its history as a women's college, President Marshall answered that she would consider this a failure. When asked the same question, Provost Woods, also hired after the transition to coeducation, replied that it would be "unacceptable and impossible to think that the history would be eradicated."[29] Nonetheless, it is not yet clear how successful the attempts to maintain awareness of Wheaton's distinctive past will be as the college hires more and more new personnel.

One attempt to reinforce awareness of Wheaton's history occurred in October 1998, when the college sponsored a conference to celebrate the tenth anniversary of coeducation. Two professors, both leaders of the Wheaton feminist community, organized the conference not only to celebrate Wheaton's transition to coeducation, but also to transmit the importance of conscious coeducation to a national audience.[30]

The conference brought more than two hundred people to Wheaton and provided an important forum for discussing issues related to single-sex education and coeducation. According to an account of the conference, most participants agreed that the Wheaton story represented an important lesson: A coeducational college must be committed to gender equity in explicit ways, and it may be the processes of education rather than its structure that are central to the goals of gender equity. That is, coeducation does not have to be "chilly" to women if it is accompanied by a philosophy, curriculum, and pedagogy committed to gender equity.[31]

Administrative appointments appear to indicate a continuing concern with maintaining awareness of the college's history and a commitment to feminism. Professor of economics Gordon Weil was appointed acting provost for the 1998–99 academic year. A leader in the transition to coeducation, Gordie Weil was an important link to Wheaton's past. In spring 1999 Wheaton appointed as provost Susanne Woods, the former dean of the college at Franklin and Marshall, who has a distinguished record in women's studies.

Provost Woods believes that Wheaton is a different type of coeducational college because of its history as a women's college. Woods has said that if she were to write about her experiences at Wheaton compared to her experiences at other coeducational institutions that were previously men's colleges or universities, she would title the piece "From Boot Camp to Tea Party." She has found Wheaton to be "astonishingly collegial." Other institutions manifest a "self-consciousness of hierarchy," whereas Wheaton has a "comfort with collaborative modes."[32]

The tension between past and present is also reflected in the admissions process. Whereas many veteran faculty believe the college should market its "different coeducation," the admissions director argues "that 17 year olds do not come to college for feminist pedagogy; and that students come to Wheaton today because it is coeducational."[33] Thus, admissions literature plays up Wheaton as an excellent small coeducational liberal arts college. There is little mention of its history as a women's college, nor any discussion of "different or conscious coeducation." Students support this perspective, as many say that they would not have applied to Wheaton had it remained a women's college.

Institutionalizing Gender Equity and Healing Wounds

The transition to coeducation remained squarely at the forefront of Wheaton's concerns during the 1990s.[34] The college's mission statement, still used today, summarizes its commitment to becoming one of the leading coeducational liberal arts colleges at the same time that it retains its historical commitment to gender balance:

> The mission of Wheaton College is to provide an excellent liberal arts educa-tion in a small, residential coeducational learning community, enabling students to understand and participate in shaping the multicultural, interdependent world of which they are a part. . . . *Wheaton teaches women and men to live and work as equal partners by linking learning, work and service in a community which values equally the contributions of men and women* [emphasis added].

Two other important indicators of the college's commitment to women are, first, the development of an Annual Women's Leadership Conference at Wheaton to help cultivate leadership skills in women students and, second, the beginning of reaching out to alumnae with an apology for their feelings of betrayal.[35] The leadership institute and conference, initiated in 2002, will be used, in part, to address the decline in women student leaders since coeducation, especially as the presidents of the student government. After the first conference, Marshall distributed a detailed memo to the President's Council summarizing what the college did well (mentoring, women administrative role models, gender balance in campus offices, women's studies minor and major, campus programs for women, programs that respond to violence against female students) and what the college would like to do better, such as addressing specific problems of distinctive groups of women, including women of color, lesbian women, women in the sciences, women athletes, and feminist women; reducing the gender gap in technological expertise; stressing the competitive as well as the relational aspects of leadership; increasing the opportunities for women-only conversations; and providing for consistent discussions of Wheaton's history as a formerly women's college. With respect to the last item, the memo stated:

> Wheaton's identity as a formerly women's college is not claimed or felt consis-tently across campus. While some in attendance believe that the college tends to be ahistorical in general, others believe that there was a deliberate breaking off from history at the time of coeducation. Throughout the room was interest and hope in fully claiming our history, and a belief that our current strength as a coeducational institution will allow this to happen.[36]

Alumnae's feelings of betrayal have begun to be addressed in college pub-lications. An article in the September 2001 alumnae/i magazine, the *Wheaton Quarterly*, focused for the first time on Wheaton alumnae's feelings following the college's decision to become coeducational. It quoted an alumna, Amber Swope '88, who called in to a National Public Radio program on women's colleges and said to host Juan Williams:

I was one of the sour grapes classes at Wheaton College as well. I remember the announcement. I remember the president coming in and just seating us all in the chapel and telling us it was a "red letter day." And we went to the trustees; we did everything we could to say "Hey, we will help with recruitment. We will do what it takes to keep this place the place that makes it so special." And they did not take advantage of that and they've been coed ever since. And my money has gone to Smith ever since.

When asked by Williams, "Do you think Wheaton is a lesser quality school because it admits men?" she replied:

I think it is a different school. I benefited from the single-sex education I received at Wheaton. And I believe that that's the kind of education I'd like to support. And because Wheaton does not offer it any longer, I don't support it.[37]

Another alumna, also quoted in the *Wheaton Quarterly*, described how over time some of her feelings changed:

"Confusion, horror, anger and resentment." That's the way Amy Wallens Green '89 described her initial response to the coed decision. . . . Green was a sophomore when she heard the announcement in Cole Chapel in January 1987, and recalls her initial frustration. "I chose Wheaton in large part because it was an all-female institution. My aunt, great aunt and grandmother were proud graduates of their classes. Wheaton stood for something in my mind and in my family and the pillars of pride and loyalty were shattered." She went on to say, "I came back to campus when a friend was attending in 96 and she shared with me her Wheaton experience. Socially, it was not my Wheaton, but academically it was stronger. . . . It was not my Wheaton, but it was a good Wheaton."[38]

President Marshall indicated that her conversations with alumnae resulted in her understanding that they felt not merely angry but betrayed. She began apologizing to them formally in her alumnae meetings—not for the decision to go coed, but for the way it was handled.[39] In an effort to heal the wounds, Marshall went on a nationwide "listening tour" to hear alumnae's views and try to bring these alumnae back to their alma mater. According to the *Wheaton Quarterly*, "a 1993 college survey revealed that more than half of those upset by the decision in 1987 had come back to embrace the college; today, even more have returned to full participation."[40]

Assessing Wheaton Today: Distinctive Coeducation?

Gender Ratios

Wheaton aims to be different from an ordinary coeducational college. To be a distinctive coeducational institution that promotes gender equity, it needs to maintain a balance of women and men throughout the college. Table 3.1 charts how well Wheaton has accomplished this (after men were admitted in 1988) for students, faculty, top administrators, and trustees. Although student enrollment has increased to more than 1,500 students, which was the goal when the decision to become coeducational was made, the male student population has not moved above 35 percent. This is consistent with the experiences of many formerly women's colleges, but not with Wheaton's stated goal of gender balance. Wheaton has also been able to improve the academic qualifications of incoming students by becoming more selective. For example, while in 1996, 20 percent of first-year students were in the top 10 percent of their high school class, by 2001 that number had increased to 29 percent.[41] The college's faculty gender ratio has remained at or about 50 percent women, which is an important goal of the college (see Table 3.1). The administrator ratio has remained overwhelmingly female.

The gender composition of the board of trustees has become increasingly female since around the time Wheaton became coeducational. However, President Marshall indicated that until recently the power on the board was concentrated with the male chairs and a small number of wealthy male trustees. With the ascension of alumna Patricia King '63 to the chair, and a number of wealthy female trustees such as Adrienne Bevis Mars '58, vice chair, and Diana Davis-Spencer '60 having influence, the board power is no longer held exclusively by men.[42]

Finances
The financial state of Wheaton has improved since coeducation. In terms of alumnae/i support, the first four years of coeducation found that each year the annual alumnae/i fund broke the previous year's high record for giving.[43] In 1995 Wheaton set a fund-raising goal of $65 million, and by 2000 it had raised more than $90 million. Wheaton was able to reduce its draw from endowment from 6 percent in 1992 to 5 percent in 2003.[44] The endowment in 2003 stood at $129 million. According to former president Marshall, her successor has inherited a fiscally sound foundation in which to launch Wheaton into the top quartile of liberal arts colleges (it is now in the third quartile).[45]

Selectivity
Between 1992 and 2002, Wheaton steadily improved its competitive position, which former president Marshall believes was in large measure due to the decision to become coeducational. For example, with respect to admissions, she noted that "the college's ability to win a diverse group of top students from around the world has grown considerably reflecting the esteem our educational programs have earned."[46] Applications increased from 1,738 in 1993 to 3,534 in 2002; the college was able to be more selective, accepting only 44 percent of

Table 3.1. Representation of women at Wheaton, 1960–2002

	% Students (Total enrollment)	% Faculty (Total faculty)	% Top Administrators (Total administrators)	% Trustees (Total trustees)
1960	100 (785)	66 (79)	57 (7)	43 (19)
1965	100 (1,100)	55 (110)	43 (7)	50 (20)
1970	100 (1,130)	45 (119)	33 (6)	43 (19)
1975	100 (1,319)	52 (116)	80 (6)	50 (22)
1980	100 (1,241)	53 (132)	80 (6)	46 (24)
1985	100 (1,089)	54 (125)	80 (6)	64 (24)
1987	100 (1,039)	—	—	—
1988	93 (1,137)	—	—	—
1990	77 (1,223)	53 (136)	80 (6)	57 (30)
1995	68 (1,300)	48 (133)	80 (6)	61 (28)
2000	66 (1,480)	49 (150)	80 (6)	67 (30)
2002	65 (1,532)	—	67 (6)	62 (32)

Source: *Wheaton College Bulletins*, 1960–2002
Note: Top administrators include president, provost, deans, vice presidents, and director.

applicants in 2002 compared to 80 percent in 1993; the percentage of first-year students in the top 10 percent of their high school class rose from 18 percent in 1993 to 43 percent in 2002; and early-decision applicants, acceptances, and enrollments increased from 42, 41, and 40 respectively in 1993 to 243, 158, and 148 respectively in 2002.[47]

Students and Gender Issues
Just as Wheaton is different today, so are societal gender relations. The majority of Wheaton students come to college out of coeducational postsecondary schools and take coeducation for granted. Although feminism today may be less prevalent than in the period of the balanced-curriculum era of the 1980s, nevertheless, the precepts of liberal-feminism appear to be largely accepted by women before they arrive at Wheaton. Obviously, changes in societal level gender relations have affected Wheaton and its students, just as Wheaton has affected them. Today the open hostility and conflict between women and men that characterized the first years of coeducation have disappeared. In 1987 the questions most often asked were: Why would a man come to Wheaton? What type of men would apply? Based on our interviews with faculty, administrators, students, and alumnae/i, it appears that in the early years three types of men applied to Wheaton: artsy intellectuals, gays, and jocks. On the one hand,

like the Vassar men of the 1970s, both gay and artsy intellectual men seemed to be drawn to a formerly women's college with its less "jocky" and machismo atmosphere. On the other hand, the Admissions Office explicitly recruited male athletes, selling them on the likelihood that they could come in and immediately play at Wheaton.

In addition to examining what type of man comes to Wheaton, a more important question may be how Wheaton women have changed, an issue that the planners did not address. Discussions with faculty, administrators, and students indicate that women who come to Wheaton today are significantly different from Wheaton women of the 1970s and 1980s. First, they appear less concerned with women's issues and are less feminist (at least in their first year), reflecting the culture at large, which is less supportive of feminism. Second, they selected Wheaton because it is coeducational. Although not all women came to Wheaton before coeducation because they were committed to women's colleges (some came for geographic or financial reasons, others because their mothers were Wheaton graduates), they all knew it was for women only, and they could have attended coeducational institutions. Wheaton women today consciously choose coeducation.[48]

The issue of gender has continued to permeate the Wheaton community. Relationships between men and women are an explicit part of its formal and hidden curriculums. Although gender issues and feminist pedagogy do not inform all classes, they clearly are part of the overall climate of the college. Discussions of gender infuse first-year orientation, men's and women's groups, a feminist theme house, and other extracurricular activities—so much that some students by their senior years get tired of discussing gender. One male student told us: "I am so sick of gender. I just want to graduate, get a job, get married, have a family, and never think about gender again." Nevertheless, most of the students we have talked with believe that they are much more aware of gender issues than are their friends who have attended other coeducational colleges.[49]

The style of pedagogy favored at Wheaton tends to be "women centered." On measures of student engagement on the National Study of Student Engagement related to the characteristics of women-centered education, including active and collaborative learning, student-faculty interactions, and supportive campus environment, Wheaton students ranked Wheaton consistently near or above the average of other baccalaureate liberal arts colleges and consistently and significantly above the average of all other four-year colleges and universities.[50]

Student leadership by gender has become somewhat more male dominant over time, but the trends are not overwhelming or entirely stereotypical. In the early years of coeducation, women dominated the student government. In 1988–89, for example, women held the positions of president, vice president, secretary, and treasurer. The following year, women were again found in three of these positions, but a man was, unstereotypically, secretary. In 1994–95 women again occupied three of these four positions, and a man was treasurer. Since then, however, men have dominated or held at least the top position in three years that we examined: in 1995–96, men held all four positions; in 2000–2001, men held two of the four positions, and these were the more stereotypical ones of president and treasurer; and in 2002–3, again men held two positions—president and, more unusually, secretary. We also examined the chairs of three college councils—the Program Council, the Educational Council, and the College Hearing Board. In general, women have been better represented among these chairs. Of six academic years examined, in only one year, 1994–95, did men hold two of the three chairs; in all other years, women held either all three chairs or, as in 2002–3, two of the three chairs.

Men and women students at Wheaton have shared some bathrooms since men were admitted in 1988. *Photo by Colleen Shea, now Colleen Shea Doherty. Marion B. Gebbie Archives & Special Collections, Madeleine Clark Wallace Library, Wheaton College.*

Gay and Lesbian Students

Beginning in the early 1990s, gay and lesbian students claimed that the gender-balanced curriculum and attention to gender issues were heterosexist and left them out of conversations. Wheaton responded by incorporating issues of sexual identity into curricular and student-life programs. As far back as 1975, lesbian students at Wheaton attempted to organize a student club, but on April 24, 1975, President Prentice vetoed the proposed Gay Student Alliance. At the time, presidential approval was required for new student organizations. In fall 1983, IRIS (Individual Rights in Sexual Freedom) was given club status by the Student Union. The first meeting of the Lesbian and Gay Alliance was held on September 24, 1989, about a year after Wheaton became coeducational. In 1990, the group changed its name to the Lesbian, Gay, Bisexual Alliance, with "transsexual" later added to the name.[51] Today, gay and lesbian students are a visible group on campus and, although there have been some reports of harassment, our interviews indicate that the climate is much less chilly than it was between 1988 and 1992. In addition, a gay and lesbian alumni group has been formed.

Minority Students

Minority students, now about 10 percent of the enrollment, also have their own student organizations. In the early years of coeducation, students of color, like gay and lesbian students, felt that their needs and cultures took a backseat to gender issues. Students of color pressured the college to broaden its emphasis on gender equity to a wider emphasis on race and ethnicity. The college responded by making the recruitment of students and faculty of color a major goal. Toward this end, President Marshall instituted a minority recruitment program, which targeted high schools in Boston and New York City and raised funds to support minority scholarships.[52] And yet in 2004 Wheaton was more predominantly white in its enrollment than it was in 1994, having increased from 84 percent to 90 percent white.[53]

Faculty Diversity

Wheaton has been more successful in increasing the racial diversity of its faculty. In 2000 the college received national attention through a first-page article in the *Chronicle of Higher Education* for its aggressive minority-faculty recruitment program. Through a targeted affirmative action policy that bypassed traditional search committee procedures, the college hired five faculty members of color. The *Chronicle* article used Wheaton's success to explore the growing national controversy over race-based affirmative action in faculty hiring and student admissions. Although most faculty, students, and administrators praised the policy, one Wheaton professor interviewed by the *Chronicle* criticized the college for reverse discrimination and pandering to the politically correct climate on campus.[54]

Today, like the liberal arts colleges Wheaton considers its peers, Wheaton remains a largely white, middle-class campus. Like its competitors, Wheaton continues to see increased diversity of students and faculty as a major goal. Additionally, the new Wheaton College interdisciplinary general education curriculum, Connections, stresses race, ethnic, and global issues as strongly as gender issues.[55] Some on campus see this as an important step forward to broaden the college's definition of diversity; others see it as evidence of the retreat from Wheaton's historic commitment to women.[56]

Wheaton in the Twenty-first Century

In spring 2003 President Marshall announced her retirement, effective June 30, 2004. Saying that twelve years was a long enough term as president and that she had successfully guided Wheaton's complete transition to a coeducational college, Marshall indicated that it was time for a new president to lead the college to the next level: to be competitive with the top twenty-five liberal arts colleges in the country.[57]

Marshall's retirement announcement brought to the fore the question of whether the next president needed to be a woman. Dale Marshall herself later reflected on the differences between 1992, when she was appointed, and 2004. She argued that it was essential in 1992 for the successor to President Emerson, the college's first woman president, to be a woman, given the controversy over coeducation. But Marshall said that she believed Wheaton had moved to a level of comfort with and commitment to coeducation and that the college could and should hire the most qualified person, regardless of gender. The announcement of the presidential search made clear to all candidates that while the college was coeducational, it would never forget its history as a women's college or the important pedagogical and curricular contributions of that history.[58]

Wheaton's statement announcing the presidential search honored Wheaton's history as a women's college at the same time that it stressed its improvements since becoming coeducational. It noted that Wheaton has "longstanding, deeply rooted commitments to gender equity, expressed today in a gender balanced curriculum and faculty, as well as to multicultural and experiential learning, and to a global perspective." The statement pointed out that the college had made the choice of coeducation "deliberately," with plans to "carry forward its core values into its new life as a coeducational institution." The challenges for the seventh president would include, it noted, making Wheaton "a school of first choice" for more of its students, and "developing ties with the community of Norton, ensuring that it and the college become increasingly attractive communities."[59]

Patricia King, Georgetown law professor, alumna from the class of 1963, and the first African American woman chair of the board of trustees, led the search for the next president. More than three hundred candidates were recruited, twelve making it to the list of semifinalists. In March 2004 the board of trustees announced that Ronald Crutcher, provost and executive vice president for academic affairs at Miami University of Ohio, would become Wheaton's seventh president, the first African American to hold that office. An experienced academic administrator, world-renowned cellist and music scholar, and founding member of the Klemperer Trio, Crutcher stressed his commitment to making Wheaton competitive with the number-one liberal arts colleges in the country and continuing to make it more diverse.[60]

Conclusions

As Ronald Crutcher begins his presidency, Wheaton College is clearly a different place than it was sixteen years ago. The transition to coeducation, now complete, has resulted in a much healthier financial and enrollment picture. The last five years have brought the largest first-year classes in its history, and the college is as large as it wants to be at present, with a total enrollment of slightly more than 1,500. And yet, the college is still grappling with the effects of coeducation and with how to implement its "differently coeducational" philosophy, curriculum, and pedagogy. Wheaton sees itself as a coeducational liberal arts college, but one that has incorporated the best lessons of women's education for both men and women. These include an explicit emphasis on gender equity in the curriculum, pedagogic practices, and student life and government; a respect for the history and traditions of the institution as a women's college; a broadening of the definition of gender equity to include attention to both men and women; a broadening of the definition of diversity to include not only gender, but also race, ethnicity, social class, and sexual orientation; and the socialization of new faculty, students, and administration into the ethos of the institution.

Wheaton's philosophy of conscious coeducation is concerned not only with maintaining equity for women but also with socializing its new male students. The 1999 accreditation report of the New England Association of Schools and Colleges concluded that Wheaton has succeeded. It pointed to "conversations with male students about their experiences at Wheaton College and their perceptions of the quality of their lives" that indicated that their "Wheaton experience is a transformative one and that they (males) are different individuals at the end of their experience here."[61]

In terms of enrollments, finances, and selectivity, Wheaton today is a much stronger college than it was before it admitted male undergraduates. The key issue is whether over time it can retain its commitment to "conscious coeducation" and be significantly different from other coeducational liberal arts colleges that have more "chilly" climates for women. Our research indicates that a successful transition from a women's college to a gender-equal coeducational institution requires attention to three factors: (1) making explicit an institutional philosophy that is committed to gender equity under coeducation; (2) carefully implementing this philosophy and constantly assessing and reevaluating its successes and shortcomings; and (3) maintaining institutional memory with regard to its history as a women's college and creating a process to socialize new students, faculty, and administration about this history. Overall, we agree with the summary of the conference that celebrated ten years of coeducation at Wheaton: The gender characteristics of an institution (single-sex or coeducational) may be less important to gender equity than processes within a college. Coeducational institutions with gender-equitable practices do *not* have to be "chilly" places for women.

Notes

This research has been supported by a grant to the authors from the Spencer Foundation, to Susan F. Semel from the Hofstra University Faculty Grants Program and the PSC-CUNY Faculty Grants Program at the City University of New York, and by Wheaton College, which provided guest house accommodations from 1996–2001. The conclusions are those of the authors alone and do not reflect the positions of the Spencer Foundation, Hofstra University, the City University of New York or Wheaton College. We would like to thank the many students, faculty, administrators, trustees, and alumnae/i who gave generously of their time, both formally and informally, and without whom this research could not have been completed. In particular, college archivist Zephorene Stickney provided valuable archival support and assistance and made our hours of research in the Wallace Library anything but a lonely experience. Wheaton College historian and professor emeritus of history Paul Helmreich shared generously his rich understanding of the history of Wheaton. We also acknowledge President Emerita Dale Rogers Marshall, Provost Emerita Hannah Goldberg and Provost Emerita Susanne Woods for helping to arrange access to the campus and to interviewees; and Professor of Education Frinde Maher for valuable feedback on our ideas.

Sections of this chapter are adapted from "The Transition to Coeducation at Wheaton College," 134–55, in Amanda Datnow and Lea Hubbard, eds., *Gender in Policy and Practice* (New York: Routledge/Falmer, 2002).

1. See Paul C. Helmreich, *Wheaton College, 1834–1912: The Seminary Years* (Norton, Mass.: Wheaton College, 1985) and *Wheaton College, 1834–1957: A Massachusetts Family Affair* (New York: Crown Books, 2001), for a detailed history of the seminary years.

2. See L. Boas, *Women's Education Begins: The Rise of the Women's Colleges* (Norton, Mass.: Wheaton College Press,1935); and R. Rosenberg, "The Limits of Access: The History of Coeducation in America," 107–29, in John Mack Faragher and Florence Howe, eds., *Women and Higher Education in American History* (New York: Scribners, 1988).

3. Patricia Palmieri, "From Republican Motherhood to Race Suicide: Arguments on the

Higher Education of Women in the United States," in Carol Lasser, ed., *Educating Men and Women Together* (Champaign-Urbana: University of Illinois Press, 1987), 49–66.

4. For a detailed discussion of Wheaton between 1912 and 1957, see Paul C. Helmreich, *Wheaton College, 1834–1957: A Massachusetts Family Affair.*

5. Bonnie Spanier, Alexander Bloom, and Darlene Baroviak, *Toward a Balanced Curriculum* (Cambridge, Mass.: Schenkman, 1984), 73–74.

6. Ibid, 77.

7. Ibid.

8. Darlene Baroviak, Frinde Maher, and Paul Helmreich, interviews by Alan Sadovnik and Susan Semel, Norton, Mass. March 12, 1996.

9. Minutes of the Board of Trustees, May 9, 1987, Appendix B, Box 2552, Wheaton College Archives, Madeleine Clark Wallace Library, Wheaton College, Norton, Mass., (hereafter WCA). Although the faculty passed this resolution, it never voted on a resolution for or against coeducation.

10. Helmreich interview.

11. Maher interview.

12. Boroviak interview.

13. Faculty Meeting Minutes, October 2, 1987, Box 2552, WCA.

14. "Students Cry SOS," *Wheaton Wire,* February 6, 1987.

15. "Eliza Wheaton Strong's Birthday Celebrated," *Wheaton Wire,* April 30, 1987.

16. Brandi Sikorski, "Colliding with Coeducation," *Wheaton Quarterly,* Winter 1994/1995, 23–24.

17. Box 4, 2556, WCA.

18. Ibid.

19. Box 4, 2557, WCA.

20. Sikorski, "Colliding with Coeducation," 24.

21. Maher interview.

22. Hannah Goldberg, interview by Alan Sadovnik and Susan Semel, Norton, Mass., March 1996.

23. Dean Sue Alexander, interview by Alan Sadovnik and Susan Semel, Norton, Mass., April 1996.

24. Alice Emerson, interview by Susan Semel, New York City, April 1996.

25. On Dale Marshall's inauguration ceremony, *Wheaton Quarterly,* Winter 1992/1993.

26. Dale Rogers Marshall, interview by Alan Sadovnik and Susan Semel, Norton, Mass., March 2004.

27. Alumnae Weekend Workshop, October 1996. On a panel on Wheaton, yesterday and today, this discussion occurred between one alumnus from the first coeducational class and two alumnae from the 1970s and 1980s. President Marshall was in the audience and responded to them.

28. Adam Bart, letter to *Wheaton Quarterly,* Spring 1995, WCA, in possession of authors.

29. Dale Rogers Marshall, interview by Alan Sadovnik and Susan Semel, Norton, Mass., May 30, 2001, and Provost Suzanne Woods, interview by Alan Sadovnik and Susan Semel, Norton, Mass., May 30, 2001.

30. "Education for the 21st Century: A Working Conference on Educating Women and Men for the Future," October 30–31, 1998, Wheaton College, Norton, Mass.

31. Kersti Yllo, "Education for the 21st Century: A Working Conference on Educating Women and Men for the Future," October 30–31, 1998, Wheaton College, Norton, Mass.

32. Woods interview.

33. Interview with Gail Berson, Director of Admissions, by Alan Sadovnik and Susan Semel, Norton, Mass., April 1996.

34. *1999 Self-Study for New England Association of Colleges and Universities,* WCA. Copy in possession of authors.

35. Marshall interview, May 30, 2001.

36. Memo, October 7, 2002, given to authors by Dale Rogers Marshall; in possession of authors.

37. "Beyond Betrayal," *Wheaton Quarterly,* Fall 2001, 6.

38. Ibid., 7.

39. "President's Message," *Wheaton Quarterly,* Fall 2002, 3.

40. "Beyond Betrayal," 7.

41. "2001–2002 President's Report: A Ten-Year Retrospective," Wheaton College, Norton, Mass., 2002, 10. WCA. Copy in possession of authors.

42. Ibid.

43. Wendy Killeen, "Wheaton President Moves On," *Boston Sunday Globe,* October 27, 1991.

44. www.wheatonma.edu/president/casestatementfull.html, accessed December 11, 2003.

45. Marshall interview, March 2004.

46. "2001–2002 President's Report," 10.

47. Ibid.

48. These findings are based on interviews and group discussions with students, faculty, administrators, and alumnae/i from 1995 to 2004. We visited the campus at least three times per year from 1996 to 2004; Sadovnik spent a sabbatical living on campus September–December 1995.

49. Student interview by Alan Sadovnik and Susan Semel, Norton, Mass., April 1996.

50. The measures of student engagement can be found on the Wheaton Web site, http://www.wheatoncollege.edu/nsse/ Characteristics of women-centered education are described by Barbara Bank, *Contradictions in Women's Education: Traditionalism, Careerism, and Community at a Single-Sex College* (New York: Teachers College Press, 2003), and Frances Maher and Mary Kay Tetrault, *The Feminist Classroom.* (New York: Basic Books, 1994).

51. Email correspondence with Wheaton archivist Zephorene Stickney, based on data in WCA, October 13, 2004.

52. Marshall interview, March 2004.

53. 1991 *Barron's College Guide* (New York: Barron's, 1991) and "America's Best Colleges," *U.S. News and World Report,* (2005), www.wheatoncollege.edu/nsse/ (accessed December 2005).

54. The search committees made some offers to candidates of color before interviewing all candidates on their shortlist. Wheaton decided that to be competitive with better-endowed institutions, it would begin searches early and make offers to candidates of color approved by the search committee and administration immediately following campus interviews rather than waiting to interview more candidates. In this way,

Wheaton would be able to hire ahead of most other competing institutions. For further information, see Robin Wilson, "What Does it Mean When a College Hires 5 Black Scholars," *Chronicle of Higher Education,* June 9, 2000, p. A16.

55. "Wheaton College Connections" brochure, 2004. Available from Wheaton College Admissions Office, Norton, Mass. In possession of authors.

56. Marshall interview, March 2004.

57. According to the controversial but important *U.S. News and World Report* college rankings, Wheaton continued to be ranked in the second tier (at 62), well behind its New England neighbors, former women's colleges Vassar (12) and Connecticut College (35); women's colleges Wellesley (4), Smith (13), and Holyoke (24); and coeducational Bates (22), Bowdoin (7), and Colby (19). For the complete list see www.usnews.com. Although President Marshall and Director of Admissions Gale Berson publicly question the validity of such rankings, our interviews with them indicate that comparison with these schools is significant and that moving up in the rankings is important. This is true at most universities that criticize these rankings but nonetheless take them seriously, as they affect student applications.

58. Marshall interview, March 2004.

59. "Wheaton: An Invitation to Apply for the Position of President of Wheaton College," www.wheatonma.edu/president/casestatementfull.html, accessed December 11, 2003.

60. Jayne M. Iafrate. "Thrive in a World that Appears to be Falling Apart: Interview with Ronald Crutcher." *Wheaton Quarterly,* Summer 2004, 30–31.

61. New England Association of Schools and Colleges Accreditation Report, 1999, WCA, 10. In possession of authors.

4

A Catholic Women's College Absorbed by a University

The Case of Mundelein College

Prudence Moylan

Mundelein College in Chicago provides an example of how, despite a record of educational innovation and cultural engagement, a Catholic women's college was unable to survive the rapid social, demographic, and economic changes that fundamentally altered its environment. Mundelein's history illustrates key themes raised about the effect of the social changes in the 1960s on Catholic women's colleges. Between 1960 and 1975 Mundelein College redesigned its curriculum and its academic calendar, built a new residence hall, adapted an apartment building for student residents, and built a new Learning Resource Center. In 1974 a Weekend College in Residence, the first in the country, welcomed a hundred new students and grew to more than six hundred students in three years. Yet by 1990 Mundelein was unable to survive the combined forces of declining enrollment and rising costs.[1]

This story has three parts. The first two chart the history of Mundelein College. The third considers how the legacy of Mundelein has had an impact on Loyola University. The period from 1960 to 1975 was characterized by innovation and optimism in the face of change. The struggle to survive as a women's college began in 1975 and intensified until in 1991 Mundelein temporarily affiliated with Loyola University Chicago. The affiliation provided a five-year legal transition period for the dissolution of Mundelein as a distinct corporation. It was during the transition that the idea for a women's center at Loyola took shape. In 1993 the Ann Ida Gannon Center for Women and Leadership became a reality, honoring the Mundelein heritage by continuing a commitment to educating women for leadership.

The BVMs and Mundelein College

The Sisters of Charity of the Blessed Virgin Mary (BVM) have a long history of providing Catholic education. Founded in 1833 when five Irish women from Dublin arrived in Philadelphia, the BVM were determined to take up the work of education in the United States. Mary Frances Clarke, the leader of the women, was assisted in forming a religious community by Reverend Terence James Donaghoe, a priest in the Diocese of Philadelphia. In 1843 the newly formed BVMs and Donaghoe answered the call of Bishop Loras to work on the frontier in Dubuque, Iowa.[2] The BVMs devoted themselves to education and took up work in parish elementary schools as well as establishing their own girls' academies. In 1867 they opened their first parish elementary school in Chicago.[3] When they started St. Mary's High School on the South Side in 1898, it was the first Catholic central high school for girls in the United States. In 1922 the BVMs established a second girls' high school, Immaculata, on the north side of Chicago.[4] The BVMs had a long-established reputation for educational excellence by the time the newly appointed archbishop George Cardinal Mundelein invited them in 1916 to found a college for women in Chicago.

It was not until 1928 that the sisters could take up the invitation. Since Catholic colleges founded by religious communities did not receive direct financial support from the Catholic Church, the BVMs undertook a tremendous financial risk in their response to Cardinal Mundelein's request.[5] Mundelein College, named in honor of the cardinal, opened in September 1930 in a purpose-built art-deco skyscraper on the shores of Lake Michigan, eight miles north of downtown Chicago. The Rogers Park neighborhood on the northern edge of the city had expanded rapidly in the 1920s and was home to a growing middle-class Irish and German population. Mundelein's first president, Sister Justitia Coffey, saw the skyscraper as an apt metaphor for the college's mission: "It is the aim of those in charge of this institution that the quality of instruction shall be in keeping with the exterior of the college—modern, complete, efficient."[6] Coffey also identified the young sisters she needed for the faculty of the new college. Mary DeCock, BVM, noted in an essay on the founding of the college: "The 1930–31 faculty roster lists at least fifteen sisters who earned masters of arts degrees between 1928 and 1930, and four who were enrolled in Ph.D. programs."[7]

When it opened, Mundelein served Chicago women who could not afford to "go away" to school. Many of the students came from the BVMs' two high schools in Chicago. Julianna Jegen recounted that as a Mundelein first-year student in 1944, she and a friend calculated that if they brought their lunch with them, they could complete four years at Mundelein for the same amount of money it would cost to attend Clarke College, a BVM college in Dubuque, for one year.[8]

Catholics in the 1960s: Gannon's Initiatives

Initiatives for change at Mundelein began in 1957 when the BVM congregational leaders made Ann Ida Gannon, BVM, the new president of the college. Appointed to the Mundelein faculty in 1951, Gannon had already established herself as a popular teacher of philosophy when she was made president. Under her leadership, Mundelein and the BVMs were eager to be included in the conversations initiated by Pope John XXIII when in 1961 he called the Second Vatican Council, which encouraged the Catholic Church to be in dialogue with the secular world. Gannon took initiatives in educating BVM sisters, developing new curricular programs, and increasing collaboration with laity.

Educating BVMs

One of Gannon's first initiatives was collaboration with the BVM congregation in the education of young members. A 1951 papal address to the first International Congress of Teaching Sisters in Rome directed women's religious congregations to properly prepare young members for ministerial work.[9] A nationwide Sister Formation movement launched in 1952 aimed at providing a college education for young members before they were assigned to work. The education program was ready by 1957 when the first class of forty-eight young BVMs, known as scholastics, arrived to complete their college education side by side with the more than 1,100 young women studying at the college.[10]

From 1957 to 1969 Gannon facilitated the enormous effort to educate young BVMs at Mundelein. Like Coffey, her predecessor, she worked with the leaders of the congregation to choose young women with the potential for college teaching and send them to graduate school to prepare them to join the faculty at Mundelein or at Clarke College. Many young members of the congregation were sent for graduate study at a wide range of universities in the United States and abroad in preparation for joining the college faculty. Between 1959 and 1972 more than forty-two BVMs who had completed master's or doctoral degrees taught for a period at the college.[11]

In the 1960s there were between fifty and sixty BVMs working as faculty or staff at the college in collaboration with an increasing number of laywomen and laymen.[12] The change agents within the college were young faculty members who were BVMs. They were the most liberal group of faculty and had the most influence on older sisters.[13] They created a college culture receptive to innovation and brought to conversations in the college and in the congregation the critical insights and the enthusiasm for cultural dialogue gained from their graduate education. Language and literature specialists in Russian, Spanish, English, and French conversed with philosophers, theologians, and historians about the global pressure for change in church and state. It was in theology that the change was most evident at Mundelein.

Ann Ida Gannon, BVM, president of Mundelein, congratulates three students for their summa cum laude scholastic standing. *Mundelein College Records, Women and Leadership Archives, Loyola University Chicago*

Theological Developments

In 1957 Gannon asked Carol Frances Jegen, BVM, to establish a Theology Department.[14] In 1960 Jegen developed a summer course for BVM high school religion teachers that became the foundation for a graduate program in theology at Mundelein. The first religious education summer session in 1961 included seventy-five BVMs and fifteen diocesan priests sent by Cardinal Meyer. A summer lecture series with eminent theologians who participated in the Second Vatican Council was an integral part of the continuing summer sessions. After 1961 the summer courses were opened to hundreds of students, mostly women religious.[15]

Changes in Governance

Like most Catholic colleges and universities in the 1960s, Mundelein established separate incorporation from its founding congregation and created a lay board of trustees, a decision that would have far-reaching consequences. This incorporation coincided with the need to clarify the independent as opposed to church-related status of Catholic colleges in order to make them eligible for federal funding. Gannon sought federal funds for dormitory and library construction. Nevertheless, she decided in 1969 to locate the Religious Studies Department in a separate building that received no federal funding rather than in the new Learning Resource Center to avoid any appearance of federal funds being used in support of religious education. When Mundelein's first lay board of trustees met on August 16, 1967, ten laymen and five BVMs, including the officers of the BVM congregation, attended the meeting as members.[16] For the remainder of Mundelein's existence, the trustees were predominantly Catholic laymen who saw themselves as helping the sisters rather than as taking full responsibility for the finances of the college. The number of laymen on the board ranged from nine to seventeen; no ordained men ever served. The first laywoman joined the board in 1968, and except for 1971, thereafter at least one laywoman always served on the board. The first African American appointed to the board, a laywoman, joined in 1988 (see Table 4.1).

BVMs maintained influential participation in the governance of Mundelein in two ways. First, the women leaders of the BVM congregation continued to serve on the board of trustees, although they were a minority of the membership. A second and less obvious source of BVM influence came through the creation of members of the corporation, who had "the right to approve or veto certain decisions of the Board of Trustees . . . [and] to approve or veto nominations for new members of the Board." The members' most important responsibility was to approve or veto board decisions "involving acts of ownership: mortgaging, selling, merging, closing the Corporation."[17] Through this legal entity the BVMs working at the college and the leaders of the congregation insured that their direct participation and approval was required for any decision on ownership

Table 4.1. Mundelein board of trustees membership, 1931–1990

	BVMs	Laywomen	Laymen
1931–67	8	0	0
1967	5	0	10
1970	5	1	12
1975	5	2	12
1980	5	4	17
1985	6	5	17
1990	7	8	15

Source: Women and Leadership Archives, Loyola University Chicago Mundelein College Records, Series A.5.1, General College Records, Trustees, Governance.

of Mundelein. Though no one could foresee the future, the legal processes that would be required for the affiliation agreement between Mundelein College and Loyola University had been created in 1967.

The Faculty

The BVMs' expanding cooperation with laity, both Catholic and non-Catholic, was also evident in the faculty. Gannon recruited women and men to join the Mundelein faculty and raised salaries to make Mundelein a competitive institution. In 1975, by the end of Gannon's tenure as president, the BVMs were no longer a majority on the faculty (see Table 4.2). Since the college was supported by the contributed services of the BVMs, one of the major causes of the financial crisis of 1990 was the trustees' failure to find alternative sources of income as the contributions of the BVMs declined.

Administrators

By contrast with the trustees and the faculty, the college administration changed little until 1983. From the college's founding until 1962, the administrators consisted of the president, the treasurer, and the dean, all sisters. The president also served as superior of the community of sisters at the college until 1963, when the two positions were separated and a new superior was appointed for the community. This was done to make clear the distinction between the community and spiritual lives of the sisters and their work at the college as faculty or staff. In 1962 the first lay male administrator, Norbert Hruby, joined the administration in a newly created position of vice president, and in 1965 another layman, Daniel Cahill, became vice president for development and

Table 4.2. Mundelein faculty, 1960–1990

	BVMs	Laywomen	Laymen
1960	60	11	6
1965	52	27	15
1970	48	30	16
1975	46	35	24
1980	41	35	22
1985	31	31	18
1990	18	37	14

Source: Women and Leadership Archives, Loyola University Chicago Mundelein College Records, Series A.5, General College Records, Faculty.

public relations. Women continued to lead the college even as laywomen administrators joined BVMs in the 1980s. Table 4.3 shows the addition of lay men and lay women in administration.

A Self-Study

In 1962 Gannon began an influential process of self-study to answer the audacious question: "Does this college have the right to exist?" While it is safe to assume she believed the answer was yes, she wanted to know what changes were necessary to assure excellence. Under the direction of Vice President Hruby, the entire Mundelein community engaged in a process of critical analysis and collaborative planning that created a lively intellectual community[18] A 1965 self-study showed that Mundelein had educated young women to take responsibility in church and family but had not educated them to be change agents in the broader society.[19] The new focus at Mundelein was to educate Catholic women to be leaders in creating and directing social change. The mission statement was updated, and the college calendar and the core curriculum were completely revised. Mundelein learned about change by doing it.

The Mission Evolves

The evolution of the mission statement in the 1960s and 1970s reflected the ecumenical energies of the Second Vatican Council and the recognition of the principles of religious freedom, as well as of the changing status of women

Table 4.3. Mundelein top administrators, 1962–90

Presidents and vice presidents			
	BVMs	Laywomen	Laymen
1962	1		1
1965	1		2
1970	1		1
1975	2		1
1980	3		1
1983	2	3	4
1985	4	4	1
1990	3	3	1

Source: Women and Leadership Archives, Loyola University Chicago Mundelein College Records, Series A.5.1, General College Records, Governance, Administrators.

in U.S. society. From its beginning, Mundelein's mission always included a practical awareness of the importance of preparation for paid employment in women's lives. The phrasing of this concern varied, but it never disappeared from statements about the purpose of the college. In 1930, for example, Mundelein claimed that it prepared a graduate "to go forth well-equipped to maintain her place in the economic world, and at the same time to claim the place that is rightfully hers as a Catholic social and civic leader."[20] From 1932 to 1962 the college claimed that "the curriculum . . . should secure if necessary the power of economic independence."[21]

By the end of the 1960s, the emphasis in the mission had shifted from the practical purpose of education for economic independence to education for personal development, specifically, "to awaken an enduring intellectual curiosity." The means to achieve this goal was a shared search for truth among faculty and students, a critical self-motivated pursuit of lifelong learning. In 1930 the graduate was prepared to be "a Catholic social and civil leader," but by 1970 the graduate was to be able to "grasp [the] . . . permanent Christian values which give ultimate meaning to life." The meaning of leadership shifted from fulfilling one's social roles to defining one's goals and roles personally.

Academic Innovations

Mundelein introduced two new academic innovations that fundamentally altered the nature of study. A new term system, a calendar of three ten-week terms, replaced the traditional long-semester system, though credits were still based on semester hours.[22] Students were to take fewer courses per term so that they could concentrate more fully on their subjects. Ideally they would take three or four courses that had a relationship in content or methodology. For example, courses in Victorian literature, modern British history, and modern philosophy would provide an interdisciplinary approach to nineteenth-century Britain. A second innovation, a new core curriculum called Basic Studies, distributed core requirements across the four years of college.[23] The traditional Western Civilization course, for example, became a senior requirement. The faculty envisioned this as a capstone experience that would enable students to integrate their liberal arts education. The students, however, did not like the new core curriculum and resented it as an unnecessary infringement on their educational choices and their maturity as seniors.[24]

At the end of the 1960s, Mundelein experimented with even greater student self-direction when it adopted further revisions of its curriculum. General education requirements were dropped and students were encouraged to create their own educational plan with advice from the faculty. An independent study program, Mandala, allowed students to create their own curriculum and completely abandon formal courses. All college committees were reorganized so that faculty and students would make decisions together about common interests. The students in the early seventies who had helped draft the collaborative practices were disappointed with the reality. Faculty and student interests did not coincide, and one group or the other was bored by the joint meetings.[25]

These dramatic innovations in the curriculum and calendar were accompanied by some turmoil in the administration. Two interim deans served from 1968 to 1970, when Robert La Du was hired as vice president for academic affairs. He presided over a creative and chaotic two years and then spent the final year of his three-year term on leave. Strong leadership in academic affairs was reestablished when Susan Rink, BVM, was appointed vice president for academic affairs in 1973. By 1978 the all-college committees had been replaced by separate associations for students and faculty, and general education requirements reinstated for all students.

Student Life

The changes at Mundelein that began in the 1960s were about more than governance, calendar, and curriculum; they were also about learning to accept and celebrate diversity. In 1965 the college created the Degree Completion Program for women who left college to marry and never returned to complete their degrees.[26] Returning women students enrolled in regularly scheduled courses, but they could also choose from a series of weekly three-hour seminars. Mundelein began an outreach to black students in 1965 and to Hispanic students in 1975.

The Mundelein community was even more radically transformed by the arrival of hundreds of teenage resident students when new dorms were provided in 1962 and 1963. Within the decade diversity was not only a classroom experience but a challenge of living together. Coffey Hall, a new dormitory named for the first president, opened in fall 1962 with 208 residents. Northland Hall, an apartment building converted to a residence hall, opened in 1963 with another 250 students. Mundelein had provided for a few resident students since 1934 but had never committed itself to being a college with responsibility for creating a resident student community. Joan Frances Crowley, BVM, was named director, later dean of residence, in 1962.

In the collection of memoirs *Mundelein Voices,* Cowley recounted her experience of life in the 1960s among the students. She recalled how students were divided over the Vietnam War. Crowley remembered sharing conversations with "three upperclassmen [who] were dating West Point cadets" and with a young woman "whose fiancé was planning to emigrate to Canada."[27] Students sponsored teach-ins to learn more about U.S. foreign policy and marched in the April 1968 protest that was broken up by the Chicago police. Crowley encouraged students who supported the war to bring officers from Fort Sheridan to campus to present another side of the argument, but they didn't follow up on the project.

Another important topic of conversations with students was "the meaning of sexual freedom" and Catholic teaching on birth control. Crowley noted the realistic assessment of the editor of the student newspaper, the *Skyscraper,* who wrote in 1966 that "unless a positive statement on birth control is forthcoming, this one point is volatile enough to call church allegiance into grave question among a large number of Catholics."[28]

The conversations on sexuality reported by Crowley and appearing in the *Skyscraper* were always about heterosexual issues. Homosexuality never appeared in the documentary record. Crowley never mentions this in her account of residence life. Anecdotal evidence from alumnae of the 1970s and 1980s affirmed that a few lesbian relationships among students in residence were known and unchallenged. Friendships and loving relationships among women were encouraged and celebrated, but no sexual dimension of such relations was publicly acknowledged. The college seemed to have had a "Don't ask, don't tell" policy that was tolerant of homosexuality among students, staff, and faculty as long as it was either an invisible or a nonassertive presence.[29]

When Crowley began her tenure in residence, the students were happy to have more liberal hours. By the end of the decade the students were proposing a "no hours" policy and an end to in loco parentis policies that assumed the college authorities could act in place of parents in the students' lives. In retrospect Cowley said of her life with students: "Their response to a decade that ran the gamut from racial confrontation to war, changing sexual mores and the challenge of a modernizing church, kept me in dialogue with myself. I learned much from them and have reason to believe the feeling was mutual."[30] Her sentiments, widely shared by faculty and staff, were to be even more characteristic of student-faculty relations in the Weekend College after 1975.

Admitting Men

In 1968 Mundelein had to address the issue of admitting men. Three years earlier, Loyola had removed the restrictions limiting women's access to programs on their Lakeshore campus.[31] Mundelein had joined the Central States College Association (CSCA), a group of small coeducational liberal arts colleges in the Midwest, in 1967. One of the advantages of association membership was the opportunity for students to take classes at member colleges. Young men from CSCA schools applied to attend Mundelein, and a decision on admitting them had to be made. Gannon was committed to the primacy of educating women. She did not want to exclude men who wished to attend Mundelein but did not want to recruit men as students. This compromise became Mundelein policy. The board of trustees and the members of the corporation agreed in 1968 to amend the Articles of Incorporation to include male students. The college lawyer did not actually register the change with the State of Illinois until 1971. In a 1968 memo Gannon stated: "It was not the intent of the Trustees to render the college coeducational."[32] On the 1971 amended Articles of Incorporation Gannon again wrote in her own hand that the change "was not intended to provide for coeducation in the full sense." Under the law, however, Mundelein was now incorporated "to provide and furnish opportunities to persons of both sexes on equal terms in all departments of higher education."[33] Gannon believed that with Loyola as a neighbor with an adjacent campus, it was unrealistic for Mundelein to become fully coeducational.

Mundelein would remain a college dedicated to educating women, but men who wished to study with women would be welcomed. After the CSCA visitors attended Mundelein in 1970, there was only an occasional male student registered among the full-time day students. After 1969, the men in day classes were more likely to be Loyola students taking advantage of a new cross-registration program for Mundelein and Loyola students.[34] Men did register at Mundelein in the graduate program and after 1974 in the Weekend College program, but only briefly did they constitute more than 10 percent of the students. The 10 percent measure was commonly accepted as the basis for saying Mundelein was a women's college that admitted men, not a coeducational college. In the 1980s when faculty were asked to suggest enrollment initiatives, one person suggested that increasing the male enrollment to 30 percent would not jeopardize the focus on women, but this was not widely supported.

Gannon affirmed her commitment to the future of women's colleges in 1973 when she claimed that women's colleges had a long tradition of practicing the respect for women that the culture was only beginning to affirm in theory: "Every aspect of a [woman's] college . . . witnesses to achievements for women in governance, faculty, academic achievement, student participation."[35]

Feminism

Feminism came to Mundelein as it came to many entities in the United States in the form of Betty Freidan's *The Feminine Mystique*.[36] Vice President Hruby asked the entire faculty to discuss it in study groups. In 1971, the faculty senate inaugurated a Women's Studies Committee that encouraged the creation of cross-disciplinary courses with a focus on women. In 1977, a Committee for Women created by interested faculty organized two conferences on women, in 1978 and 1979, supported by the Illinois Humanities Council.[37] The Committee for Women then began the process of formalizing the women's studies minor. They surveyed the curricular offerings and interviewed department chairs, learning that more than twenty relevant courses were offered in six departments. They invited Gerda Lerner to speak on the politics of women's studies in February 1982.

The work of the Committee for Women stirred up controversy over the meaning of feminism at a women's college. In March 1982 fifty-two faculty signed an open letter to the committee expressing concern that feminism was a narrow ideology and would not serve students well in their goal to compete in the real world defined by men.[38] Undaunted and with administrative support, the committee planned the September 1982 faculty orientation around the theme "Educating Women Leaders in the 1980s" and proposed a women's studies minor, which was approved by the Curriculum Committee in 1983. The 1989 peace studies minor integrated feminist perspectives, and the John D. and Catherine T. MacArthur Foundation supported the creation of a Center for Women and Peace in 1990.[39] Feminism in its many guises, rather than being unnecessary at a women's college, was the inevitable outcome of teaching women and men to think critically.

Several of the men at Mundelein in these years later wrote in *Mundelein Voices* reflecting on the importance of feminism. Steven Schmidt, who joined the religious studies faculty in 1976, said: "Here I learned to know my first intellectual stirrings of feminist thought. . . . Gifted feminist colleagues confronted me daily. . . . The man's world was always in question . . . and gradually I began to know the full meaning of self-criticism and gender honesty."[40] David Block, a Weekend College student, recalled writing "a précis on a classic feminist reader response essay by Patrocino Schweickart" in Brooks Bouson's literature class. He said: "I quickly came to see that almost everything I have ever read can be seen through a feminist view that forces the reader to notice that the heroes are male, the enablers are female, and that the literature game has been rigged for more centuries that one can count."[41] Michael Fortune, a professor of English, who also taught in the Religious Studies Graduate Program, reflected on the lives of men and women and "concluded that among most couples . . . a subtle understanding of the subordinate role of women lay at the base of their relationship."[42] His experience at Mundelein led him to decide "it was up to women to demand equal acceptance for the situation to change, and it was up to males to assist their efforts wherever possible." He determined to help by teaching writers of both sexes.

Race

Appreciation of gender diversity evolved over the decades, but issues of race awareness at Mundelein emerged quickly. According to Crowley, race awareness was divided into before and after 1968.[43] Before 1968 race was not acknowledged as an issue. Roommate assignments for new first-year and transfer students were made based on identifying shared interests in student essays without regard to race. In 1965 twenty-eight students and eight faculty joined the Selma march with broad support from the Mundelein community. A small number of students who protested the student council's decision to use student activity funds to support the marchers were generally ignored. After the death of Martin Luther King Jr. in April 1968, the black students met in an overnight session and emerged with a list of demands. The college administration responded positively to this confrontation, providing black students with meeting space, expanding course offerings and hiring practices to acknowledge diversity, and supporting McCuba, Mundelein College United Black Association, their new student organization. Diane Allen, a McCuba founder, recalled the "subtle white barriers" experienced by black students: "Black music was not played at mixers; weekend trips to colleges were planned for colleges that had few Black students; Humanities III, the music appreciation course included no Black composers or musicians."[44]

Since it was only in 1965 that Hruby developed a proposal for "outreach to Negro students" and only in 1966 that the Education Program launched Upward Bound, a federally funded summer program designed to help aspiring minority high school students to succeed in college, only a small percentage of black students were enrolled.[45] In fall 1970 registration figures indicated that the minority enrollment of seventy-six students was double that of 1969.[46] Nevertheless, the college community had accepted the challenge of a steep learning curve on the issue of race in the United States.

Mundelein's outreach to Hispanic students did not begin until the 1970s.[47] The Hispanic Institute that provided a course of study for ministers serving Hispanic Catholics in Chicago was launched in 1972 through the graduate religious studies program. The Education Department inaugurated the Bilingual/Bicultural Program in 1975. Ford Foundation grants supported outreach to young Hispanic women undergraduates through the Hispanic Alliance begun in 1981. The next year Hispanic students created their own organization, Hispanics for the Advancement of Our Culture and Education (HACE), which was reorganized in 1986 as Latins United for Our Cultural Heritage (LUCIR).

Changing Demographics

During the 1960s, changes in student demographics and student choices brought new challenges to Mundelein. As the Illinois higher-education system provided opportunities for more students to go to public colleges, the percentage of students in private colleges in Illinois declined from 50 percent in 1960 to 29 percent in 1970.[48] In the 1980s, with the exception of Hispanics, few of whom went to college, the number of eighteen-year-olds in Illinois declined by 19 percent.[49]

Mundelein's proportion of full-time younger day students declined for several reasons. Girls' high schools, Mundelein's traditional feeder schools, began to close in the 1970s. The two BVM high schools closed, St. Mary's in 1973 and Immaculata in 1981. Girls who did attend single-sex high schools often

Two celebrating students, representative of the diversity Mundelein was able to attract. *Mundelein College Records, Women and Leadership Archives, Loyola University Chicago*

did not want to continue their education in a single-sex college. Many alternatives became available to young women as formerly men's institutions became coeducational and the states rapidly expanded their higher education institutions with both community colleges and four-year institutions. The changes in Catholic culture after the Second Vatican Council meant that Catholic families no longer felt required to send their children to Catholic colleges. The success of the graduates of Catholic institutions often led parents to want to send their children to institutions with more cultural prestige. The rising cost of private higher education had put it beyond the reach of young women from working-class families. The result of these factors was that the number of students in college increased even as the distribution changed.

A few developments enabled colleges like Mundelein to do better than might have been expected. The private colleges in Illinois were able to benefit from expanded state support for higher education after 1958 through the Illinois Financial Assistance Act and Illinois State Scholarship Awards. The federal government programs for student loans also enabled Mundelein to increase financial assistance to students.[50]

Enrollment, Enrollment, Enrollment

The appointment of Susan Rink, BVM, as academic vice president in 1973 signaled an end to the shockwave of change in the 1960s. Her most pressing challenge was to increase enrollment. In 1970 there were 1,311 students registered in the fall term, including 72 graduate students, for a total of 1,127 full-time-equivalent (FTE) students. In the fall of 1973 there were 1,110 undergraduates enrolled, for an FTE of 887. For an institution that depended on tuition revenue, this was a precipitous drop.

In 1974 Gannon and Rink began a Weekend College in Residence.[51] Initially, the program was advertised with the hope of getting thirty students, but nearly a hundred students registered for classes. For the remainder of the 1970s, enrollment remained fairly stable (see Table 4.4).

Though the total number of students remained fairly stable from 1975 to 1980, the number of full-time students declined precipitously (see Table 4.5). Full-time students constituted 65 percent of enrollment in 1975 but only 41 percent in 1985. The number of part-time students exceeded full-time students

Table 4.4. Mundelein enrollment, 1960–90

	Day	Cont. Ed.	Weekend College	Other	Total
1960	1,005	0	0	195[a]	1,201
1965	1,199	108	0	144	1,351
1970	808	263	0	38[b]	1,108
1975	578	316	432	53	1,380
1980	445	212	688	9[c]	1,354
1985	387	119	579	0	1,085
1990	311	85	515	6	917

Source: Women and Leadership Archives, Loyola University Chicago Mundelein College Records, Series H.2.1, Registrar Reports, Enrollment.

[a] Young members of religious communities of women, most of whom were BVMS known as scholastics, who attended Mundelein between 1957 and 1970.

[b] Special students who were not registered for a degree and visiting students from other schools in the Central States Colleges Association, including nine men in 1970.

[c] Students from a special program for the National Association of Banking Women.

for the first time in 1981. The numbers do not tell the full story of changing demographics in the student population. Part-time students were generally older students, so age became a challenging aspect of diversity at the college. The success in recruiting women students over the age of twenty-three changed the climate of the college, but the change was gradual. Since the continuing-education students were older women who attended weekday college classes, the weekday program had 894 students compared to 432 weekend students. But viewed from another perspective, Mundelein had 748 students over twenty-three and only 578 who were younger. Weekend classes were not open to younger undergraduates without special permission, which was granted, but only rarely, to juniors and seniors.

For the most part the older and younger students had separate classes. In general, the older women enjoyed being in class with younger students, but the younger students were less enthusiastic. They named the older women DARs for Damned Average Raisers.[52] Faculty generally found the diversity in the intergenerational classroom a positive contribution but noted the challenge of classroom climate. Mundelein did not take on the challenge of creating an intergenerational climate except when individual faculty addressed the challenge in a specific course. By the fall of 1980 adult students over twenty-three outnumbered younger students by 916 to 476.

Although men did enroll in the Weekend College, college policy was not to actively recruit men, so the total number of male students remained low (see Table 4.6).

Since the 1960s, the college had made a commitment to increase recruitment of minority students. The changing demographics of the city of Chicago facilitated this intent. Mundelein enrolled 26 percent minority students overall in 1985 when the Catholic women's colleges averaged 14.6 percent minority enrollments.[53] By 1990, when overall enrollments had dropped (from 1,085 in 1985 to 911), the percentage of minorities had increased to slightly greater than

Table 4.5. Mundelein full-time students, 1970–90

	Day	Cont. Ed.	Weekend Evening College	Total
1970	846	91		937
1975	546	125	233	904
1980	436	109	173	718
1985	348	44	62	454
1990	298	38	93	429

Source: Women and Leadership Archives, Loyola University Chicago Mundelein College Records, Series H.2.1, Registrar Reports, Enrollment.

Table 4.6. Mundelein student enrollment, 1982–90

	Day	Cont. Ed.	Weekend Evening College	Total
	Female/Male	Female/Male	Female/Male	Female/Male
1982	421/9	205/15	562/47	1,188/71
1985	385/2	119/0	476/103	980/105
1990	311/0	84/1	461/54	856/55

Source: Women and Leadership Archives, Loyola University Chicago Mundelein College Records, Series H.2.3, Registrar Reports, 1981–90.

35 percent, and the percentage of black students was just twice as great as the percentage of Hispanic students (see Table 4.7).

Mundelein continued its founding mission to serve Chicago-area women, many of them the first in their families to attend college, but the cost of education in private or independent colleges had increased dramatically since 1930. In the 1980s, Mundelein had significantly more students from poor families than the national average, which meant that more financial aid was devoted almost entirely to the younger day students.[54] Table 4.8 shows the increases in aid despite a drop in enrollment.

Rising Costs

When Ann Ida Gannon, BVM, was appointed president in 1957, the college had a balanced budget. Under Gannon's leadership the college expanded to include

Table 4.7. Mundelein minority enrollment in Day/Cont. Ed./Weekend College, 1982–90

	Black	Hispanic	Asian	Indian	Total (including whites)
	Total (%)	Total (%)	Total (%)	Total (%)	
1982	98/33/97	43/12/38	13/4/9	1/4/0	
	228 (18)	93 (7)	26 (2)	5 (0)	1,254
1985	73/23/87	42/6/29	16/3/6	0/0/1	
	183 (17)	77 (7)	25 (2)	1 (0)	1,085
1990	57/12/135	52/8/37	11/5/7	1/0/2	
	204 (22)	97 (11)	23 (2.5)	3 (0)	911

Source: Women and Leadership Archives, Loyola University Chicago Mundelein College Records, Series H.2.3, Registrar Reports, 1981–90.

Table 4.8. Mundelein tuition revenue and student aid, 1960–85

	Enrollment (FTE)	Tuition revenue	Student aid
1960	1,065	$ 556,170	$ 87,396.
1965	1,283	$ 1,104,756	$ 255,653
1970	1,128	$ 1, 244,741	$ 283,569
1975	1,004	$ 1,997,777	$ 598,197
1980	1,186	$ 3,418,858	$ 1,544,400
1985	807	$ 4,305,583	$ 1,484,696
1990	726	$ 5,755,195	$ 2,230,272

Source: Women and Leadership Archives, Loyola University Chicago Mundelein College Records, Series I.1.2, Treasurer/Business Officer Reports. Financial Records, Annual Audits, 1938–91.

Note: Enrollment figures for 1985 are not included in the annual audit so comparable figures are taken from the enrollment reports from the registrar. Enrollment for all years except 1985 includes summer school. If summer school were included in the 1985 figure, it would be higher.

two dormitories, a new-construction and a renovated apartment building, and a new Learning Resource Center, as well as another residential property in the neighborhood. Gannon also expanded the faculty to include more laymen and laywomen as well as more young sisters. She established competitive salaries and provided support for advanced study for both lay and religious faculty.

In 1960 the college had a surplus of $18,000 revenue over expenditure, but the auditors provide a note that presaged difficulty in the future. In 1938 in order to meet the requirements for endowment income required for accreditation by the North Central Association, auditors devised a way to account for the contributed services of the sisters. Each sister's salary was defined according to what would have been paid to a layperson in her position, and the total of sisters' salaries donated to the college was capitalized at 5 percent in order to create a "living endowment.[55] The auditors' note in 1960 explained that the college would have had a deficit of $275,000 if not for the contributed services of the sisters.

Between 1960 and 1965 the assets of the college increased from $4 million to $8 million, but costs increased as well. The deficit was $268,000 but contributed services amounted to $405,000. In the decade from 1960 to 1970, the college had transformed itself into a nationally recognized residential women's college, but the costs of this transformation rose faster than the number of students. The FTE enrollment in 1960 was 1,065 and in 1970 was 1,128. Tuition nearly quadrupled, from $360 to $1400 per year. Instructional salaries went from

$120,753 to $474,615. By 1970 the assets had increased to $13 million, but the deficit had nearly doubled, to $517,000, and contributed services amounted to just under $316,000, no longer enough to cover the deficit.[56]

Federal Funding for New Initiatives

The college had established an Office for Public Relations and Development by 1970, but raising money for a small Catholic women's college was not easy. Gannon recounted several instances of approaching corporate foundations only to be dismissed because women's colleges did not contribute to the corporate interest—they had no corporate officers who were graduates of women's colleges. Gannon's experience is a glimpse into the culture of gender inequality in corporate life that began to change only when legal challenges to these customs were successful. State and federal government programs were the main sources of financial support. Illinois State scholarships were available to students at public and private colleges. Financial help to address the challenges of a diverse institution came primarily from federal programs.

Mundelein was not alone in facing financial challenges as a result of the rapid changes in higher education and in the Catholic Church in the 1960s. The American Association of Catholic Colleges and Universities addressed this problem regularly in meetings and in its journal. One of the experts on this issue, Paul C. Reinert, S.J., president of St. Louis University and friend to Gannon, alerted her to the federal government's program for Advanced Institutional Development. With the help of Margaret Irene Healy, BVM, Gannon was able to insure that Mundelein qualified as a "developing institution" before she left the presidency in 1974. Susan Rink, BVM, the new president of Mundelein, continued to work with Healy in writing the proposal that was funded in 1975. In the decade from 1975 to 1985, Mundelein received nearly $2.5 million in federal assistance as a developing institution under Title III of the Higher Education Acts of 1965 and 1972.[57]

The federal funds supported a variety of initiatives at Mundelein. Faculty and administrators learned the terminology and the practice of strategic planning and management by objectives. The clarity with which goals and objectives had to be stated, the timelines for achieving objectives, and the necessity of evaluation increased the accountability and the transparency of the work of faculty and staff. Everyone learned to read enrollment reports and auditors' statements. Curricular and advising programs for students were developed and student satisfaction was measured. The funds made the development of computer resources possible and paid for faculty development so that computer-assisted learning was actually implemented. Maintenance of the physical plant was possible, though the needs remained greater than the funds available. The recognition provided by federal funding also helped to gain support from foundations and corporations. The boost in enrollment and funding that the Weekend College and federal grants brought in the 1970s not only provided encouragement but also provided good practice in planning and developed an institutional perspective among faculty, staff, and students.

From Financial Stability to Financial Crisis

By 1980 enrollment at Mundelein had again fallen into decline. Competition for adult students increased, as many colleges developed satellite campuses and taught evening and weekend courses. More women entered the workforce and no longer had the time to return to college to complete their education on weekdays. Fewer nontraditional students enrolled for full-time study on weekends.

Consultants hired by Mundelein found that it was difficult for the college to coordinate its recruiting efforts aimed at three distinct populations.[58] The diversity of Mundelein's students had created confusion in the public mind. As the success of the Weekend College was publicized and recruiting for it in the media made Mundelein's programs for nontraditional students familiar, people began to think that Mundelein was only for adult students. Young women, and more importantly their families, did not identify Mundelein as a college that served their needs and interests. The decline in the numbers of young students made Mundelein appear to be a school where older students were the priority because they were the majority.

Disagreements over admissions policy led to tensions between the faculty and administration. Rink consolidated the admissions offices for day, continuing education, and weekend college in 1978, hoping to enhance administrative efficiency. She made the decision without consulting the faculty. In response, the faculty organized the Faculty Association to gain a greater voice in college governance. Though the new Faculty Association was accepted by the administration and the faculty was better able to define its contribution to the success of the college, the tension between faculty and administrative responses to enrollment issues remained.[59] The faculty supported the effort to increase day-program enrollments but was often more interested in expanding the nontraditional student population.

During the 1980s, administrators tried to recruit from among traditional-age college students, who would ideally be full-time students for four years. This ideal college student was increasingly rare except in the most selective of institutions. College students were transferring between or among schools, and increasingly they were taking more than four years to complete a college degree. Mundelein also recruited transfer students and created transfer agreements with the community colleges to make this process easier. However, the number of full-time day students continued to decline.

The precipitous decline of full-time adult students between 1975 and 1985, more than 60 percent for continuing education and 70 percent for weekenders, was not addressed by the consultants or the administration in developing recruitment strategies.[60]

Financial Troubles and Mundelein's Demise

Despite declining enrollments, Mundelein maintained financial stability, however precarious, until the mid-1980s. But declining enrollments and dramatic growth of the deficit pressured the college toward a radical break with its past. Part of the sudden decline of Mundelein's financial status was the result of administrative decisions. John Richert succeeded Rink in 1983 after a difficult and controversial search for a new president. No single candidate had the support of the whole Mundelein community, and after being interviewed, some candidates were unwilling to take the position. Although many of the faculty strongly opposed selecting John Richert, a committee of trustees and BVMs decided to offer him the presidency. He had improved enrollment at St. Mary's College in Omaha, Nebraska, and promised to take bold initiatives to do the same at Mundelein. He made it clear that he believed it was necessary "to spend money to make money" and that increasing enrollment would require new investments in recruiting and in development.

Richert also focused on recruiting traditional-age students. He increased emphasis on the athletic program and hired consultants. This was a decade when the eighteen-year-old population in Illinois declined by 19 percent except among Hispanics. Richert was unable to increase enrollment.

After only one year, both faculty and BVM administrators shared a concern about the cost of Richert's initiatives. When Rink left the presidency in 1983, Mundelein had an operating surplus of $36,000.[61] Richert, however, rapidly increased the number of vice presidents and associate vice presidents from three to eight, which increased administrative costs by $750,000 from 1983 to 1985. By 1985 the operating-fund deficit was $1,484,696, and enrollments had not increased.[62] That same year, Mundelein bought out Richert's five-year contract after only two years of service.

A significant change in administrative leadership was unable to stem the declining enrollments. In 1985 the board of trustees appointed as president Mary Brenan Breslin, BVM, a Mundelein alumna and long-time vice president for finance.[63] Mary Murphy, BVM, was appointed academic vice president after the departure of Jeffrey Willens, one of Richert's new administrators who stayed only one year. Breslin and Murphy had worked together at Mundelein since the 1960s and were good friends.

Like her predecessor, Breslin was convinced that full-time day students offered the only hope of financial stability, based on predictable tuition income. Her efforts to recruit a traditional-age student population were no more successful than Richert's, however, though they were less extravagant. The Admissions Office developed no new initiatives to recruit adult students. The budget for recruiting full-time weekday students was nearly double the budget for recruiting Weekend College students, a reflection of the recruitment emphasis.[64] From 1985 to 1990, as the number of weekday and weekend students continued to decline, the accumulated deficits grew to nearly $3 million. A new mortgage backed by the congregation of the Sisters of Charity, BVM, refinanced the debt, but strict repayment requirements were imposed. The mortgage debt at Mundelein doubled to $6,262,533 in 1990 after the refinancing that allowed for consolidating the debt.[65]

In 1990 with an enrollment of 726 full-time-equivalent students, it became clear that the college would be unable to meet its repayment obligations. The contributed services of the BVMs at Mundelein that had offset the debt until 1970 totaled $149,269 in 1990. The changes in the membership of religious congregations, including the BVMs, meant that this amount would only get smaller over time. The college could not continue on its present course.

From Temporary Affiliation with Loyola to Dissolution, 1991–96

From November through January of 1991, various committees and consultants addressed the future prospects for Mundelein.[66] One option was simply to close the college. A group of faculty, the Vision Committee, proposed making Mundelein a college for adult students with a special focus on women. A committee of trustees, administrators, and faculty, the Long Range Planning Committee, emphasized Mundelein's Catholic character as its primary heritage. Overtures for an affiliation were made to De Paul University and to Loyola. DePaul was uninterested but Loyola responded favorably. Joseph Sullivan, chair of the board of trustees at Mundelein and a member of the board of trustees at Loyola University, had successfully merged several businesses and saw this as a reasonable possibility.

Loyola University Chicago, founded by the Jesuits in 1870 as St. Ignatius College, became a university in 1908 and began a move to its Lakeshore campus in the Rogers Park neighborhood of Chicago, which was geographically contiguous to Mundelein. The BVMs had a long history of collaboration with the Jesuits in Chicago, beginning with their work in Holy Family Parish in the 1870s. The Jesuits had supported the BVMs' mission at Mundelein from 1930, serving as faculty in theology and philosophy and as chaplains. Faculty- and student-exchange programs developed after 1966 when Loyola admitted women to all programs on the Lakeshore campus. Loyola had recently sought to expand by creating a landfill in Lake Michigan but had been refused permission on the basis of a little-known environmental law protecting the Lake Michigan lakebed.[67] The Mundelein property, though more expensive than landfill, would provide Loyola with a lakefront expansion. Mundelein's Catholic heritage would fit nicely with the Jesuit educational mission at Loyola.

Carolyn Farrell, BVM, replaced Breslin as president in late February 1991 and joined negotiations on affiliation that had begun.[68] She had redefined her own understanding of the BVM commitment to women's leadership as mayor of Dubuque, Iowa, in 1980, as a fellow at the Hubert Humphrey Institute for Public Affairs at the University of Minnesota in 1988, and as the first director of the Women's Office established by the BVM congregation in 1989, where she developed a noninstitutional approach to educating women for leadership.[69]

Administrators announced the negotiations on affiliation on March 19, 1991, and informal groups of students immediately held rallies and protests. The student government prepared a report for the trustees that detailed student concerns regarding the affiliation and sponsored a panel discussion, "Save Our College," to seek support.[70] One of the students, Meg Ivo, summed up the importance of Mundelein for many women:

> For sixty years, Mundelein College has been a place for the empowerment of women. Mundelein's educational programs and the Mundelein community as a whole provide unique opportunities for free and open discourse among women. This atmosphere has proven itself time and again to produce strong leaders.[71]

Karen Veverka, another student, highlighted the value of a community of learning: "Our students have a closeness and an open relationship with the faculty that is unique to this institution. We do not wish to lose this." Dina Grammatis added: "We are being taught to be aware of global events around us, so that we are able to educate and inform others." Meg McCarthy said: "We have grown in a sense of unity among ourselves and each other regardless of race or creed. This has been a refreshing component in the social structure of Mundelein, seeing as it is simply not present in other areas of our lives and of the world." Alicia Rangel noted that "the tradition of Mundelein is . . . the richness of the liberal arts, . . . the joy of learning, and the building of a community that lasts a lifetime."[72] When the BVMs hosted a farewell gathering for the students, Mary Alma Sullivan, BVM, expressed the pride the sisters felt in hearing the students' statements on the mission of Mundelein.[73]

Despite student concerns, the trustees signed the preliminary agreement with Loyola on April 11 and approved the final agreement on June 10, 1991. The facts on Mundelein's financial condition forced the pace of decision making. Mundelein and Loyola faculty in the Communication Departments made a video documenting the event.[74]

During the brief negotiation, there had been little time to develop a plan for

Mundelein students protest the proposed merger of Mundelein with Loyola University, 1991. *Mundelein College Records, Women and Leadership Archives, Loyola University Chicago*

recognizing the Mundelein heritage within Loyola. Mundelein undergraduates were invited to become Loyola students and until 1993 were allowed to choose whether their degrees would come from Mundelein or Loyola. Many tenured Mundelein faculty were given appointments with rank and tenure, after a hurried interview process, in their respective departments at Loyola. However, several tenured Mundelein faculty were not offered or did not accept Loyola appointments and sued Loyola over its failure to honor their tenure in the affiliation process. After several years the lawsuit was decided in favor of the Mundelein faculty.[75] Nontenured faculty and some tenured faculty in programs that Loyola did not have were given five-year contracts in 1991. Most administrative and staff employees at Mundelein were offered positions at Loyola and many accepted, but staff positions were subject to the financial resources at Loyola, which by 1994 were under strain.

The affiliation agreement stipulated support for an annual Conference on Women and a limited commitment to continuing the Weekend College Program. Loyola used the name Mundelein College for its adult program, formerly University College, from 1991 to 2003, when the adult program was renamed the School of Professional Studies. The BVM/ Mundelein heritage was commemorated in 2001 by a brass plaque on the skyscraper, renamed Mundelein Center in 2003.

The affiliation process was expected to take five years. In 1991 Farrell accepted an appointment as associate vice president at Loyola with responsibility for overseeing the process. The rhetoric of affiliation and the creation of Mundelein College of Loyola, focusing on the historic tradition of cooperation between the Jesuits and the BVMs, was basically a legal requirement to allow for all the affairs of the Mundelein Corporation to be completed in a five-year transition. It created some confusion but also eased the pain of Mundelein's demise. Raymond Baumhart, SJ, president of Loyola, along with Gannon and Farrell, emphasized that affiliation was a new stage of partnership in educational mission. The respect given by Loyola leadership to Mundelein administrators, faculty, staff, and students made a painful process bearable.

Mundelein students and alumnae grieved the loss of their alma mater. Mary Griffin, a much loved faculty member, dean of the college 1960–66, and the inspiration for the Weekend College, gave the final baccalaureate address on June 9, 1991. She affirmed with the students the love of the college on the shores of Lake Michigan where "you gained knowledge and skills . . . but most of all where you learned how to live, how to create, how to celebrate."[76] She then used a tradition learned from Christian communities in Nicaragua who honor their heroes by reciting their names and asking the community to respond "Presente!" (Be present). As she called upon the leaders and the students of Mundelein's past, the assembly responded "Presente!" Having called forth this Mundelein community, she issued this challenge:

> Loyola may have thought it was acquiring a splendid piece of lakeside property. . . . What it is really taking on is a vast spiritual assemblage with a dangerous memory. The memory of a college where women know what it is to be equal. And those of us affiliating with Loyola aren't likely to settle for less! Part of your job—graduates of 1991—is to keep alive that dangerous memory.[77]

Then sounding a more hopeful note, she recalled the words of T. S. Eliot—"To make an end is to make a beginning"—and concluded with the hope that the new beginning in affiliation with Loyola would bring the students "a bright future filled with promise."[78]

The Ann Ida Gannon Center for Women and Leadership

Once the five-year transition to legally dissolve the Mundelein Corporation was under way, Farrell realized that without a more permanent physical and financial commitment to educating women for leadership than had been specified in the affiliation agreement, the Mundelein heritage would disappear. When Farrell became the Mundelein president in February 1991 and a participant in the negotiations on affiliation, she asked if Loyola had a women's center but never got a clear answer. By the fall of 1991 Farrell had learned that in fact Loyola did not have a women's center and that faculty and student proposals to create one had been rejected. As part of her responsibility for achieving a successful affiliation, she initiated a dialogue with Loyola women, Focus on Women. The yearlong conversation among Barbara Bardes, dean of Mundelein College; Kathleen McCourt, dean of the College of Arts and Sciences; and Susan Ross, associate professor of theology; and others led to a vision of a women's center that would support research and teaching on women as well as serve undergraduate women students. Farrell had found a way to give material reality to the BVM/Mundelein legacy within Loyola through her new relationships with Loyola women leaders.[79]

Realizing that before this idea could be presented to the Loyola administration she needed a name and financial support, Farrell received Gannon's permission to use her name and a pledge of financial support from Dennis Keller, the founder of DeVry Institute and Keller School of Management, whom Gannon had befriended when he was a young man. Farrell presented the proposal for the Gannon Center to the Loyola president, John Piderit, SJ, and the Development Office. Its appeal, she argued, was partly that it would enable fund-raising from Mundelein alumnae, many of whom were confused or unhappy about the fate of their alma mater. Piderit agreed that all funds contributed by Mundelein graduates could be designated for the Gannon Center Endowment. The endowment campaign was supported at the outset by a $200,000 contribution from Virginia Piper, a generous benefactor to Mundelein in the past and a friend of Gannon's, and by a $150,000 contribution from the Sisters of Charity, BVM. With the generous support of Mundelein alumnae, the endowment goal of $3 million was reached in 1999. In 2005 the endowment had more than $4 million, much more than Mundelein had ever had.[80]

The Gannon Center's mission to recognize women's leadership in its many guises—past, present, and future—was now on a sound financial footing. The center has facilitated linking existing projects with new initiatives that promote women's leadership. The Loyola Women's Studies Program worked closely with the center even before moving its office there in 1997. The Women and Leadership Archives has an active collection policy and also holds the Mundelein College Archives. The Annual Women's Conference, conferences on women in business and women in science, a Visiting Scholar Program, research support for faculty and graduate students, and a scholarship program for undergraduate women students are among the center's activities.

The Gannon Center moved in 2005 into the newly renovated Piper Hall, the lakeside mansion that served as the Mundelein Library from 1934 to 1969 and was home to the Religious Studies Department from 1969 to 1991. An elegant gathering space has been provided for the university community on the first floor. The second and third floors have been designated for the Gannon Center offices, the archives, the Women's Studies Program, and a common area for student and faculty gatherings. Through the renovation of Piper Hall as a space for the Gannon Center for Women and Leadership, the spirit of intellectual community and hospitality characteristic of Mundelein College has been reestablished. In 2002 the BVMs honored the two hundredth anniversary of the birth of Mary Frances Clarke, their founder, by a gift to three places where her spirit was being made visible.[81] The Gannon Center was one of the three, even though it is a part of Loyola University and the BVMs have no institutional connection with it.[82] Gannon and Farrell followed in Clarke's footsteps, creating new and productive relationships to continue to educate women for leadership in society and in the Church. Mundelein College as a corporation was dissolved, but the BVM mission as lived by Farrell continues in the relationships that the Gannon Center has encouraged within Loyola and sustained among Mundelein alumnae and the BVM congregation.

Still the questions asked by the student government leaders in 1991 remain.

> Why does American society allow a school with good academic programs and effective leadership training programs to fail financially? In other words, this crisis is symbolic of what appears to be happening more and more in higher education; fewer and fewer people are receiving the opportunity to receive a college education at the institution of their choice. Is the value of women's experience being phased out?

> What larger symbol of failure are we sending to our own students and to women in general? . . . there are so few institutions of higher education run by women for women, when one fails the ramifications are much more widespread.

> Is the Catholic Church (specifically the Jesuits) ready to allow women to continue to control their own destiny even though affiliation may occur?[83]

The student questions for the board of trustees in 1991 were prescient. One answer may be provided by the work of centers for research on women on how much of women's experience is validated by coeducation. The Gannon Center at Loyola represents a twenty-first-century pioneering effort as the only center committed to women's leadership in a Catholic coeducational institution. Loyola University, through its support of Farrell's initiatives in creating the Gannon Center, has taken the lead in responding to the challenge posed by Mundelein students in 1991—to educate women and men in a way that recognizes both their diverse experience and their full equality.

Notes

1. The Catholic context for women's higher education is provided in a recent collection of essays, Tracy Schier and Cynthia Russett, eds., *Catholic Women's Colleges in America* (Baltimore: Johns Hopkins University Press, 2002).
2. Ann M. Harrington, *Creating Community: Mary Frances Clarke and Her Companions* (Dubuque, Iowa: Mount Carmel Press, 2004), 36, 42–46.
3. M. Jane Coogan, BVM, *The Price of Our Heritage*, Vol. 1, 1831–1869 (Dubuque, Iowa: Mount Carmel Press, 1975), 378–79.
4. Ibid., 269–70, 403.
5. Mother Isabella Kane, superior of the congregation, and Sister Justitia Coffey, appointed first president and superior of the yet to be realized college, were directly involved in the purchase of property, the design of the building, and the supervision of construction. They secured all the funding for the enterprise.
6. Mundelein College Records, Women and Leadership Archives, Loyola University Chicago (hereafter MCR), Z Shelf List. 2A.1 Scrapbooks 1930–41, 1930–33; newspaper clipping, September 21, 1930.
7. Mary DeCock, "Creating a College: The Foundation of Mundelein, 1929–1931," in Ann Harrington and Prudence Moylan, eds., *Mundelein Voices: The Women's College Experience, 1930–1991* (Chicago: Loyola Press, 2001), 17.
8. Julianna Jegen, conversation with the author.
9. Information in this paragraph comes from Ann M Harrington, "A Class Apart: BVM Sister Students at Mundelein College, 1957–1971," in Harrington and Moylan, *Mundelein Voices*, 123–27.
10. MCR, Series E 6.2 Administration, Enrollment Reports.
11. MCR, Series A.5.3,.General College Records, Compilation of Personal Information, Faculty, 1957–58, 1965–66.
12. In this essay the term "laywoman" or "layman" identifies those who have not taken religious vows, though in the technical distinctions of canon law women with religious vows are laypersons. Members of the Roman Catholic Church are designated in two groups—ordained and nonordained, that is, clerics and laypersons. Men who are members of religious congregations, those who take vows, may be cleric or lay, but all women members of religious orders are laypersons since they cannot be ordained. See *Dogmatic Constitution on the Church*, Vatican II, *Lumen Gentium*, November 21,

1964, in *Vatican Council II: The Conciliar and Post Conciliar Documents*, vol. 1, new rev. ed. (Collegeville, Minn.: Liturgical Press,1984), 388, 403.

13. MCR, Series C.3.h, Institutional Planning, Institutional Analysis, Norbert Hruby, "Truth and Consequences: Mundelein College Emerges from Analysis."

14. The information on the religious studies program is based on Jegen's account; see Carol Frances Jegen, BVM, "Working with the People: The Religious Studies Department 1957–1991," in Harrington and Moylan, *Mundelein Voices*, 106–22.

15. Those who had completed three summer sessions received a certificate in religious education. The request for graduate courses came from this group. Under Jegen's leadership an undergraduate major in religious studies was approved in 1968, and a graduate program in religious studies in 1969. More than seven hundred students representing many parts of the United States and ten countries in Latin America, Africa, and Asia had completed an MA in religious studies by 1990. Mundelein College was the center of a theological program that shaped Catholic religious education not only in Chicago but also in a national and world context. In addition, when the BVMs began their congregational renewal in 1968 in response to the Vatican decree *Pefectae Caritatis,* they were among the most theologically well-educated congregations in the United States ("Decree on the Renewal of Religious Life," Vatican II, *Perfectae Caritatis,* October 28, 1965, in *Vatican Council II,* 611–23). The details on individual religious congregations were the results of a sisters survey conducted in 1967; see Marie Augusta Neal, SND de Namur, *Catholic Sisters in Transition: From the 1960s to the 1980s* (Wilmington, Del.: Michael Glazier, 1984)

16. MCR, Series A.5.1, General College Records, Board of Trustees, Governance Lists.

17. MCR, Series A.5.1.a-c, General College Records, Members of the Corporation, Administration. BVMs who had worked at the college for one or more years elected five of their number to serve two-year terms as members of the corporation. These five BVMs in turn selected three trustees, one of whom was the chairperson, to serve as members for a one-year term. Ex-officio members included the president, first vice president, and treasurer of the BVM congregation and the president of Mundelein, who chaired the members.

18. Norbert Hruby, "The Golden Age of Mundelein College: A Memoir, 1962–1969," in Harrington and Moylan, *Mundelein Voices,* 183. Hruby brought with him "Maurice Donahue's Concept of an Institutional Self-Study Process," which would be the basis for restructuring Mundelein. The institutional analysis (IA) Hruby developed had three components: first, "searching questionnaires to be administered to . . . faculty, administration, students, alumnae and even husbands of alumnae"; second, "study groups . . . of faculty, administrators and students to inquire in depth into the governance, the curriculum, the library and even the parietal rules . . . ; and third, "an advisory committee of eminent educators and scholars . . . whose responsibility was . . . to react to the reports of the study groups."

19. Robert Hassenger, a faculty member in the Psychology Department, assisted Hruby in implementing the self-study and wrote on the results of the study in Robert Hassenger, ed., *The Shape of Catholic Higher Education* (Chicago: University of Chicago Press, 1967). Hassenger also wrote about Catholic higher education in Philip Gleason, ed., *Contemporary Catholicism in the United States* (Notre Dame, Ind.: University of Notre Dame Press, 1969).

20. MCR, Series A 2.2a4, General College Records, Sponsorship and Mission, Early Mission Statements.
21. Ibid.
22. MCR, Series C.4, Institutional Planning, ConCur. Term system.
23. Hruby, "Golden Age," 185–86.
24. Author's experience in teaching the course to seniors in 1968 and in course evaluations.
25. MCR, Z Shelf List, 2B.4 N4.1, Official Set of *Skyscrapers: Skyscraper,* April 18, 1969, included *Hades* 1, 1, an experimental newspaper that reported on the open discussion on sex by seven students. The focus was entirely premarital sex.
26. Hruby, "Golden Age," 186.
27. Joan Frances Crowley, BVM, "Remembering 1962–1969," in Harrington and Moylan, *Mundelein Voices,* 178.
28. Ibid., 159, 171.
29. These assumptions are based upon the author's conversations with students, alumnae, and colleagues while a faculty member at Mundelein College from 1966 to 1991.
30. Crowley, "Remembering 1962–1969," 180.
31. MCR, Series EE.3, Administrative Reports, Loyola/Jesuit Records, James F. Maguire, President of Loyola, to Gannon, December 22, 1965.
32. MCR, Series A. 1.1, General College Records, Charter/Revisions, memo signed by Gannon as Chair of the Members of the Corporation, 1968.
33. MCR, Series A.1.1, General College Records, Amended Articles of Incorporation approved by the State of Illinois.
34. MCR, Series EE.3, Administrative Reports, Loyola/ Jesuit Reports, memo from Robert LaDu, Academic Vice President at Mundelein, to Mary Brenan Breslin, BVM, Director of the Business Office, January 19, 1970, confirming tuition and fees for exchange agreements in 1969.
35. MCR, Series A, 2.2.a2, General College Records, Sponsorship and Mission, Mission/ Catholic, Ann Ida Gannon, BVM, "Identity and Purpose—Musts for the Independent College," *AAUW Journal,* November 1973, 15–17.
36. MCR, Series C.3, Institutional Planning, Institutional Analysis.
37. MCR, Series F.7.2c, Academic Affairs, Special Academic Programs, Committee for Women, vol. 2, 1981–82.
38. Ibid.
39. MCR, Series F.7.6, Academic Affairs, Special Academic Programs, Peace Studies.
40. Stephen Schmidt, "Mundelein College: Catholic Substance, Ecumenical Ethos, 1976–1991," in Harrington and Moylan, *Mundelein Voices,* 242–43.
41. David Block, "Reminiscences of a Mundelein Junkie," in Harrington and Moylan, *Mundelein Voices,* 258.
42. Michael Fortune, "The College on the Curve," in Harrington and Moylan, *Mundelein Voices,* 231–32.
43. Crowley, , "Remembering 1962–1969," 171–76.
44. MCR, Z Shelf List, 2B.4 N4.1, Official Set of Skyscrapers, editorial, *Skyscraper,* October 4, 1968.
45. MCR, Institutional Planning, Institutional Analysis, Hruby: Sears Grant; Upward Bound.

46. MCR, C.4, Conference on Curriculum, Program Initiatives 1960–1991.

47. MCR, Series F.9.11 and F.9.12, Academic Affairs, Other Academic Programs, Hispanic Programs, Bilingual-Bicultural Programs.

48. MCR, Series K1.3a, Admissions, Scholarships, Financial Aid, Admissions, Taken from G. J. Froehlich, *Enrollment in Institutions of Higher Learning in Illinois: 1971, 1972* (Bureau of Institutional Research, University of Illinois Urbana).

49. Elaine El-Khawas, "Demographics of the Decade: A Closer Look," *Journal of the Association of Catholic Colleges and Universities* 6, 1 (summer 1985): 17–20.

50. MCR, Series K, Admissions, Scholarships, Financial Aid. Pell grants were introduced in 1973.

51. MCR, Series F.9.3, Academic Affairs, Other Academic Programs, Weekend College. Also, details on the process are found in Mary Griffin, "Reinventing Mundelein: Birthing the Weekend College, 1974," in Harrington and Moylan, *Mundelein Voices*, 215–24.

52. Marianne Littau, "Damned Average Raisers: The Continuing Education Program," 206; and Hruby, "Golden Age," 186–87, both in Harrington and Moylan, *Mundelein Voices*.

53. J. Patout Burns and David M. Johnson, "Trends in Enrollments and Finances in Catholic Colleges and Universities" *Journal of the Association of Catholic Colleges and Universities* 7, 1 (summer 1986): 8–19.

54. MCR, Series K.1.3.d, Admissions, Scholarships, Financial Aid, Admissions, Miscellaneous Studies, Ingersoll, Williams Report.

55. MCR, Series I.1.2, Treasurer/Business Officer Reports, Financial Records, Annual Audits 1938–1991, Audit Report 1960. Gannon reported that this practice was invented by Altschuler, Melvoin, and Glasser, the Mundelein auditors, and was adopted by many Catholic institutions.

56. MCR, Series I.1.2, Treasurer/Business Officer Reports, Financial Records, Annual Audits 1938–1991, Audit Reports 1960, 1965, 1970.

57. MCR, Series C. 6, Institutional Planning, Major Federal Institutional Development Grants, Advanced Institutional Development Grant (AIDP) and Supplementary Institutional Development Program (SDIP).

58. MCR, Series K.1.3.d, Admissions, Scholarships, Financial Aid, Admissions, Miscellaneous Studies. Several admission consultants advised Mundelein College in the period after 1975: Johnson and Associates, 1975; Campbell Report, 1982; Bozell, Jacobs Report, 1988; Ingersoll, Williams Report, 1990.

59. MCR, Series F.3.2a, Academic Affairs, Faculty Association, Suggestions on enrollment development.

60. MCR, Series K.1.3.d, Admissions, Scholarships, Financial Aid, Admissions, Miscellaneous Studies.

61. MCR, Series I. 1.2, Treasurer/Business Officer Reports, Financial Records, Annual Audits 1938–1991, Audit 1983.

62. MCR, Series I.1.2, Treasurer/Business Officer Reports, Financial Records, Annual Audits 1938–1991, Audit 1985.

63. MCR, Series A1.6g, General College Records, Affiliation with Loyola; Series E9.1, Administration-Presidents, Mary Brennan Breslin, BVM.

64. MCR, Series K.1.3.d, Admissions, Scholarships, Financial Aid, Admissions, Miscellaneous Studies, Chart H, Ingersoll Williams Report, 1990.

65. MCR, Series I.1.2, Treasurer/Business Officer Reports, Financial Records, Annual Audits 1938–1991, Audit 1990.
66. MCR, Series A1.6g, General College Records, Affiliation with Loyola, Vision Committee, Blue Ribbon Committee, Long-range Planning Committee, Ingersoll Williams Report; Series EE.3, Administrative Reports, Loyola/Jesuit Reports.
67. A 1987 plan to put sports fields on a twelve-acre landfill was abandoned in 1989 after a judge ruled against the project. Fran Spielman, "Turning Landfill into Lakefront Park," *Chicago Sun Times,* June 27, 2002, www.greatlakesdirectory.org/il/062702_landfill_lakefront.htm, accessed August 25, 2004.
68. MCR, Series A1.6g, General College Records, Affiliation with Loyola; Series E.10, Administration-Presidents, Carolyn Farrell, BVM.
69. Loyola University Chicago, Women and Leadership Archives, Farrell Papers.
70. MCR, Series A1.6g, General College Records, Affiliation with Loyola, *Skyscraper,* April 6, 1991.
71. MCR, Series A1.6g, General College Records, Affiliation with Loyola. All the students' comments are found in summary in "Student Rally for the Preservation of Mundelein College," April 5, 1991.
72. Ibid.
73. Ibid., Program for BVM open house for students, Mary Alma Sullivan, BVM, Chairperson.
74. Bren Murphy; Mary Pat Haley, BVM; and Mary Alma Sullivan, BVM, *A College of Their Own* (Chicago: Loyola University, 2000).
75. Yohma Gray, Elvira Hasty, and Judith R. Myers, *Plaintiffs vs. Loyola University of Chicago an Illinois Not-For-Profit Corporation, and Mundelein College an Illinois Corporation, Defendants,* Circuit Court, November 7, 1996, www.nacua.org/documents/Mundelein_College_Case_1996.htm, accessed August 25, 2004. On appeal, Gray was awarded annual salary through September 30, 1996, $262,371; Hasty received the same judgment in the amount of $205,349; Myers's claim was denied.
76. Mary Griffin, "Mundelein College Baccalaureate Address, June 9, 1991," in Harrington and Moylan, *Mundelein Voices,* 283.
77. Ibid., 285.
78. Ibid.
79. The details in the story on the creation of the Ann Ida Gannon Center for Women and Leadership come from an interview by the author with Carolyn Farrell, May 3, 2004.
80. When the original endowment goal was reached in 1999, Gannon Center fund-raising was directed toward renovation of Piper Hall.
81. Details from a telephone interview by the author with Mary Ann Zollman and Peggy Nolan, vice presidents of the Sisters of Charity of the Blessed Virgin Mary, May 6, 2004.
82. The other gifts were given to Carmel High School and Clarke College, both institutions established by the Sisters of Charity of the Blessed Virgin Mary.
83. MCR, Series A1.6g, General College Records, Affiliation with Loyola, Mundelein Student Government Report.

5

Texas Woman's University
Threats to Institutional Autonomy and Conflict over the Admission of Men

Claire L. Sahlin

Texas Woman's University, founded in 1901 as the Girls Industrial College, is the nation's largest university primarily for women and one of only two public universities of its kind in the United States. Established by an act of the twenty-seventh Texas State Legislature to educate "white" girls of Texas in the liberal and industrial arts, it was the last public university for women in the United States to accept men into all its academic programs. Although men began to enter health-science programs in 1972 and graduate programs in 1973, it was not until 1995 that male students were allowed admission into all areas of the university, including all undergraduate majors of the General Division. Although the institution now welcomes men as students, its growing body of almost eleven thousand students remains less than 10 percent male.[1] As TWU has expanded and adapted to dramatic social changes throughout its one-hundred-year history, the university has maintained its mission to educate primarily women even as it frequently has been forced to campaign vigorously for its institutional autonomy and negotiate passionate conflicts over men's admission into its academic programs.

Texas Woman's University Today

The 270-acre main campus of the university is located just a few blocks from the town square of Denton, Texas, a historic and rapidly expanding city of approximately a hundred thousand bordered by horse ranches and small farms on the northern edge of the Dallas–Fort Worth metropolitan region. The distinctive features of this campus include high-rise dormitories and administrative buildings visible from many miles away, neoclassical brick buildings and an attractive colonnaded library named for TWU's first female president (Mary Evelyn Blagg Huey, 1976–86), a nondenominational chapel designed by prominent Texas architect O'Neil Ford, as well as well-maintained flowerbeds, fountains, a golf course, and turtle ponds. Texas Woman's University also includes the Institute of Health Sciences in Dallas and Houston, which offers clinical experiences and classroom training to students pursuing health professions. The Dallas Center consists of one site (established in 1966) near the Parkland and St. Paul hospitals and another (established in 1977) near Presbyterian Hospital, while the Houston Center (established in 1960) is located in the Texas Medical Center complex.

The university, which is organized into eight colleges and schools, offers a wide range of undergraduate and graduate programs in the liberal arts and professional fields. It is especially known for its programs in traditionally female-identified fields such as nursing, allied health professions, nutrition, school librarianship, social work, dance, and teacher education. The institution offers nationally recognized programs in occupational and physical therapy and graduates more new nurses than any other nursing program in the state. Designated by the Carnegie Foundation as a Doctoral/Research University—Intensive, Texas Woman's University is ranked fifth in the United States in the number of doctoral degrees awarded each year in health sciences.[2]

Athletics also plays a significant role in the life of the university, which boasts Olympic competitors, including high-jump gold medalist Louise Ritter, among its alumnae and competes at the NCAA Division II level in gymnastics, soccer, basketball, volleyball, and softball. Intercollegiate athletics have been a part of the school since 1915 when the school began competing with other colleges in tennis, and throughout the twentieth century students participated in a wide range of intercollegiate and intramural sports, including swimming, softball, field hockey, golf, archery, and riflery.[3] The institution's characteristic emphasis on athletics has especially increased since the 1970s, when TWU became recognized as Association for Intercollegiate Athletics for Women (AIAW) national champions in track and field as well as in softball. More recently, TWU has become known for its successful gymnastics team, which has won the USA collegiate title seven times since 1993.

Reflecting the institution's mission primarily to women, all the university's presidents since 1976 have been women, and currently five out of the nine members of the board of regents and 50 percent of the university's vice presidents are women. Seventy-one percent of the 263 tenured and tenure-track faculty members are also women, a statistic that has been typical throughout the history of the institution, while 88 percent of the tenured and tenure-track faculty members are classified as "white."[4]

According to statistics from fall 2003, the total number of students is approximately 9,700, which includes slightly more than 800 men or approximately

8.3 percent of all students. During the past ten years, the institution's total enrollment has ranged from a high of 10,090 in fall 1994 to a low of 7,928 in fall 2001, but the percentage of men has never reached more than 9.8 percent, which it attained in 1998. Almost 35 percent of the students are from ethnically underrepresented groups, including 18.1 percent African Americans and 10.6 percent Latina/os;[5] the total percentage of ethnic minorities has steadily increased during the past decade from 20.4 in fall 1993.[6]

The university actively recruits nontraditional-age students and provides services for women with children, including family housing, which it has provided in Mary Hufford Hall since 1983. The average age of students is thirty-one, and a large proportion of the enrollment—45 percent—consists of graduate students.[7] In addition, 45 percent of all students, including approximately 30 percent of the undergraduates, attend the university on a part-time basis;[8] many of them work to support themselves and/or their families. The vast majority of students (93 percent) are from the Dallas–Fort Worth area and other parts of Texas;[9] 78 percent of undergraduates commute or live in off-campus housing, according to statistics from 2001.[10] Approximately 80 percent of undergraduates transfer into the university from other institutions of higher learning, with half of them transferring from community colleges.[11] Based on standardized test scores and other measures, many undergraduates at TWU, approximately 45 percent in 2002, were considered underprepared for university-level studies and in need of remedial courses.[12] In light of these demographics and in the face of lower appropriations for higher education from the Texas legislature, Texas Woman's University currently faces challenges associated with ensuring the academic success of its diverse students, including increasing their rate of retention, rate of graduation, and preparation for job opportunities offered in the state.

Early History

The Girls Industrial College of Texas was established in Denton after years of lobbying throughout the 1890s for an educational counterpart to the all-male Texas Agricultural and Mechanical (A&M) College, which opened in 1876. Active agitators for the women's institution included leaders of the Women's Christian Temperance Union (WCTU), the Texas Federation of Women's Clubs (TFWC), the Texas Woman's Press Association, and the Texas State Grange and Patrons of Husbandry, an agrarian organization that worked to improve education throughout the state. They envisioned an independent educational institution in which women from the entire state would receive practical training that could enhance their economic security, increase their opportunities, and prepare them for their future lives as wives and mothers. In their view existing colleges, including the coeducational University of Texas, which was founded in 1883, did not sufficiently meet the specific needs of the women of Texas.[13] One staunch promoter of the college for girls, Archibald Johnson Rose, a leader in the Grange who served on the board of directors at Texas A&M, declared: "Do [girls] not need an industrial college, too, where they can receive a practical education which will prepare them for some vocation in life, in order that they may not work in the cotton fields from necessity. Certainly the State will not do less for her girls than her boys."[14] Another powerful campaigner, Helen M. Stoddard, president of the Texas WCTU, reported that the WCTU promoted the school in order to make broad, affordable, and practical educational opportunities available to women of all social classes. Stoddard advocated a "three-fold education of the head, heart and hand" of the young women of the Lone Star state, in order that they might become self-reliant and not compelled to marry out of economic necessity.[15]

Legislation to create the school, which was modeled after the Industrial Institute and College for the Girls of Mississippi (today, Mississippi University for Women), did not pass easily, however, because of powerful opposition to the idea of creating a separate educational institution for women, concerns about its funding, and uncertainty over whether such a school should be independent or connected with another institution.[16] Some legislators argued that an education in childcare and housekeeping was unnecessary for girls, since "instinct is all a woman needs to carry her successfully through all the vicissitudes of raising a family."[17] Others seemed to fear that educating women would make them too independent, which would be detrimental to the state of Texas; one legislator even predicted that if women learned how to support themselves, they "would cease getting married, and within fifty years there wouldn't be a baby born in the State."[18]

After at least a decade of debate, a bill, which narrowly passed in 1901, established the "Texas Industrial Institute and College for the Education of the White Girls of the State of Texas in Arts and Sciences," and in the following year, the city of Denton—attractive to many for its proximity to the railroad, healthy agricultural economy, and absence of saloons—was selected as the site of the school.[19] Then, in 1903 after the first building was constructed, 186 students, mostly from small towns and farms across the state, enrolled in classes taught by fourteen faculty members, ten of whom were women. The school was governed by President Cree T. Work and the board of regents, which included three politically influential women and agitators for women's suffrage, Helen M. Stoddard, Mary Eleanor Brackenridge, and Eliza S. R. Johnson, who became the first female regents of an educational institution in Texas.[20] Their presence on the board of regents set the precedent for a significant proportion of women to serve on each board; in 1927 a law, which is still in effect, established that at least four of the nine members of the board of regents must be women.[21] From 1979 onward, the board often has consisted of more than its required minimum number of female regents, frequently with as many as seven serving overlapping terms.[22]

From the time of the institution's earliest history, the curriculum followed the motto suggested by Stoddard, "We learn to do by doing," and combined studies of literature, mathematics, science, and the fine arts with vocational training in such areas as cooking, laundering, childcare, sewing, photography, typing, bookkeeping, beekeeping, horticulture, and dairying.[23] President Work, a strong supporter of women's rights and an incisive critic of male dominance in the workplace, established a curriculum aimed at increasing women's choices and occupations, enabling them to be economically self-supporting, trained for work in industry and commerce, and well-prepared to be wives, home managers, and mothers.[24] At the same time, he and the regents, intending that the school become more than simply a trade school, instituted courses in literature, language, and science.[25] This emphasis on practical training in conjunction with literary studies has continued in the face of steady growth, as well as controversies concerning the value of single-sex education. For many decades, beginning in 1911, the university offered extension programs in home economics to the women of the state; lectures and demonstrations on topics related to homemaking reached thousands of women across Texas on a specially equipped railway car that toured with Texas A&M's agricultural train that provided programs for farmers.[26] Graduate degrees began to be offered in 1930, and ever since, graduate education has been an integral part of the university, with nearly half of all students now pursuing graduate degrees.[27] Reflecting changes in the scope of curricular offerings, the institution has been renamed three times: the College of Industrial Arts in 1905, Texas State College for Women in 1934, and Texas Woman's University in 1957.

The historical development of the school is intimately connected with the history of the city of Denton, including one of the most shameful events in the city's past. From 1920 to 1922, the school, which had grown to more than 1,500 students and was engaged in efforts to expand and enhance the stature of the college even further, led a successful campaign to relocate a thriving African American community of almost sixty families, known as Quakertown, away from its location only one block down the hill from the school. Joining efforts with city officials to create a municipal park on the families' properties, university officials and professors, in concert with local women's clubs and business leaders, promoted the forced relocation of the African American households; white segregationists who ran the college and the city regarded the close proximity of Quakertown to the school as a blight, danger, and obstacle to the further progress of the college for young white women. As Michele Powers Glaze writes: "Although the creation of a city park fulfilled a valid civic need, it camouflaged the deeper desire of administrators at the college and business leaders to minimize contact between the black community and the all-white

The Texas Pioneer Woman Statue on the TWU campus
indicates that not only beauty was held up as a female ideal. *The
Woman's Collection, Texas Woman's University*

women's campus."[28] The removal of Quakertown to a less-desirable location
more than one mile southeast ruptured close bonds between some displaced
families, shut down businesses, and forced African American workers to walk
much longer distances to work, including to the women's college where many
were employed as cooks and custodians.[29]

   In the following decade, two campus landmarks representing the resource-
fulness and distinctive contributions of women embraced by the university—the
Pioneer Woman statue and the Little Chapel in the Woods—were erected.
These landmarks also embody the paradoxes of Texas Woman's University as
an institution. As Vivian M. May points out: "TWU itself symbolizes a place
of both convention and subversiveness, propriety and risk taking, domestic
femininity and public leadership."[30] The Pioneer Woman, a fifteen-foot marble

statue representing the pioneering women of Texas, was donated by the state to the school in 1938 in recognition of the centennial of Texas's independence. The inscription at the foot of the statue stresses the courage and ingenuity of the pioneer woman, "the unsung saint of the nation's immortals," who ministered to her family on the frontier and "lived with casual unawareness of her value to civilization."[31] The other landmark, an interdenominational chapel dedicated by Eleanor Roosevelt in 1939, is decorated with a series of ten stained-glass windows on the theme of women ministering to human needs. Executed by students and partly based on identifiable historical women, the windows highlight the ideal woman in her role as mother and also portray women's contributions to society through their professional lives as nurses, teachers, scientists, dancers, writers, orators, social servants, and musicians. Throughout the years, the chapel has been a site for quiet meditation as well as a popular location for weddings, including thousands of weddings between students from TWU and Texas A&M.[32] By simultaneously embodying ideologies of traditional femininity and paying tribute to women's valor and contributions outside the home, these campus landmarks depict the school's emphasis on providing, in the words of David Gold, "benefits to women and society within politically acceptable margins, while at the same time seeking to extend those margins."[33]

For many decades, Texas Woman's University maintained a close bond with Texas A&M, its male institutional counterpart. Although located more than two hundred miles apart, the two universities shared identical school colors and many traditions, while students from both schools regularly participated in each other's social activities, including formal luncheons, dances, football games, and panel discussions on dating and marriage. One highlight of every year was the Aggies' selection of a football sweetheart from TWU to present during half-times at their annual football games in Dallas and Fort Worth. These traditions persisted through the early 1970s and gradually disappeared after Texas A&M accepted women into all of its programs in 1971 and TWU students, who increasingly commuted to campus, began gradually to rely less on the university to provide them with their primary opportunities for socializing.[34]

Despite the long-standing emphasis on cultivating relationships with the men of A&M, some concern has surfaced throughout the history of TWU that the single-sex education of the university promotes lesbianism. This persistent stigma, rooted in a fear of homosexuality, is not unique to this institution; scholars have documented its pervasiveness at women's colleges throughout the country.[35] In fall 1963 one student who withdrew from the university charged a group of students for making unwanted homosexual advances toward her and other students in a dormitory. Her charges brought unwelcome attention to the school when the *Fort Worth Star-Telegram* reported her story on November 4, 1963, in large headlines on the front page of its morning edition and insinuated

Traditional ideals of beauty and charm are reflected in the selection of the TWU Redbud Princesses of 1961. *The Woman's Collection, Texas Woman's University*

widespread homosexuality on the campus.[36] This led school administrators to report that they had conducted a formal investigation that found the charges to be false. With many considering this incident a crisis for the school, President John Guinn believed that the reputation of the school had been slandered, held assemblies with students and faculty members, and was forced to appease a state representative who threatened to launch a full state investigation into sexual "irregularities" at the school.[37]

During President Guinn's administration, TWU admitted its first African American student in the fall of 1961, when the board of regents, citing legal requirements, voted to abolish the policy of admitting only white women, after explicitly discouraging or resisting the desegregation of the school since at least 1952. In 1961 one African American student from Dallas was admitted into the nursing program, and in the following year six additional African American women entered the university.[38] TWU lagged behind many Texas public institutions of higher education in accepting African American students into its programs of study, but it was not the last university in the state to do so either; threatened with lawsuits and forced by the courts, the University of Texas accepted African American students at the Galveston Medical Branch in 1949 and into its School of Law in 1950, while the state teachers colleges in Huntsville, Nacogdoches, and Commerce did not begin the process of integration until 1964.[39] At TWU, the gradual inclusion of African American women and Latinas, who attended the school from at least the mid-1950s, into the student population has been one of the institution's most momentous historical changes. The campus community has become rather ethnically diverse, and this diversity continues to increase among students on the undergraduate, master's, and doctoral levels, while not increasing to any significant degree among administrators or the faculty. In fall 1993 minority students were slightly more than 20 percent of the total enrollment of 9,702,[40] and by fall 2004 more than one-third of TWU students were classified as belonging to a minority group.

The Beginnings of Coeducation in the 1970s

The first men to enroll in courses at TWU were a handful of graduate students from other area universities, who participated in a cooperative program instituted in 1968 between TWU, Texas A&M University-Commerce, and the University of North Texas (formerly known as North Texas State University) to coordinate graduate programs and share institutional resources. Men tended to enroll in these courses to meet their scheduling needs or to take courses not offered elsewhere. The program also allowed women from TWU to enroll in graduate courses at the other institutions belonging to this Federation of North Texas Area Universities.[41]

In the fall semester of 1972, when the size of the university had increased to more than 6,200, the first men were admitted into selected degree programs at TWU. In order to comply with legal provisions against sex discrimination in Titles VII and VIII in the Public Health Service Act, qualified men were permitted to enter programs of study in the Institute of Health Sciences, which offered course work in nursing, occupational therapy, physical therapy, and health-care services. Eight men in nursing and one in physical therapy registered in fall 1972;[42] this historic event was chronicled in the student paper, which described it as a "notable occurrence" that was "not quite as exciting as being the first man on the moon." Motivated to attend TWU by its program offerings and affordable cost, the first male students in degree programs described experiencing difficulties finding male restrooms and joked about sometimes having to hold open the doors for practically the entire student population.[43]

In the summer of 1973, men also began to be admitted into all degree programs offered by the Graduate School, in compliance with Title IX of the Higher Education Act Amendments of 1972. To reflect the changes in admissions policies, the 1973 university catalog was more gender-neutral in its presentation than previous catalogs and eliminated the long-standing description of the school's mission as "developing women who combine such characteristics as competence and charm, culture and self-reliance, enthusiasm and poise, character and tolerance."[44]

Undergraduate programs in the General Division, which included bachelor's degrees in the humanities, natural sciences, social sciences, physical education, dance, and the fine arts, were reserved for women until the board of regents made its highly controversial decision to admit men in 1994 (discussed in detail later).[45] Although large numbers of male students did not flock to TWU after the health-science and graduate programs were opened to them, men comprised 4.6 percent of the total student enrollment of 8,054 by fall 1975, when the university first opened dormitory rooms to men.[46] The percentage of men on the campus steadily increased until the early 1980s and reached a high of 9.8 percent in 1998.

Some students in the early to mid-1970s became anxious that leadership on the campus would be assumed by the newly admitted male students and attempted to take action to reserve positions in student government exclusively for women. In September 1973 a proposal both to bar men from participation in student organizations and to change the name of the Campus Government Association to the Women's Student Government Association was put forward and narrowly voted down. Proponents of this change had envisioned the formation of a separate student council for men if their numbers ever became significant. The editor of the student newspaper, who supported the proposal, urged the adoption of "protective measures" to help ensure that the school remained an institution for women, arguing that "the capable and intelligent women on this campus [should] . . . not . . . let themselves be run over or dominated by a male minority."[47] Similarly, Vice President for Student Affairs Catherine Williston advocated for the proposal in order to preserve the historical, woman-centered identity of the university and encouraged male students to establish separate student organizations.[48] Opponents of the proposed measure, on the other hand, rejected it as discriminatory against men and likely to prevent the kind of competitive interaction with men that was needed as preparation for the "real" world.[49] Bobby J. McCracken, one of the earliest male students, submitted an editorial to the student newspaper in mid-September 1973, which stated that he was shocked to learn that some desired to exclude men from student government and asserted that he, as a student, deserved an equal voice in student government. He concluded his letter by affirming himself an equal member of the student population: "When I decided to come to TWU, it was with the understanding that I would be treated just as a student should be and not be denied the dignity of a voice in my school. I hope that there are others here who feel that I as a man have the right to be given the dignity of being called a Student of Texas Woman's University."[50]

Controversy about admitting men continued throughout the following year, as alumnae and newspaper editors expressed discomfort with it;[51] some students continued to propose policies to permit the exclusion of men from student organizations, including the planning committee for the annual Redbud Festival, which culminated in a beauty-queen pageant.[52] (This pageant has now been replaced by an awards ceremony that recognizes student and faculty service to the community.) Other students made overtures to welcome men to the campus; for example, in 1975 Deborah Martinez, a junior, broke tradition—much to the surprise of her peers—by adopting a male student as a "little brother," the first-year student to whom she would offer guidance about campus activities.[53] Male students also sometimes formed organizations of their own, such as the Texas Men's Association, which was established in 1974 to support new male students on the campus.[54]

For more than twenty years, from 1972 until 1994, male students were generally tolerated or welcomed, albeit sometimes with reservations, into the Graduate School and programs of the Institute for Health Sciences, even while it was recognized that large numbers of them were not likely to attend the university with its women-centered emphasis and name. Male students had a minority presence in the institution, which increasingly emphasized its distinctive mission to women in the second half of the 1980s. Faculty and students, as Professor Turner Kobler of the English Department remarked in his commencement address in May 1994, frequently supposed that male students who attended TWU must be exceptional and confident men who knew exactly why they pursued degrees at the school, since they often endured teasing from friends and family members who questioned their sincerity in pursuing a degree at a women's university.[55]

Between 1972 and 1994, the presence of male students on campus was often a point of curiosity and sometimes a source of resentment, yet it was generally accepted, even as the concerns and special needs of female students were considered to be of primary significance to the school.[56] Men who chose to attend TWU were generally attracted to the school by its reasonable tuition and fees, as well as by its distinctive graduate programs and programs in the health sciences. For example, Derek Storey, like other male students, entered TWU in 1991–92 to pursue his goal of becoming a physical therapist, according to a profile that appeared in the *Dallas Morning News.* Although his girlfriend, family, and friends raised questions about his motives for attending a women's university, the university offered attractive academic programs and was more affordable for him than other institutions in the area. Initially apprehensive, Storey reported that attending TWU was an enriching experience, stating that "you get a whole new perspective being around women all the time."[57]

Threats to Institutional Autonomy:
The Antimerger Campaign of 1986

While Texas Woman's University was adapting to male enrollment on campus, it faced a significant challenge to its institutional autonomy. Over the years, threats to the identity and existence of TWU have arisen repeatedly from proposals to merge the university with another institution, the University of North Texas, a publicly funded, significantly larger state university located only two miles from the TWU campus. The history of TWU is intertwined with the history of the University of North Texas, which was privately founded in 1890 to train teachers for the North Texas region and grew throughout the twentieth century into a large (now more than thirty thousand students) co-educational, comprehensive, state-supported university.[58] Periodically, Texas state legislators have questioned the existence of two public universities in the same relatively small town; they frequently have enjoined the two universi-ties to coordinate their programs to avoid duplication and occasionally have introduced bills to merge the two universities in an effort to save money for the state by eliminating overlapping programs and administrative positions. Faculty and students at TWU, living somewhat in the shadow of the larger and slightly older institution, have consistently resisted attempts to consolidate the two schools in any fashion, fearing that a merger would bring an end to separate educational opportunities for women in the state. This concern for preserving the institution's independence was expressed early in the history of the school by President Francis M. Bralley (1914–24), who declared: "As long as I have anything to do with it, the College of Industrial Arts will never be the tail of any other educational organization in Texas."[59]

Usually prompted by difficult economic times or declining enrollments, serious considerations of a merger have taken place in 1933, 1953, 1979, and most recently in 1986.[60] During those years, organized campaigns—spearheaded by university presidents, the Alumnae Association, and sometimes the Texas Federation of Women's Clubs—were successful in halting discussions about combining the two universities. Reflecting on the merger threat of 1979, Dr. Mary Evelyn Blagg Huey, the seventh (and first female) president of TWU, appointed in 1976, vowed to continue the autonomous identity of the single-sex school: " 'In the years ahead we will place emphasis on the recognition that TWU is a unique institution.' ... History shows ... 'how long we have been able to resist our suitors.' "[61] Repeated challenges to the continued existence of the school have resulted in strengthening the institution's independence and its mission as an educational institution for women.

In 1986 the Select Committee on Higher Education in the State of Texas seriously considered a merger between TWU and UNT as part of a larger plan to save money by restructuring higher education across the state.[62] The select committee's plan was, in effect, a proposal to close Texas Woman's University, which had declined in enrollment from 9,023 in 1977 to 7,966 by fall 1986, by consolidating programs and literally shutting the doors of its buildings.[63] Most supporters of the plan argued that significant taxpayer expenses could be saved by eliminating administrative positions and duplicate programs. Some also claimed that by combining resources a more enriching curriculum could be offered to the women currently enrolled at TWU. Many, furthermore, who publicly expressed their point of view in the local press asserted that women's colleges were unnecessary and outmoded. Herman W. Vaughan, a businessman who wrote a guest column in the local newspaper, argued that while TWU had a "unique and valuable role" educating women when no other alternatives were available, "it is doubtful that special need exists today."[64] Elise Wade, who sent a letter to the *Dallas Morning News*, attributed the general success of graduates from well-known women's colleges to the outstanding overall quality of the institutions rather than to their single-sex environment. In her words: "Unfortunately, TWU is not comparable to Vassar."[65]

In spite of these arguments and serious consideration of the economic consequences of a merger, the select committee eventually rejected the proposal to consolidate the two Denton universities after some heavily orchestrated campaigning and the presentation of reports detailing how a merger would not even reduce costs. Both TWU and North Texas strongly resisted the plan, but opposition was most notable at TWU, which, under the direction of a new president, Dr. Shirley Chater (appointed in 1986), circulated petitions, held rallies of 1,500–2,000 participants, and sent ten busloads of supporters to Austin when the select committee met for its deliberations in October 1986. Vocal university officials, staff members, and students—sporting T-shirts that read "8,000 women can't be wrong" and waving signs that read "It's not merger, it's murder"—expressed pride in the university, as well as in TWU's stature as the largest university for women in the country.[66] Some defenders of TWU's autonomy drafted reports establishing the high cost of a merger to the local economy, while many others argued for the necessity of a women's university and the distinctive benefits afforded women at TWU, which at the time was 92.5 percent female out of a total enrollment of almost eight thousand.[67]

Epitomizing the perspectives of TWU's staunchest supporters, Molly Ivins, the noted syndicated columnist from Texas, published a column in the *Dallas Times Herald* arguing for the continued existence of the school for two primary reasons—the excellence of its programs within Texas, particularly those that train nurses and other health-care professionals, and above all, the continued need for empowering women in a sexist society. "Texas women still need a college of their own," she wrote, because women need the opportunity to gain confidence, unlearn their training to be deferential to men, and develop their wit and intellect in a less competitive single-sex environment. Such a separate educational institution is especially needed in Texas, she claimed, which "suffers from an especially virulent case" of sexism. She quipped that while some Texas women might be driven to become especially tough and funny simply as a result of being presented with the Kilgore College Rangerettes dancing drill team as their principal role models, many others need a supportive educational

Dr. Shirley Chater, TWU's president, testifies before the Select Committee on Higher Education during the 1986 merger crisis. Strong and vocal opposition from TWU supporters convinced the select committee to abandon its proposal to merge TWU with the University of North Texas. *The Woman's Collection, Texas Woman's University*

environment such as Texas Woman's University to develop independence of thought and leadership skills.[68]

Students and alumnae who publicly supported TWU during the antimerger campaign of 1986 also described the school as a nurturing environment that distinguished itself from coed universities by attending to the unique needs of women students who needed support as they often juggled their course work with demanding family lives. They pointed out that TWU, where the age of students in 1986 averaged 30.4, offered smaller classes, individualized faculty attention, encouragement to participate in extracurricular activities, and services for nontraditional students, including older women and single mothers, who could live on campus with their children.[69] One visible alumna, Millie Hughes-Fulford, a payload-specialist astronaut at NASA who graduated from TWU in 1972 with her doctoral degree in radiation chemistry, lent support to TWU's cause by publicly explaining why she attended the university: While other universities discouraged her from pursuing a doctoral degree as a young mother of a three-month-old baby, TWU encouraged her studies and even designated her one of their prestigious National Science Foundation fellows.

Hughes-Fulford described TWU as an inspiring learning environment where other women were also intent on pursuing professional careers.[70]

In response to the twin threats of a merger and a recent enrollment decline, the university developed a new mission statement and identity that emphasized—rather than downplayed—its role as a women's university; such a development was considered necessary for the survival of the institution. While some felt that mission statements from the 1970s and early 1980s tended to minimize the school's historic purpose to educate women, the newly articulated university mission, which first appeared in the 1987 General Catalog, explicitly called attention to TWU's "special mission."[71] It pledged "a learning environment that fosters the advancement of women and supports their aspirations to achieve their fullest potential" and sought to "to encourage women to develop intellectual, humanitarian, and leadership skills that will advance their potential for service in all areas of human endeavor."[72] These statements, which were formulated to counteract opposition to TWU's continued independent existence, powerfully shaped and still continue to mold the identity of the university. Men were included in the mission, but it was clear that the primary purpose of the school was to provide educational opportunities for women.[73] By December 1988 the institutional mission was modified again to include minority and adult students and "to serve as a resource and depository for information and knowledge about women and their particular contributions to the history and progress of the State of Texas, the nation, and the world."[74]

Controversy over Admitting Men to the Undergraduate General Division, 1994–96

Steve Serling and the Board of Regents' Decision
In 1994 Texas Woman's University was the only remaining freestanding publicly funded university in the nation that excluded men from some of its undergraduate majors, including those in business and the liberal arts and sciences. During that year, it was confronted with serious challenges to its policy of excluding men from undergraduate degree programs coordinated by the General Division. Initially provoked by a prospective male student who challenged the policy, the board of regents abruptly altered the admissions policy on December 9, 1994, to allow men to be accepted into all programs of the university. The decision, which was upheld in court two years later, triggered a highly publicized firestorm of campus protests and a lawsuit filed against the regents by a coalition of students, faculty, and alumnae. The controversy that erupted over the place of male students in the university prompted stakeholders in the university to articulate their divergent understandings of the identity and purpose of TWU. The ensuing debate was symptomatic of underlying tensions that existed about gender and the changing status of women in U.S. society.

In the late spring of 1994, a thirty-five-year-old airline mechanic from Denton County, Steven Serling, caught the attention of Texas politicians when he raised challenging questions about the fairness of TWU's exclusion of men from some of its undergraduate programs. In spite of the school's name, Serling apparently did not realize when he applied to the nursing program in January 1994 that the university served primarily women; after gaining acceptance, he also seemed to have initially misunderstood the school's policies, mistakenly believing that he would not be allowed to take any elective courses outside his nursing major, despite information he was provided by the associate vice president for academic affairs.[75] Nevertheless, he was opposed to the university's exclusion of men from most undergraduate degree programs and made phone calls and sent letters to Texas legislators and officials, including Governor Ann Richards. In his letter to the governor, he asserted that TWU's admission policy was a case of reverse discrimination supported by taxpayer funds. Observing that discrimination against blacks, Jews, and Catholics was no longer acceptable, he asked the state to provide a rationale for continuing policies that barred men from TWU's undergraduate programs in the liberal arts and sciences.[76] Later that year the *Fort Worth Star-Telegram* quoted Serling: "I'm a homeowner, a taxpayer, a veteran—why should any woman from anywhere in the world have more access to public education in this country than I do? It was simply unfair."[77] He also asserted: "I think the idea [of the need for a women's university] is a bunch of garbage. . . . Throughout the country women hold 50 percent of jobs, which means this doesn't hold up in the real world; it has no merits."[78] Moreover, "if their self-esteem is so low that they can't sit in a classroom with someone of the opposite gender and still learn, then they [female students at TWU] need professional help. . . . An academic environment is not the answer to their problems."[79] Although Serling did not hire an attorney to initiate legal action against the school, such a possibility lurked just below the surface. Furthermore, Texas state senators, including Steven A. Carriker, who became aware of Serling's complaints, began to investigate the constitutionality of TWU's policy and considered raising the issue in the next legislative session, which was scheduled to begin in January 1995.[80]

At the beginning of the fall semester of 1994, TWU's enrollment was at its peak with more than 10,100 students, representing better than a 10 percent increase over the previous fall semester, and included 881 male students—approximately 8.7 percent of all students. More than 50 percent of TWU's courses enrolled men.[81] By this time, Serling's grievances had become well known at TWU and even around the country. TWU's ninth president and the first African-American in that post, Dr. Carol Surles, had assumed her duties in mid-August. She was forced immediately to face this issue, which threatened the continued identity of the school, when she was contacted by Texas legislators and nationwide media, including CNN, which interviewed her on

September 7. . Throughout the fall 1994 semester, the new president publicly defended the admissions policy on the grounds that TWU offered women greater opportunities for leadership in an environment that is "less distracting and more free of gender bias."[82]

Many faculty, students, staff, and alumnae also defended the school's enrollment policy. Supporters of the policy included men such as Charles Blank, an occupational therapy major who publicly declared: "I am proud to be a part of this university. . . . Evidence shows that coed universities show preferential treatment to men. So why is Serling trying to obliterate the one place where women can learn to be self-fulfilled individuals?"[83] More than 850 individuals signed a petition in favor of maintaining the policy, which they believed empowered women and affirmed their full development. Under the leadership of sociology graduate student Dawn Tawwater-King, the TWU chapter of the National Organization for Women sponsored the petition drive and presented the long list of signatures to Dr. Surles before the end of September.[84] Tawwater-King and other student activists report that they received reassurances from the university administration about the institution's continued adherence to the policy; they were told that although their petition drive was appreciated, it was unnecessary since the university would never consider a change in policy to admit men into all programs.[85]

Hence, when the TWU Board of Regents met later that semester on December 9 and voted six to one (with two regents absent) to open all programs in the General Division of the university to men, their decision was met with shock, disbelief, and anger throughout the campus. The regents, likely wishing to forestall negative publicity, did not openly solicit input for their decision from campus constituencies, and few individuals knew very far in advance of the meeting that the regents would be voting on the policy. Campus student leaders and some faculty caught wind of the regents' agenda on the day before the scheduled meeting and quickly rallied approximately two hundred people, mostly students, to attend. At the meeting, students sang, clapped, and waved signs, while nearly thirty passionate individuals testified unanimously against changing the admission policy in the two minutes that each was allotted. The series of speeches was followed by private discussion among the regents in executive session and then by their vote in favor of opening all programs to qualified male applications. Despite their decision, the board of regents also unequivocally affirmed TWU's continued and distinct mission "to provide undergraduate and graduate education . . . that empowers and affirms the full development of women." Their vote was immediately followed by a proposal to "create a task force of faculty, staff, and students, to determine how to implement policy in a way that will not alter the university's mission: its commitment to women."[86]

Ironically, the lone vote cast against the change in policy came from a male regent, Don Reynolds, the vice chair of the board, who believed that the change in policy was made without sufficient study of all possible legal options and constituted a step toward the gradual disappearance of the university.[87] Those who voted in favor of the change feared potential legal action against the school and wished to avoid the resulting legal expenses of attempting to defend the school's policy. The highly publicized case of Shannon Faulkner's successful litigation in 1994 against the Citadel, the publicly funded all-male military college of South Carolina, was clearly in the regents' minds; many individuals, including Claude Watson, president of the Dallas chapter of the American Civil Liberties Union, were beginning to favorably compare Steve Serling's case with Shannon Faulkner's. The regents also were aware of the recent decision of the federal court against the constitutionality of the admissions policy at the exclusively male Virginia Military Institute.[88]

Furthermore, the regents wished to bring the issue to a close before the Texas State Legislature convened in January 1995, since some senators had threatened to bring TWU's policy up for scrutiny despite public statements by Kenneth H. Ashworth, the Texas commissioner for higher education, who said that the state stood ready to defend the school.[89] Ashworth had publicly disclosed that TWU's mission had been studied during the merger crisis of the mid-1980s and had been found by legislators to be beneficial to women.[90] Some regents and university administrators may have feared that if the legislature decided to scrutinize the mission of the school, senators and representatives would perhaps challenge the name of the school or even reopen the question of merging the university with another institution like the University of North Texas. Overall, the regents wished to be in control of the changes that they felt the school would inevitably need to face, rather than being forced to bow to changes imposed from the outside.[91] As Jayne Lipe, chair of the board of regents, wrote in an open letter dated December 12, 1994, to the TWU community: "We want to control our own destiny. If we are to ensure the university's future as an institution primarily for women, it is imperative to take the initiative in this matter."[92]

Activism against the Changed Admissions Policy: The Preservation Society and the Coalition

The board of regents, accustomed to a relatively quiet and conservative campus climate, probably never envisioned the maelstrom of emotion and intense backlash that their decision engendered. A group of about seventy-five shocked and outraged students immediately gathered off campus at the home of NOW president Dawn Tawwater-King, who had previously participated in protests against the Gulf War, to plan public demonstrations and contemplate acts of civil disobedience. Calling their group the TWU Preservation Society, the students quickly organized themselves into committees and planned daily rallies and sit-ins for the following week. These students as well as large numbers of offended faculty, staff, and alumnae were incensed by the regents, who many believed had betrayed them by underhandedly changing the policy without soliciting their input or providing adequate notice of their agenda.[93]

During the week of December 12, 1994, infuriated students, faculty, and staff held a series of daily protest rallies, sit-ins at the Admissions Office, and candlelight vigils, receiving national attention from news media. Student protesters, sometimes aided by faculty members who gave them access to rooftops, hung large banners from the buildings, tied black armbands of mourning around campus signs, wrote graffiti messages with chalk and shoe polish on windows and sidewalks, distributed flyers by hand and by fax, and wore armbands and t-shirts in support of preserving TWU's single-sex undergraduate programs. To make symbolic statements, students removed the letters "Wo" from the "Texas Woman's University" sign on a highly visible walking bridge and dressed the Pioneer Woman statue in a black hood and cape. Throughout the week of final exams, crowds hoisted signs lambasting the board of regents with such slogans as "Raped by the Regents" and "Almost a Century of Tradition, One Hour of Stupidity"; other signs asserted the desire for the university to maintain its single-sex mission—"It's TWU, Not TMU," "The W Stands for Woman," and "Better Dead than Coed." Some protesters were concerned about the future identity of the school and were alarmed that the regents' decision might be a "death warrant" for the university, which they feared could eventually become the "UNT East Campus." During graduation at the end of the week, a few graduating students wore black veils and protest signs, while the Preservation Society led a silent protest outside the ceremonies.[94]

Campus organizers from the TWU Preservation Society took direct inspiration from the campaign against coeducation at Mills College, where students almost shut down the campus and successfully lobbied in 1990 to reverse the board of trustees' vote that threatened to make the college completely open to men. As part of their campaign, they began to explore legal options, raise money, and seek outside assistance from leading feminist figures. One student organizer, Jennifer Foreman, for example, called *Ms.* magazine to speak with Gloria Steinem to solicit her support. Steinem, who arranged to speak with the student by phone on the following day, reportedly had been following the case and expressed great sympathy for the students' cause.[95]

In mid-December a group of approximately fifty faculty, alumnae, and students formed another group in protest: The Reverse the Vote Coalition. By December 28 they filed a class action lawsuit against the TWU Board of Regents charging that (1) it had violated the Texas Open Meetings Act by not providing timely (at least seventy-two hours in advance) and adequate notice of the agenda of their meeting on December 9, as well as by improperly discussing the issue in executive session; and (2) it did not have the statutory authority to change

TWU's fundamental mission for women, which had been enacted by the Texas State Legislature in 1901. The suit also asked for a legal judgment concerning the constitutionality of TWU as a historic educational institution primarily for women, based on the belief that the Fourteenth Amendment did not disallow a publicly supported single-sex undergraduate educational institution.[96]

During the monthlong holiday break between semesters, the TWU National Alumnae Association Board voted to censure the regents for both their decision and their disregard for concerned constituents of the university.[97] Also during this interim period, editorial pages of newspapers continued to hotly debate the regents' decision. When the TWU community returned for the spring 1995 semester on January 17, five undergraduate men enrolled in General Division programs.[98] These students included Sam Childers, an assistant in the TWU Office of Admissions, who wished to attend school where he worked and ironically had a direct view of the campus protests and sit-ins in December. In a newspaper story about him, he said that he did not take the protests personally and that he enjoyed pursuing his degree in history where the campus was beautiful and the classes are smaller than at the University of North Texas, in spite of feeling "kind of odd" in otherwise all-female classrooms.[99]

At the beginning of the spring semester, campus protests led by the Preservation Society kept the new admissions policy before the public eye. The Preservation Society briefly led a "girlcott" against the TWU bookstore in order to provide a symbolic display of the students' economic power and also continued by night to drape banners from campus buildings and write graffiti on windows and sidewalks. By the end of January, despite growing sentiment on campus that the protests were becoming tiresome and the graffiti an eyesore, the Faculty Senate joined the Alumnae Association in denouncing the board of regents for failing to adequately inform faculty members of its agenda.[100]

Visible campus protests culminated during a twelve-day period at the end of January and early February. Administrators had decided to restrict signs and banners to the free-speech area in response to heightened campus tension and repeated defacement of the Preservation Society's banners and graffiti messages on campus windows. In response, members of the Preservation Society, which was still determined to continue their campaign to garner additional support by heightening awareness of the importance of single-sex education for women, decided that they wished to use their physical bodies as a perpetual twenty-four-hour protest in the middle of the campus.[101] On January 30, members of the Preservation Society built a tent city on the campus lawn.[102] Vowing not to leave until they were arrested or the regents rescinded their decision, about thirty students declared themselves the TWU Preservation Nation and pitched about two dozen tents in which they lived, ate, and studied until the TWU director of public safety forced them to leave almost two weeks later. Although some Coalition faculty members believed the protesters were hurting their common cause, the tent city garnered increased support from some sympathizers, kept the issue at the forefront of campus attention, and received national attention from the press, which described the protestors as reminiscent of the "flower children from the 60s."[103] Nevertheless, several people harassed the Preservation Nation, including skateboarders in the middle of the night, pickup truck drivers who blasted loud music and threw bottles, a man who mooned them, and others who yelled obscenities about their purported sexuality.[104]

In early February, in response to a rumor that the Texas legislature was proposing a bill to merge TWU with the University of North Texas, some faculty members of the Coalition publicly called for the tents to come down and the protests to be halted. They feared that the Preservation Society and their tent city were hurting TWU's reputation and that the public protests were excessive in light of the pending lawsuit against the board of regents. Student activists, in turn, reaffirmed their resolve to continue their protest; Tawwater-King addressed the rally, declaring: "We believe what we are doing is the right thing, and we will continue doing it, and we ask you to join us."[105]

On the day following this rally, university authorities dismantled the Preservation Nation's tents and forced the student campers to leave. The fourteen-year-old son of one of the protesters had burned himself during the night trying to extinguish a small fire that his propane heater had ignited. Consequently, campus officials felt they needed to halt the protest out of consideration for the safety of its participants. They also may have wished to both eliminate negative publicity and evacuate the campsite before President Surles's inauguration ceremony took place one week later.[106] This, in effect, brought the major activities of the Preservation Society to a standstill, leaving the lawsuit filed by the Coalition as the foremost remaining challenge to the new admissions policy.

Toward the end of the following year, on November 14, 1996, U.S. District Court judge Paul Brown, ruling on the Coalition lawsuit, decreed that the board of regents both had exercised its proper authority to alter the admissions policy and in fact had been constitutionally obligated to open all academic programs at the university to men. Basing his decision on the Supreme Court ruling in July 1996 concerning violations of women's equal protection rights by the Virginia Military Institute's admission policy that excluded women, Judge Brown asserted that "the former TWU admissions policy [excluding men from some undergraduate programs] violated the Equal Protection Clause of the Fourteenth Amendment." To bolster his judgment, he cited the U.S. Supreme Court decision of 1982 concerning Mississippi University for Women, which ruled it unconstitutional to exclude male students from its nursing program, since it could not be shown that the policy of excluding male students from the nursing program compensated for discrimination against women.[107]

According to the judge's discussion of the case, the plaintiffs' argument that single-sex education benefits women and contributes to their success was based on overly broad generalizations about gender differences similar to those presented to uphold the male-only policies at VMI and did not constitute a sufficiently persuasive justification for preserving TWU as a single-sex institution (7–8). Furthermore, the judge rejected the plaintiffs' argument that male students could pursue comparable programs at UNT or other Texas institutions rather than attend TWU. He reasoned that men do not have the opportunity to attend an all-male university in Texas and also asserted that insufficient evidence was provided to show that other universities provide opportunities and an environment comparable to those at TWU (8–9). According to the ruling in this case, "the Court recognizes the significant contribution TWU has made to the education of woman [sic] and understands the feelings of those who would like to keep an all-female admissions policy, but this policy cannot continue under the present law. Plaintiffs have not met the constitutional requirement of showing that the use of single-sex education at TWU is substantially related to an important governmental interest" (9). Under the Constitution, however, TWU must accept men into all programs but may remain "a university for women, with a curriculum and atmosphere to meet women's needs" (5).[108]

Coeducation and the Development of Women's Studies

Ironically, men's admission into all programs indirectly led the university administration to champion the creation of the M.A. degree program in women's studies—the first freestanding degree in women's studies in the state of Texas. Once the university's admissions policy was changed, the administration actively sought ways to strengthen TWU's mission and adopted women's studies as an integral part of their strategic plan. Although documented interest in creating a women's studies program had existed at TWU since 1972 and dedicated individuals endeavored for many years to formalize a one, the university did not institute an official program until 1992, shortly after it became possible for undergraduates to minor in women's studies and the first coordinator of the program, Brenda Phillips, was hired. The case of women's studies at TWU confirms Leslie Miller-Bernal's observation that "women's colleges have not led in the development of this new, multidisciplinary field of study, probably because it has seemed less necessary in institutions whose raison d'être is women."[109] Yet when the identity of a woman's college is threatened, an active women's studies program can be used to strengthen its institutional distinctiveness, as in the case of TWU.

The earliest appeal for a women's studies program arose from students in February 1972 who circulated a petition and gained unanimous support from the Campus Government Association to add women's studies courses to the curriculum.[110] The student leader in this effort, Sandra Sparks, a graduate student in English, believed that such courses were needed especially at TWU, since it was a woman's university. "We're considered the largest women's university in the nation," she was quoted in the student newspaper as saying, "but yet we don't have any type of women's study courses, and we need them."[111] A campus group identifying itself as the Students' Human Rights Movement also took up the cause of adding women's studies courses to the curriculum in spring 1972. This movement was an immediate outgrowth of student protests by the TWU chapter of the NAACP, which had received censure from the university for attempting to show a controversial film about Angela Davis, whose highly publicized trial was taking place.[112] Students belonging to the NAACP chapter and hundreds of others joining in solidarity with them vigorously rallied on behalf of racial equality at TWU and a long list of other demands, which included greater housing choices, protection of students' privacy in dormitories, increased access to contraceptives and pregnancy counseling, greater respect for those who belonged to nonmainstream religions, and the creation of ethnic studies and women's studies programs at TWU.[113]

Significantly, the efforts of the TWU Students' Human Rights Movement to force the university administration to address its grievances were energized throughout the spring of 1972 by the ideas of the women's liberation movement and the campus visits of several prominent feminist leaders, including U.S. District Court judge Sarah T. Hughes, Texas gubernatorial candidate Frances "Sissy" Farenthold, Margaret Sloan, and Gloria Steinem. Steinem, a graduate of Smith College, was known at TWU for her enthusiasm for women's colleges; she believed in their potential to "serve as one big radicalizing place where women learn about their history and where they can develop the self confidence they might otherwise lose."[114] During her twelve-hour visit to TWU with Margaret Sloan, who later became chair of the National Black Feminist Organization, she praised TWU's female students, stating that "TWU is an example of women's problems all over the country . . . but there is much more cooperation and few boundaries between races of women here; this is rare. It is a great tribute to the women on this campus. . . . I would say that this is the best campus we have visited, because it is all women."[115]

Student demands did not directly lead to the creation of an organized women's studies program, but some faculty responded by offering more courses that focused on women, and an ad hoc committee of faculty from the College of Arts and Sciences developed a rationale for creating new courses in this area, citing strong student interest and "national interest in the women's movement" while explicitly rejecting any discussion of a degree program in the field.[116] The first women's studies course that appeared in the TWU catalog was a sociology course, Women in American and World Society, which was added in the 1974–75 academic year.[117] Throughout the 1970s and 1980s, other courses related to women were added to the curriculum, while interested faculty and staff invited speakers to campus, planned symposia, and met together on an

A women's liberation march in 1971 with Betty Friedan and Gloria Steinem reveals feminist sentiment on the TWU campus. *The Woman's Collection, Texas Woman's University*

irregular basis to work on long-range planning for the creation of an official program of study. In fall 1981 Elizabeth Snapp, the director of the TWU libraries, and Joyce Thompson, chair of the Women's Studies Committee, brought a consultant to the campus with the assistance of a grant from the National Endowment for the Humanities in order to receive outside advice concerning possibilities for establishing a program in women's studies at TWU. The consultant, Leonore Hoffmann of the Borough of Manhattan Community College, believed that great potential for an intellectually enriching program existed at TWU, where stimulating courses focusing on women were being taught and members of the Women's Studies Committee were committed and hardworking; however, she expressed concerns that faculty and student interest might not be widespread or sufficient enough to sustain a program.[118] Some faculty apparently considered women's studies to be too radical for the TWU campus, while others who believed that women's issues should be integrated throughout the curriculum did not see a need to develop a separate program.[119]

Dedicated faculty and staff during the 1970s through the mid-1980s dreamed of the creation of degree programs in this emerging field and launched studies of their feasibility. However, the generally conservative climate of the university and the Denton area, coupled with a belief that a separate women's studies program was unnecessary at a woman-centered university, contributed to a general lack of strong support for developing this field of study. In 1985–86 a Women's Curricular Emphasis Committee, which was formed to help strengthen the women-centered identity of the university, explicitly rejected creating a formal program in women's studies and instead advocated incorporating feminist perspectives throughout the university. Carolyn Rozier, acting vice president for academic affairs at the time, stated that "gender-balanced curricula in which the female perspective is included in all courses—not just women's studies offerings . . . is one of the reasons that research shows a positive correlation between women's colleges and women achievers."[120] The Women's Curricular Emphasis Committee, which brought ideas about feminist pedagogy to the fore, sponsored faculty-development workshops and meetings to promote the empowerment of women students and their education for leadership, to the pleasure of some faculty and the discomfort of others.[121]

In the latter half of the 1980s and early 1990s, momentum toward developing a women's studies program with its own course offerings, mission, faculty oversight, and budget began to build within the institutional environment that was embracing its newly articulated special mission, one that "fosters the advancement of women and supports their aspirations to achieve their fullest potential."[122] Jean Saul, chair of the Women's Studies Committee, enhanced the visibility of women's studies by inviting speakers to the campus and hosting programs for faculty development. In 1990 a preliminary proposal for a master's degree was written under her leadership, while an external consultant was enlisted to provide guidance and the vice president for academic affairs, Patricia Sullivan, provided necessary support for the emerging program. By 1992, after the program had been placed administratively under the direction of Joyce Williams, chair of the Sociology and Social Work Department, the first course offered directly by the women's studies program was approved and taught by Saul along with the newly appointed coordinator of women's studies, Brenda Phillips.[123] By 1994 the women's studies program took another major step forward: A women's studies component was added to the new undergraduate general educational core curriculum in order to lend greater support to the university's mission, thus requiring each undergraduate student to take one course in the field. This general education requirement, which still is in existence at TWU, has led to the multiplication of undergraduate offerings in women's studies, including courses related to women and business, health, mathematics, music, dance, visual art, law, politics, psychology, literature, and philosophy. The requirement of taking one of these courses, which students sometimes resist, has frequently inspired some feminist students to work for political change, while challenging all students to consider the significance of social inequalities and the meaning of social justice.

Ironically, the regents' decision to open all academic programs to men gave top-level university administrators the final impetus to fully support the development of the first degree program in women's studies in the state of Texas. In her open letter to the TWU community, which explained the reasons for the board of regents' decision to change the admissions policy, the chair of the board, Jayne Lipe, specifically mentioned building "more outstanding programs in women's studies" as one of the ways to support the continued mission of TWU.[124] As a direct outgrowth of the regents' change in the admission policy, the university developed a strengthened resolve and strategic plan to enhance its "primarily for women" mission, which provided the necessary institutional support for developing a master's degree program in women's studies. At the same time, passion for defending TWU's mission for women during the protests of 1994–95 transformed into enthusiasm for creating the state's first degree program in women's studies.

While President Surles considered graduate degrees in women's studies a potentially significant part of the curriculum even before she assumed the presidency of the university, the board of regents' 1994 decision required her to strengthen TWU's mission primarily for women, which for her naturally included a strong women's studies program.[125] Surles publicly supported and encouraged retaining women's studies in the undergraduate core curriculum, as well as the development of the master's degree program, to preserve the university's woman-centered focus in the face of coeducation. In her presidential inaugural address on February 17, 1994, Surles twice mentioned the need for advancing women's studies at TWU;[126] in subsequent public speeches she continued to reiterate her support for further developing the program in order to help preserve the mission of the university. "Women are first at TWU, then men," she explained. "We have a university-wide commitment to remain woman centered. We are deliberate in planning to focus on the needs of women and ensure that TWU remains focused on the needs of women."[127] For Surles, women's studies was a key element of this vision for the university.

In response to Surles's directives and building on the previous efforts of faculty members, a proposal for the MA degree in women's studies was unanimously approved by the board of regents in December 1996 during the same meeting in which the federal judge's final ruling in the Coalition-initiated lawsuit was announced. The new MA degree program directly supported the university's new strategic plan, "Pioneering Our Future," in its emphasis on creating an educational environment that empowers women. This plan, which included the development of a "nationally ranked master's program in Women's Studies as a foundation for a doctoral degree program," was developed by a special task force that descended from the board of regents' mandate in December

1994 to preserve the university's mission for women, which emerged at the same time that the board authorized the inclusion of men into all programs.[128] In this way, then, the new coeducational policy of TWU helped pave the way for the creation of the master's degree program in women's studies.

Since its inception in 1998, the master's degree program in women's studies has attracted graduate students from across the state of Texas, throughout the United States, and from other countries, including Canada, Uganda, Zimbabwe, India, and Nepal. By August 2004, eleven students with wide-ranging academic interests graduated with degrees in women's studies, and by the spring of 2005, approximately forty students, including the program's first three male graduate students, pursued this program of study.

Promoting the University's Distinctive Mission

In addition to its programs in women's studies, the university currently displays its mission primarily to women, especially women of the state of Texas, through special library collections, public exhibits, and various academic and student-support programs. The Woman's Collection in the Blagg-Huey Library houses a rich gathering of works on the history of U.S. women and is considered to be one of the oldest and largest such collections in the United States. Established in 1932 at the instigation of President Louis H. Hubbard, who desired to collect biographies of women who could "serve as role models" for the university's students, the Woman's Collection is the official archive for the Women Airforce Service Pilots (WASP) of World War II and includes the records of many Texas women's organizations, including the Texas Federation of Women's Clubs, the Texas Federation of Business and Professional Women's Clubs, and the Texas Association of Women's Clubs (formerly the Texas Federation of Colored Women's Clubs).[129] The Woman's Collection also includes the university archives, which provide a valuable depository of information about the history of women's education in the state. Furthermore, it is known for its extensive culinary library, as well as for wide holdings on women and the military and the women's suffrage movement.[130]

Three exhibits on the Denton campus highlight the university's mission as well. Since 1983, the Blagg-Huey Library has displayed the "Texas Women: A Celebration of History" exhibit, an outgrowth of the Texas Woman's History Project sponsored by the Texas Foundation for Women's Resources, a nonprofit educational organization that later founded in Dallas the Women's Museum: An Institute for the Future.[131] Also on permanent display at TWU is the Texas First Ladies Historic Costume Collection, a large display of inaugural gowns worn by First Ladies of the Republic and State of Texas, which the Texas Society of the Daughters of the American Revolution presented to the school in 1940. This collection now includes clothing from Miriam "Ma" Ferguson, the wife of a governor and herself the first female governor of the state, as well as dresses worn by wives of U.S. presidents, including Mamie Eisenhower, Lady Bird Johnson, and Barbara Bush. The third noteworthy display on the Denton campus is the Texas Women's Hall of Fame exhibit of biographies and photographs of over one hundred Texas women honored for their achievements by the Texas Governor's Commission for Women.

Other expressions of the university's distinctive mission, including its mission to minority students and adult learners, are visible in research centers, degree programs, and student services. These include the multidisciplinary Institute for Women's Health, a research center with a mission to promote health and prevent disease among the girls and women of Texas; the Science and Mathematics Center for Women, offering activities and events designed to encourage women and girls to pursue careers in science and mathematics; the Women in Engineering program, supporting qualified undergraduate women pursuing careers in engineering; and the Multi-Ethnic Biomedical Research Support program, providing research opportunities, financial support, and faculty mentoring to ethnically underrepresented undergraduate and graduate students. Other offerings include an emphasis on gender analysis and feminist scholarship within the doctoral programs in rhetoric as well as counseling psychology; an online certificate program in women's health physical therapy; the women's health clinical nurse-specialist and women's health nurse-practitioner programs; and a range of mentoring and women's leadership programs offered through the Office of Intercultural Services. Annual symposia on topics such as women in music and women in aviation, as well as cooperative programs with TWU's sister university, Mukogawa Women's University in Nishinomiya, Japan, also uphold the university's mission.

Furthermore, student organizations and other programs sponsored by the Division of Student Life provide support for underrepresented student populations. Student organizations that reflect the diversity of TWU's students include a chapter of the National Association for the Advancement of Colored People, the Asian Students Organization, the Hispanic Organization for Leadership and Advancement, African American sororities, a Latina sorority, and PRIDE, which provides support for lesbian, gay, bisexual, and transgender (LGBT) students and sponsors an outdoor music festival celebrating LGBT rights. The Counseling Center offers a range of services to help meet specific needs of female students, including support groups specifically for African American women, Latina women, Asian women, and lesbian and bisexual women. Interestingly, the Counseling Center has been offering for the past five years a group specifically for men seeking support while attending TWU—a reflection of the institution's outreach to male students, who remain a numerical minority. A men's support group has never been formally organized, however, due to insufficient enrollment.[132]

Still Primarily for Women

Opening the undergraduate General Division to male students had only a small immediate effect in fall 1995, although it had indirect effects on strengthening programs like women's studies. In 1995 the male enrollment—907 out of a total of 10,090 students in the university—represented only a 0.5 percent increase in male students over the previous fall semester. Steven Serling, the prospective student who precipitated the policy change, did not register. Although the population of male students has fluctuated slightly from one year to the next, men have comprised only 8.3 to 9.8 percent of all students since 1995.[133] A study by sociology doctoral student Amitra A. Hodge revealed that undergraduate male students surveyed in 1998 selected TWU principally because of its academic offerings, location, and reputation.[134]

Attempts occasionally have been made to launch organizations for male students, including a male fraternity, and sometimes male students have assumed positions of campus leadership, but men have decidedly remained a relatively small presence at Texas Woman's University, whose name remains unchanged and mission remains primarily for women.[135] The mission statements that were developed in the late 1980s are relatively the same; the wording has been adjusted slightly to be more inclusive for male students, but the addition of the phrases "primarily for women" and "especially for women" reinforce the impression that the university remains faithful to its primary task of providing educational opportunities for women with special emphasis on offering programs for minority students and adult learners. According to the TWU *General Catalogs* published since 1999, "it is the special mission of the Texas Woman's University . . . to provide undergraduate and graduate education of the highest quality in a learning environment that empowers and affirms the full development of students, primarily women; . . . to provide minority students, primarily women, an academic and social environment for learning, involvement, and leadership development; . . . [and] to provide educational programs to meet the needs of adult students, especially women, who wish to resume or initiate collegiate or graduate study."[136]

Student enrollment fell from 10,090 in 1995 to 7,928 in 2001, a drop that may have been primarily a result of diminished efficiency in administrative offices and a lack of coordinated publicity about the school. Some also have speculated that prospective students may have been reluctant to apply to TWU in the aftermath of the tumultuous 1994–95 academic year, which attracted so much publicity. Additionally, uncertainty about the identity of the institution after men were accepted into all programs likely contributed to the downward trend. Indeed, during this period of declining enrollment, some efforts were subtly made to increase the student population by recruiting more men, and questions about TWU's mission primarily to women were sometimes raised.

Recently, however, under the leadership of President Ann Stuart (appointed in 1999), student enrollment reached a record high of nearly eleven thousand after employees of the university joined together to reverse the downward trend and increase their responsiveness to prospective and enrolled students. Texas Woman's University remains a unique, state-supported institution that continues to exist in order to provide affordable and quality educational opportunities primarily for women, in spite of legal requirements that the university admit men into all programs of study. As a review of this institution's history discloses, its future and its continued autonomy lie in strengthening its institutional mission even further by developing its distinctive programs of study, particularly those in direct support of the empowerment and leadership of women.

Notes

I would like to thank Ann McGuffin Barton, Dawn Letson, and Tracey MacGowan of the Woman's Collection at Texas Woman's University for their assistance; I also appreciate assistance and encouragement provided by Greg Hardin, AnaLouise Keating, Linda Marshall, Dru-Ann Merriman, and Jon C. Nelson. I am especially grateful to Brenda Phillips, who had the foresight to document through photographs and tape recordings the tumultuous activities of the 1994–95 academic year at TWU and who also laid the foundation for the graduate program in women's studies at TWU.

1. *Fact Book* (2004), Office of Institutional Research and Planning, Texas Woman's University [hereafter TWU], B-5, B-9, B-10, and I-7, www.twu.edu/o-irs/factbook/fbcontents.html, accessed January 4, 2005.
2. "About TWU," www.twu.edu/aboutTWU.htm, accessed August 4, 2004; and "TWU Measures of Excellence," www.twu.edu/twunews/TWU-Brags/bragshomepage.htm, accessed August 8, 2004.
3. Phyllis Bridges, *Marking a Trail: The Quest Continues, A Centennial History of the Texas Woman's University* (Denton, Tex.: Texas Woman's University Press, 2001), 17, 28–30.
4. *Fact Book* (2004), H-3.
5. Ibid., I-6, B-25, B-5, B-9, B-10, and I-7.
6. Access and Equity 2000: The Texas Educational Opportunity Plan for Public Higher Education, September 1994 through August 2000," Institutional Six-Year Plan submitted December 1, 1994 (Denton, Tex.: Texas Woman's University, 1994) 3, TWU Archives.
7. *Fact Book* (2004), I-6.
8. Judith Bean, "Undergraduate Retention and Graduation Report from the Task Force on Academic Success," June 18, 2004, 5, TWU internal document; *Fact Book* (2004), I-6.
9. *Fact Book* (2004), B-14.
10. "Common Data Set," Office of Institutional Research and Planning, TWU, www.twu.edu/o-irs/factbook/twucds.htm, accessed August 8, 2004.

11. Bean, "Undergraduate Retention and Graduation Report," 5.

12. Ibid., 7.

13. TWU, *A Self-Study* (Denton: TWU, 1961), 1–2, TWU Archives.

14. Quoted in Joyce Thompson, *Marking a Trail: The History of Texas Woman's University* (Denton: Texas Woman's University Press, 1982), 1.

15. Helen M. Stoddard, "Denton Address, September 1903, Address at the Opening of the College of Industrial Arts, Denton," in Fanny L. Armstrong, *To the Noon Rest: The Life, Work, and Addresses of Mrs. Helen M. Stoddard* (Butler, Ind.: L. H. Higley, 1909), 183–96; and Thompson, *Marking a Trail,* 2.

16. Ibid., "Denton Address, 1903, at the Laying of the Cornerstone of the College of Industrial Arts, January, 10, 1903," in Armstrong, *To the Noon Rest,* 183–86; and Dawn Letson, "Industrial Education for White Women: The Establishment of Texas Woman's University," paper presented to the Southern Association for Women Historians, June 2–5, 1994, Rice University, Houston.

17. Armstrong, *To the Noon Rest,* 187; and Letson, "Industrial Education for White Women."

18. Armstrong, *To the Noon Rest,* 125; and Letson, "Industrial Education for White Women."

19. Thompson, *Marking a Trail,* 2–3.

20. Ibid., 2–6.

21. Edmund Valentine White, *Historical Record of the Texas State College for Women: The First Forty-Five Years, 1903–1948,* Texas State College for Women Bulletin 364, December 1, 1948, 5–7, TWU Archives.

22. For a list of current and past members of the TWU Board of Regents, see TWU Archives, www.twu.edu/library/archives/archive_regents.htm, accessed August 9, 2004.

23. Stoddard, "Denton Address, September 1903," 191–92. Stoddard noted that this motto was taken from John Amos Comenius (d. 1670), a Czech educational reformer who advocated equal educational opportunities for women.

24. Thompson, *Marking a Trail,* 4–5.

25. Ibid., 5–8. For a sensitive treatment of instruction in writing at TWU in its early years, see David Gold, "Beyond the Classroom Walls: Student Writing at Texas Woman's University, 1901–1939," *Rhetoric Review* 22 (2003): 264–81.

26. Thompson, *Marking a Trail,* 34–35.

27. *Fact Book* (2004), B-25.

28. Michele Powers Glaze, "The Quakertown Story," www.dentonhistory.org/Quaker.html, accessed August 9, 2004.

29. Ibid.; Mark Odintz, "Quakertown, Texas," *The Handbook of Texas Online,* Texas State Historical Association, www.tsha.utexas.edu/handbook/online/articles/view/QQ/hrqgk.html, accessed August 9, 2004; and Kelly Melhart, "Preserving Memory of an Erased Neighborhood," Star-Telegram.com, posted December 30, 2003, www.dfw.com/mld/startelegram/ news/local/states/texas/northeast/7597730.htm, accessed August 9, 2004. Also see the following fictional accounts of this event: Lee Martin, *Quakertown* (New York: Dutton, 2001), and Carolyn Meyer, *White Lilacs* (San Diego: Harcourt Brace Jovanovich, 1993).

30. Vivian M. May, "The Ideologue, the Pervert, and the Nurturer, or, Negotiating Student

Perceptions in Teaching Introductory Women's Studies Courses," in Barbara Scott Winkler and Carolyn DiPalma, eds., *Teaching Introduction to Women's Studies: Expectations and Strategies* (Westport, Conn.: Bergin and Garvey, 1999), 23.

31. Bridges, *The Quest Continues,* 27.

32. Ibid., 33–36, 38.

33. Gold, "Beyond the Classroom Walls," 267.

34. Thompson, *Marking a Trail,* 120; Bridges, *The Quest Continues,* 38–40, 51.

35. Leslie Miller-Bernal, *Separate by Degree: Women Students' Experiences in Single-Sex and Coeducational Colleges* (New York: Peter Lang, 2000), 206–7.

36. Guy Draughon, "Girl Claims Fear Forced TWU Dropout: Dorm Life Charged Unnatural," *Fort Worth Star-Telegram* (Morning), November 4, 1963, 1, 8; and "Top Regent Challenges TWU Deviate Charges," *Fort Worth Star-Telegram* (Evening), November 4, 1963, 1, 2.

37. "President, Student Leaders Refute Charges, Plan Steps," *Daily Lass-O,* November 4, 1963, 1; "TWU Upheld After Charges," ibid., November 5, 1963, 1; "TWU: The Feeling That Crisis Is Over," *Denton Record-Chronicle,* November 6, 1963, 1, 2; "State Official Backs TWU," *Daily Lass-O,* November 8, 1963, 1; "Letters to the Editor from the People," *Fort Worth Star-Telegram,* November 10, 1963; "Regents Reaffirm Faith in TWU," *Daily Lass-O,* November 12, 1963, 1.

38. Amilcar Shabazz, *Advancing Democracy: African Americans and the Struggle for Access and Equity in Higher Education in Texas* (Chapel Hill: University of North Carolina Press, 2004), 203–4; Yvonne Barlow, "Alumna Still Vocal on Educational Issues," *Daily Lass-O,* December 4, 1991, 6; Integration File, TWU Archives. A full account of the history of TWU's relationship to the African American community in Denton and the racial integration of the school remains to be written.

39. Shabazz, *Advancing Democracy,* 66–89, 211–17.

40. Office of Institutional Research, TWU, *Fact Book* (1996), 38.

41. Susan Benshoof, "Males in TWU Classes," *Daily Lass-O,* March 15, 1972, 4.

42. Amitra A. Hodge, *The Perceptions and Experience of Undergraduate Males on a Predominantly Female Campus,* Mellon Studies in Sociology 34 (Lewiston, N.Y.: Edwin Mellen Press, 2002), 34.

43. Patricia Couch, "Male Students in Special Program," *Daily Lass-O,* September 29, 1972, 2.

44. TWU Bulletin, Catalogue Issue 1972–1973, April 1, 1972, 39.

45. *Fact Book* (2004), A-5.

46. Office of Institutional Research, TWU, *Fact Book* (1988), 5; "Male Students Find Home," *Daily Lass-O,* September 4, 1975.

47. Susan Benshoof, "Look Closely at Name Change," *Daily Lass-O,* September 11, 1973, 2; and "CGA Name Change Proposal Fails," ibid., September 19, 1973, 1.

48. "Williston Gives View on Issue," *Daily Lass-O,* September, 14 1973, 2.

49. "Students React to WSGA" and "Staff Presents Opinions," ibid.

50. Bobby J. McCracken, letter to the editor, in "Students React to WSGA," ibid.

51. See *Daily Lass-O* articles: Vicky Waddy, "Southworth Recalls TSCW Campus Life," March 27, 1974, 1; Marie Butler, "'Love Affair' with TWU Drives Ex-Lass-O Editor," May 1, 1974, 1, 4; and editorial, "Male Dominance . . . No," September 27, 1974, 2.

52. See *Daily Lass-O* articles: editorial, "UWA Wants Redbud," October 29, 1974, 2; "UWA

Again to Submit Proposal for Redbud," November 8, 1974, 1; "ERA Proposal Tabled by CGA," April 16, 1975, 1; "CGA Vetoes One Section of Proposal," April 23, 1975, 1, 3; editorial, "Last Night's 'Real World,'" April 23, 1975, 2.

53. "Big Sister Acquires New Brother," *Daily Lass-O,* October 29, 1975, 4.

54. "Proposed Platform Issued for Newly Formed TMA," *Daily Lass-O,* November 8, 1974, 1.

55. Turner Kobler, "TWU Graduates: Who Do They Think They Are," TWU Commencement Address, May 14, 1994, "Commencement Addresses," TWU Archives.

56. The TWU yearbook, *The Daedalian,* 1975, 45, devotes an entire page to men on campus with the heading "Males Still Face Growing Pains."

57. Toni Y. Joseph, "The Education of Derek Storey," *Dallas Morning News,* January 28, 1992.

58. Robert S. La Forte, "University of North Texas," *Handbook of Texas Online,* Texas State Historical Association, www.tsha.utexas.edu/handbook/online/articles/view/UU/kcu53.html, accessed May 20, 2004.

59. Quoted in "Many Changes in Customs, Campus over Years," *Daily Lass-O,* April 23, 1976, 1.

60. For 1933, see *The Daedalian,* 1933, 35, 243, and the *Lass-O,* January 12, 1933, for accounts of the opposition of students and alumnae to save the institution from consolidation with North Texas State Teachers' College during the Great Depression. For President L. H. Hubbard's defense and rationale for single-sex education, see also "Hubbard Explains Exclusive Assets of Girls' Schools," *Lass-O,* January 19, 1933, 1. For 1953, see Thompson, *Marking a Trail,* 132–33.

61. Quoted in Thompson, *Marking a Trail,* 227.

62. See Anti-Merger Campaign, Box 34, TWU Archives.

63. Bridges, *The Quest Continues,* 77.

64. Vaughan, "'Doubtful' TWU Still Needed." Vaughan also contended that graduates from distinguished East Coast women's colleges like Radcliffe, Wellesley, Smith, and Barnard normally would be expected to become leaders, pursue graduate degrees, and earn higher incomes simply because most come from economically advantaged backgrounds—not because they attended a college for women. He continued his argument against TWU's continued existence by claiming that TWU and Douglass University, affiliated with Rutgers University, were the only remaining public universities in the United States for women. According to Vaughan: "Forty-eight states do not have public universities for women. Forty-eight states can't be wrong!"

65. Elise Wade, letter to the editor, "Maybe Schools Should Merge," *Dallas Morning News,* September 19, 1986.

66. *TWU Update,* July 7, 1986, 1–2; Susan Rogers, "Students Campaign to Save TWU," *Dallas Morning News,* October 3, 1986.

67. Lauraine Miller, "An Identity All Its Own," *Dallas Morning News,* December 10, 1986; *Fact Book* (1988), 17.

68. Molly Ivins, "Keep Texas Woman's U.," *Dallas Times Herald,* July 13, 1986. Interestingly, a TWU alumna, Gussie Nell Davis, was the founder of the Kilgore College Rangerettes and served as their director from 1940 to 1979. For a faculty member's public defense of TWU, see Joyce Williams, "University for Women Is Still Vital," *Dallas Morning News,* September 10, 1986.

69. On average age of students, see Miller, "An Identity All Its Own." On other advantages, see Sherrie Taylor, "Student Questions Validity," *Denton Record-Chronicle,* October 20, 1986; and Miller, "An Identity All Its Own."

70. Miller, "An Identity All Its Own"; Millie Hughes-Fulford to the TWU Alumnae Association, October 29, 1986, Anti-Merger Campaign, Box 38, TWU Archives.

71. Joyce E. Williams, "History and Background of Women's Studies at TWU," typescript, 4–7, TWU Women's Studies Program files.

72. *General Catalog, 1987–89,* TWU, 6–7.

73. Faculty and the regents responsible for the university's mission statement generally were committed to the view that an educational environment that places women at its center will be particularly effective in developing women's self-confidence and leadership skills by providing nurturing role models, mentoring, and courses focusing on women. As Ann Walker, acting dean of the School of Physical Therapy, stated in the 1986 *Pioneer,* TWU's yearbook: "In a woman's university the students have the opportunity to study women's issues at a high level, which makes them more aware of their opportunities as women. Leadership skills are developed first hand and women consequently can be confident competitors in a society that is male-dominated" (133).

74. *General Catalog, 1989–91,* 5–6.

75. Lenni Lissberger, "Male Student Refuses to Attend," *Lasso,* August 24, 1994, 1; "Setting the Record Straight: Media Misinforms on TWU's Male Admission Policy," *Lasso,* September 14, 1994, 3.

76. Steve Serling to Governor Ann Richards, April 26, 1994, TWU Archives.

77. Justin Bachman, "'Joe Average' Initiated TWU Admissions Change," *Fort Worth Star-Telegram,* December 12, 1994.

78. Sarah Farr, "Women's School Accused of Discrimination," *Daily Illini* Online Archive, October 26, 1994, www.dailyillini.com/archives/1994/October/26/clips.html, accessed May 22, 2004.

79. Kevin Caston, "Man Protests TWU Policy," *Dallas Morning News,* August 21, 1994.

80. Ibid.

81. Kathleen Gigl and Ann Hatch, TWU Press Release, September 9, 1994, 3, Coeducation, Box 174, TWU Archives.

82. Kit Lively, "Discrimination or Compensation? Questions Raised over Right of Texas Woman's U. to Bar Men from Some Majors," *Chronicle of Higher Education,* October 12, 1994, A23.

83. Charles Bank, "Not All Male Students Disagree with University Admissions Policy," *Lasso,* September 7, 1994.

84. The petitions are deposited in Carol D. Surles, Box 169, TWU Archives. See also the Denton NOW Newsletter distributed by the Denton/Texas Woman's University Chapter of the National Organization for Women, 1, 6 (October 1994): 1–2, Coeducation, Box 174, TWU Archives.

85. This account of the views of student activists is partially based on presentations by Dawn Tawwater-King, Sharon Snow, Chrissy Marks, and Jennifer Foreman at the National Women's Studies Association, University of Oklahoma, Norman, Oklahoma, June 22, 1995, during a roundtable session entitled "Single Sex vs. Co-Education: The TWU Case." For a tape recording of this session, Preservation Society, Box 148, TWU Archives.

86. TWU Board of Regents Minutes, December 9, 1994, 3, TWU Archives.

87. April M. Washington, "TWU Regents Defend Their Decision," *Denton Record-Chronicle*, December 13, 1994.

88. Caston, "Man Protests TWU Policy"; Lively, "Discrimination or Compensation?"

89. Same Howe Verhovek, "At a Mostly Female University, a Fight to Keep It Thus," *New York Times*, December 16, 1994.

90. See Lively, "Discrimination or Compensation?"

91. President Carol D. Surles to Ms. Jayne Lipe, chair of the TWU Board of Regents, November 21, 1994, Carol D. Surles, Box 169, TWU Archives; April M. Washington, "Regents Make TWU Coed," *Denton Record-Chronicle*, December 10, 1994.

92. Jayne Lipe, Open Letter to the TWU Community, December 12, 1994, 1, Coeducation, Box 174, TWU Archives.

93. Many also accused the regents of intentionally scheduling their vote to coincide with the end of the semester when students were studying for final exams and leaving for their holiday break, since the fateful board meeting occurred on the Friday preceding finals week.

94. For videotapes of the protests, Brenda Phillips, Box 234, TWU Archives. See also Justin Bachman, "Texas Woman's Goes All Coed" and "Coed Vote Protested at TWU," *Fort Worth Star*-Telegram, December 10 and 13, 1994; Washington, "TWU Regents Defend Their Decision"; April M. Washington, "Surles Hopes for Unity" and "Protesters Unite for TWU Fight," December 14 and 15, *Denton Record-Chronicle*; Verhovek, "At a Mostly Female University."

95. Brenda Phillips, Box 234, TWU Archives.

96. Law Offices of Griffin, Whitten, and Jones, "Status Report to All TWU Supporters from Attorneys Representing the Coalition, Re. Civil Action No. CV-95CV20, *Myers, et al v. Lipe, et al,*" June 30, 1995, Coeducation, Box 174, TWU Archives. Three lead plaintiffs were named in the suit: Bettye Myers, representing the alumnae; Joyce Williams, chair of the Department of Sociology and Social Work, who represented the faculty; and Tami Lankford, representing the students.

97. Packet from the TWU National Alumnae Association, January 1995, Coeducation, Box 174, TWU Archives.

98. Hodge, *Perceptions and Experiences of Undergraduate Males*, 42; Nita Thurman, "Odd Man In," *Dallas Morning News*, January 30, 1995.

99. Thurman, "Odd Man In."

100. Darcie A. Mason, "Faculty Senate to Admonish Regents," *Lasso*, February 1, 1995, 1, 12; see also B. J. Easton, "Surles Addresses Rumor at Faculty Senate Meeting," *Lasso*, February 15, 1995, 1.

101. Sharon Snow, presentation during a roundtable session entitled "Single Sex vs. Co-Education: The TWU Case," National Women's Studies Association, University of Oklahoma, Norman, Oklahoma, June 22, 1995.

102. Jessica DeLeon, "Pitching a Protest," *Denton Record-Chronicle*, January 31, 1995.

103. April Washington, "Reaching Back to the Sixties: TWU Students Use Tent City to Protest College Going Co-Ed," *Harlingen* [Tex.] *Valley Morning Star*, February 14, 1995. Many TWU students and faculty who stopped by the campsite to pick up informational flyers and envelopes for sending letters to Texas state legislators reportedly responded much more positively to the tent city than they had to the previous demonstrations.

104. Sharon Snow, presentation during a roundtable session entitled "Single Sex vs. Co-Education: The TWU Case,"

105. Linda Stewart, "NT Merger Rumor Riles TWU Students," *Dallas Morning News*, February 10, 1995.

106. Maintenance workers were enlisted to remove the tents, and a group of six student protesters refused to emerge from one of them. After pleading by some faculty members, the remaining students were taken into police custody by the TWU director of public safety and then released pending possible disciplinary action by the university, which never materialized.

107. U.S. District Court for the Eastern District of Texas, Sherman Division, 4:95cv20, *Bettye Myers, et. al., Plaintiffs, v. Jayne Lipe, et. al., Defendants*, 9, November 14, 1996, Coeducation, Box 174, TWU Archives. Succeeding citations of this source appear as page numbers in parentheses in the text.

108. See Kelley Reese, "Court Upholds TWU Decision," *Denton Record-Chronicle*, December 6, 1996. At the same time that he rejected the constitutionality of all-female programs at TWU and upheld the decision of the board of regents, the federal judge ruled that the regents had violated the Texas Open Meetings Act by not adequately disclosing on the agenda their intention to vote on changing the admissions policy to include men in all programs of the General Division. Although the regents provided advance notice of the topics to be discussed in their meeting, the wording of the agenda item pertaining to changing the admissions policy was too vague and not commensurate with the gravity of and public interest in this issue. This violation, however, did not supersede the issue of the constitutionality of TWU's admissions policy.

109. Miller-Bernal, *Separate by Degree*, 344.

110. Julie Fernandez, "Women's Studies Courses Sought," *Daily Lass-O*, February 17, 1972, 4; and "CGA Asks New Course on Women," *Daily Lass-O*, February 23, 1972, 1.

111. Fernandez, "Women's Studies Courses Sought," 4; see also "Panel Viewing Women's Studies," *Daily Lass-O*, March 9, 1972, 1.

112. *The Daedalian*, 1972, 46; "NAACP Given Social Probation," *Daily Lass-O*, March 8, 1972, 1.

113. *The Daedalian*, 1972, 46; Rhonda Fulbright and Jackie Grey, "100 Gather: Grievances List Read," *Daily Lass-O*, March 10, 1972, 1.

114. Odilia Mendez, "Steinem, [Florynce] Kennedy Sound Out," *Daily Lass-O*, February 3, 1972, 2.

115. Quoted in *The Daedalian*, 1972, 50–51.

116. "Panel Viewing Women's Studies."

117. Thompson, *Marking a Trail*, 197.

118. Williams, "History and Background of Women's Studies," 3.

119. Leonore Hoffman, Women's Studies Consultant from the National Endowment for the Humanities, to Texas Woman's University Community, November 10, 1981, Women's Studies, Box 38, TWU Archives.

120. *The Pioneer*, 1986, 99.

121. Williams, "History and Background of Women's Studies," 3–6.

122. TWU, *General Catalog, 1987–89*, 6.

123. Williams, "History and Background of Women's Studies," 9–10.

124. Lipe, Open Letter.

125. Carol Surles, unpublished manuscript on the development of women's studies at TWU, 1, TWU Women's Studies Program files.

126. President Carol D. Surles, "Inaugural Address," February 17, 1995, Carol D. Surles, Box 169, TWU Archives.

127. Angel Holmes, "A Woman-Centered University: Surles Reaffirms TWU's Mission," *Daily Lass-o,* March 6, 1986, 1.

128. Texas Woman's University, *Strategic Plan for Texas Woman's University: Pioneering Our Future* (Denton, Tex.: Texas Woman's University 1997), 7, TWU Archives.

129. "About the Collection," Woman's Collection, TWU Libraries, *www.twu.edu/ library/ woman/wm_about.htm*, accessed August 5, 2004.

130. Metta Nicewarner, "Woman's Collection, Texas Woman's University," *Handbook of Texas Online,* Texas State Historical Association, www.tsha.utexas.edu/handbook/on-line/ articles/view/WW/lcw1.html, accessed August 5, 2004.

131. Ellen C. Temple and Candace O'Keefe, "Foundation for Women's Resources," *Handbook of Texas Online,* Texas State Historical Association, *www.tsha.utexas.edu/handbook/ online/ articles/view/FF/vrfqb.html*, accessed August 5, 2004; and "Foundation for Women's Resources," Women's Museum: An Institute for the Future, *www.thewomensmuseum.org/ i_foundation.html*, accessed August 5, 2004.

132. E-mail correspondence from Donald Rosen, PhD, director of the TWU Counseling Center, August 5, 2004.

133. Hodge, *Perceptions and Experience of Undergraduate Males,* 43; *Fact Book* (2004), B-27.

134. Hodge, *Perceptions and Experience of Undergraduate Males,* 94.

135. Linda Stewart, "Big Men on Campus: Phi Kappa Psi Colony Becomes TWU's First Fraternity," *Lasso,* August 25, 1995, 31A and 35A.

136. *General Catalog, 1999–2001,* TWU, www.twu.edu/gencat/99–01/geninfo.html, accessed May 31, 2004.

6

Wells College

The Transition to Coeducation Begins

Leslie Miller-Bernal

Since opening in 1868, Wells College has remained remarkably the same in several respects. It is a very small college with close, familylike ties among members of the academic community;[1] the setting in Aurora, New York, continues to be rural, with the college situated in a village of fewer than a thousand people on the eastern shores of Lake Cayuga, twenty miles from the nearest small city, Auburn; the curriculum is traditional liberal arts, with education as the only preprofessional program; and the college is still a women's college. And yet Wells is different today from the college that students of just thirty-five years ago knew. Today's students are no longer predominantly wealthy, and many more belong to racial and ethnic minorities. Admissions are less selective, student retention is a matter of concern, and the college seems less up-to-date, as no new buildings have been constructed on campus for about thirty years, although some have undergone renovations. Such changes pale in comparison to the major change the board of trustees announced in October 2004: Beginning in fall 2005, men students would be admitted.

This chapter examines the attempts of Wells College to respond effectively to the educational challenges of the last third of the twentieth century, when almost all formerly men's colleges became coeducational and many women's colleges admitted men. Problems with enrollments and finances led the college to implement such innovative ideas as a women's leadership institute and dramatic tuition cuts, but the same problems resurfaced. My basic argument is that while remaining a women's college pleased internal constituencies and avoided conflict, only admitting men has the potential to resolve the college's structural difficulties.

In discussing events at Wells College, particularly from 2003 to 2005, I have utilized an insider's perspective, as well as official documents. Not only am I a senior faculty member at the college, but given that my recent research has dealt with single-sex and coeducational institutions, and the transition of some colleges from the former to the latter, I played an active role in the discussions of coeducation at Wells. Indeed, the trustees read some professional papers I had written, and I was asked to speak to them and to the larger college community about my research.

The Beginnings

Similar to Vassar College, which opened just three years earlier, Wells College owes its existence to a businessman with no experience with higher education. Henry Wells (1805–78), the founder of Wells, Fargo and Company, lived in the small village of Aurora. One of Wells's friends was Ezra Cornell, who planned to establish a university in Ithaca, about twenty-five miles south. Although Cornell tried to encourage his friend to establish a college for women as part of Cornell University, Wells wanted to found his own institution. Wells Seminary and Cornell University both opened in 1868, Wells with just 36 women and Cornell with 412 men.[2]

Wells had the title of seminary only for its first two years, but it retained the characteristics of a seminary longer. Strict rules, even bells, regulated students' lives. The curriculum was a mixture of secondary- and college-level work, taught at first by women who had no college degrees and a few male professors from Cornell. A majority of the students studied in the Preparatory Department; a minority completed the collegiate course. A key focus of the college was the refinement of its wealthy women students. Practical study was deemed unnecessary, since students were not expected to earn their own living but rather to marry high-status men. The college required French, on the other hand, since it was believed to be indispensable for cultivated women. Wells offered many music and arts courses for similar reasons.

Henry Wells's strengths and limitations as the founder of the college had profound consequences for the way the college developed. On the one hand, Wells's belief that women's intellects were stunted by their lack of education fueled his desire to better their situation. In a speech he wrote for the inauguration of the college, he noted that while it was "commonly said" that a woman's mind was "not capable of attaining to a high order of discipline," he was "not acknowledging this" but rather wanted to "give her the opportunity." And yet Wells was no radical; he hoped that by educating women, he could keep them from agitating for suffrage. His views also fit squarely into the Republican motherhood ideology: Women needed to be educated so that they could better raise sons for their future leadership roles. Wells did not design the college to educate women identically to men; the 1871 catalogue, for example, mentioned that the mathematics course was as "extensive as is desirable for young ladies." Henry Wells's speeches focused on the advantages of a small size to enable the college to function as a "home" for its "refined" students and the importance of Christianity for the college's educational program.

While Wells gave the initial land and about $200,000 to the college, he did not establish an endowment, as Matthew Vassar did for the college he founded. The resulting financial insecurity made the college dependent on tuition money from students. Tuition dependence in turn made it reluctant to abolish the Preparatory Department, even though having such a department prevented the college from being perceived as a "true" college. Pressure from alumnae, including the college's best-known alumna, Frances Folsom, who in 1886 married U.S. president Grover Cleveland in a White House ceremony, finally led to the closing of this department in 1895. Another consequence of a shaky financial foundation was that the college continued to enroll only wealthy women, since it did not offer scholarships for capable but poorer students. Although Henry Wells could not have foreseen all these consequences, by the end of his life he did acknowledge that he, a "comparatively uneducated man," had made "errors" in his attempt to "found, build, and put into successful working . . . the proper management of a woman's college."[3]

The College in the First Two-Thirds of the Twentieth Century

As a result of support and pressure from students, alumnae, faculty, and presidents, Wells College gradually became a financially secure, strong liberal arts college for women, with a sound curriculum and qualified faculty equivalent to if not surpassing those at other private liberal arts colleges. Endowment topped $1 million by 1923, the same year that the college established a rigorous honors program. In the late 1920s Wells instituted comprehensive exams for seniors, and in 1931, Phi Beta Kappa accepted the college's chapter application.[4]

Wells defined itself as a pure liberal arts college and took pride in having no practical courses.[5] As a women's college for wealthy students, Wells retained its emphasis on refining students. Students had teas where they practiced being hostesses; dining required formal dress and proper manners; and students' voices and posture were monitored and improved.[6] Not all students accepted these values. Some wanted help in finding jobs, which the college responded to by opening a Placement Bureau in 1928, although at first it had no specially trained staff.[7]

Applications to the college rose during the 1920s, permitting greater selectivity in admissions. Not everyone viewed the growth of the college as desirable. President Kerr D. Macmillan argued forcefully in the early 1920s for keeping Wells's enrollment at about two hundred, similar to the size of a Cambridge or Oxford University college, in order to be able to retain its emphasis on the college as a "family."[8] But by the late 1920s, Macmillan began to realize some of the disadvantages of low enrollments, such as lower prestige and the "uneconomical" nature of very small colleges.[9] Macmillan raised the question of what "small" really meant. But by then it was too late to grow, as the country was entering the Great Depression. Wells and many other colleges had difficulty in maintaining the size of their enrollments, never mind increasing them.

After the Depression, college officials increasingly saw larger enrollment as desirable. In 1941, for example, the treasurer argued that the college's financial position would always be "critical" with an enrollment of fewer than three hundred.[10] In 1959 the trustees approved the growth of the college to five hundred students, a number reached just three years later, in 1962.[11]

Wells's enrollment remained quite homogeneous by religion, social class, and race for the first half of the twentieth century. Even though the college had a couple of Jewish students by the late 1920s, it advertised itself as a Christian, nondenominational institution, a description it did not change until the 1960s. For a time in the 1920s, students were required to take a course on the life and teachings of Jesus Christ, and the college held the baccalaureate service in the local Presbyterian church.[12] Virtually all students had to be wealthy to attend Wells, since the college offered few scholarships until the Great Depression. By the 1950s, however, about one-quarter of the college's students received scholarships; not surprisingly, these turned out to be some of Wells's academically strongest students.[13] Wells occasionally enrolled a few Japanese students, but the college did not enroll its first black student until 1960.

Although Wells College was not one of the prestigious Seven Sisters colleges, it did have a good academic reputation that improved after World War II. Entering students' median scores on verbal SATs rose between 1953 and 1959 from 479 to 530, and those on math SATs increased from 456 to 531.[14] One way the college attempted to increase its status was to decrease the percentage of women on the faculty. From 70 percent in 1928, women's representation on the faculty fell to 42 percent by 1965.[15] Women remained well represented on the board of trustees, however—close to half between 1928 and 1965—but the chair of the board was always a man, as was the president of the college.

The 1960s and 1970s: From Plenty to Scarcity

The 1960s were good years for Wells College, as they were for many educational institutions. Wells's enrollments for each of the seven years between 1966 and 1972 were more than six hundred students, the highest in the college's history. The college was able to be selective, accepting about one in two applicants for the class entering in the fall of 1965.[16] In anticipation of its centenary, Wells launched a capital campaign in 1960 to raise $5 million by 1968. The college built a new student union, a dormitory, a library, and by the mid-1970s, a fine-arts building. College planners thought about becoming coeducational or opening a coordinate college for men students, but such plans never materialized.[17]

The euphoria of high enrollments and sound finances did not last long. President John Wilson recognized the dire implications of many men's and some women's colleges becoming coeducational. In his inaugural address in 1969 he warned that if the present national "preoccupation" with coeducation continued, it would not be possible to sustain "a first-class, single-sex undergraduate college," even though, he noted, women's colleges do have a "special character."[18] When enrollment started to drop, entering students' academic qualifications also declined, as acceptance rates rose to achieve even the smaller entering classes. President Wilson responded to this challenge by establishing committees to make recommendations about ways to make Wells more attractive.[19] Exchanges with other schools, increased financial aid for students, and summer programs to use the campus when it is most beautiful were all implemented.[20] Such attempts did not raise enrollments to 1960s and early 1970s levels. While the drop was not steady, enrollment never reached even 550 again. The year that President John Wilson left Wells, 1975, enrollment stood at 481, the first time in fourteen years that the enrollment was fewer than 500 (see Figure 6.1).[21]

Characteristics of the student population changed as enrollment fell. Students were less and less likely to come from wealthy families and more likely to come from families in which they were the first to attend college. This had financial implications for the college. The budget for financial aid increased approximately 300 percent between 1967 and 1975. By the late 1970s, about half

Figure 6.1. Wells total students, 1965–2003

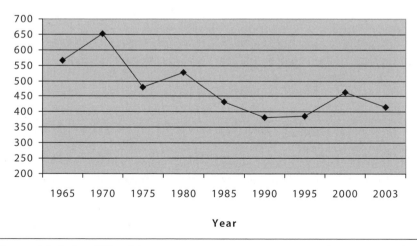

Source: Admissions Office data.

the students received financial aid from Wells, requiring the college to spend about $500,000 each year.[22] Using the endowment to meet some of these needs meant that Wells began to have deficits and the endowment dwindled. Some people made the dire prediction that the college would fold.[23]

A More Feminist Institution

At the same time that the college was experiencing financial and enrollment difficulties, it became a more feminist institution. The women's movement made college constituencies more aware of the discrimination women faced in the larger world and focused their attention on what a women's college could do to enhance its students' lives. Students played an active role in these changes. By the late 1960s, Wells had enough African American and Latina students for them to establish a Black and Latin Women's Society. Students formed a Women's Resource Center in 1973, which maintained a library, showed films, and sometimes brought speakers to campus to talk about such issues as health, reproduction, and sexual identity.

Women began to appear more prominently in the college hierarchy. In 1976, the trustees appointed Wells's first woman president, Frances "Sissy" Tarlton Farenthold, a lawyer and national political figure who had been a founder and first chair of the National Women's Political Caucus, as well as a member of the Texas House of Representatives. That same year the college appointed a woman as academic dean, Nenah Fry, a historian from Wilson College, a small women's college in southern Pennsylvania. Women's numbers on the faculty rose, too, increasing from 28 percent in 1969–70 to 42 percent in 1984–85. Women already made up half the board of trustees in 1969–70, and their number increased slightly, to 58 percent, by 1984–85.[24]

The increasing number of women among the top administrators led to new initiatives to support women's higher education. During President Farenthold's administration, for example, Wells and four other women's colleges used a Carnegie Corporation grant to form the Public Leadership Education Network, PLEN, for sponsoring seminars on current policy issues in order to encourage young women to be active in the public domain. Sports received more attention with the construction in 1979 of a large athletic facility with indoor tennis courts and practice space for such team sports as lacrosse and soccer. President Farenthold also appointed a Women's Studies Committee in the late 1970s, which at first had only a small budget to bring speakers to campus. When the college instituted curricular minors in 1980, women's studies became a minor.[25] Not until fourteen years later, however, did it become a major field.[26]

At the Turn of the Twenty-First Century:
"A Utopian Society in the Middle of Nowhere"

The Wells campus community in recent decades "looks" different from the Wells of former years.[27] About one in five students identify themselves as "persons of color."[28] Although the approximately forty-five-member faculty is overwhelmingly white, there are about five U.S. minority faculty members, including two who identify as Native Americans, and several men originally from African or Asian countries. The college has also been able to fill a few administrative and staff positions with women of color. Recently Wells has begun to acknowledge and celebrate the history of the village of Aurora as an Iroquois site through several Native American festivals and summer archeology courses on Haudenosaunee excavations in or near Aurora.

Students of color have not always felt the college has done enough to support them, however. In the spring of 2002, some minority students and their allies held a sit-in outside the dean of the faculty's office, demanding that the college establish a Minority Affairs Office and appoint more diverse faculty. The administration has made diversity a priority; several committees on diversity exist, and speakers on diversity frequently come to campus. Overcoming the traditional European American ethos may not be easy. An African American student, for example, wrote an article for the student newspaper in which she described various difficulties in being a minority student on campus, including receiving racist comments from other students and being asked, in class and out, questions about black people. "I should get a salary for being a professor, I teach so much . . . I spend most of my days explaining my race to people," she complained.[29]

Lesbians, bisexuals, and transgendered students are more visible than in the past, apparently comfortable in expressing their sexual and gender identities. The alumnae magazine has photos of the activities of the Wells LBQTA (Lesbian, Bisexual, Questioning, Transgendered, and Allies) group, as well as notices of lesbian alumnae who have had "commitment ceremonies" in the class notes section[30] Gay students sometimes hold "zap" panels during which straight students can ask them questions about being a lesbian. A major campus event is the annual Big Dyke Party, and in recent years the student newspaper has carried a column, "Out Loud," dealing with issues of concern to gay students. A few faculty members are also openly gay. And yet students sometimes complain that the Admissions Office downplays the roles of the Women's Resource Center and LBQTA association.[31]

Another contrast with the past is that Wells students now get much more help with career preparation. Internships, which give varying amounts of college credit and which students may now take at any time during the calendar year, are an important part of what the college calls "experiential learning." Many major fields either require or permit internships to count toward major requirements. Students say that they get ideas for careers that they might want to pursue through doing internships. The popularity of internships is indicated by the statistic that 82 percent of the class of 2002 held one or more internships during their college career, and 28 percent of students who had internships in January of their senior year were offered future employment by their sponsors.[32]

Many Wells students credit their self-confidence and success to attending a women's college, even if they are also defensive about their college choice. College talks and publications have often mentioned the advantages of single-sex education for women, using statistics from the Women's College Coalition on the outstanding achievements of women's college alumnae.[33] At the same time, students are aware how unusual it is to attend a women's college and describe having to "defend" their choice to high school friends and explain, "No, we're not all lesbian." As a student wrote in the college newspaper: "We're Wells women—some of the strongest in the world. If anyone confuses strength or pride with man-hating, I have enough confidence in you all to tell them where they can stick their stereotypes."[34]

The increasing activism of Wells students may be a function of the changes in the types of students who attend the college—more minority and less privileged—as well as a manifestation of their rejection of traditional passive roles for women. The confidence that a Wells education instills, and a sense that the institution truly belongs to them, may be other contributing factors. In recent years, students, faculty, and staff have organized annual symposia on service and activism in the academy.[35] In spring 2003, students protested the trustees' unwillingness to make new faculty lines tenure-track and presented a petition to trustees about how tenured faculty are necessary for academic program quality and continuity.[36]

The Wells College curriculum has not changed much over the decades. It remains steadfastly liberal arts with only such minimal changes as programs in education that enable students to become certified as teachers, computer science in conjunction with mathematics, and since 1994, the major field of women's studies. And yet the number of faculty has decreased substantially, from about seventy in the early 1970s to fifty by 1988, and about forty-five today. At the same time, the number of staff has increased; for example, to accomplish more fund-raising, the Development Office went from three people in 1964 to ten in 1993.[37]

Wells College received national attention in the early twenty-first century because of its business relations with its wealthy alumna Pleasant Rowland, '62. Rowland, who made her fortune through the American Girls Collection, a series of historical dolls that she sold to Mattel in 1998, had previously given the college money for renovating and redecorating interiors of several buildings on campus. In May 2001 Rowland's negotiations with the college led to the creation of the Aurora Foundation, "a partnership designed to improve and preserve commercial properties" previously owned by Wells, which was expected to "revitalize the village of Aurora's economy."[38] The Aurora Foundation received at least $4 million from Rowland's own foundation, and the college contributed seven properties, valued at $1 million, including the historic Aurora Inn. By fall 2003 the village of Aurora had undergone a facelift, the most obvious change probably being the inn's complete renovation to a luxurious standard.[39] Pleasant Rowland's involvement in the community caused a great deal of controversy, however, as some residents of Aurora believed that historic aspects of the village were being destroyed. Since Wells College's president supported Pleasant Rowland's gift and foundation, faculty and staff who lived locally and who were opposed to the facelift also tended to oppose the president when she began to push for coeducation.

Continuing Problems with Enrollments and Finances

Although there have been better and worse years for Wells College's enrollments, the general trend since the early 1970s has been downward. Even the college's enrollment goals have been scaled down. In 1972 a planning body mentioned 800 as the number of students the college should have; in 1987 a committee said that its aim was for 500 students, and in 2001 the goal being discussed was 450 students.[40] The 1980s began with somewhat more than 500 students, but starting in 1983, enrollment fell below 500 and once even below 400 (in 1987, when there were 377 students).[41] The 1990s saw enrollments of 300–400, and in 1997 they fell slightly below 300 full-time equivalents (FTEs).[42] At the turn of the twenty-first century, Wells had 462 students, the most in more than a decade, but in 2003 the number had fallen again, to 415 (see Figure 6.1; note that the numbers refer to total head counts rather than FTEs).[43] Enrollments in the late 1990s and early years of the twenty-first century would have been even lower had it not been for a sizeable group of transfer students, between 28 and 45 each year, of whom somewhat more than a third were older than the traditional age for college students. Given that the campus was designed for a student population of between 500 and 600, as a college committee report noted, the "physical size dwarfs the students and staff and adds to the sense of isolation and quiet."[44]

Retention of students has also been a problem. Between 1976 and 1990, the graduation rate varied from a low of 54.3 percent to a high of 68.2 percent, with an average of about 61 percent for those fifteen years.[45] In the 1990s, the five-year graduation rate averaged about 62 percent.[46] Of 122 first-year students who entered in fall of 2000, 57 remained in the fall of 2003, which means that the graduation rate in 2004 was no higher than 47 percent.[47]

Entering students' academic qualifications declined during the 1970s too.

Combined SAT scores dropped about 100 points in seven years, from 1,168 in 1970 to 1,065 in 1977. This decline has not continued, however. Between 1999 and 2003, the average SAT scores for students entering Wells remained relatively steady, between 1,132 and 1,149. [48] Because national recentering occurred in 1995–96, these latter scores were about 100 points higher than they would have been before recentering and so almost equivalent to students' scores in 1977.[49] Given that acceptance rates have been high, averaging over 85 percent since 1969, it is perhaps surprising that the SAT averages have not been lower.[50]

A major way Wells has tried to attract students is by giving financial aid. Three-quarters or more of entering students have been offered financial aid since the mid-1980s.[51] In the mid-1990s, Wells gave aid to almost all its students—95 percent.[52] This percentage subsequently dropped somewhat; 81 percent of the class of 2006, and 76 percent of the class of 2007, received need-based financial aid. These percentages were still high in comparison to those at other colleges, since in 1999–2000, an average of 44 percent of students in private nonprofit four-year nondoctorate-granting institutions received institutional aid (58 percent received federal aid).[53] Even though Wells's tuition is quite low in comparison to that of other private colleges, $13,592 in 2003–4 (with board and other fees amounting to $7,530), the college still finds it necessary to subsidize students' education to maintain enrollment.[54]

The finances of the college have been affected by these enrollment trends, of course, but improvements in the stock market, a successful capital campaign, no debt, some large gifts to the college, and continuing alumnae support, all have made Wells a richer institution than it was in the 1970s. Without taking inflation into account, Wells's endowment increased threefold between 1980 and 1987, from $7 to $21 million.[55] In 2000 Wells completed a successful fundraising campaign that raised over $58 million.[56] A year later, the college received the single largest gift in its history, a bequest of about $20 million from Ruth Price Thomas for scholarships and endowment. But given the major drop in the stock market in the second half of 2000, this gift mainly helped the college recuperate its endowment, which had declined more than $18 million between June and December. In June 2002, Wells's endowment stood at $54 million, about $5 million less than it had been two years earlier.[57]

The annual expenditures of the college in the early years of the twenty-first century (about $15 million) have been about $3 million more than revenues. Wells trustees had a "long-standing policy" that the annual draw on endowment should not exceed 5 percent of the market value averaged over twelve quarters. But Wells spent above that recommended amount for many years, ranging from 11 to 14 percent between 1997 and 2002. In 2003 the board of trustees asked the administration to try to reduce the college budget so that the draw on endowment did not exceed 3 percent and requested that departments across campus cut budgets by 17 to 26 percent.[58]

The College's Long-standing Response to Institutional Problems: Anything but Coeducation

The college has responded to downturns in enrollments and finances since the 1970s by establishing many planning committees and task forces. Trustees' early response to these problems was to mandate that the academic dean and faculty committees work together to reduce curricular offerings and the number of faculty. By 1980 five faculty positions had been cut.[59] Every president since then has tried to come up with an innovative approach that would "save" Wells. Presidents have formed committees or hired consultants, and often done both. This focus on survival has thus cost the college a great deal of money and required a large time commitment of from faculty and administrators, and sometimes from students and trustees as well.

Some committees in the early and mid-1980s gave careful consideration to making Wells a coeducational college. A significant segment of the faculty favored this option. A twenty-five to twenty straw vote of faculty in early October 1987 showed that a small majority wanted the president and the board of trustees, "in appropriate consultation with the Wells community," to consider "coeducation and pricing." Faculty were careful to explain, however, that the vote "did not constitute an endorsement or rejection of coeducation," as they wanted the college to "continue to explore whatever other means there may be to improve the attractiveness of the college."[60] In great contrast to faculty, when students were polled about their views of coeducation, 83 percent said that they wanted the college to remain for women only.[61]

Between 1988 and 2002, coeducation was not seen as a possibility. Presidents and trustees favored other approaches to survival. Some of the ways the college used to boost enrollment, for example, teaching a few Wells courses in the two closest cities (Ithaca and Auburn) and establishing a Women's Leadership Institute, were later abandoned. Other initiatives continue today: cross-registration at Cornell, Ithaca College, and a community college that enables students to take a few courses at these other institutions; three-two programs that allow students to work toward particular master's degrees after three years at Wells; and a leadership transcript that lists students' extracurricular activities on an official document. While none of these approaches led to a long-term solution to Wells's problems, some had a small positive impact on enrollment, at least for a few years.

The major innovation during these years was when Wells, at the advice of a consultant, "slashed" tuition by 30 percent beginning in the fall of 1999.[62] Given that over 80 percent of students received financial aid, this action was not as financially risky as it might have seemed. The college increased its advertising budget at the same time that it got publicity for this innovative step. Enrollments did rise, from 325 full-time students in 1998 to 381 in 1999 and to 436 in 2000 (see Figure 6.1). College constituencies felt optimistic as the endowment also rose with stock market gains. In 1999 the trustees voted unanimously to build a new science facility, which architects estimated would cost about $18 million.[63]

This upturn in enrollments was short-lived, however, and construction on the science building never began.[64] In February 2003, President Ryerson reported at a faculty meeting that, given the erosion of "positive trends in enrollment," she would be forming a planning group with the goal of stabilizing the "residential count" at 450 students.[65] This college planning group, SWAT (Sustainable Wells Action Team), worked on ideas that would make year-round use of Wells's physical setting—"a lakeside campus in a rural environment." It hoped that the college would build "on things that we already do well . . . possibly recommending that the College create one or more parallel endeavors ('centers') that are visible and externally fundable."[66] Similar to previous attempts to increase enrollment and income, SWAT considered some graduate programs, at least in education; new and distinctive major fields such as peace and global studies; and such "cash cows" as summer institutes in foreign languages and workshops at the college's book-arts institute. Rather late in SWAT's deliberations, coeducation was brought up as another possibility. According to one faculty member on SWAT, planning-group members had earlier decided that coeducation should not be discussed because it would dominate and prevent consideration of these other important ideas.[67]

The Coeducation Option: Momentum Builds

The SWAT proposals did not seem to generate much enthusiasm among the trustees. They appeared to realize that they were not sufficiently capable of making much difference in Wells's enrollments and finances. At the last minute, less than twenty-four hours before SWAT members were due to make detailed presentations in early October 2003, a faculty committee member asked me to speak to the trustees about my research. I made just a few points in the short time allotted me: Many women's colleges face enrollment and associated financial difficulties; these problems result from an irreversible trend toward coeducation since the late 1960s; and women's colleges that admit men can, with careful planning, remain good places for women students while increasing their enrollment substantially. A few trustees told me afterward that this information was very different from what they had previously understood, as they thought that women's colleges that had admitted men were not doing well.

Gradually faculty, students, staff, and alumnae became aware that President Ryerson and the trustees were seriously considering coeducation. Early in the spring semester of 2004, faculty endorsed looking into coeducation by a three-to-one margin—not at an official meeting, but at an open meeting of a committee. At their request, the president then met informally with faculty to discuss why she saw the need to consider "expanding" the college's "audience."[68] She agreed that in the spirit of shared governance, she would form a group composed of several faculty and administrators to examine research related to women's colleges and the transition to coeducation. Ultimately the president decided that it was important to have outside consultants to be sure to obtain "objective" advice.[69]

Factions among the faculty became clearer over time. A few faculty, perhaps four or five, remained adamantly opposed to admitting men and argued that the real problems were the lack of a strategic plan and inadequate administrative leadership. The administration was accused of lack of "transparency," with a couple of faculty arguing that the president favored coeducation only so that it would fail and the college could be turned into a nonacademic institute of some sort. Some faculty who originally favored coeducation changed their minds as students began to speak out passionately against admitting men. Among the faculty who believed that coeducation was the only way to solve persistent enrollment and financial problems, many of whom had been at Wells a long time, only a few were willing to identify themselves publicly once the students began protesting. Others tried to take a middle-of-the-road position, arguing that the college should try coeducation first in graduate programs.

Students and alumnae seemed much more unanimous in their opposition to coeducation. Both groups used electronic media to communicate with each other, as well as with other campus groups. Students sent e-mails to the entire college community to make their opinions known. Alumnae collected more than three hundred signatures on an anti-coeducation petition that they put on a Web site. In their e-mails and at meetings, students argued emotionally, saying how upset they were by even the idea of men students at Wells. They also tried to suggest ways the college might increase enrollments, for example, by making cross-registration at Cornell University easier. Many said that by becoming coeducational, Wells would lose its uniqueness, and some predicted that this change would lead to the "downfall" of the college. Students used other methods of protest as well, for example, a day of silence. Not only did they not speak in their classes, but also they appeared in large numbers outside the room where the faculty were holding an official meeting. Invited inside, they stood silently throughout the meeting.

By the second half of spring semester 2004, coeducation was the major topic of conversation and meetings. President Ryerson organized two information sessions at which the college treasurer and I spoke to a combination of faculty, staff, and students. Major faculty committees held open meetings in which all who wished to could express their feelings and ask questions. A top administrator said in a faculty committee meeting that coeducation was not the "right path" for the college at this time. Speaking in favor of admitting men seemed more and more difficult to do, a fact noted by one senior faculty member at a communitywide meeting.

The May 2004 board of trustees meeting on campus turned out to be anti-climactic. Trustees decided that they were not ready to make a decision on coeducation but needed more information. They were even unwilling to say when exactly they might be ready to take a vote. Tensions did increase in the days before the trustees' meeting, however, notably when a recent alumna member of the board of trustees resigned. She claimed that her decision was "not due to the issue of coeducation," but she did say that she viewed coeducation as "a divisive measure" to take "attention away from the long-standing issues which face our community." These long-standing issues were those also brought up by some anti-coeducation members of the faculty: lack of "collaborative planning," and an administration that was viewed as "tired and uncommitted to the mission of the institution." Students also made their anti-coed sentiments known by many posters in places that the trustees would be certain to see, among them: "Improve What We've Got . . . Don't Make Us What We're Not," "Coeducation Silences Wells," "Co-ed = Less Students (Do the Math)," "Save Our Sisterhood," and "Single Sex Education Is Alive and Wells."

The Coeducation Decision

When the college reopened in late August 2004, the campus community immediately returned to the coeducation issue. For the first time, President Ryerson mentioned the word "coeducation" in her remarks during the opening convocation. Students used a personal publishing, or blogging, site to express their feelings. Many professed their love of Wells, such as the one who said "Wells College f—ing rocks. It's an amazing, unique, f—ing fabulous single-sex institution and I want it to stay that way." Quite a few declared their intention of transferring should the trustees decide to admit men. Some criticized the president; some mentioned protests at other women's colleges, particularly Mills, when the admission of men was announced; and some argued that there were other solutions to Wells's problems besides coeducation.

As the trustees' early October meeting approached, students' protests grew more visible. One morning in late September, more than sixty students lined up outside the registrar's office to request transfer forms. At one of the most revered traditions, the odd-even basketball game, which key administrators attend, students came dressed in black. Students also gathered information to present to the trustees by surveying student and faculty opinions on coeducation. While fewer than half the students responded, almost all who did expressed anti-coeducation feelings; 88 percent said they were against coeducation, for example, and 43 percent said they would transfer if the decision were made to admit men. Given the intensity of students' feelings, and the belief that the trustees' views might yet be swayed, these results were not really surprising. One of the questions on the survey—whether a student had come to Wells because it was a women's college, in spite of its single-sex character, or whether they had been indifferent to this characteristic—reveals how much answers to this questionnaire were affected by the context. All previous research done at Wells found that the vast majority of students said that they had enrolled "despite" the college's single-sex character. Yet just before the trustees came to campus in 2004, almost two-thirds (60 percent) claimed that they had come "because" Wells was a women's college.[70]

The results of the faculty survey showed that faculty's views differed substantially from students' opinions. Fewer than half the faculty, twenty individuals, filled out questionnaires. They were not asked directly if they supported coeducation but rather if they would leave if Wells became coeducational. Seventeen of the twenty (85 percent) responded no, one was uncertain, and two said yes. Faculty made mostly positive comments about coeducation on the survey, but some expressed negative views. One faculty member wrote, for example: "The argument that Wells has exhausted all recruitment efforts is suspicious. Efforts only work if they are attempted and maintained over time." Two examples of positive comments were: "I am convinced this is our best, if not only, chance to survive as a college," and "I support going co-ed and hope that it will mean co-equal."[71]

The dean of the faculty, Ellen Hall, also conducted a special meeting on September 28 to learn more about faculty's views so as to convey them to the trustees at their upcoming meeting. Thirty-four faculty filled out a short survey, in which almost half, sixteen (47 percent), said that they agreed with the "possible transition of Wells to a coeducational institution," ten (29 percent) said they did not agree, and almost one-quarter, eight (24 percent), said they were "unsure." Some new concerns voiced at the meeting included the worry that not enough resources would be committed to a possible transition to coeducation; that faculty needed to "resolve their differences for the good of the college" for either decision to be successful; that "benchmarks" were needed to know whether a decision had "succeeded"; and that a coeducation decision would be unfair to students and to faculty who had come to Wells thinking that it would be a women's college.[72]

When the trustees appeared on campus, students began to protest in earnest. They lined the steps to the building where trustees were meeting, trying to block their way unless they agreed to vote no on coeducation.[73] They sang songs at designated times and chanted until they were hoarse. With all these activities, as well as members of campus security and journalists from newspapers and television stations milling about, the campus seemed unusually lively and exciting. A few students told me how much they were enjoying the protests, the first they had ever participated in.

The following description of the protest, written by a student on the blogging site, conveys some of students' feelings:

> I left class to go to the protest. Well over 150 students were there, I believe. We blocked the entry to the library, where the trustees were meeting, signs in hand, chanting "VOTE TODAY, VOTE NO WAY" and other things. I got my feminist t-shirt in the mail just beforehand, so I wore that. We had every entrance blocked! Campus security tried to get us to move as we were a "fire hazzard," [sic] but we didn't budge. Then, a male trustee came and tried to get through us. We kept blocking him. . . . but he pushed us down—poor D—got the worst . . . he just barged on through, yelling at us about blocking the door. Outraged, we stayed a bit and moved inside . . . then outside to where all the trustees were actually entering the library. All of us lined up on the bridge, shouting protests at them as they walked by. Some people were crying, I almost did too. I had to leave for tennis . . . but I wished I could have stayed.

Students did not just protest, however, but used their positions on the Student Affairs Committee of the board of trustees to present their ideas about ways other than coeducation Wells could improve enrollments and finances. Student representatives to this committee reported feeling positive about their meeting with the trustees and enjoyed the reception they received from students and alumnae when they went for a drink afterward at a local bar.

Faculty and trustees also met, as is usual when the trustees hold their meeting on campus. Trustees got to hear the views of faculty vehemently opposed to coeducation, as well as of faculty who favored the change. Members of the board were noncommittal, however, and did not even promise that they were going to vote on the issue at this meeting.

Nonetheless, on Saturday morning, October 2, 2004, the announcement finally came. "The Wells College Board of Trustees affirms our commitment to liberal arts education. In order to provide and sustain the highest quality educational experience, we aspire to grow enrollment by admitting women and men at Wells College commencing with the 2005–2006 academic year." The actual vote was not revealed, but the president later affirmed that it had not been unanimous. A majority was all that was needed.

Postdecision Protest

Students knew what they wanted to do once the decision was announced: Shut down the campus. They took over the main administration building, where many classes are also held, and pitched tents outside when they were told that, due to fire regulations, they could not sleep in the building. Using electronic communication, they enlisted the support of alumnae, asking for food and money donations. Some faculty held classes, but attendance was sparse. At designated hours, students sang and shouted protest slogans. One student wrote in her blog: "I feel like I am getting closer to my Wells sisters by the minute. . . . Protesting and chanting [are] . . . an empowering experience."

Fall break was scheduled to begin only a week after the trustees' decision. This meant that most classes had scheduled exams during this week of protest. Deans sent out guidelines for students and urged faculty to "be gentle" with the students whose involvement in the protest meant that they were not doing their academic work. Many students chose to take their exams, but not in the usual places. They could be seen outside near other protestors writing in their blue exam books.

Students were proud of the media coverage the protest received. A student wrote to me when she was informing me about her decision not to attend class: "We have appeared in newspapers around the world now and the strength of the movement is growing." Not only did newspapers in the nearby cities of Auburn, Syracuse, and Ithaca cover the protest, but reports appeared on national television (CNN, Fox News), as well as in *USA Today* and on nationally syndicated wire services. A couple of months later, National Public Radio featured a story on the protest.

The administration organized informational sessions for faculty and staff. Some of these meetings were tense, as people expressed emotional reactions to the coeducation decision and the ongoing protest. The president and the chair of the board of trustees also wrote to staff and faculty explaining how they were communicating with all segments of the college community and providing background to the decision. One fact that emerged was that the college's charter had actually been changed in 1969, permitting it to enroll men students. No one on campus had been aware of this. But the major message the president and board chair tried to get across was that the coed decision had been made carefully, not hurriedly. Their message ended with these positive words: "We chose change over decline. And we are committed to our future."

Two developments in the protests at Wells seem to have been unique. One, a hunger strike, was short-lived but dramatic, with the seven participating students explaining that their strike was "a metaphor for the way the body of Wells would waste away as a result of the decision to admit men." The other, parents' involvement, was sustained and led to a decision by the parents of two students to file a legal suit against the college. About ninety parents held their own demonstration during Parents' Weekend in October; some also sent emotional e-mail messages to faculty, saying they felt "cheated" and that they had been "victims of a set-up job." The parents who became leaders of this anti-coed faction said that their "main concern" was that parents had been left out of the decision-making process. Parents developed their own Web site, asking for donations to help defray the estimated $30,000 legal expenses. The legal suit claimed that the college engaged in "deceptive acts," since students thought they would be attending a women's college for four years at the same time that the board of trustees was developing plans to admit men students. It also argued that the students had been "irreparably harmed" by the decision to admit men and asked that the college not be allowed to admit men until 2008, by which time the students in question would have graduated.

In December, a little more than two months after the coed decision, a judge ruled on temporary and permanent injunctions on the college's recruitment of men. He decided emphatically against the suing parents, saying that there was "no evidence of misrepresentation, deceit, deception, dishonesty or hiding of the facts," or of "fraud, breach of contract or irreparable harm to the students." In fact, he concluded that the issue was "more about change" and that "preserving the college" was more important than "inconvenience to two students."[74] The decision against the injunctions did not prevent the main suit from proceeding, but ultimately the parents decided not to pursue further action.

Students' active protests declined during the fall semester of 2004, but they did not disappear entirely. Students held a vote of no confidence in the administration at a student government meeting in early November. While a majority of those who voted (85 of 156, or 54 percent—64 percent if one removes the 24 abstentions) agreed with the motion of no confidence, more than 200 students did not vote, which enabled the administration to say that only a small minority of students agreed with the motion. By early November only a few tents remained outside, and they seemed to be empty, as they were blowing away in the wind. They were finally taken down on November 18, but the grass underneath had gone brown, leaving a visual reminder of their former presence. The "Out Loud" column of the student newspaper in early November commented that the "dating scene" on campus seemed to be getting back to normal—"normal craziness, anyway." The writer wondered whether the earlier protests had led to greater closeness of students and more "hooking up" than usual.[75] The minutes of the students' representative council in mid-November revealed ordinary student preoccupations with class elections, social activities, club meetings, and so on. The only reference to the coed vote was the statement that the student government was "working on the transition process. We want to make sure that women maintain leadership positions at Wells."

Some faculty also tried to obtain a vote of no confidence in the administration. Attendance at the faculty meeting was unusually high, and speakers were serious and polite. Some made moving statements about the need to support the decision in order for it to succeed; one noted her original opposition to the decision but gradual recognition that it was necessary. She argued that an alumna president who had been at the college for about a decade was the best

Wells students protesting trustees' decision to admit men students took over part of the campus's main administration building. Here, several days into the protest, they vote to continue their occupation and refuse to go to another building to meet with members of the administration. The black cloths over their mouths symbolize a protest slogan: "Coeducation silences." *Photo by Laura Bartlett and Sarah Clement.*

person to lead the college through the transition. The motion of no confidence was never made, as it was clear that it would have been soundly defeated.

Alumnae were not as unanimously opposed to coeducation as many members of the college community believed. Although a large number of alumnae signed an online petition protesting the coeducation decision (more than 750 by mid-November 2004), the alumnae office received almost twice as many letters favoring the decision (278 of 465, or 60 percent) as opposing it (151, or 32 percent—the other 8 percent were unclear). Even more important from the college's perspective, alumnae who wrote in support of the decision tended to be the large donors. Supporters of the decision gave about ten times more money to the college in 2003–4 than those opposed (approximately $3,496,000 versus $344,000). Alumnae who supported the decision often wrote that they were sad but would rather see the college admit men than close its doors; they also said that they were "proud" of the trustees and administration for taking this "courageous" step. A few wrote that the decision should have been made thirty years earlier; as one succinctly expressed it: "Hooray! Finally!" Those opposed often said that they would not give any more money unless the situation was reversed (one dramatized this sentiment by saying the college had received its last dollar from her and wrote out a check in that amount). One said that she was sending her gift to Mills College instead. Opposed alumnae also expressed the view that the college had not taken enough "aggressive and creative" steps to remain a women's college. They tended to blame the president and urged her to resign.[76]

By December, Wells had accepted a few men students, and more had attended admissions days at the college. One male prospective student wrote to current students on their blog site, pleading with them, "Please don't hate me," and expressing the hope that he would "have a chance to win some of you over at some time in some way." He also noted that he was gay and so posed "no sexual threat." Many of the responses of Wells students were negative. One said that although she "love[d] gay men," he was "in for a hate fest." Others argued that he would never be able to experience "the real Wells" as the "campus culture is going to be vastly changed." About a week after this exchange, a student wrote that she had begun to hate the "power struggle" among people in the protest and was upset by students planning to be "nasty to men" who might want to fit in somewhere, just as she had.

During spring semester 2005, there were few visible signs of protest. Nonetheless, when prospective students visited campus, tensions were evident. In one case a current student felt that she had been prevented from recruiting a possible sports team member because admissions personnel knew that she had been involved in the fall protest and feared what she might do or say. In another instance, male visitors made a comment about a widespread lesbian poster; they were reputed to have asked, "Do you do that around here?" When these same men students were careless or somewhat disruptive in the dining hall, current students shouted at them, "Go home! We don't want you here!"[77]

Applications to Wells increased dramatically, as predicted. By March 2005, around a thousand applications had been received, with 20 percent coming from men. In previous years, the total number of applications had been only about four hundred. While most faculty and administrators were very pleased with these figures, some remained worried that enrollment would not reach the target of 135 first-year students. About two-thirds of these applications were online, whereas in previous years only one-third had been online. Students who apply over the Internet appear not to be as serious about their intentions as those who apply on paper, so the "conversion rate" was uncertain. Yet most faculty believed that the entering class was going to be large, and some worried about how they would handle the increased numbers. By June 2005 it appeared that the entering class would be 134 students, including twenty-two men.[78]

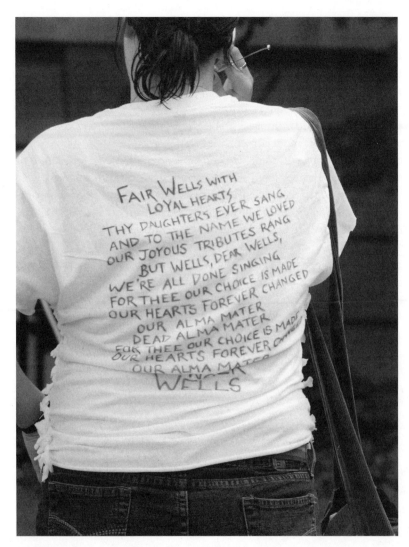

Among the T-shirts students had made for the protest, this one changed the lyrics of the college song to express a student's views of making Wells College coeducational. On the front it said, as all the T-shirts did, "Save Our Sisterhood." *Photo by Laura Bartlett and Sarah Clement.*

Conclusions: A New Chapter for Wells College

Students and alumnae of Wells are intensely loyal to and proud of their college.[79] And yet in the last thirty years, they have been a select group, not only because few seventeen- and eighteen-year-old girls will consider a women's college, but also because up to one-half of the women students who begin at

Wells leave before they graduate. Those who remain benefit from the close, personalized attention they get from faculty; many leadership opportunities in a wide variety of campus clubs; such special academic programs as study abroad in Denmark, England, France, Germany, Ireland, Italy, Japan, Mexico, Spain, Sweden, and Senegal; and extensive availability of internships. Wells is a college where feminism is taken seriously, and lesbian, bisexual, and transgendered students are generally accepted. There is also little to no concern about sexual harassment, especially from peers.

Older alumnae's image of "their" college does not fit today's Wells. Student characteristics have changed, from mainly white, Protestant, upper or upper middle class to a greater percentage of minority students, many from the working or lower middle class. Older alumnae, however, dominate key parts of the Wells hierarchy. Between 50 and 65 percent of the trustees have been alumnae over the past thirty years; between 1989 and 2003, chairs of the board were alumnae, and the man who became the chair in the fall of 2003 is married to an alumna; a large number of administrators, including the president since 1995, are alumnae. Part of the reason that Wells may not in the past have considered coeducation seriously may be that significant proportions of alumnae did not

At the fall 2005 convocation, President Lisa Ryerson, far left, lights the candles of students who in turn light those held by other members of the Wells College community, all standing outside in a large circle. This tradition now includes men students. *Wells College Office of External Relations.*

understand that Wells cannot revert to the college they once knew. As Wells's situation became more precarious, however, many alumnae, especially the large contributors, began to see coeducation as necessary for survival.

The committees that were set up about every five years to try to increase enrollment and improve finances belied the view that tinkering with programs would be sufficient to ensure institutional survival. Faculty, administrators, staff, trustees, and to a lesser extent, students gave hundreds or perhaps thousands of hours to studying Wells's problems and trying to come up with solutions. The difficulties Wells faced since the late 1960s could not be resolved by piecemeal approaches. Wells did not have many of the options open to other colleges. Given its rural location, twenty miles from the nearest small city of Auburn, it does not have the catchment area necessary for evening or part-time graduate programs. Some consultants suggested that Wells might be able to develop outstanding professional programs, but they have also noted that implementation would be akin to "starting a new institution." Such programs are expensive and take time, perhaps five or ten years, to develop the kind of reputation that would begin to increase enrollment.[80]

Wells did not embrace the idea of coeducation quickly or easily. Administrators and the trustees only reluctantly came to understand that admitting men was necessary for the college's survival. Despite the evidence that other former women's colleges have flourished after becoming coeducational, some faculty and staff continued to believe that Wells was different. The same arguments that had been made in the 1980s were again brought up: The college has not tried all methods of increasing enrollment; what the college should do is proudly proclaim that it is a women's college; becoming coeducational will mean that Wells will lose its market niche; and the financial situation is not really desperate, since the college has no debts.

The real question seems to be, How did Wells overcome these objections and vote to admit men? The leadership of the president seems critical. Lisa Marsh Ryerson is both an alumna and the longest-serving president in the past thirty years. She tried other approaches to solving Wells's persistent problems but saw what short-lived effects they had. As the chair of the Women's College Coalition, she heard about the struggles of other women's colleges, even those that were proclaiming to the public that they were doing well. Having a few senior faculty who argued strenuously for coeducation may have helped as well.[81] Getting the needed vote of the trustees was not easy and required on-campus leadership backed up by research from consultants who, as outsiders, were seen as objective.

Wells now faces the challenges faced by other former women's colleges: how to be loyal to its history, serious about the education and support of women students, and yet welcoming to men. Various constituencies are yet to be convinced that this is possible—not only many students and alumnae, but also some faculty, staff, and parents. Making the transition in the twenty-first century has one advantage: Wells can look to many other former women's colleges for examples of what is important to do and what is best to avoid. While no two colleges are exactly alike, administrators have rightly concluded that Wheaton College in Massachusetts is similar to Wells. They are both small liberal arts colleges in relatively isolated locations with only undergraduate students and a long history of being women's institutions. In fact, Wheaton administrators came to Wells to talk about their college's commitment to "conscious coeducation" (see Chapter 3). Wells's struggle to institutionalize gender equity while increasing enrollments and finances has begun.

Notes

I wish to thank the following people at Wells for helping me gather the information for this chapter: A. Shilepsky, Professor of Mathematics; Helen Bergamo, Archivist; Ann Rollo, Vice-President for External Affairs; and Susan Sloan, Director of Admissions. Other people have helped me look for and obtain needed photos: Janet Mapstone, Graphic Designer; Kelly Tehan, Communications Director; and two students, Laura Bartlett and Sarah Clement.

1. In 2000 Wells was one of only 62 private baccalaureate colleges in the United States with fewer than five hundred students. As there are 527 private baccalaureate colleges, this means that Wells's enrollment puts it in the smallest 12 percent. Of course, the percentage of *students* who are educated in these small institutions is much lower, since large institutions enroll many students. See *Chronicle of Higher Education*, August 29, 2003, 15.
2. See Charlotte Williams Conable, *Women at Cornell* (Ithaca, N.Y.: Cornell University Press, 1977), for information about Cornell University's beginnings. For information about early Wells College, I have relied mainly on Jane Marsh Dieckmann, *Wells College: A History* (Aurora, N.Y.: Wells College Press, 1995), and Leslie Miller-Bernal, *Separate by Degree: Women Students' Experiences in Single-Sex and Coeducational Colleges* (New York: Peter Lang, 2000).
3. Temple Rice Hollcroft, "A History of Wells College," n.d., 148–49, Wells College Archives, Louis Jefferson Long Library, Aurora, N.Y. (hereafter WCA).
4. President's Report, 1929–1930, 102–3, and Phi Beta Kappa folder, WCA.
5. David O. Levine, *The American College and the Culture of Aspiration, 1915–1960* (Ithaca, N.Y.: Cornell University Press, 1986), 102–3.
6. Alberta Prigge '32, Class Folders, and *Wells College Catalogue*, 1936–37, WCA.
7. John Rosseel Overton McKean, *Wells College Student Life, 1868–1936* (EdD thesis, Cornell University, 1961), 211.
8. Kerr D. Macmillan, *The College Home*, Wells College Bulletin 1920, WCA.
9. President's Report, Wells College Bulletin 1928, 32, WCA.
10. Treasurer's Report, Wells College Bulletin 1941, 17, WCA.
11. *Wells College Express*, November 1960, 4, and January 1962, 4, WCA.

12. President's Report, 1928, 11.
13. *Wells College Express,* March 1963, WCA.
14. L. J. Long, "A Report of Progress, 1950–60," WCA.
15. Dieckmann, *Wells College,* 330.
16. Wells College enrollment data, 1965–1990, Admissions Office.
17. *Self-Evaluation Report,* Middle States, 1967, WCA.
18. "Dr. Wilson Talks on Wells Co-education," *Courier,* November 18, 1969, WCA.
19. Wells's acceptance rate rose from 69 percent in 1967 to 89 percent in 1977, and the academic qualifications of entering classes dropped. The combined SAT scores fell about one hundred points between 1970 and 1977 (from 1,168 to 1,065). See *Self-Evaluation Report for Middle States,* January 1979, WCA.
20. Dieckmann, *Wells College,* 273.
21. Table based on Wells College catalogues and Dean of Students Office Retention Reports, Personal Loan, A. Shilepsky.
22. *Self-Evaluation Report for Middle States,* January 1979, WCA.
23. Dieckmann, *Wells College,* 214–15.
24. Miller-Bernal, *Separate by Degree,* 168.
25. Dieckmann, *Wells College,* 216; Miller-Bernal, *Separate by Degree,* 169.
26. *Wells College Catalogue,* 1994–95, WCA.
27. The quote in the subhead is from the student newspaper, the *Onyx,* in an article on survival tips for women. The authors recommended taking such precautions as having a list of important phone numbers, approaching one's car with car keys in hand, etc., even though Wells might seem to be a very safe "utopian" environment. Johanna Vining and Elyse Doyle, "Survival Tips Every Woman Needs to Know . . ." *Onyx,* October 2001, WCA.
28. In the class of 2007, for example, of a hundred entering students, nineteen were self-identified as "persons of color." Data sheet from director of admissions, 2003, personal copy.
29. Tomarra Campbell, "Being Black Me," *Onyx,* December 2001, WCA.
30. See, for example, the photo of Wells students and alumnae participating in the Washington, D.C., Millennium March, *Wells College Express,* Spring 2001. Wells LBQTA sponsored the event and received support from the student government association.
31. See *Onyx,* nos. 5 and 6, April 2002, for complaints about this issue, WCA.
32. "Evidence of Success," *Wells College Express,* p. 9, Spring 2003, WCA.
33. Ibid., pp. 5–8, *Wells College Express,* Spring 2003, WCA.
34. Rachel Young, "Passive Prisses or Amazon Women? Stereotyping Single Sex Institutions," *Onyx,* April 2002, WCA.
35. See, for example, *Onyx,* February 2002, WCA.
36. Minutes of the Wells College Faculty Meeting, May 13, 2003, WCA.
37. Dieckmann, *Wells College,* 232.
38. "Aurora Express: Aurora Renaissance," *Wells College Express,* Summer 2001, pp. 16–17, WCA. The plans to renovate the Aurora Inn created a great deal of controversy, with a group of about eight village residents, most of whom were connected to the college, suing on the grounds that the plans violated historical preservation requirements.
39. Wells has two seats on Aurora Foundation; Pleasant Rowland is the board chair, and

she appointed two additional board members. David Curren, "The Right Twigs for an Eagle's Nest: Pleasant Rowland's Views on Philanthropy," *Wells College Express*, Summer 2003, pp. 18–21, WCA.

40. See Dieckmann, *Wells College*, 208, for a discussion of the 1972 goal of having eight hundred students by 1980. The *Executive Summary of the Committee for the Twenty-First Century*, May 2, 1987, mentions on page 4 the aim of "500 students within 3 to 7 years." In fall 2001, the *Express*, the college's alumnae magazine, mentioned that one goal of strategic planning was to "create a close-knit learning and social environment for 450 residential students," p. 7.

41. Enrollment numbers vary a bit depending on the source of information. Sometimes the numbers refer to total students, including part-time students and students who are not matriculating; other times, they refer only to full-time students (my preference when this number is separated from the others); and at still other times, they refer to full-time equivalents. Numbers also vary with time of the year, given attrition that occurs once the academic year begins. Even if precise numbers vary, the trends discussed remain the same.

42. Occasionally the Admissions Office reports on the college choices of students who were admitted to Wells but decided not to attend. In September 1991, for example, the dean of admissions reported that Wells "lost" 147 applicants to other private colleges, 45 of them to other women's colleges (31 percent), and 38 to public colleges. Wells's major competitors were Mt. Holyoke, Wellesley, Bryn Mawr, Simmons, Randolph-Macon, Syracuse, and Clark. See Minutes of the Regular Faculty Meeting, September 10, 1991, WCA.

43. Enrollment figures come from the registrar and Office of Admissions. They are headcount figures, which are always higher than full-time equivalents.

44. *Report of the Committee for the Twenty-First Century*, 1987, WCA.

45. Wells College Retention Task Force, Subcommittee Report, *Executive Summary*, July 1991, WCA. A retention of 65 percent to graduation was about average in 1990 among the following colleges, considered peers of Wells: Mt. Holyoke, Hood, Mills, Simmons, Randolph-Macon, Sweet Briar, and William Smith. At all private four-year comprehensive and liberal arts colleges, the median for 1988–90 was 85 percent, however. "A Brief Review of Market Factors Affecting Women's Colleges," Wolf Organization, 1990, WCA.

46. Wells College, Cohort Retention for Cohorts of 1993–1999, data from the registrar.

47. Minutes of the Wells College Faculty Meeting, September 2003, personal copy.

48. *Self-Evaluation Report prepared for the Middle States Association*, January 1979, 124, WCA. SAT scores for 1999–2003 are from the Wells College Admissions Office.

49. For information on the goals and mechanics of recentering, see www.madison.k12. wi.us/cso/news/96–97/satscore.htm, accessed September 27, 2003. Information from 1999–2003 comes from the information about entering classes that the director of admissions gives faculty each September .

50. For the thirty-four years between 1970 and 2003, the average acceptance rate was 88 percent. In eleven years the acceptance rate was over 90 percent, and twice, in 1976 and 1985, it was 96 percent. Data from the Wells College Office of Admissions.

51. Pleasant T. Rowland, "For Wells—That She May Bloom," position paper, 1987, WCA.

52. Diane Hutchinson, Focus on the Future group presentation, Wells College, March 10, 1997.

53. Information on average percent of students in different kinds of institutions of higher education comes from the *Chronicle of Higher Education,* August 29, 2003. Information on financial aid of Wells students and their retention comes from Minutes of the First Regular Meeting of the Wells College Faculty, September 9, 2003, WCA.

54. In 2002–3, slightly more than two-thirds of private four-year institutions had tuitions of $15,000 and above. *Chronicle of Higher Education,* August 29, 2003, 27.

55. Dieckmann, *Wells College,* 222.

56. "Milestones in Women's Giving," *Wells College Express,* p. 19, Summer 2003, WCA.

57. President's Report, *Wells College Express,* Fall 2002, WCA.

58. Minutes of the Fifth Regular Faculty Meeting, February 11, 2003, WCA.

59. Miller-Bernal, *Separate by Degree,* 171.

60. Minutes of Special Faculty Meeting, October 5, 1987, personal copy.

61. Dieckmann, *Wells College,* 227.

62. Other recommendations of the Critical Issues Action Committee that were implemented at least to some degree were to strengthen the popular education program and to increase ties to other educational institutions in the area, particularly Cornell University.

63. "Special Report: Campus Planning at Wells College," *Wells College Express,* pp. 16–24, Spring 2001.

64. In spring 2006, the second semester that Wells was coeducational, construction on the science building began.

65. Minutes of the Fifth Regular Meeting.

66. Minutes of the Meeting of the Wells College Faculty, May 13, 2003, WCA.

67. Personal communication, September 26, 2003.

68. A Message to the Community from the Faculty Advisory Committee, Wells College, March 2004, personal copy.

69. Some faculty criticized the choice of consultants, noting that Easton, the firm that was doing research on women's colleges and the effects of admitting men, had no experience in higher education. The other consultant was charged with looking at financial implications.

70. Representative Council Meeting Minutes, September 28, 2004, Wells College, personal copy. Previous research done at Wells in the late 1990s found that of all the reasons listed for applying to Wells College, the three most common were size of college (75 percent of students), student-faculty ratio (74 percent), and academic reputation (65 percent). Being a women's college was the least-chosen reason by far, with only 7 percent of students giving that response. Critical Issues Action Committee research, Wells College, 1998.

71. Results of survey of faculty, e-mail from member of Collegiate Council, September 30, 2004.

72. "Summary Report on Dean's Faculty Forum on Coeducation," September 28, 2004, Wells College.

73. A male member of the board of trustees pushed protesting students aside angrily, including one who was on crutches. She lost her balance but did not fall. This incident, as well as another one involving a tall male faculty member who tried to get by students

who were blocking a stairwell, made some faculty believe that the campus was getting an idea of the kind of violence one could expect once men students enrolled. Personal notes from a community meeting.

74. David L. Shaw, "Judge: Wells Can Go Coed," *Syracuse Post Standard,* December 17, 2004.

75. Rachel Porter, "Outloud." *Onyx,* November 9, 2004, WCA.

76. Information provided by the vice president for external affairs, Ann Rollo, February 2005.

77. These incidents were described to me by various members of the campus community, some of whom presumably heard about them through other students. Hence the descriptions were not identical in all details.

78. A year later it appears that the entering first-year class for fall 2006 will be around 170 students, of whom about 40 are men. Personal communication, Susan Sloan, Director of Admissions, May 25, 2006.

79. Slightly more than three-quarters of alumnae who give money are "loyal donors" who give every year, "well above average among peer institutions." "Relationships that Endure," *Wells College Express,* Summer 2003, p. 8, WCA.

80. Wolf Organization, Wells College Planning Project, Summary of Interim Presentations, n.d., WCA.

81. The key person in this regard is professor of mathematics Arnold Shilepsky, who for more than twenty years has collected information on women's colleges compared to former women's colleges. The data he has amassed show convincingly that former women's colleges are stronger in applications, enrollments, selectivity, finances, and faculty salaries than are continuing women's colleges.

PART III

Case Studies of Women's Colleges
That Have Remained Single Sex

The four institutions in Part Three are women's colleges that have survived as single-sex institutions. Like those in the previous section, they represent the variety among women's colleges. Mills College is secular and independent; Simmons College has vocational roots; Spelman College is historically black; and the College of Notre Dame is Catholic. Together, these chapters document many of the financial and social challenges that women's colleges face today, when the vast majority of women students prefer a coeducational environment.

Like many women's colleges, Mills College faced declining enrollment and financial stress during the 1980s. The board of trustees decided to admit men in 1990, but their announcement was met with such determined protest that the college recommitted itself to single-sex status. Determination is not enough to maintain a college, however. In Chapter 7, Marianne Sheldon documents not only the well-known protests that erupted at Mills in the early 1990s, but also the more quiet efforts to develop new sources of revenue and higher enrollments in the ensuing years. Sheldon, now associate provost for graduate studies and professor of history at Mills College, was at Mills during the 1990 coed strike.

In Chapter 8, Susan Poulson reviews the unique history of Simmons College, which was founded to benefit working-class women in the Boston area by offering vocational education. For several decades, its class association, as well as the discrimination at other institutions that propelled students to Simmons's more open enrollment, provided a steady pool of applicants. However, changes in the marketplace of higher education have shrunk that pool. Virtually all institutions now are open to minorities, and fewer women seek a vocational education in today's economy. In response to these developments, Simmons has increasingly emphasized its liberal arts program, developed a graduate program twice the size of its undergraduate population, formed a consortium with nearby institutions, and emphasized the attractiveness of its location in the heart of Boston.

Spelman College, Frances D. Graham and Susan Poulson note, defies the trend of declining enrollments and finances. Although all U.S. institutions of higher education are now open to black men and women, Spelman College during the past forty years has increased not only its enrollment but also the academic qualifications of enrolled applicants. Additionally, the college has created several innovative programs, improved its physical plant, and dramatically increased its endowment. It has done so, Graham and Poulson assert in Chapter 9, by creating a strong and empowering environment for the academic and social development of young black women. It also benefits from its urban location in Atlanta next to Morehouse College (a historically black men's institution), generous philanthropy, and careful financial management.

In Chapter 10, Dorothy M. Brown and Eileen O'Dea, SSND, reveal that administrators at Notre Dame College of Maryland struggled with a decline in applicants and with financial concerns, both typical in many women's colleges. However, by reaching out to nontraditional students, developing a graduate program and a weekend program, and enrolling half its students on a part-time basis, Notre Dame has been able to maintain itself as a predominantly women's college and resist suggestions for a merger with a nearby Catholic university. Brown, as former interim president of the college, and O'Dea, as vice president for mission and former vice president of planning, offer unique insights from their extensive experience within the College of Notre Dame of Maryland.

7

Revitalizing the Mission of a Women's College

Mills College in Oakland, California

Marianne Buroff Sheldon

For more than a century, Mills College has been a nationally recognized independent, liberal arts college for women. Beginning in the 1920s, the college also developed graduate programs for women and men. At present, Mills enrolls about 735 undergraduate women and 475 graduate women and men. It is the only undergraduate women's college in the San Francisco Bay Area and, along with Mount St. Mary's in Los Angeles and Scripps in Claremont, one of three women's colleges in California. The parklike 135-acre campus is located in the foothills of Oakland, California, a diverse urban community with a population of about 400,000. The prominent California architect Julia Morgan designed many of the buildings on campus.

Mills received national media attention in 1990 when the board of trustees decided to transform Mills into a coeducational undergraduate college and dramatic protests erupted. The quick reversal of that decision was followed by a reaffirmation of the college's commitment to the education of women and a determination to revitalize its mission as a women's college.

The College's Beginnings

The history of Mills College begins with the founding of the Young Ladies Seminary in Benicia, California, in 1852, three years after the forty-niners descended upon California seeking gold. Two years later, Mary Atkins, a graduate of Oberlin College, took over the seminary, and in 1865 Susan and Cyrus Mills purchased it. Susan Mills, a graduate of Mount Holyoke Seminary, and Cyrus Mills, a graduate of Williams College, had been educational missionaries in Ceylon. Inspired by the achievements of such pioneers in women's education as Mary Lyon, the founder of Mount Holyoke, they came to California with the dream of founding a seminary. The curriculum designed by Susan and Cyrus Mills included mathematics, astronomy, moral philosophy, painting, Italian, and botany. After purchasing the seminary, they moved it in 1871 to Brooklyn Township, about five miles outside the city of Oakland. In 1885 the State of California chartered Mills as a nonsectarian college for women, the first chartered women's college west of the Rockies. Its first bachelor's degree candidates graduated in 1889. In 1920, a School of Education and a School of Graduate Studies were established. The master of arts degree was first awarded by Mills in 1921 and the master of education degree first awarded in 1929.

Mills's isolation from other institutions of higher learning shaped its early history. Although the University of California was admitting women in the 1870s, Mills was the only women's college in the West until 1927, when Scripps was founded. The college curriculum approved by the trustees in 1885 was said to be similar to that of Harvard College. Speaking at Mills in 1899, David Starr Jordan, the first president of Stanford University, observed: "This College stands for serious education. It is not a finishing school, but a building school. It works to form character, not to give accomplishments; to meet demands not of society, but of life."[1] However, because the growth of enrollment at the college level was slow, students continued to be accepted into the preparatory secondary program during the administration of President Susan Tolman Mills (1890–1909). In 1909 there were 84 college students at Mills and 115 young women at the preparatory level. The last secondary class graduated from Mills in 1911, but the institution struggled in the years after Susan Mills's retirement to complete the shift from seminary to college.[2]

Becoming a National Institution

Under the energetic leadership of President Aurelia Henry Reinhardt (1916–43), the college expanded its enrollment, physical campus, and academic development. When Reinhardt arrived at Mills in 1916, the enrollment stood at 212. When she retired in 1943, it had reached 656 (the third-highest total in the history of the college to that point), in spite of significant financial and enrollment challenges during the 1930s Depression (236). In addition to the dramatic expansion of the student population, President Reinhardt presided over the implementation of a comprehensive administrative structure, the development of a campus facilities plan, the construction of some important new buildings, and the creation of a comprehensive college curriculum. Simultaneously, the college's reputation shifted from that of a purely regional institution to one with a national standing, as evidenced by the growth in the out-of-state student population: from 32 percent in 1931–32 to 45 percent in 1939–40 (93).

In the ten years following the establishment of the School of Graduate

Studies in 1920, the college awarded Masters of Arts degrees to fifty candidates. In 1935 two men were enrolled in the graduate program, beginning a tradition of coed graduate education at Mills that continues to the present (103). By the early 1960s Mills was offering three graduate degrees—master of education, master of arts, and master of fine arts. In the 1960–61 academic year, fourteen of the sixty-four graduate students were men, about 22 percent of total graduate students, a percentage that has remained remarkably stable down to the present.[3]

In spite of the emergence of a small group of male students at the graduate level, Mills steadfastly retained its mission as a liberal arts undergraduate institution for women. Mills's official mission statements have been updated periodically to reflect changing programs and perspectives, but its fundamental mission has not changed. From time to time, the pressures of finances and enrollment led the college to consider the coed option at the undergraduate level, similar to what has occurred at most other women's colleges in the nation. During the Great Depression with an enrollment low of 387 in 1933, President Reinhardt thought about but then rejected the suggestion of a merger with Stanford.[4] The coeducation debate, along with the gradual expansion of higher-educational opportunities for women, encouraged Mills to define more explicitly the meaning and importance of single-sex education for women. In the 1920s Aurelia Henry Reinhardt put forth a philosophy on how Mills should meet the needs of its students:

> A woman's college must define a woman's responsibility—always manifold, but especially significant in three directions: her world-old responsibility in the home must first be understood, then ennobled and beautified, if possible; her newer responsibility as neighbor and citizen must make her ready to improve her community in health and housing, in educational and recreational facilities, as well as in conditions of labor and living; her responsibility as an economic factor in a country where, on the one hand, women make ninety per cent of all expenditures in the home, and where, on the other hand, eight per cent of the workers in industry are women, must find her trained in social economics.[5]

President Reinhardt believed that in the early twentieth century women's colleges were particularly suited to preparing women to participate in spheres of activity beyond their homes.

The next president of Mills College, however, elaborated an educational philosophy that embraced, to a considerable extent, more traditional and stereotypical expectations for women. Lynn Townsend White Jr. (1943–58), a strong advocate of humanism and the liberal arts curriculum, took up the challenge of defining the mission of educating women with the publication of his book *Educating Our Daughters* (1950). White's treatise explicitly called attention to the crucial role of women's colleges: "The task of formulating and elaborating a type of higher education truly appropriate to women will be carried on primarily in the women's colleges."[6] His most frequently quoted observation called attention to the ways in which the prevailing ideals of marriage and motherhood shaped the education of women in the 1950s: "Why not study the theory and preparation of Basque paella, of a well-marinated shish kebab, lamb kidneys sauteed in sherry, and authoritative curry, the use of herbs."[7]

In fact, White was continuing a curriculum that had long integrated subjects thought to be of practical or vocational use to women. As far back as 1911 when Mills ended its secondary curriculum, vocational classes such as Home Sanitation and House Construction, Millinery, and Catering continued to be offered alongside such traditional liberal arts courses as Latin, history, poetry, and biology. During World War I the college began to offer courses in stenography, typewriting, bookkeeping, and office organization. In the 1940s Mills majors included dietetics and institutional administration, medical technicianship, occupational therapy, premedicine, and prepharmacy. In the 1950s under the leadership of President White, career-related majors expanded to include interior design, laboratory techniques, medical records librarianship, merchandizing, nursing, and personnel work. Indeed, between 1951 and 1960 Mills offered a BS degree in fields with a "high concentration in studies with specific vocational goals."[8] Such a distinction between the BA and BS degrees was probably a reflection of the tension that existed between liberal arts and vocational majors.

The Boom Period of the 1960s

The 1960s marked a significant point of growth and development for the college, reflecting the general boom in U.S. higher education. Total undergraduate enrollment grew from 691 in 1960, to 709 in 1965, to 852 in 1970. Indeed, the boom in enrollment was sustained throughout the 1970s; undergraduate enrollment peaked at 907 in 1971, but remained above 800 through 1979. In the sixties the Mills curriculum turned away from the explicitly feminine vocational focus of earlier years. In January 1960, the college discontinued its majors in business studies (which included such courses as Stenography, Typewriting, Bookkeeping, and Office Organization), home economics, merchandizing, occupational therapy, and personnel.[9]

While by the 1960s Mills's earlier focus on traditional job preparation was no longer seen as relevant, a new academic vision had not yet been defined. The college presented the well-rounded liberal arts education as the best preparation for the future, but not much explicit attention was given to the needs and interests of women per se. Lynn White's successor, Easton Rothwell (1959–67), noted somewhat ambiguously in his inaugural address: "I can promise you that

Mills College will continue to graduate young women who will look the future full in the face. They will be educated to see their world in balanced perspective, and to perform their share of what must be done to bring human relations into harmony with science."[10] Interestingly, Mills students only slowly began to demand changes during the 1960s. The climate of student discontent, protest, and activism that prevailed in nearby Berkeley did not have a dramatic impact on the Mills campus until the end of the decade.

What was described as "the greatest on-campus activism Mills has seen" exploded over the issues of racism and "student power."[11] In the spring of 1968 a group of Mills African American students formed the Black Students Union and presented a list of demands to the incoming president, Robert Wert (1967–76) that asked the college to "commit itself to the securing and hiring of two full-time black professors and a black on-campus advisor for the academic year beginning September, 1968."[12] At that time only about 3.5 percent of students were African American, and the Mills faculty included just one part-time African American instructor. At an open all-campus meeting held in May 1968, college administrators promised to expand efforts to hire African American faculty members, to hire a student advisor trained in supporting minority students, and to recruit more minority students.[13] Shortly thereafter, an African American professor and an African American assistant to the dean of students were hired, and commitments were made to recruit additional faculty of color. In 1969–70 a Department of Ethnic Studies was created, although initially faculty in the department tended to have either part-time or joint appointments.[14]

The emergence of student protest on the Mills campus coincided with the development of concerns about changing patterns of enrollment and financial pressures. In 1960, out of 691 undergraduates, only 27 (4 percent) were designated as commuting students. But by 1971, with a peak undergraduate enrollment of 907, the number of nonresidents had jumped to 274 (30 percent).[15] That development's financial implications greatly concerned college administrators.[16] In addition, growing inflation led to the spiraling cost of faculty and staff salaries as well as of construction and maintenance. Since these rising expenditures coincided with the decline of tuition revenue, income from the endowment, and foundation support, Mills began to experience serious budget constraints. President Wert observed in 1969: "I know of no area in the college which can now sustain further reductions of expenditures without damaging the scope and quality of our operation."[17] Nevertheless, in 1975 Wert had to admit that for the preceding seven years, expenditures had exceeded income: "Obviously, an institution can't survive if spending surpasses income for long. If we continued in this fashion, our deficits would have to be covered by endowment capital, causing a constant and growing drain on our resources."[18]

Early Discussions of Coeducation

In this climate of financial and enrollment difficulties, Mills College constituencies began to discuss coeducation. As early as 1963 an article on coeducation appeared in the *Mills Quarterly,* "Is There a Future for Women's Colleges?" The author of the article was Mervin B. Freedman, an associate with the Institute for the Study of Human Problems at Stanford University. Earlier that year, Freedman and Mills president Easton Rothwell had participated in a conference titled "Conference to Plan a Program of Research on Problems Affecting the Education of Women." Freedman, noting the current "uncertainty about the future" of women's colleges, saw little about the curriculum of women's colleges that was distinctive: "Surely when we look about us at women's colleges we see little or nothing to suggest that the women's college possesses a special educational virtue; . . . there is little difference between the curriculum of the women's liberal arts college and that of a comparable men's or coeducational institution."[19] Freedman did not believe, however, that women's colleges had outlived their usefulness. He argued that women's colleges ought to "help restore to American higher education some of the joy in life and learning" and "restore to us our esthetic sense, our awareness of the complexity of nature and life."[20] Such vague objectives probably did not satisfy all on the Mills campus. Indeed, throughout the 1960s the issue of coeducation continued to be actively explored and vigorously debated.

Under Easton Rothwell's leadership, Mills undertook a study of the feasibility of establishing a coordinate college for men on the campus. Although a 1965 study yielded information about the legal issues and costs, Rothwell's successor, Robert Wert (1967–76), was not "persuaded that Mills should grasp so eagerly for men."[21] Wert, however, echoed the concerns raised by Mervin Freedman about the lack of a compelling academic argument for the existence of women's colleges: "The fact is that we have no precise idea of the comparative educational effects of women's colleges, men's colleges and coeducational ones. Our best judgment is that some students thrive in each of these situations, just as some perform better in small colleges and others in large universities." Wert concluded: "I want Mills to show clearly that a women's college is a special place; that it brings a range of influences to bear upon its students which cannot be duplicated elsewhere; that it creates an academic and social mood distinct from that of other colleges and that it develops and changes by drawing inspiration and vigor from its own unique circumstances."[22] But the research to support such aspirations was still forthcoming in 1967, and so the debate over the merits of coeducation continued.

Students overwhelmingly favored coeducation in the late 1960s. The student newspaper, the *Mills Stream,* conducted a poll in 1969 which found that 79 percent of students who responded (187 of 238) favored Mills going coed. Students who supported the coed position observed that Mills is "unnatural without men," that the male perspective in the classroom was absent, and that opportunities for nonromantic friendships with men were lacking. Students who wanted Mills to remain a women's college felt that the campus did not need men because they were "only a distraction."[23] Some observers on campus concluded that student discontent with the all-female campus could also be addressed by efforts to provide exchange programs or other kinds of links with coed institutions. The May 1969 issue of the *Mills Quarterly* that reported the debate ended with a summary of the basic questions that remained unanswered, questions that would still be there twenty years later: "Does a college have to resemble society to be relevant to it, or should it create artificial situations to counteract failings of that society? What would Mills' going coed entail? If Mills went coed, what men would apply? Does the faculty favor going coed? And how do the alumnae see it from their unique vantage point?"

Coeducation was still "a hot topic" at Mills in 1970, although the discussion at this time does not seem to have been highly emotional, confrontational, or urgent.[24] Underlying the discussion was concern about the challenge of recruiting young women to a women's college. The *Mills Quarterly* reported in early 1970 that only 6.6 percent of high school senior girls expressed interest in attending a women's college.[25] Although 1971 represented the peak of undergraduate enrollment at Mills (907 students), the director of admissions lamented the fact that the college was admitting a higher percentage of applicants than it had in the past: "It is clear that we must develop a larger number of applicants. . . . Our experience in this regard is consistent with like institutions with whom we are competing for a shrinking pool of young women seeking education at a single-sex college."[26] In addition, the college believed it was still struggling with "the image of Mills as an exclusive club of rich girls."[27] The director noted with pride that one-quarter of undergraduates were "of minority group background" but expressed great concern about the need to recruit more resident students. The opening of new residence halls on the campus led to an increase of about two hundred residential spaces in three years, leading the admissions director to complain: "Empty beds present a formidable challenge to a Director of Admissions."[28]

Responding to Women Students' Changing Interests

Concerns over enrollment were a major factor in Mills's development of new academic programs designed to be responsive to the needs of women. Faculty, administrators, and students focused attention on the importance of preparing women for careers previously closed to them. By the late 1960s, Mills faculty were becoming knowledgeable about the new research on the educational socialization of women. They believed that the college should focus its academic program in ways that responded to the findings of this research. For example,

Mills mathematics and computer-science professors described how the development of a computer-science program at Mills was in part a response to concern with the discrepancy between the number of college men and the number of college women who took advanced math classes. They wished to overcome circumstances that could serve as a "filter" for future career decisions.[29]

Mills succeeded in getting significant financial support from the federal government, as well as from national foundations and corporations, for some of its educational initiatives. The college received one of the initial grants under the Women's Educational Equity Act of 1974 to develop a curricular/career model project aimed at assisting women to enter scientific and technical fields.[30] Since the 1960s Mills had been active in developing undergraduate courses in computer science.[31] In 1974 Mills created a Department of Mathematics and Computer Science and initiated "a comprehensive program to increase the participation of women in regular mathematics and computer-science courses."[32] By 1976 it offered twelve courses in computer science and in 1977 developed an extensive "computer literacy program." The department could now cite an article in the *Mills Quarterly* headlined, "The New 'Women in Science' Program Is Booming with Students."[33]

The adoption of additional career-oriented majors continued despite concern about the antagonism between them and liberal arts education. In the fall of 1974, Mills developed a new interdisciplinary major called administration and legal processes (ALP). This major, explicitly designed to prepare women for careers in law, business, and government, was initially supported by a grant from the Carnegie Corporation.[34] In 1980 an interdisciplinary major in communications was introduced.[35]

Women students' rising aspirations led Mills to provide additional resources for career guidance and preparation. In 1973, with the support of a grant from the Fund for the Improvement of Postsecondary Education (FIPSE), Mills established a Center for Career Planning charged with providing undergraduates with self-assessment tools, vocational awareness, and job-search information. The new center focused particularly on the importance of reversing career gender stereotypes and patterns of job discrimination. To that end, the center began to work with Mills faculty to relate career information to the academic program, "to effectively blend career planning with the academic development of students throughout their years at Mills" and to develop internships for students that would relate academic and work experiences. The center also began to cultivate its alumnae network more actively as a resource for undergraduates seeking career guidance and expanded its work-study and internship programs.[36]

By 1975 the Mills College faculty and administration were ready for a comprehensive discussion of "how the curriculum might adapt to meet the needs expressed by new generations of students."[37] In February 59 of the 111 Mills faculty and ten administrators attended a campus conference that considered a range of proposals including incorporation of more non-Western studies into the curriculum, development of interdisciplinary perspectives, and responses to the needs of students of color and nontraditional-age students. Discussion at the conference was focused particularly on the need to identify an academic core crucial to the mission of Mills as a women's college. In response, a group of faculty presented a proposal for the creation of a new major in women's studies.

The growth of the feminist movement and the expansion of knowledge about and by women in the 1960s and 1970s in almost all academic disciplines encouraged the development of a more integrated and comprehensive study of women. In the early 1970s Mills did offer a few courses that focused on women, for example, a sociology course on women in contemporary society, and an English course on women writers. In 1975–76 the Mills catalogue observed: "Systematic study of the role and status of women in society is an academic area in which a college for women has particular responsibility."[38] In the following year, women's studies was formally organized into a major at Mills.

The college's leadership gradually came to embrace not simply the idea of educating women, but the very special role of the women's college in this process. Mills president Mary Metz (1981–90) wrote in 1982:

> In the last few years, researchers have documented the fact that women's colleges have played a unique role in educating women for distinction and accomplishment far beyond what one should expect from colleges of our size. The learning environment that prevails on our campus is at once challenging and encouraging, one in which the only limits set on women are self-defined. Women's colleges encourage women to think in terms of possibilities rather than limitations and provide the kind of education that turns possibilities into realities.[39]

At the same time, the college was also taking steps to enhance athletic and sports opportunities that high school girls were coming to expect. The expanded national media attention given women athletes in the 1970s, along with the growing emphasis on health and fitness, had an impact on the Mills campus. A new facility for dance and athletics was completed in 1971. The organization of intramural sports teams on campus—soccer, inner-tube water polo, softball, volleyball, and tennis—boomed. Intercollegiate sports competitions also grew. Despite limited resources, Mills competed in four team sports (tennis, crew, volleyball, and basketball) and three individual sports (fencing, badminton, and judo). Mills Athletics Department leaders believed themselves to be "in the avant-garde of private women's colleges" with respect to organizing intercollegiate competitions.[40] In the early 1980s, Mills College became a full member of the National Collegiate Athletic Association (NCAA) at the Division III level. This change led to increased efforts to recruit prospective student athletes to the college. A new director of athletics was hired; new cross-country and swimming intercollegiate teams were formed; and intramural offerings increased from six to twenty-eight. For the first time, intercollegiate sports activities received funding from the general Mills College budget. Finally, a Committee on Athletics was established to recommend "actions the College should take in order to insure that the athletic program at Mills College will be responsive to the athletic needs and interests of Mills students in the coming decade."[41]

Recommitment to Being a Women's College

If the college had been suffering some kind of identity crisis in the early 1970s, it had certainly become less acute by the middle of the decade.[42] The decline in interest in the coed option at Mills might have been related in part to the growth of the feminist movement, which was accompanied by a renewed commitment to the importance of women's colleges. At a national conference on the future of women's colleges held on the Mills campus in January 1973, President Wert spoke on the topic "The Important Role of the Woman's College."[43] In the same year, the college received a Ford Foundation grant to undertake studies of women's education at coed and single-sex colleges and to host another national conference on the topic.[44] Perhaps, too, the development of new academic initiatives such as the programs in administration and legal processes and computer science contributed to the renewal of faith in the mission of the college. Mills was successful in expanding its outreach to some new groups of undergraduates, most notably "resumers," women twenty-three or older at the time of enrollment. In 1980 there were 63 "resumers" on campus; in 1985, 159; and in 1986, 170, the high point in these years.[45] Enrollment of undergraduate minority students was fairly stable: 1977, 23.9 percent; 1980, 18.8 percent; 1985, 20.2 percent; 1990, 20.9 percent.[46]

The unanticipated growth of graduate student enrollment in the 1970s was probably also a factor that supported maintaining Mills as an undergraduate women's college. Larger numbers of graduate students certainly increased tuition revenue, and they also enriched the quality of campus life. A self-study completed in 1980 noted that "the graduate programs at Mills never dominate their discipline[s], as they may do at some research universities. Here, the graduate programs exist to support the undergraduate education in that the presence of a few highly trained, mature students in classroom and studio clearly enhanced the quality of a Mills education."[47] Although very little institutional effort was expended upon graduate student recruitment before about 1978, the number of graduate students increased from 64 in 1960 to 101 in 1970 and 150 in 1980.[48] Explanations for this growth typically centered on the outstanding reputation of the faculty, as well as on the college's Bay Area location, program flexibility, and moderate fee structure. At this time, Mills offered MA degrees in dance, education, English, music composition, and music history; MFA degrees in art technique and music performance and literature; and several credential and degree programs in education.

The strong growth of the graduate programs continued into the 1980s. Graduate enrollments in fact doubled from 145 in 1981 to 290 in 1988.[49] At the same time, new graduate programs were added to the curriculum: an MFA in creative writing, MA in interdisciplinary computer science, and MA in graduate liberal studies.[50] Although Mills's graduate programs had been attracting men since the 1930s, the percentage of male graduate students remained relatively constant: 22 percent in 1961, 24 percent in 1971, and 21 percent in 1980.[51]

The appointment of Barbara White as president of Mills College in 1976 was in many ways a reaffirmation of the mission of Mills as a women's college. Her presidency followed more than thirty years during which Mills College was headed by three male presidents—Lynn White, Easton Rothwell, and Robert Wert. At the start of her presidency, Barbara White set forth a clear statement on the mission of Mills, which was approved by the board of trustees in 1978: "The mission of Mills is to help able, aspiring women develop their potential to the full. The college does so by offering a liberal arts education of the highest quality, with an environment that provides special reinforcement and challenge for women."[52] The statement of academic purpose drafted and approved by the Mills faculty in 1979–80 echoed this determination to remain a women's college.[53]

College officials remained concerned about the state of college finances and the level of undergraduate enrollment throughout the late seventies and into the eighties. Operating-budget deficits at the college prompted the faculty to create an informal faculty-salary bargaining group in 1976 and, two years later, to elect a new faculty governing body called "the council," charged with the task of reviewing the college budget.[54] The need for sustained and focused academic planning was obvious. A 1980 self-study document pointed out that Mills would "face the critical need in the eighties" for "intensive planning" if it was going "to retain its position as an institution of high quality," as such planning was widely recognized as necessary in this "crucial decade for higher education in general and for small liberal arts colleges in particular."[55]

Studies of Mills's circumstances and the challenges that it faced continued. In November 1979, in preparation for a capital campaign, the board of trustees authorized the formation of task forces charged with studying alumnae leadership, faculty support, financial aid, financial planning, and new programs. A few months later, an ad hoc advisory committee on enrollment was created to study student recruitment and retention. Consensus on an emerging strategy was developing: Enlarge the college's endowment, increase the number of students admitted and retained, and develop "educational initiatives that will attract students by combining a sound liberal arts education with sufficient pre-professional background to enter the arts, the sciences, the professions, or the public service."[56] All these planning efforts were clearly based on the premise that "the College will remain a college for women." Yet the Mills accreditation self-study, completed in 1980, sounded an ominous note when it concluded: "The role of a college for women, however, may prove the subject of an intensive future review if the College finds that the larger society will not support this distinctive service."[57]

A Decade of Self-Study and Planning

The arrival of a new president, Mary S. Metz, in 1981, marked the beginning of a decade of self-study, consultation, and planning that initially produced a renewed sense of energy and optimism on campus. In 1981 President Metz instituted a comprehensive long-range planning process that involved all segments of the Mills community. She established a new Planning and Budgeting Committee, and within a year the college adopted a new set of "all-college goals" in order to link planning with budgeting.[58] Although the initial intent seems not to have been to identify dramatic new paths for the college, underlying concerns about the viability of a liberal arts college for women continued to surface.

A marketing plan completed in the spring of 1983 by outside consultants noted that "the potential consequences of any further deterioration in Mills's ability to recruit able students are serious" and urged the college to create a distinctive "model for the education of women that in its totality sets the College apart from every other competing institution."[59] One of the central recommendations of the consultants was to develop an identity for Mills as "an elite college for a small number of very promising women who will attain positions of leadership in our society."[60] The consultants' report served as a focus of discussion for faculty and administrators, but it did not precipitate dramatic new curricular initiatives at the college.[61] Nonetheless, for a time in the mid-1980s Mills enrollments improved. Undergraduate enrollment increased from 715 students in 1983 to 810 in 1987, reversing the decline evident in the 1970s. Graduate numbers also grew in these years, from 185 in 1983 to 246 in 1987.

The finances of Mills improved in the mid-1980s too. The college had begun the decade with a serious operating deficit for the fiscal year ending June 1981. Mills launched a five-year $35.5 million capital campaign in 1984, and within a year almost half the goal had been achieved.[62] An $8 million gift from an alumna in 1984 also enabled the college to strengthen existing academic programs and introduce some new ones, including a new major in business economics. By the mid-1980s, the college had achieved a balanced operating budget, and the market value of the endowment had risen from about $28 million in 1981 to $48 million in 1986.[63] In 1987 the college celebrated the official announcement of the largest foundation grant ever received by Mills, $5.8 million from the F. W. Olin Foundation for the construction of a new library.[64]

In November 1985, amidst these promising signs, President Metz announced the board of trustees' approval of an ambitious new strategic plan for the next ten years. While reiterating the mission of Mills as a liberal arts women's college, the plan outlined a bold set of goals to "assure the distinctiveness of Mills College in the future and to reinforce its appeal to high quality students in an increasingly competitive market."[65] The three basic goals of the 1985–95 plan were: (1) to move Mills's ranking into the top twenty-five private liberal arts colleges in the United States; (2) to increase enrollment and to have more students in residence by increasing the number of undergraduate students from 774 in 1986 to 850 in 1990, and to 1,000 in 1995, and the number of graduate students from 216 in 1986 to 250 in 1995; and (3) to attract more high-ability students while maintaining diversity. Academic excellence, national prominence, and fiscal strength were the guiding principles of the administration.

But if 1985 represented a high point of optimism, the outlook soon changed. Although undergraduate enrollment had been on the upswing since 1984 when there were 739 undergraduates, it peaked at 810 students in 1987 and declined again in 1988 to 749 students. In 1989 it increased only slightly, to 777 undergraduates. Graduate enrollment increased until 1988, when there were 290 graduate students, but declined to 264 in 1989. In fall 1990 graduate enrollment had begun to grow again, reaching 270, thereby exceeding the 1985–95 strategic plan goal of 250. But undergraduate enrollment stood at only 774, thereby failing to meet the 1985–95 strategic plan undergraduate goal of 850 (see Figure 7.1).

Concern mounted over the failure of undergraduate enrollment to increase. On the basis of a study begun in 1986, the Office of Planning and Research concluded that Mills's position with respect to undergraduate student recruitment was different from that of eastern women's colleges because Mills faced greater competition from the state university system with its lower tuition: "Mills's competition was dominated by the California university system, led strongly by UC Berkeley and followed by UC Santa Cruz, UC Davis, San Francisco State University, and UC Santa Barbara." The challenge was then how to educate prospective students to the advantages of a Mills undergraduate education, how to demonstrate that "we are better than the competition": "We should do more to make students aware of the high reputation of our teaching faculty. Our faculty and curriculum are the cardinal strengths of Mills. We must find concrete ways to illustrate the commitment of our faculty to the students."[66]

The dramatic drop in the stock market in October 1987, and its consequent impact on the value of the college's endowment, intensified the pressure to increase enrollment. These new constraints forced the board of trustees to mandate reductions in staff and expenditures and to use funds from the 1984

Figure 7.1. Mills enrollment, 1960–2002

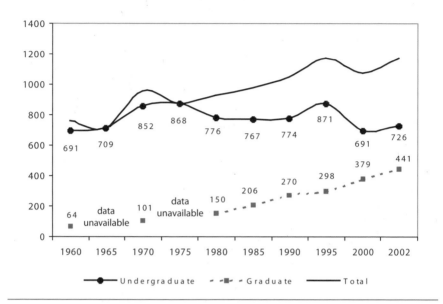

$8 million gift to the college to balance the 1988–89 budget rather than to support new programs. Responding to the call to cut faculty positions, Mills's faculty undertook a comprehensive curricular review in the spring of 1989 but was not able to recommend significant faculty reductions.[67]

The administration turned to outside consultants for information and advice. In 1988–89 the board of trustees hired Cambridge Associates, a financial-planning firm, to undertake a study of the college's financial policies and resources; the Boston Consulting Group to identify ways for the college to achieve a more stable financial situation; and Communicorp Georgia to study admissions strategies. From some perspectives, Mills remained a strong institution. For example, the six-year capital campaign, with an original goal of $35.5 million, ultimately raised $73 million. However, the report of Cambridge Associates concluded that, based on a widely used model for financial equilibrium, Mills had failed to meet the basic criteria for long-term fiscal health. The college, it contended, had not met renewal and replacement needs, spent too much of the yield from the endowment, and allowed its expenses to grow more rapidly than its revenues. The 1988–89 operating budget had a deficit of approximately $212,000, and the projected deficit for 1989–90 was $609,000.[68] Although there was disagreement over the applicability of the Cambridge model of financial equilibrium, trustees, administrators, and faculty generally agreed that declining undergraduate enrollment was indeed a grave concern.

Facing an Uncertain Future

A pivotal moment for the reassessment of the college's future occurred in spring 1989. President Mary Metz and the board of trustees made the decision to begin an eighteen-month planning process to consider "strategic options to lead Mills from strength into the 21st century."[69] President Metz argued that the college was not "in crisis." Mills "is in control of planning its future. It is not reacting precipitously to outside forces," she wrote.[70] She did believe, however, that Mills had been too small for too long. While an undergraduate enrollment of 1,500 to 2,500 seemed desirable from a revenue perspective, at its high point in 1971 Mills's undergraduate enrollment stood at only 907. And there were further disconcerting observations. The Boston Consulting Group reported that Mills did not compete well with other women's colleges, spent too many of its tuition dollars on financial aid, and attracted students less able or willing to spend a significant proportion of their income on education. The growth of the financial aid budget relative to the growth of tuition had become a significant concern. As a percent of tuition and fees, undergraduate financial aid increased from 29.5 percent in 1972–73 to a high of 39.3 percent in 1987–88. Because graduate tuition was only half of undergraduate tuition, the growth in the number of graduate students did not have as positive an effect on net tuition revenues as comparable growth in undergraduate enrollment would have had.[71]

Over the summer of 1989, the board's Strategic Planning Committee studied the college's mission. Gradually, a number of options emerged: (1) to increase enrollment and strengthen the academic program while remaining a women's college; (2) to maintain the current enrollment but reduce faculty, staff, and services while remaining a women's college; (3) to increase enrollment by becoming a coeducational institution; (4) to affiliate with another educational institution. In the fall of 1989 President Metz made clear her preference for remaining a women's college and growing, but she acknowledged the challenge this presented. Although "it would be wrong for Mills to become co-educational and become like all other co-educational liberal arts colleges," if Mills did decide on coeducation, it had to continue its commitment to women's education, not just "as rhetoric bouncing off the Campanile," but as reality in all parts of its life.[72] How that could be accomplished while simultaneously attracting male undergraduates was never fully discussed.

Mills decided on its goal by fall 1989: "To develop a strategy that will reverse declining enrollment and position Mills to fulfill its mission academically and be financially viable over the long term."[73] The board established four subcommittees to investigate and report in November on the various options and also set up a process for informing faculty, students, staff, and alumnae. In addition the board formed an external advisory committee, chaired by former University of California, Berkeley chancellor Roger Heyns, to ensure that the process was equitable and responsible. From the outset, the Mills Board of

Trustees stated explicitly that it was to be the final decision maker: "The College will use an inclusive decision-making process. Faculty, staff, students, and alumnae will participate in the process of generating and evaluating options and strategies. Ultimately, the Board of Trustees will make the decision it judges to be in the best interests of the College, after weighing the information and recommendations from the College's constituencies."[74] At a special meeting held in December, the Mills faculty gathered to discuss these developments. President Metz reiterated that before the end of the academic year, "we must develop a plan that is congruent with our values and educational philosophy and has a high probability of solving the College's enrollment and economic problems."[75] After receiving reports from the four subcommittees, the board's Strategic Planning Committee eliminated from consideration two of the four original options: maintaining the current enrollment while preserving the traditional mission of the college, and affiliating with another educational institution.

Making the Decision to Admit Men

The Strategic Planning Committee had to consider many issues as it deliberated on the two remaining options. In order to decide whether to increase its size as a women's college or become a coeducational institution, Mills's constituencies needed to review with care "the case for single-sex education, and at the same time consider the effects, both negative and positive, of a decision to become a coeducational college."[76] The Committee tried to answer many questions, including: What strategies had other women's colleges used to help them be more successful? And on the other side, What were the negative aspects of coeducation and how could they be eliminated or at least minimized? Trustee Virginia Smith, chair of the board's Strategic Planning Committee observed: "The burden of proof is on Option 1 [growing while remaining a women's college]."[77]

In retrospect, that coeducation had become a viable consideration for the future of Mills should not have been particularly surprising. That possibility had been debated in the not too distant past and had not been unilaterally rejected by all constituencies. In fact, however, it came as a shock to most members of the Mills community to discover that in 1989, the college was seriously considering coeducation. Throughout much of the 1989–90 academic year, students continued to believe that the board of trustees would not choose the coeducation option.[78] As late as February 1990, a prominent Mills faculty member noted that President Metz had been "very consistent" in her position "that co-education is a last-resort option."[79] Although some supporters of the coed option argued that there was no longer a need or place for single-sex educational institutions, most of them emphasized financial rather than ideological imperatives. For many members of the Mills community then, it seemed that the only motive for Mills to go coed was financial—and not all agreed that coeducation would in fact be a financial solution. [80]

In contrast to Mills students in the 1960s, the majority of students in the late 1980s were strongly opposed to the college's becoming coeducational. An editorial in the *Mills College Weekly* in early September 1989 condemned the coed option: "Other means of solving the financial crisis must be pursued before the most important characteristic of Mills is lost. Ignoring the tradition and changing the essence of Mills as [a] women's college many well alleviate the fiscal hardships of the college, but the solution would be in exchange for the loss of Mills' identity."[81] Signs of the depth of the opposition to coeducation also appeared, most notably when a group of students protested by organizing a sale of T-shirts emblazoned with such slogans as "Better Dead than Coed" and "Mills College: Not a Girls' School Without Men, but a Women's College Without Boys." In November, the *Weekly* surveyed Mills students' attitudes toward coeducation. Although about half the students who responded to the survey believed that Mills would in fact "go coed in the next five years," an overwhelming majority registered their dissatisfaction with coeducation. Eighty-seven percent of freshmen and sophomores surveyed said that they would transfer if Mills went coed while they were there, and 94 percent said they would not encourage others to apply to Mills if it became coeducational.[82] News of the debate filtered out to some of the local newspapers. The September 17, 1989, issue of the *Oakland Tribune* carried an article entitled, "All-Women Mills May Go Coed: Money Squeeze Forces 137-Year Old College to Reassess Its Mission."

Faculty opinion on the coed issue was not unanimous or fixed.[83] At a meeting on March 5, 1990, the faculty agreed to the president's request to postpone a previously scheduled vote on the two options until more information could be gathered and presented to them. However, the debate within the faculty was beginning to heat up. Already one senior faculty member had called upon the faculty not to remain silent but to speak out in support for women's education: "Let's speak out now! . . . We cannot remain silent, we cannot be neutral in the face of this death threat to the essence of Mills' identity."[84] Others called attention to studies of the advantages to women of single-sex education.[85]

The potentially divisive and disruptive nature of the debate among the faculty was becoming clear. One academic department issued a memo declaring that it had "decided unanimously to support the implementation of coeducation at Mills. . . . We are convinced that coeducation is an inevitable trend in American education and we are even more convinced that it is a necessary step for Mills at this time."[86] The head of that department contended that their action had been taken to refute the perception that Mills faculty were unanimous in their support of keeping Mills a women's college. In fact, he believed, it had become "politically dangerous" for faculty to express their support for coeducation: "We are disheartened by what we perceive as a growing tendency toward suspicion of each other as 'the enemy' on the primary issue of coeducation."[87] One longtime faculty member observed that being on campus "feels as if one is involved in a household in which the husband and the wife are trying to decide whether or not to get a divorce."[88] But although the debate was becoming more emotional and more heated, for the most part it did not divide the faculty along clear lines of gender, age, or length of service at the college.

Across the campus, the coeducation debate was on in full force by spring 1990, with emotions running high. At its February meeting the board of trustees gave President Metz the task of appointing a new campus committee, the Vision 2000 Committee, charged with creating visions of Mills based on the two options under consideration—a larger women's college or a coeducational college. Dr. Metz pointed out that "each vision needs to depict a college that is distinctive, provides an education of high quality, and is financially sound."[89] The Vision 2000 Committee, made up of four Mills faculty members, a student, an alumna, and two nonvoting administrators, prepared two scenarios, both directed at increasing undergraduate enrollment to a thousand students by 1995.[90] Faculty, staff, and students discussed the committee's report during the spring, and it was then submitted to the board of trustees for action in early May. Although views varied widely, most of the undergraduates and most of the alumnae stood opposed to the college's admitting men to the undergraduate program. Letters from alumnae poured into the *Mills Quarterly* in the fall of 1989 and spring of 1990. In February 1990 it was estimated that alumnae opinion was about 78 percent in favor of Mills remaining a women's college.[91] Even Warren Hellman, chair of the Mills Board of Trustees, acknowledged: "The sentiment is obviously overwhelmingly to remain a women's college."[92]

The small size of the Mills undergraduate population seemed to many of the college's leaders to make for a precarious situation. In fall 1989 there were 777 undergraduate women at Mills, which was then less than half the size of Mount Holyoke (1,939) and about a third the size of Wellesley (2,145). In 1990 there were, according to the Women's College Coalition, only ninety-four women's colleges in the United States, a drop from about three hundred in 1960.[93] In recent years, Wheaton, Goucher, Marymount, and Colby-Sawyer had decided to admit men, and Chatham College was debating the issue at the same time that Mills was.[94] Recognizing the vulnerability of a case that rested solely on financial considerations, board of trustees chair Warren Hellman argued: "Everybody says you shouldn't do something just for financial reasons. But money is not the cause, it's the symptom. Not enough people are willing to pay enough to buy the mission of Mills College to make it financially viable."[95]

Students' Opposition to Coeducation

Students held marches, vigils, demonstrations, and town meetings and organized petitions and pledges in the early months of 1990 in support of keeping Mills a women's college. The words "strong women, proud women, Mills women" gradually evolved into a theme that came to be repeated over and over in the months before the board of trustees was set to announce its decision. The students' president argued that admitting men to the undergraduate program "destroys the whole mission of the college, which is the empowerment of women." And Mills president Metz seemed to be in agreement: "It's a great dilemma because of the evidence that attending women's colleges makes a difference in the lives of women. It has truly empowered women, and they've gone on to do greater things."[96]

By the middle of April, groups of students were beginning to meet to develop a strategy for influencing the outcome of the debate on the coed issue. Students wrote letters to faculty lobbying them for support, tied yellow ribbons around the eucalyptus trees on campus, wore yellow armbands, adapted civil rights resistance songs to their cause, and organized press conferences. When the faculty gathered on April 23 to vote on the Vision 2000 report, students lined the path to the building where the faculty meeting was held and left yellow roses on the seats in the meeting room. As the college chaplain would later observe, "The campaign was underway."[97]

The faculty voted fifty-seven to twenty-six, with one abstention, against admitting male undergraduates to the college. Two days later students held a rally, attended by more than 350 students, alumnae, and staff, to oppose the coed option.[98] Faculty continued to debate the likely financial implications of a coed decision. "There is a market out there that won't consider going to a single sex college, and that's the market that could give us our greatest initial gains," wrote one supporter of coeducation. "By going coed, Mills would actually be losing its distinctive niche in the market," countered an opponent. Others rejected a purely economic analysis of the issue: "Even if it's not an easier path, I would still favor staying a womyn's college. What womyn have achieved here far outweighs much of the economic arguments of the coed issue."[99] One day before the board of trustees was scheduled to vote on the issue, a group of Mills students shaved their heads to protest against the possibility of the college going coed. The mood was tense, emotionally charged, and perhaps a bit despairing. "I feel like there's nothing I can do," said one student.[100] The headline of the *Tribune* on the morning of May 3, 1990, put it succinctly and starkly: "Decision Time for Mills College."

The Coeducation Decision and the Strike

A few minutes before two o'clock in the afternoon of May 3, 1990, the bells of El Campanil rang to signal that the board of trustees had reached a decision. The campus community came together for the announcement. Standing at the back door of earthquake-damaged Mills Hall, Warren Hellman, chair of the board of trustees, and Mary Metz, president of the college, announced that the trustees had voted to change the mission of the college and admit men to its undergraduate program by the fall of 1991. Most of the words of the speakers were drowned out by the cries, shouts, screams, and jeers of those who had come to hear the announcement. Hellman later said that the thirty-five-member board voted "overwhelmingly" to become coed because it really "had no other choice" if the college was to remain financially viable.[101] In a photograph that was reprinted in newspapers and shown on television throughout the country, a group of Mills students, clutching at one another, reacted with tearful, anguished cries.

That photo, however, did not capture the spirit of energy and resistance that quickly came to the forefront. At a meeting held that evening, students called for a boycott of classes. For the next two weeks, all normal activities on campus came to a virtual halt. Students blockaded campus buildings, put up banners proclaiming the strike, held rallies, and established communication channels. The *New York Times* observed: "Tears of sorrow have turned to shouts of defiance at Mills College, where students have vowed to shut the school until the board of trustees reverses its decision to end the institution's 138-year tradition as a women's college."[102]

The extent of students' outrage and their determination were most probably what inspired others in the Mills community to question the decision made by the board of trustees. The idea of bringing about a reversal of the decision, something that seemed unthinkable on May 3, within a week began to emerge as a distinct possibility. "A Glimmer of Hope," said the *Tribune* on May 8. Informal meetings among faculty, students, staff, and alumnae led to the development of a variety of plans for supporting the college if the trustees' decision were reversed. The Board of Governors of the Alumnae Association of Mills College came out in support of the students and organized a new, large fund-raising drive. Students and staff promised to assist with fund-raising and student recruitment and retention. The faculty proposed increasing their teaching load on a "plus one" basis without additional compensation; in addition to teaching five courses, full-time faculty would teach an additional course, preferably in the new general education program, or perform some other significant form of college service. Faculty members also agreed to maintain the current size of the faculty. All the proposals attempted to respond to the enrollment and financial issues that had been raised by the trustees.

The students ended their strike on May 17, one day before the board of trustees was scheduled to meet to reconsider its decision. On May 18 Warren Hellman stood on the steps of the College Tea Shop and held up a banner reading, "Mills: For Women Again." The board of trustees proclaimed the following resolution: "WHEREAS the alumnae, faculty, students, staff, and administration of Mills have overwhelmingly demonstrated their commitment to the college's mission for the education of women, WHEREAS these constituencies have translated that commitment into action through the proposals they have developed to maintain the health and vitality of Mills as a women's college. . . . NOW, THEREFORE BE IT RESOLVED THAT: the Board of Trustees' May 3, 1990 Resolution Nos. 2 and 3, which provide for the admission of men to Mills College's undergraduate programs by the fall of 1991, be and are hereby rescinded."[103]

The news was greeted with joy and a new sense of pride. The celebration was tempered, however, by the realization that the trustees had also set out some clear goals: increase undergraduate enrollment to nine hundred by 1993 and one thousand by 1995; decrease the overall faculty-student ratio from 1:10 to 1:13 by imposing a three-year faculty hiring freeze to reduce the number of faculty through attrition; reduce the financial aid–to–tuition ratio to about 30 percent by 1995 from a high of about 39 percent in 1987–88; increase the $72 million endowment by $10 million; increase the percentage of alumnae giving annually from 39 to 50 percent; and implement the curricular changes outlined in the proposals submitted to the board of trustees.[104] The headlines of the *San Francisco Examiner* proclaimed on May 19, 1990: "Mills Women Win Struggle; Now Comes the Hard Part." Another comment made by some members of the national press was that it was ironic to celebrate "separatism" at all-female Mills and yet simultaneously condemn discrimination at all-male Virginia Military Institute.[105]

Mills after the 1990 Crisis

A major upheaval in the college's chief administrative offices occurred shortly after the board reversed its decision. Although not all the changes were the direct consequence of the strike, within two years there were new people in many offices. Mary Metz resigned as president in June 1990; she was replaced on an interim basis by Virginia Smith, a member of the Mills board of trustees and former president of Vassar College. In 1991 Janet L. Holmgren, former vice provost of Princeton University, assumed the presidency. In the same year, new appointments were also made to the positions of dean of students and dean of admission. A new vice president for institutional advancement and a new provost and dean of the faculty were appointed in 1992. Under the new college leadership, in an atmosphere of optimism and energy, efforts to implement the agreed-upon strategies began. Curricular enhancement activities flourished. Alumnae giving increased dramatically, reaching 45 percent of solicited alum-

Mills College students celebrate the moment in 1990 that became famous—when trustees, responding to students' vigorous protest, rescinded the decision to admit men undergraduates. *Photo by Peg Skorpinski, Mills College Archives.*

nae in the first year, thus allowing the Alumnae Association to give $940,000 to the college in 1990–91.[106] Although undergraduate enrollment in 1992 was the same as in 1990 (774), with the aid of a freeze on undergraduate tuition it grew to 824 by 1993, 863 by 1994, and 871 by 1995. The benchmarks set by the board of trustees in 1990 had not been reached, but clearly the trend was in the right direction.

In the aftermath of the "crisis of 1990" there was an obvious need to develop institutional consensus on college goals and plans. After two years of planning, Mills adopted in 1993–94 a new strategic planning blueprint, "Moving Mills to 2002." That document set forth goals, strategic objectives, and integrative initiatives that explicitly connected financial and physical resources with institutional purposes and academic programs. The four strategic objectives listed were building enrollment to one thousand undergraduate and four hundred graduate students; fostering outstanding academic programs that prepare women for leadership in a global society; enhancing the campus working and living environment; and strengthening the financial position of the college and increasing its endowment to $250 million.[107] Recognizing the challenges to enlarging the undergraduate enrollment, the college supported a number of special initiatives. Undergraduate tuition and fees were frozen at 1992–93 levels for three years in an effort to stabilize the cost of attendance. With the assistance of a major grant from the James Irvine Foundation received in 1992, Mills launched a major effort to enrich multicultural education. Finally, the college began a new initiative to expand enrollment of graduate students, strengthen existing graduate programs, and create new graduate programs.[108] Supporting all these initiatives was a new capital campaign, timed to culminate with the celebration of the Mills sesquicentennial in 2002.

The commitment to enhancing and supporting diversity at the college was notably strengthened in the poststrike years. The contributions of women of color and of lesbians to the success of the 1990 strike had been particularly visible. Both these groups of students had their own special reasons for wanting Mills to remain a women's institution, and both were clear that Mills had to be a college for all women regardless of their race or sexual orientation.[109] As a result, struggles against racism and homophobia became more overt on campus.[110] Ethnic diversity among both Mills undergraduates and the faculty grew. In 1990 about 21 percent of undergraduate students were "American minorities"; in 1995 about 32 percent of undergraduates were "U.S. students of color"; and in 2002, 33 percent of undergraduates were students of color and 11 percent were multiethnic.[111] In 1990 "ethnic minorities" counted for about 5 percent of the full-time faculty; in 1995, people of color were about 16 percent of the full-time faculty; and in 2002 people of color were 20 percent of the full-time Mills faculty.[112] For a number of years including 2003, *U.S. News and World Report*'s "America's Best Colleges" has listed Mills as one of the most diverse liberal arts colleges in the United States. President Janet Holmgren has explained her vision for the college as providing "a supportive, challenging environment where we can experience, understand, and respect women in all our diversity."[113]

Diversity has come to be understood broadly as encompassing "difference" and including sexual orientation. Going back to the 1980s, a number of student organizations focused on issues associated with sexual identity have been organized—the Mills Lesbian Union, the Mills Lesbian BiSexual Union, the Mills Queer Alliance, Queer Melanin, and most recently, Mouthing Off. These organizations have generally sought to create unity among the lesbian, bisexual, and transgendered members of the Mills community and to provide a support network for women with questions about their sexuality. As the Mills community's sensitivity to issues of race, ethnicity, and sexual orientation has evolved, a new awareness of the multifaceted nature of students' identities has emerged. Campus student services have worked to identify new ways to address this understanding of diversity and its implications for student life and academic success. In addition, there are indications that diversity has been embraced across the Mills community. For example, beginning in October

1992, the *Mills Quarterly* began to list "commitment ceremonies" in its Class News section along with marriages, births, and deaths.

The reaffirmation of Mills's traditional mission as a women's college led to a new curricular emphasis on women's leadership. A 1993 gift from a Mills alumna who had spoken out passionately in 1990 in favor of keeping Mills a women's college established an endowed fund, as well as a faculty chair in women's studies. The women's studies program was thus effectively positioned to support the education of women in the liberal arts tradition with an emphasis on multiculturalism.[114] At the same time, a new Women's Leadership Institute was created on campus, an idea that had been discussed in the early 1980s.[115] President Holmgren supported the creation of a center that would promote leadership programs and activities for women with a wide range of career and life experiences. The Women's Leadership Institute held a national symposium, "Summit on Advancing Women's Leadership in Science," in 1994; led a delegation from Mills to the United Nations Fourth International Women's Conference in Beijing in 1995; hosted an international conference for women college presidents in 1996; and held a summit on women in legal education in 1997.[116]

The establishment of the Women's Leadership Institute was a logical consequence of Mills's renewed commitment to women's education. Encouraging and preparing women to be leaders have become important parts of the mission of the college.[117] Two of the 2001 academic initiatives, an undergraduate major in public policy and an MBA graduate program, explicitly focus on providing the information, skills, and perspectives, as well as the mentoring and networking opportunities, needed by women aspiring to leadership positions. In addition, the founding of the Institute for Civic Leadership in 2001 has allowed Mills students another opportunity to advance their leadership capacities, as well as to promote the civic purposes of higher education.

In accord with the college's mission of fostering women's leadership, both historical and current data demonstrate Mills's especially strong achievements in the hiring of women faculty and administrators. In the decades between 1960 and 2002, the percentage of women on the faculty ranged between 46 and 64 percent (see Table 7.1).[118] Furthermore, women have long been strongly represented among the college officers. The last three college presidents have been women, and since 1960, at least half the college officers have been women.[119] Finally, the trend has been toward more women than men serving on the board of trustees. Between 1960 and 2002, the proportion of women on the board ranged from 29 to 75 percent; between 1990 and 2002, from 68 to 75 percent (see Table 7.1).[120]

Mills trustees have long been, and remain, informed and passionate advocates of women's education. A few years ago, Jadwiga Sebrechts, president of the Women's College Coalition, spoke at Mills and observed that "a women's college is a place where women are in charge—whether as trustees . . . , as senior administrators . . . , as faculty . . . or as student leaders—where female leadership has become a norm and has internalized itself as an expectation. It is a place of abundant female role models for achievement and ready mentors to midwife the success of other women."[121] On these grounds, Mills has succeeded admirably. Throughout the college community, high expectations and confidence in women as leaders prevail.

Changing Goals: The College's Record since 1990

Over the course of the decade following the strike, it became clear that some of the ambitious enrollment goals set out in the early 1990s were not attainable. In addition, certain distinguishing characteristics of the Mills undergraduate student population were also becoming evident. Like many other women's colleges in the 1990s, Mills experienced a decline in undergraduate enrollment. From a poststrike high of 871 in 1995, the number of undergraduates declined to 691 in 2000; since then, the number has increased to 722 in 2001 and 726 in 2002. The average high school grade-point average of entering first-year students rose from 3.27 in 1990 to 3.55 in 2002.[122] Acceptance rates have declined somewhat,

Table 7.1. Women on Mills faculty and board of trustees, 1960–2002

	Faculty		Trustees	
	Total	**Women (%)**	**Total**	**Women (%)**
1960	88	48 (55)	34	12 (35)
1965	92	43 (47)	41	12 (29)
1970	113	53 (47)	32	13 (41)
1975	107	52 (49)	33	15 (45)
1980	113	67 (59)	32	15 (47)
1985	65[a]	34 (52)	31	16 (52)
1990	70	35 (50)	32	22 (69)
1995	69	40 (58)	34	23 (68)
2000	92	54 (59)	40	30 (75)
2002	88	51 (58)	39	29 (74)
2003	91	52 (57)	39	30 (77)

Source: Mills College Annual Catalogues.
[a] From 1985, numbers of full-time faculty, tenured and nontenured, were available in college reports to agencies. They do not include regular part-time faculty, which is why their numbers are lower than in previous years.

indicating that selectivity has slightly improved, from about 80 percent in the mid-1990s to 73 percent more recently.[123] During the same period the number of nonresidential students has continued to grow, from a little over 25 percent of the undergraduates in 1990 to about 43 percent in 2002.[124] Associated with this development has been the growth in the numbers of transfer and resumer students. In the early 1980s transfer students made up less than 25 percent of the entering class; by 1990 transfers comprised 38 percent of the incoming class; and between 1998 and 2002 they were close to 50 percent of the entering class each year.

This pattern is distinctive to Mills. The other women's colleges to which Mills compares itself have much lower percentages of transfer students in their entering classes. Similarly, Mills has had a consistently higher percentage of undergraduates who are resuming students, that is, students who are twenty-three years or older. In 1980 less than 10 percent of the undergraduates were resumers; in 1990 that number had increased to 15 percent; in 1995, 31 percent; between 1999 and 2002, between 19 and 26 percent. Data from peer institutions indicate that less than 10 percent of undergraduate students at peer institutions are resumers. One additional characteristic of the Mills student population is the significant proportion of first-generation college students. At present, slightly over 20 percent of the undergraduate students are first-generation.[125]

In the poststrike decade, aided in part by positive national economic forces, the college endowment grew to a high of about $177 million in 2000 but did not reach the $250 million goal. Recent downward economic trends shrank the endowment to $146 million in June 2002. On the positive side, the college's capital campaign has increased alumnae and foundation giving. By the summer of 2004, the college had exceeded its $100 million capital campaign goal.

The strategic plan endorsed by the board of trustees in early 2003 set new and perhaps more realistic goals for the college: an undergraduate enrollment of 800 and a graduate enrollment of 550 for the next five years. That plan also defined the elements of a "nonnegotiable" foundation for the future as including liberal arts education for women; graduate programs for women and men; a vibrant residential college community; high caliber, academically qualified students; diversity; and education that enlarges the choices of graduates in careers and contributions to society.[126]

Some of the shortfall in undergraduate enrollment has been compensated for by increases in graduate enrollment. In 1993–94, with a graduate student population of 313, the strategic planning document "Moving Mills to 2002" put forward an enrollment goal of 400 graduate students. That plan prompted the development and implementation of a Graduate Education Initiative in the mid-1990s aimed at strengthening existing graduate programs and supporting the development of new ones.[127] Between 1995 and 2002, the number of graduate students increased almost 50 percent, from 298 in 1995 to 441 in

2002.[128] In addition to ongoing programs in music, dance, writing and literature, art, computer science, education, and premedical training for liberal arts
students, Mills introduced two new graduate programs. In 1999 the Education
Department launched an advanced graduate program in educational leadership
culminating in the EdD degree. In 2001 the college began an MBA program that
includes a 4 + 1 component allowing undergraduates to obtain the degree in
only one additional year. In accord with a theme heard throughout Mills, both
these new graduate programs emphasize development of students' leadership
potential. Growth at the graduate level has made it possible for the total enrollment at the college to increase at a time when undergraduate enrollment has
improved only slightly.

Although the graduate student population is coed, women continue to
predominate. Between 1999 and 2003 the percentage of male graduate students
ranged from 20 to 24 percent, a figure not that different from 1990 when men
comprised about 22 percent of graduate students.[129] As President Holmgren
observed in 2003: "Graduate programs, as always, will be open to men, but they
will be distinctively ours because we understand how women achieve." Those
graduate programs build on the liberal arts curriculum but also seek to address
new professional opportunities for women. From that perspective, the college's
leadership has argued that "The vision that animates the [Mills Strategic] plan
is no less than a new paradigm for a women's college."[130]

Conclusions: Continuing Challenges

The Mills College strike of 1990 was a watershed event in the history of the college. Moreover, its influence has extended beyond the college. Robert Rhoads,
the author of *Freedom's Web: Student Activism in an Age of Cultural Diversity*,
studied "key student movements of the 1990s." In his view, "the most important"
of these movements "might well have been the Mills College Strike of 1990."[131]
Mills women, Rhoads observed, demonstrated

> a deep conviction that there was a great need and benefit in preserving women's
> space within the larger landscape that is American higher education. Their
> struggle was about much more than merely keeping men out; it was about
> women's education and the place of women in a society that has been largely
> male dominated.[132]

Thirteen years later that space continues to be preserved. The many positive
accomplishments at Mills include innovative academic programs, construction
and renovation of campus residential and academic facilities, and enhanced
recruitment and retention efforts. But much work still needs to be done and
clear challenges remain. Achieving the undergraduate enrollment goal of eight

hundred by 2007 will require focus and determination. In addition, the college must identify budget strategies that increase the college's endowment and support priority funding goals.

On the tenth anniversary of the strike, former chair of the board of trustees Warren Hellman observed: "The strike did many positive things for the College, but it did not solve all the problems."[133] Chatham College faced the coed challenge at precisely the same moment that Mills did and also rejected that option. Esther L. Barazzone, president of Chatham, recently observed that being an undergraduate women's college is not easy.[134] Barazzone's comment is, in fact, appropriate to the array of liberal arts colleges in the United States today. Higher education faces many daunting challenges, but they are particularly acute for women's colleges. Mills is attempting to create what President Janet L. Holmgren has called "a dynamic model of education for the 21st century": "Mills is well on its way to becoming a comprehensive higher educational institution for women—true to our mission but evolving to embrace education for women in the 21st century."[135] The need is clear; the determination is evident; the opportunities have been identified; but the challenge to identify and create a successful paradigm for a women's college will be ongoing.

Notes

I would like to thank Eda Regan and Terra Schehr for their research assistance with this chapter and the Meg Quigley Women's Studies Program at Mills College for providing a summer stipend to support this project.

1. Rosalind A. Keep, *Fourscore and Ten Years: A History of Mills College* (Oakland: Mills College, 1946), 97. Keep's book is the primary history of Mills College from its founding to 1943.

2. George Hedley, *Aurelia Henry Reinhardt: Portrait of a Whole Woman* (Oakland: Mills College, 1961), 78; succeeding citations of this work appear as page numbers in parentheses in the text.

3. "The Best Way Out Is Back," *Mills Quarterly*, February 1961, 96.

4. Hedley, *Aurelia Henry Reinhardt*, 233.

5. Keep, *Fourscore and Ten Years*, 123.

6. Lynn Townsend White Jr., *Educating Our Daughters: A Challenge to the Colleges* (New York, Harper and Brothers, 1950), 57.

7. Ibid., 78.

8. Marge Thomas, "Mills College: Paying Attention to Business," *Mills Quarterly*, November 1985, 40–41.

9. Ibid., 41.

10. C. Easton Rothwell, "The Inaugural Address, October 8, 1959: The Lamp Burns with a Clearer Flame," *Mills Quarterly*, November 1959, 63.

11. Jean Bayne, "Don't Do It Just to Be Fashionable," *Mills Quarterly*, February 1969, 4.

12. "Black Student Union," *Mills Quarterly*, May 1968, 31.

13. Ibid., 31–32.

14. *Self-Study Report to the Accrediting Commission for Senior Colleges and Universities Western Association of Schools and Colleges,* submitted November 15, 1980, 96–105, College Archives, Special Collections, F.W. Olin Library, Mills College; "Black Student Union," 30–31.

15. *Mills Facts and Trends, 1990–1991,* 1, table 2G. College Archives, Special Collections, F.W. Olin Library.

16. Robert J. Wert, "Balancing the Books," *Mills Quarterly,* August 1973, 15.

17. Ariel Eaton Thomas, "The Black Students: They Have Their Dreams Too," *Mills Quarterly,* May 1969, 17.

18. Robert Wert, "Mills Must Use the Present to Prepare for an Uncertain Future," *Mills Quarterly,* Summer 1975, 7.

19. Mervin B. Freedman, "Is There a Future for Women's Colleges?" *Mills Quarterly,* August 1963, 3; letter from Peter J. Crosby Jr. to Lawrence W. Larson, December 8, 1965, College Archives, Special Collections, F.W. Olin Library.

20. Freedman, "Is There a Future," 4.

21. "The Inaugural Address of Robert J. Wert, Ninth President, Mills College, October 18, 1967," *Mills Quarterly,* November 1967, 28. An interesting intuitive observation countering this perspective appeared in the Mills catalog of 1948: "Mills is a woman's college because the intellectual growth of young women and their discovery of their own capabilities are aided by an environment not dominated by masculine attitudes." *Bulletin of Mills College Catalogue Issue, March 1948,* 4. College Archives, Special Collections, F.W. Olin Library

22. "Inaugural Address of Robert J. Wert," 29, 30.

23. "Students Think about Co-Education," *Mills Quarterly,* May 1969, 19–20.

24. Ariel Eaton Thomas, "Creative Academic Revolution," *Mills Quarterly,* February 1970, 7.

25. Ibid.

26. Beth Cobb, "A New Look at Admissions," *Mills Quarterly,* November 1971, 6.

27. Audrey Bowers, "Admissions: Years of Decision," *Mills Quarterly,* February 1971, 8.

28. Cobb, "A New Look at Admissions," 4; Bowers, "Admissions," 4–9.

29. Lenore Blum and Steven Givant, "Preparing Women for Careers in Mathematics," *Mills Quarterly,* November 1981, 16–22.

30. *Self-Study Report,* 121.

31. Lenore Blum, "The New 'Women in Science' Program Is Booming with Students," *Mills Quarterly,* Summer 1975, 14.

32. Blum and Givant, "Preparing Women for Careers," 16.

33. Blum, "New 'Women in Science' Program," 14.

34. "A New Advisory Council for ALP," *Mills Quarterly,* Fall 1975, 15; *Self-Study Report,* 148.

35. *Self Study Report,* 36.

36. "Center for Career Planning: Helping Students Get Where They Want to Go," *Mills Quarterly,* May 1977, 13.

37. Peggy Webb, "The Faculty Foresees Changes in Mills Future," *Mills Quarterly,* Summer, 1975, 9.

38. Mary S. Metz, "A Room of Her Own: Women and the College Curriculum," *Mills Quarterly,* November 1982, 13; *Bulletin of Mills College, Catalog for 1975–76,* 151.

39. Metz, "A Room of Her Own," 16.

40. Memo from Patrice Griffin to Committee on Athletics, April 14, 1980; *Annual Report, 1980–1981,* Health and Movement Studies Department, May 29, 1981, Department of Athletics Archives, Mills College.

41. *Self-Study Report,* 185–86; *Mills Facts and Trends, 1982–1983,* 2.

42. "Everybody Owns a College," *Mills Quarterly,* August 1972, 17.

43. "Women's Colleges," *Mills Quarterly,* February 1973, 5.

44. "Mills News," *Mills Quarterly,* August 1973, 8.

45. M. Thomas, "Going Grey: Campus Colors Are Changing in America," *Mills Quarterly,* April 1994, 7–8; *Mills Facts and Trends, 1982–1983,* table 2.J; *1985–1986,* table 2.J; *1990–1991,* table 2.J.

46. *Mills Facts and Trends, 1981–1982,* table 2.I; *1985–1986,* table 2.I; *1990–1991,* table 2.I.

47. *Self-Study Report,* 151.

48. "Best Way Out Is Back," 96; "The Graduate Program," *Mills Quarterly,* May 1973, 14; *Mills Facts and Trends, 2002–2003,* 1, section 3.E; *Self-Study Report,* 155.

49. Graduate Studies Task Force, *Interim Report,* November 1989, 4. College Archives, Special Collections, F.W. Olin Library.

50. "Building on Strength: Grad Studies at Mills," *Mills Quarterly,* Summer 1996, 10.

51. "The Graduate Program," *Mills Quarterly,* May 1973, 14; "Best Way Out Is Back," 96; *Mills Facts and Trends, 1981–1982,* 2, table 3.D.

52. "The Mission of Mills," *Self-Study Report,* appendix I, attachment 1.a.

53. "Statement of Academic Purpose," *Self-Study Report,* appendix I, attachment 1.b.

54. *Self-Study Report,* 38–41; *Fifth-Year Report to the Western Association of Schools and Colleges,* submitted November 15, 1985, 39.

55. *Self-Study Report,* 39.

56. Ibid., 47.

57. Ibid., 53.

58. *Fifth-Year Report,* 11–12.

59. Executive Summary, *Mills College Student Recruitment Marketing Plan,* prepared by Jan Krukowski Associates, June 1983, 3–5.

60. Ibid., 15.

61. Helen Longino, "An Education with Which to Build the Future," *Mills Quarterly,* November 1983, 1–11; *Fifth-Year Report,* 5–6.

62. *Fifth-Year Report,* 6.

63. Ibid., 39–43. *Mills College Self-Study 1991 Submitted to the Western Association of Schools and Colleges for Reaffirmation of Accreditation,* September 16, 1991, 10, College Archives, Special Collections, F.W. Olin Library.

64. "College Receives Largest Foundation Grant," *Mills Quarterly,* November 1987, 2–5; "Special Colloquium Honors Olin Grant," *Mills College Weekly,* September 18, 1987.

65. Memo from Mary S. Metz to the Mills Community, November 8, 1985, in *Fifth-Year Report.*

66. Elizabeth Griego, "Why Did Our Freshmen Choose Mills? Who Didn't Come, and Why?" *Mills Quarterly,* May 1988, 7.

67. *Mills College Self-Study 1991*, 28–31.
68. Ibid., 29, 47. "Announcements," *Mills Quarterly*, November 1989, 4–5; memo from Campus Strategic Planning Committee to the Mills Community, August 23, 1989. College Archives, Special Collections, F.W. Olin Library.
69. Memo from Campus Strategic Planning Committee.
70. "Announcements," *Mills Quarterly*, November 1989, 4.
71. Ibid.; memo from Campus Strategic Planning Committee.
72. "Announcements," 4–5.
73. Memo from Campus Strategic Planning Committee.
74. Ibid.
75. Memo from Mary S. Metz to Members of the Faculty, November 29, 1989. College Archives, Special Collections, F.W. Olin Library.
76. Ibid., attachment, Excerpts from Minutes of the Strategic Planning Committee of the Board of Trustees of Mills College, November 3, 1989.
77. "Alumnae Respond to College's Plan for Future," *Mills Quarterly*, February 1990, 16.
78. Melissa Stevenson Dile, "Reflections of a Reluctant Revolutionary," *Mills Quarterly*, Spring 2000, 14.
79. Marilyn Chandler, "The Co-education Debate: A Chance for Reappraisal, Redefinition, and Recommitment," *Mills Quarterly*, February 1990. 9.
80. Ibid.
81. Editorial, *Mills College Weekly*, September 8, 1989. The student campus newspaper was called the *Mills Stream* through December 9, 1985. As of February 7, 1986, it became the *Mills College Weekly*.
82. Editor's Note, *Mills College Weekly*, December 8, 1989.
83. For the faculty, the debate over the future of the college was also another opportunity to reassess the curriculum. In addition to serving on the task force committees associated with the options under consideration by the board of trustees, faculty members also worked in 1989–90 on committees charged with investigating academic programs in environmental studies, Pacific Rim/Asian studies, and enlarging the women's studies program. The faculty, particularly those committed to maintaining Mills as a women's college, also discussed revising general education requirements.
84. Edna Mitchell, letter to the editor, *Mills College Weekly*, February 9, 1990.
85. See, for example, Helen Longino, "Liberal Arts Education for Women," *Mills Quarterly*, February 1990.
86. Mary Lane, "Psychology Professors Endorse Coeducation," *Mills College Weekly*, March 9, 1990.
87. Ibid.
88. Ibid.
89. *Mills College Self-Study 1991*, 32.
90. Ibid., 33.
91. "Letters," editor's note, *Mills Quarterly*, April 1990, 5.
92. Peter Monaghan, "Mills College Faces a Demographic and Educational Dilemma: Can It Admit Men but Remain a Leader in Women's Education?" *Chronicle of Higher Education*, April 4, 1990, p. A37.
93. "Women's College Struggles to Keep Its Identity," *New York Times*, March 7, 1990.
94. "Agony for a Campus: Go Co-Ed?" *Los Angeles Times*, April 15, 1990.

95. Monaghan, "Faces Demographic and Educational Dilemma."

96. "Women's College Struggles."

97. Linda A. Moody, *Mills—For Women Again: A Consideration of Race, Gender, and Religion in the Effort to Remain a Women's College* (Oakland: Mills College, Office of the Chaplain, September 22, 1992), 7.

98. "Students, Alumnae at Mills Protest Coed Proposal," *San Francisco Chronicle*, April 26, 1990; "Mills Counts Down to Trustees' Decision Date," *Mills College Weekly*, April 27, 1990.

99. Janet Camarena, "Professors Questions Coed Statistics," *Mills College Weekly*, April 6, 1990.

100. "Mills College Agonized by Pressure to Admit Men," Associated Press, May 3, 1990.

101. "Men at Mills," *Oakland Tribune*, May 4, 1990.

102. "Shock Turns to Action to Bar Men at a College," *New York Times*, May 6, 1990.

103. Marge Thomas, "Sixteen Days," *Mills Quarterly*, July 1990, 15–16. The July 1990 edition of the *Mills Quarterly* contains a day-by-day account of the May 1990 student strike. In addition, Moody, *Mills*, summarizes the events of May 1990.

104. *Mills College Self-Study 1991*, 3.

105. "Hypocrisy at Mills College," letters to the editor, *Washington Post*, May 21, 1990; Ellen Goodman, "Feminism's Déjà Vu: Separatism Becoming Fashionable Again," *Boston Globe*, May 25, 1990.

106. *Mills College Self-Study 1991*, 3–4.

107. *Mills College Self-Study 1998 Submitted to the Western Association of Schools and Colleges for Reaffirmation of Accreditation*, December 9, 1998, 35–39.

108. Ibid., 39–42.

109. Moody, *Mills*, 23–24.

110. "Mills Community Focuses on Issues of Diversity," *Mills Quarterly*, April 1992, 3.

111. *Mills College Facts and Trends 1990–1991*, table 2.I and *1995–1996*, table 2.G; *Diversity at Mills: Spring 2003*, 4. College Archives, Special Collections, F.W. Olin Library.

112. *Mills College Facts and Trends 1990–1991*, 5, and *1995–1996*, 5; *Diversity at Mills*, 7.

113. President Jan Holmgren, "Sexual Orientation and Mills College: A Personal Statement," *Mills Quarterly*, Summer 1995, 7.

114. *Mills College Self-Study 1998*, 361–65.

115. "Alumnae Respond to College's Plans," 17.

116. *Mills College Self-Study 1998*, 85.

117. See, for example, the 2003 brochure on the college's current strategic plan, "Expanding Avenues to Leadership." College Archives, Special Collections, F.W. Olin Library.

118. Percentages are based on an analysis of the faculty listed in the college catalogues every five years between 1960 and 2002. In these years, the number of faculty ranged between 84 and 144 with an average of 105.

119. In 1960, 1965, and 1970, 3 of the 5 college officers were women; in 1975 and 1980, 3 of 6 officers were women; in 1985, 4 of 6; in 1990, 6 of 6; in 1995, 5 of 6; in 2000, 4 of 7; and in 2002, 5 of 7.

120. Percentages are based on an analysis of the members of the board of trustees listed in the college catalogues every five years between 1960 and 2002. In these years, the number of trustees ranged from thirty-one to forty-one with an average of thirty-five.

121. Jadwiga S. Sebrechts, "This Special Place," *Mills Quarterly*, Winter 1999, 5.

122. *Mills Facts and Trends 1994–1995*, section 2.D; *2003–2004*, section 2.D.

123. "Best Colleges," *U.S. News and World Report*, 1995 and 2005.

124. *Mills Facts and Trends 2003–2004*, section 2.E.

125. These conclusions have been constructed from data collected in successive years of *Mills Facts and Trends* with the assistance of the Mills Office of Institutional Research and Planning. Comparative analysis is based on date from the Integrated Postsecondary Education Data System (IPEDS).

126. *Expanding Avenues to Leadership: The Mills College Strategic Plan for 2003–2007.* College Archives, Special Collections, F. W. Olin Library.

127. *Mills College Self-Study 1998*, 41–42, 123–24.

128. *Mills Facts and Trends 2002–2003*, 1, section 3.E.

129. Ibid., section 3.B; *Mills Facts and Trends 1991–1992*, table 3.E.

130. *Expanding Avenues to Leadership*, 2003.

131. Robert A. Rhoads, "Student Activism in the 1990s and the Importance of the Mills College Strike," *Mills Quarterly*, Spring 2000, 10.

132. Ibid., *Freedom's Web: Student Activism in an Age of Cultural Diversity* (Baltimore and London: Johns Hopkins University Press, 1998), 18.

133. David M. Brin, "In the End, We All Won: An Interview with Warren Hellman, Chair of the Board of Trustees in 1990," *Mills Quarterly*, Spring 2000, 19.

134. Audrey Williams June, "Remaining the Province of Women," *Chronicle of Higher Education*, August 1, 2003, A28.

135. Janet L. Holmgren interview by Marianne Sheldon, Oakland, CA, August 28, 2003.

8

Simmons College

Meeting the Needs of Women Workers

Susan L. Poulson

For more than a century, Simmons College has held a "distinctive niche" in the realm of women's colleges and in the crowded market of Boston-area higher education.[1] Unlike most non-Catholic women's colleges, which traditionally educated women from privileged households, Simmons served women from the working class. Its vocational emphasis offered a step up the economic ladder, as well as the likelihood of job security, to women who were otherwise vulnerable unskilled laborers and dependent wives. When many colleges and universities discriminated against or discouraged applicants from immigrant groups, especially Jews, Simmons welcomed them.[2] As long as other institutions discriminated against working-class women and society restricted women's employment, Simmons found an eager pool of applicants.

Since the 1960s, however, seismic shifts in higher education and in women's employment have altered the terrain for Simmons College. As other institutions became more accessible to women and to the working class, and as the notions of women's employment expanded to include more white-collar and professional jobs, the traditional pool of Simmons applicants shrank. Through the past few decades, administrators at Simmons have struggled to redefine its unique form of education and to maintain its viability as a women's college.

John Simmons

In a city that has long been associated with the education of the elite, Simmons College stands out as an exception. In its early years, Simmons educated working-class women, a population largely marginalized in the world of private higher education. Its benefactor, John Simmons, directed that Simmons Female

College train women students "to acquire an independent livelihood."[3] Born in 1796, Simmons himself had witnessed firsthand the low pay and tenuous nature of traditional women's employment, and had noted how easily unforeseen events could deprive a woman of a breadwinner, leaving her destitute. Simmons pioneered the mass production and standardization of men's suits, replacing the tailor's practice of custom suit making. In the early years of Simmons's enterprise, women made the suits by doing piecework. Simmons traveled to their homes and paid them per piece cut and sewn. Following the invention of the sewing machine, Simmons was able to centralize suit production in factories; women played a vital role in his urban industrial workforce.

Before his death at the age of seventy-five, Simmons used his fortune to create a women's college. He had become one of the largest landholders in Boston, with an estate worth more than $1.7 million. His personal fortune sadly contrasted with his monetary wealth, however; all his sons had died an early death. With no male heirs to continue his business and oversee his real estate investments, Simmons decided to use his vast wealth to educate the women who earned their living by the sweat of their brow. He intended to use his wealth to educate women like those who worked in his factories and helped build his fortune. Simmons wanted a women's college with a vocational emphasis; this quality has varied over the years but has always been a unique and defining feature of Simmons College.

The Early Years

The final shape of Simmons College was determined by people and events after the death of Simmons in 1870. The Boston fire of 1872 destroyed most of the buildings in the Simmons estate and delayed Simmons's founding by nearly three decades. In 1899 Simmons Female College became incorporated under the direction of the Simmons Corporation, a group of prominent local men and women. In addition to several influential lawyers and businessmen, the corporation included two educators, Edgar H. Nichols, a founder of the Browne and Nichols Preparatory School, and Professor William T. Sedgwick, the head of the Department of Biology and Public Health of the Massachusetts Institute of Technology; two philanthropists, Frances R. Morse and Marion C. Jackson; Fanny B. Ames, the wife of a prominent clergyman; and Edward H. Bradford, a leading physician. Corporation members struggled to define the exact nature of the new college, especially its mission, its students, and its location. In his will, Simmons stipulated that the college should teach "medicine, music, drawing, designing, [and] telegraphy." These programs would require, however, a medical school and a music school, as well as some form of technical instruction—an ambitious if not impossible agenda for the money he left behind. With almost no formal schooling himself, Simmons probably had little idea what lofty expectations he set for the college. However, he also left flexibility in the language, instructing that the college teach "other branches of art, science and industry."[4]

During the corporation's first year of operation, its members debated whether the institution should be a charitable institution aimed at vocational training for poor girls, or whether it should be more collegiate in nature. They followed the advice of Dr. Henry LeFavour, a former dean of Williams College, who was hired to create a plan for organizing the college. The corporation endorsed LeFavour's plan and hired him to be the first president of Simmons.[5] He proposed a four-year college that would have "a technical college of high standard, receiving girls who have already a foundation of general knowledge and graduating them well equipped with both a broad intellectual or artistic foundation and a specialized technical training that will open to them some avenue of remunerative labor."[6] The type of occupation, however, should not be too low, the Simmons's estate attorney advised in 1901. A Simmons education would not be used "to train for one's own housework nor to become a servant."[7]

Most existing women's colleges were in rural, often bucolic, settings. However, to serve the immigrant population of the working class, Simmons administrators decided to locate the college in the heart of Boston, close to a large Irish neighborhood and easily accessible by public transportation. Located along the Boston Fenway, a long, sinewy waterway banked by parkland, the college sits today amidst numerous educational and cultural institutions. To one side is the Isabella Gardner Museum with its widely admired collection of medieval art. To the other side are two colleges: Emmanuel College, a Catholic institution founded in 1919 by the Sisters of Notre Dame de Namur, and Wheelock College, a small institution with a mission "to improve the quality of life for children and their families," which was founded in 1888 by Lucy Wheelock, a leader in the U.S. kindergarten movement.[8]

The first students were clearly of the kind that John Simmons had in mind when he founded the college. About half the 102 students who attended already held positions as bookkeepers, clerks, or stenographers, one quarter were teachers, and the rest held various jobs. In order to keep tuition low, the Simmons estate subsidized the operating costs of the college.[9] As a low-cost, easily accessible vocational institution, Simmons had a ready pool of applicants for more than sixty years.

However, many in Boston and in higher education viewed Simmons not as a true college but as a "high-grade technical school."[10] Ironically but understandably, the Association of Collegiate Alumnae (ACA), the predecessor of the American Association of University Women, the umbrella organization for women's higher education, fought against state recognition of Simmons as a women's college. In 1905, Simmons College Corporation applied to the Massachusetts legislature for permission to grant degrees, but the ACA argued that Simmons was not collegiate in nature and should not be recognized as a true college. Like any marginal group seeking respect and recognition, the ACA sought to uphold the prestige of women's higher education by supporting only institutions that fostered the traditional liberal arts curriculum in place at most other colleges and universities. However, the ACA was successful for one year only; in 1906 the legislature granted Simmons the right to award degrees.[11]

In its early years, Simmons College reflected the expanding sphere of women's work during the Progressive Era. In 1902, the first year in which students matriculated, there were programs in secretarial work, librarianship, general science, and "domestic engineering;" Simmons had acquired the School of Housekeeping previously established by the Women's Educational and Industrial Union.[12] The next year it also absorbed the Boston Cooking School, which contrasted with the typical Simmons vocational emphasis by offering a program "for the more thoughtful and effective administration of a private home, even when their course of study does not adequately prepare them for self-maintenance."[13] In 1904, the college began preliminary nursing education in collaboration with nearby hospitals and, together with Harvard, opened the School for Social Workers, one of the earliest such schools in the United States.[14] The college also offered a joint program in horticulture with the Bussey Institute of Amherst Agricultural College, whereby students would spend two years at Simmons and then two years at Amherst Agricultural College.

Simmons College continued to grow in the years between World Wars I and II. In 1918, Simmons acquired full responsibility for the Prince School of Education for Store Service, a postgraduate retailing school formerly affiliated with the Women's Educational and Industrial Union.[15] In 1919, Simmons expanded its nursing education and established the School of Public Health Nursing, which offered a variety of degrees to women who most often worked for area hospitals. In 1922, Simmons began a graduate school. From 1928 until 1934, Simmons offered degrees through its School of Landscape Architecture; it closed after just six years for lack of students. From 1931 until 1942, Simmons also granted degrees to students who took some courses from the Bouve-Boston School of Physical Education.[16]

Simmons developed loyal alumnae, who provided critical assistance in the early years. The Alumnae Association was formed by the first class on the afternoon of their graduation. In the early years, alumnae contributions were relatively small. However, in the 1920s, a more organized association worked hard to raise money for their institution. The combined efforts of students, who sold pencils on street corners, and alumnae, who operated a secondhand shop and lunch wagon in downtown Boston, raised more than a million dollars for the endowment in the early 1920s.[17] In 1933, when Simmons College's first president, Henry LeFavour, retired, there were nearly 1,600 students and

147 faculty members. The physical plant had grown from one leased house to a handsome main building, two dormitories, nine residence houses, and a dining hall.[18]

The College at Mid-Twentieth Century

By the 1950s, Simmons College had built a suitable physical campus, operated with balanced budgets, created a curriculum that prepared women for work, and educated about 1,400 students each year.[19] The college continued to benefit from the restrictions of other institutions. So long as the more prestigious institutions discriminated against the newer immigrant populations, especially Jews, Simmons received applications from "superb students who might otherwise have gone to Radcliffe or Wellesley."[20] The low tuition also attracted students; from the 1930s through the 1960s, Simmons's tuition was half of Wellesley's.[21]

During the domestic era of the 1950s, Simmons still focused on vocational education "in which there is a place for college women."[22] As the 1960 catalogue stated, the college offered education in "most of the professions which women find interesting"; however, their employment would be limited by the social parameters of the era.[23] Undergraduate students took a year of general studies and then took courses in one of nine schools: business, education, home economics, library science, nursing, publication, retailing, science, or social science. The tenth school, social work, was open to graduate students only.

Simmons students of this era were conventional in their expectations and choices. As Morris Keeton and Conrad Hilberry note in their study of Simmons College during this period, the intellectual ability of students at Simmons was "somewhat lower" than at other women's colleges:

> We find that the girls at Simmons, when compared with their counterparts at such other Massachusetts colleges for women as Smith, Radcliffe, and Wellesley, indicate much less interest in pursuing graduate work, reflect substantially less interest in literature and the arts, come from families of more modest socioeconomic status, and have a much greater interest in academic work leading toward a career.[24]

While pleased with being at a women's college, many students recognized that they were not at an elite women's college. "We are conscientious; we study hard; we do our work; we like our classes; we like our teachers," a Simmons student commented. "But we aren't intellectuals. In the dorm, we talk about dates but not about books." "When a Harvard man wants a fun date he calls a Simmons girl," another Simmons student observed. "If he wants intellectual talk, he calls a Radcliffe girl."[25] About 85 percent of students married, including 46 percent who married within one year after graduation. Of those, 91 percent had children.[26]

Before feminism, women at Simmons rarely protested the societal norms that subordinated women. Although sex discrimination was widespread in the early 1960s, less than 0.5 percent of women felt a serious handicap "simply by the fact that you are a woman." A 1960 editorial in the *Simmons Review*, for example, chastised women for their lack of progress in holding political office: "One of the major obstacles barring women from high office is an obstacle of their own making. . . . [Women] demand equality of opportunity when they should be preparing themselves to handle the prizes they seek . . . They must build a philosophical acceptance of their ability to handle leadership."[27] However, in a 1960 poll, 28 percent of recent Simmons alumnae agreed with the statement that "a woman should find her only real satisfactions in her role as wife and mother."[28]

Yet Simmons alumnae also defended women's working outside the home, even when these women had families. In 1959, J. Garton Needham, vice president of Simmons College, began a self-study to assess the role, purpose, and effectiveness of Simmons as a women's college. After polling eight hundred graduates from the 1940s and 1950s and interviewing fifty alumnae, Needham found a high level of satisfaction with the nature of a Simmons education. Alumnae felt that the unique mix of professional and liberal education enabled them to gain employment otherwise hard to get "in a man's world." They point out, Needham writes,

> entirely without rancor, that this is still a man's world, and that the very fact of man's masculinity gives him a long head start toward employment and success. The male college graduate can often obtain and progress on a job without too much consideration of what he studied in college. The woman, unless she is prepared and content to resign herself to a menial, subordinate role, needs an added advantage, some special impetus, such as only a specialized college education can provide.[29]

Many of those who had worked as housewives felt that their earlier work experience, which had been "substantial and responsible, rather than dull and routine, . . . built up a bulwark against the threatening ignominy of being 'just a housewife.' As one phrases it her earlier work experience reminds her that she is, after all, worth something."[30]

The alumnae who worked outside the home also defended themselves against the stereotype that such women were unhappy and neglectful of their families. "They actually contend that they are better wives and mothers than they would be otherwise, that they look upon work as a diversion to their family cares, to the dull drudgery of unrelieved domesticity," Needham states. With remarkably prescient thinking, many alumnae rebuffed the prescribed roles for women.

Much of the life of many women is governed largely by the nature of her place in the eyes of the dominant sex, so-called. . . . But, these graduates observe, a woman desires also to be accepted and respected as a person. More than once I was reminded that on the job a woman is judged, in the long run, by what she can accomplish, not simply as an object of male attention. Thus one of the outcomes of the college experience, and quite possibly from a women's college in particular, is the opportunity for women to develop a sense of individuality, of personal integrity, of importance as persons rather than as 'man-traps,' the image that society so often ascribes to them.[31]

Redefining and Reorganizing in the Early 1960s

In the early 1960s, in response to internal and external factors, Simmons fundamentally altered its educational philosophy and practice by repositioning itself in the pool of institutions of higher education. It redefined the curriculum, which had changed little since the founding of the college, and it reinterpreted the educational philosophy of how to help women earn "an independent living."

Broad changes in access to higher education altered the social norms that had fed Simmons a steady stream of talented students. In the 1950s and 1960s, many institutions opened their doors to nontraditional students, thereby reducing the number of potential applicants to Simmons. Further, the tremendous growth of community colleges across the country brought additional competition; their offerings tended to resemble the kind of education one would traditionally receive at Simmons—at a much cheaper cost. "If the goal of a Simmons education remained only success in initial employment," Simmons president William E. Park reported in 1965, "it had to be recognized that the two-year colleges could do this job just about as well as Simmons and in half the time." Plus, he noted, they were inexpensive and could drive Simmons out of business.[32]

In these years a better-educated and more ambitious Simmons faculty desired a more collegiate feel to their institution.[33] Many were eager to increase the stature of the institution by strengthening the liberal arts curriculum, which traditionally only supported the curricular needs of other majors. Many faculty hired in the 1950s and 1960s wanted to expand their departments in order to offer a liberal arts major to students.

These faculty aspirations coincided with a shift in the career aspirations and rising academic qualifications of Simmons students. Previously, a good job for a woman may have been in an area such as retail management, nursing, or social work. However, as the concept that women could and should hold any job replaced the traditional notion of women's occupations, many young women aspired to postgraduate education, which required a significant liberal arts education. The average Simmons student's SAT score rose from a 502 verbal and 466 mathematics score in 1956 to a 600 verbal and 596 mathematics score in 1965. More classically prepared students required more complex offerings at the college level.

In response to such developments, Simmons began to make fundamental changes in its mission and in the nature of its education. Supported by a Carnegie Corporation grant, a small but influential group of Simmons administrators and faculty undertook a comprehensive study of the college's direction and goals in 1963. The Self-Study Committee reinterpreted Simmons's original mission statement to reflect the changing role of women and to bring greater coherence to the tangential programs within the college. Its study included in-depth questionnaires and interviews of first-year students, seniors, alumnae, and faculty. The committee entertained a variety of questions, including whether Simmons should become coeducational; this option, however, was rapidly pushed aside.

In 1965, the Self-Study Committee report's recommendations were widely endorsed by the faculty and alumnae.[34] The foremost proposal was to strengthen the liberal arts orientation of the curriculum. While endorsing Simmons's mission, in which "career preparation . . . should continue to be the focus for future planning of the College," the report redefined how to achieve those ends. Since young women have a variety of career aspirations and tend to have "multiple and discontinuous roles" in U.S. society, the report recommended Simmons offer a flexible education "with primary emphasis upon liberal education which embraces professional education."[35] To this end, the college completely reoriented its mode of instruction from a school-based to a department-based structure. The traditional school-based curriculum, the committee concluded, produced duplication of effort, uneven application of general education standards, and a tendency toward narrow and technical training. Such an education was inadequate to meet the needs of "women in American society in the years ahead."[36] In the next few years, Simmons changed to a departmental system in which all students were required to take standardized general education courses.

The committee also recommended that Simmons create a continuing education program to serve adult students. Begun in 1963, Simmons's Office of Continuing Education became one of the first in the Boston area. Its leaders attributed much of its success to the component of individual counseling, which encouraged hesitant women to attend college. In 1992, Simmons named the Continuing Education Program after Dorothea Lynde Dix, a renowned nineteenth century activist who reformed prisons and care for the mentally ill and advocated education. At a time of nonexistent higher education for women, Dix educated herself by frequenting Boston's libraries and public lectures. Upon her death in 1887, Dix left a $50,000 scholarship fund for needy students, which later became the Dix Loan Fund of Simmons College.[37] Not only has the Dix Program served the needs of nontraditional students, but it also has been a growing source of revenue for the college over the years.[38] It has grown gradually from 31 students in 1964 to 105 in 1974, 136 in 1984, 205 in 1994, and finally to 288 students in 2004.[39]

The Self-Study Committee's consideration of coeducation was short-lived. As the pool of potential students from traditional immigrant and working-class groups shrank, admitting men would have easily doubled the number of candidates and enabled the college to expand while also increasing the academic quality. However, key faculty and administrators felt that by giving up its single-sex status, Simmons would become more like the other coeducational institutions in the area and thus be forced to compete with Boston's vast number of well-funded coeducational institutions. Coeducational, vocationally oriented Northeastern University, as one longtime Simmons faculty commented, "is good, big, and around the corner."[40]

Rather, Simmons sought to strengthen and diversify its course offerings through mutual arrangements with nearby institutions. An alliance with the New England Conservatory in 1962 enabled students at each school to enroll for credit in some courses at the other. Later called the Colleges of the Fenway, this program expanded to include several nearby institutions: Emmanuel College, Massachusetts College of Art, Massachusetts College of Pharmacy and Health Sciences, Wentworth Institute of Technology, and Wheelock College. Not only could students cross-register, but faculty could and did integrate their classes. In the 1960s, students studied biology at Simmons while studying geometry at Emmanuel.

Changes in Campus Culture

Simmons was not exempt from the social turmoil undergone by many U.S. campuses in the 1960s. One such change was the declining emphasis upon domesticity and traditional rituals. For example, the student newspaper stopped regularly featuring formal engagement announcements. In 1961 Simmons discontinued the traditional Baccalaureate Mass, which had involved the president and a prominent representative of the Boston clergy since the earliest years of the college.[41] A year later, the Prince School of Retailing ended its annual fashion show and merged into the School of Business Administration.[42] At the annual home economics banquet, students no longer modeled clothing they had sewn. The traditional Christmas Cotillion, which connoted social pretense, became the Winter Weekend in 1969. Students also ended the long-standing Frosh-Junior Wedding traditions in which a junior "groom" married a first-year "bride." One observer felt that these traditions faded because "students are moving away from the overly cute traditions toward mature and intellectually oriented ones."[43] Students would rather have meaningful rituals, such as meeting with professors at a coffee hour to "make good talk" outside the classroom.

Simmons also became less insular. In the early 1960s there was little involvement in social problems, and campus newspaper coverage of such issues was limited to a brief review of national and international news. The tumult of the decade, however, spurred greater engagement. Simmons College created a Civil Rights Club, for example, and had a chapter of the Students for Democratic Society as early as 1965.[44] This awareness of social and political issues continued into the 1970s. In the spring of 1972, for example, the *Simmons News* reviewed an Equal Employment Opportunity Commission finding of discrimination at AT&T, the Married Women Credit Act, and the celebration of International Women's Day.

Simmons College increasingly promoted careers for women. Simmons continued to respond to the 1963 self-study recommendation that it develop a comprehensive counseling program to address the needs of women students and graduates that would focus on "the relationship of the undergraduate educational programs to the career plans of individual women."[45] The types of career plans emphasized changed as well. While in 1965 the *Simmons News* featured an article on two scholarships available for college graduates to attend the Katherine Gibbs School for Secretarial Studies, by the early 1970s, there was more coverage of nontraditional careers.[46] In 1972, for example, the Alumnae Association began a series called "Images of Women" in which alumnae spoke on campus about their various careers.

Ethnic and Religious Diversity

If the political climate of the 1960s transformed the campus culture at Simmons, new recruitment strategies of that era altered the student population. When most Boston colleges and universities were Anglo-Saxon and Protestant, the majority of students at Simmons were neither Anglo-Saxon nor Protestant. In the early 1960s Jews and Catholics accounted for just over half the students, while one-third was Protestant. Yet there was little racial diversity. Although a black woman graduated at Simmons as early as 1914 and there were a few black students over the years, they were significantly underrepresented, and until the 1960s, there were no black tenured faculty or administrators. Asian students were likewise rare.[47]

When the civil rights movement of the 1950s and 1960s highlighted racial inequities, Simmons responded by aggressively recruiting minority students and faculty. In what Simmons administrators called "a significant change in admissions practices," the Simmons Committee on Disadvantaged Young People tried to "seek out, to encourage, to make special concessions to, and to provide financial assistance for students [usually black] who would not ordinarily have the opportunity for higher education."[48] By 1968, the Special Scholarship students constituted nearly 5 percent of the first-year class. While the acceptance rate for students overall was 40 percent, Simmons accepted 75 percent of the Special Scholarship applicants. Simmons also began a financial aid program for minority students. In 1971, for example, black students were only 22 percent of financial aid applicants but received 50 percent of Simmons's financial aid.[49]

To attract minority students and address minority needs, Simmons further altered its curriculum. In the mid-1960s, faculty and administrators created an Urban Youth Teacher Preparation Program, a Seminar for Women in Urban and State Politics, and a Program in Home Economics and Social Work for Continuing Education Students from Poverty Areas.[50] These initiatives brought Simmons black faculty and black students;[51] in early 1969, Simmons initiated a black studies program (now the Department of African American Studies). Several students formed a Black Student Organization (BSO), which then protested the status of blacks on campus. The BSO gave the president a list of ten demands they wanted from Simmons College, including an increase in black staff and faculty, as well as the development of new courses related to black issues.[52] In 1976, Elizabeth Rawlins, then associate professor of education, became the first black faculty member to receive tenure.[53] In the early 1980s, Simmons established a Task Force on Race Awareness to teach the Simmons community "how to live, work, and communicate with individuals different from themselves."[54]

The Emergence of Feminism

From within and without, feminism affected Simmons. However, because it was a women's college, this transformation was more evolutionary than confrontational, without the considerable resistance to gender equity sometimes seen at other types of institutions.

Feminism first came to campus through the campus media. The *Simmons Janus,* the student newspaper, reported on the forcible takeover of a Harvard University building by a group of feminists who then held workshops in karate, silk screening, guerrilla theatre, and auto mechanics and who painted slogans such as "Sisterhood Is Powerful" and "Smash Phallic Imperialism."[55] The student newspaper featured articles about sexuality and birth control, as well as advertisements for abortion providers.[56] Two physicians spoke on campus about the methods and availability of abortion.[57] Women's liberation groups emerged. In the 1970s students began a "Mr. Simmons" contest, a raunchy takeoff on a female beauty pageant in which men competed for the title in evening wear, swimwear, and question-and-answer events, during which the largely female audience often "screeched and hooted."[58] In 1978, Simmons began to sponsor a Women's Month, which featured issues affecting women in the United States and around the world.[59] In the 1980s students organized an annual Mother-

Daughter Weekend as a counterpart to the popular Father-Daughter Dance. In recent years, however, these reactionary traditions have become less popular and take place irregularly or not at all.[60]

Most important for Simmons, however, was feminism's effect on how students experienced the college. In March 1971, the *Simmons Janus* editors lamented that Simmons had a majority male faculty, that only four of the fourteen department chairs were women, and that Simmons had never had a woman president. "What is more discouraging," the editors continued, "is the fact that the situation just outlined has had seventy-one years to root itself deep within the spirit of 300 The Fenway."[61]

In April 1971 the Simmons American Association of University Professors Salary Committee reported that "there is clear evidence of discrimination against female faculty members at Simmons College." The report noted that women faculty were disproportionately situated in the lower ranks of faculty and that half the female faculty was concentrated in three "sex-typed" professional areas: home economics, nursing, and social work. The report also concluded that "administrative power is almost exclusively a male prerogative," pointing out that men dominate the top administration: The only position held by a woman was that of dean. Less than one-third of the Simmons Corporation was women, and only one of the seven corporation committees had a woman chair.[62]

Some Simmons faculty members also developed feminist ideals. In 1971 Athena Theodore, associate professor of sociology at Simmons, wrote a report, "Sex Discrimination at Simmons College," for the American Association of University Professors. She also believed that women faculty should join with women students to change the status quo: "We are women and are going to somehow share the same fate, and maybe we can change things."[63]

Since the late 1950s Simmons has nearly doubled the size of its faculty. In 1958 there were 99 faculty members; in 2000, there were 181. Like other women's colleges, Simmons had a relatively high percentage of women faculty members. In 1980, for example, women accounted for slightly more than half the full professors, as well as half the overall faculty. Since then, the percentage of women in the faculty has risen; by 2000, they accounted for 73 percent of the faculty (see Table 8.1).

Similarly, the representation of women is rising in top administrative positions and on the board of trustees. In 1960 and 1970 Simmons had only one woman of four chief administrators (a category that includes the president, vice presidents, and academic deans); in 1980 and 1990, three of six, and by 2000, six of ten.[64] Similarly, the board of trustees has gone from about half women in 1960 (ten of twenty-one) and 1970 (twelve of twenty-five) to three-quarters women in 2000 (twenty-one of twenty-seven).[65]

Table 8.1. Simmons faculty, 1958–2000[1]

	1958	1969	1980		1990		2000	
# of faculty	99[a]	129[a]	149		138		181	
			%M	%W	%M	%W	%M	%W
Rank								
Full	21	22	48	52	67	33	32	68
Assoc.	24	32	56	44	20	80	36	64
Asst.	34	52	27	73	25	75	19	81
Instr.	20	23	*36*	*64*	*20*	*80*	*0*	*100*
Total			44	56	38	62	27	73

Sources: *Simmons College Report to the New England Association of Colleges and Secondary Schools, Inc.*, March, 1969, 1.5; *Self-Evaluation Report of Simmons College*, 1980, Chart #2, Faculty Profile; *Simmons College Self-Study Report*, September 1990, Institutional Faculty Profile Chart; *Simmons College Self-Study Report*, September 2000, Faculty Profile Chart, all in Simmons College Archives.
[a]Data by gender for 1958 and 1969 unavailable.

The Graduate School of Management

Rising expectations and career aspirations are reflected in the founding of the Simmons Graduate School of Management (SGSM) in 1974 by Anne Jardim and Margaret Hennig, both Harvard management professors.[66] Although federal law required it to be coeducational, it was the only U.S. graduate business school specifically designed for women. The courses were designed to help women "understand the rules that set men and women apart—and men ahead—in business."[67] The feminist movement, Hennig once told *Working Woman* magazine, did a disservice to women by "deny[ing] any differences between men and women, because these differences meant inferiority. We are just beginning to hear women say, 'We are of genuine value unto ourselves.'"[68]

Over the years, the SGSM has developed innovative programs distinctive from other MBA programs. In addition to regular course work, the school offers residential management programs in which students reside on campus and take condensed courses. For example, the school developed a Middle Management Program designed to help women move up the corporate ladder. During the ten-week course, the women reside on campus and receive full salary and benefits from their employer.[69] The SGSM also may accept candidates who have not earned a bachelor's degree.

The curriculum has two general areas of study: functional courses and behavioral instruction. Women learn to improve their basic business skills in areas such as finance and accounting and—as in the six-day "Managing with Influence Seminar"—are taught "to manage one-to-one interactions, to conduct efficient meetings, to improve their stand-up presentations, and to write persuasively."[70]

Simmons College and the SGSM received an unexpected boost when nearby Garland Junior College closed in the mid-1970s and in March 1976 Garland's board of trustees transferred its name, physical facilities, and other assets to Simmons.[71] Some of the buildings were sold shortly after their acquisition; today, the rest house the Graduate School of Management.

Athletics

As a historical urban institution for working women, Simmons placed little emphasis on athletics. Whatever physical improvements could be made often focused on new classroom buildings or dormitories. As late as 1976, a student wrote to the *Simmons Janus:* "It's something hardly anyone ever talks about. It's something hardly anyone ever thinks about. This something is sports at Simmons and believe it or not, it does exist."[72] However, as women have become more interested in athletics and expect better opportunities and facilities, athletics at Simmons have improved significantly.

After the class of 1980 issued a white paper demanding an athletic center, administrators began efforts to fund and build one.[73] In 1989 Simmons opened a sports and fitness center in the midst of its residential complex. Since then, varsity sports have grown in numbers and talent. The college now has eight NCAA Division III varsity intercollegiate teams and recruits most of its athletes from high school. Simmons also participates in the Colleges of the Fenway program, designed to promote the health and physical fitness of its participants. Begun in 1988, the Lifelong Exercise and Activities Program offers a variety of recreational activities like yoga classes, intramural basketball, or, the most popular, an aerobic hip-hop dance class. Student media give significant coverage to Simmons athletics, and the college now touts its athletic program as an attractive feature. At Simmons, college promotional literature declares:

> Women athletes are the top—and only—priority in the varsity sports program. Unlike coeducational institutions where women's teams often take a back seat to men's programs, Simmons gives its "Sharks" the best practice times, outstanding equipment and facilities, funding, and the undivided support of nearly 1,300 students who cheer on the athletes and encourage them to succeed in a spirited environment.[74]

A Time of Challenge: Shrinking Enrollment

In the 1980s and 1990s, trends begun in the 1960s came to fruition. By the early 1980s Simmons had become more like other colleges. It had a strong liberal arts program buoyed by general education requirements. It had shed its more traditional, insular culture and become an effective promoter of women's careers. It was engaged in empowering black women through financial assistance and curricular efforts. And yet, it did all this while still retaining a vocational emphasis in its identity and its curriculum.

By the early 1980s, Simmons also suffered from the same symptoms as many women's colleges of that era: shrinking enrollment, declining revenue, and an aging physical plant. Between 1969 and 1980, there was a 32 percent drop in applications. As fewer students applied, Simmons began to accept a larger percentage of applicants to keep enrollment numbers up. In 1969, for example, Simmons accepted 40 percent of 1,987 applicants; in 1980, 83 percent of 1,361 applicants ; in 1983, 89 percent of applicants.[75] As costs rose in the early 1980s, President William Holmes sought to dramatically increase the size of the entering class, even as the number of applicants declined. In 1981, for example, 1,562 students applied for admission, but by 1989, applications had dropped 27 percent to 1,146 (see Table 8.2).[76]

Although these higher rates of acceptance sustained student enrollment for a time, Simmons paid in the declining academic quality of its students. By 1980 the median SAT scores fell to 910, and one in seven students came from the bottom half of their high school class.[77] Many faculty became concerned

Table 8.2. Simmons undergraduate enrollment, 1958–2000[1]

	1958–59	1968–69	1978–79	1989–90	2000
Students applied	1,281	1,987	1,361	1,222	1,184
Students accepted	579	798	1,130	1,015	845
(and %)	(45)	(40)	(83)	(83)	(71)
Yield, in %	51	47	39	35	32
Enrollment					
Full-time	1,176	1,454	1,521	1,342	1,090
Part-time		94	207	13	145

Sources: *Simmons College Report to the New England Association of Colleges and Secondary Schools, Inc.*, March 1969; *Self-Evaluation Report of Simmons College*, 1980, Undergraduate Characteristics, 1958–78, 128; *Simmons College Self-Study Report*, September 1990, "Student Admissions Data"; and *Simmons College Self-Study Report*, September 2000, Student Admissions Data, all in Simmons College Archives.

about the marginal performance of some students and some faculty worried that the once-solid academic reputation of Simmons was beginning to suffer.[78]

Simmons's enrollment still declined, however, and this trend is attributable to two factors. First, fewer women students wanted to study at a women's college (see Chapter 1). A 1984–86 study by the Women's College Coalition found that only about 4 percent of high school seniors would even consider a women's college.[79] Second, the number of high school students was in relative decline during the 1980s, a period of retrenchment between the baby boom and the anticipated resurgence from baby-boom children, who would be of college age in the late 1990s.

Simmons used another tactic to offset the slackening undergraduate enrollment: graduate enrollment. During the 1980s Simmons established two new graduate schools, the Graduate Program in Management (renamed the Graduate School of Management in 1981) and the Graduate School for Health Studies, as well as graduate programs in communications management, severe special needs, and liberal studies and graduate nurse-practitioner subprograms.[80] Graduate enrollment increased and eventually surpassed undergraduate enrollment. Indeed, today Simmons has nearly two graduate students for every one undergraduate, and graduate credit hours increased fourfold during the 1990s (see Table 8.3).[81] Although Simmons has long been identified as a women's college, its graduate programs by rule of law are coeducational; however, because of the subject matter, women make up roughly 85 percent of graduate students.[82] In 1998, for example, 82 percent of graduate students were enrolled in education programs.[83]

Table 8.3. Simmons enrollment, 1958–2000

	1958	1969	1979	1990	2000
Undergraduate	1,176	1,548	1,728	1,355	1,235
Full-time	1,176	1,454	1,521	1,342	1,090
Part-time		94	207	13	145
Graduate	268	654	976	1,289	2,060[a]
Full-time	256	592	976*	368	612
Part-time	12	62		921	1,448

Sources: *Simmons College Report to the New England Association of Colleges and Secondary Schools, Inc.*, March, 1969; *Self-Evaluation Report of Simmons College*, October 1980, Student Enrollment, 1958–78, 134; *Simmons College Self-Study Report*, September 1990, Student Admissions; *Simmons College Self-Study Report*, September 2000, Student Admissions Data, all in Simmons College Archives.
* This number includes part-time enrollment.
[a] In 2000, graduate enrollment included 1,787 women and 273 men.

In the 1980s, administrators were also fully aware of the problem of declining enrollments, which were compounded by rising costs. In the short term, as faculty concern about declining student quality came to a head in 1985, President Holmes decided to admit fewer applicants. The result was a precipitous drop, from 420 entering students in 1984 to 369 in 1985, but the SAT median score stabilized at 920 and rose to 970 by 1988.[84]

As a more long-term response to the declining enrollments, Simmons changed its recruiting strategy to increase its applicant base. The strategy involved not only more outreach to minority students through "early awareness" programs such as Upward Bound and Junior High School Science Program, but also changing Simmons itself to make it more attractive to the minority community. This included hiring an "independent, highly visible affirmative action officer," more financial aid to AHANA (African, Hispanic and Native American) students, active recruitment of AHANA faculty and staff, diversity workshops for all employees, the creation of an Asian studies program and a Latin American/Hispanic studies program, and the integration of AHANA materials into the curriculum.[85] In more recent years, minority students—many of whom are international students—have indeed been a growing constituency at Simmons. Since 1990 the percent of African American, Asian American, and Native American undergraduate and graduate students has doubled. Nearly one of every seven students is a member of a minority, compared to fewer than one in ten in 1990 (see Table 8.4).[86]

Diversity is even greater at the undergraduate level. In 1996, for example, 23 percent of undergraduates were from minority groups or were international students: African American, 83; Latina/o, 38; Asian American, 88; Native American, 2; other, 105, including 58 international students.[87] As former associate dean Elizabeth Rawlins notes, diversity in the 1970s generally meant

Table 8.4. Simmons minority enrollment

	1990	1996
African American	81	155
Latino/a	54	62
Asian American	63	131
Native American	5	9
Other[a]		193
% of total enrollment	7	15

Source: *Simmons College 1996–7 Fact Book*, 14.
Note: Numbers include graduates and undergraduates.
[a]Includes 133 students designated "international"

educating African Americans. After a "redefinition of diversity," however, the college now recruits from a variety of minority groups.[88]

Also, since the college-age population was declining most rapidly in Massachusetts and the Northeast, Simmons began recruiting from a wider geographic area. In 1980, about 8 percent of students were from outside the Northeast; by 1990, that number had risen to 20 percent.[89] The college also sought to increase its international student population. Using a strategy similar to recruiting U.S. minority students, it sought to recruit more foreign-born faculty and staff, internationalize the curriculum, and give more financial aid and cultural and social support to foreign students.[90] Among foreign students, the largest constituency is Asian. Indeed, a significant rise in the number of Asian and Asian American students has resulted in recent years in an East Asian studies program. A Caribbean Culture Association caters to students from that region. In 1995, Simmons hired its first dean of multicultural affairs.[91]

Simmons has a growing religious diversity as well. Christians are served by the Christian Fellowship and the Catholic Students Organization, led by a part-time Catholic chaplain funded by the Archdiocese of Boston; Jewish students have Hillel and access to a kosher kitchen and kosher meals; and Muslims are served by the Muslim Student Association.[92] Recently, the Multi-Faith Council was founded by a group of students interested in exploring issues of religious pluralism.[93]

In the early 1990s Simmons again considered the admission of men as a means of addressing the recruitment problem. In the 1990 Simmons self-study report prepared for the decennial reaccredidation visit, a faculty committee discussed but did not recommend coeducation as a possible alternative. The change would alleviate the declining student population and enhance its quality, the report noted, but it would also result in a loss of identity as a women's college and alienate students, faculty, and alumnae. The report did not endorse this alternative but suggested that the college still explore the nature of education at other colleges, such as Goucher and Wheaton, that had already gone coed.[94] Although there was no quantification of student sentiment about the admission of men, many Simmons students loudly expressed support when Mills College rescinded its decision to adopt coeducation in 1990.

The 1990s: Crisis and Opportunity

In the early 1990s, reduced enrollments and rising costs strained Simmons yet again. Turmoil in top administrative ranks further damaged morale. Therefore, in 1993, Simmons made the long-awaited appointment of its first woman president, Jean Dowdall. Dowdall, however, faced significant problems. Simmons continued to experience challenges in attracting quality students. There were deep fissures between professional faculty and arts and sciences faculty. In

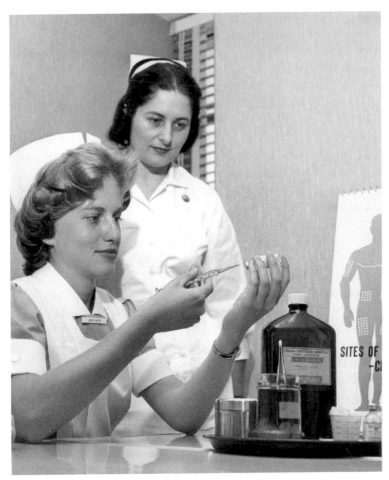

The Simmons emphasis on vocational education has continued, but new areas have been added and the student population has further diversified. Nursing fieldwork, c. 1961 *(Photographer unknown)*; a chemistry lab, c. 2000. *(Photo by William Mercer) Simmons College Archives.*

1995, this and other issues resulted first in the resignation of the provost, then of the dean of the College of Arts and Sciences, and ultimately, of President Dowdall. Morale at Simmons reached a new low, with many faculty frustrated and unhappy. Students, too, felt the decline.

In the mid-1990s three developments raised Simmons from its nadir. First, demographic changes worked in Simmons's favor as the children of baby boomers reached college age and increased the pool of potential students. Second, the strong economy brought significant increases to donations and the endowment. Aided by a buoyant stock market, the endowment tripled during the 1990s, from $59 million in 1990 to $186 million in 1999. (By comparison, the endow-

ment in 1958 was $5.6 million; in 1969, $9.2 million; and in 1979, $16 million.)[95]
While alumnae contributed about 70 percent of the funds, about 30 percent
came from "outsiders" who were supporters of Simmons as a women's college.
With this and borrowed money, the college began long-overdue projects such
as renovating dormitories and enlarging the student center.

Finally, however, administrative and curricular planning enabled the college to improve its recruitment. Under the new president, Dan Cheever, who
had faced similar problems as head of nearby Wheelock College, Simmons
developed a more cohesive vision of the mission and plans for the future of the
college.[96] Administrators revised admissions policies, developed a comprehensive strategic plan and a master plan for facilities and technology, and began
centennial and capital campaigns that brought in millions of dollars to Simmons.[97] Simmons also benefited from major curricular changes initiated by the
faculty and Dean Chet Haskell that enabled students to follow a more flexible
curriculum that could reflect their individual interests and career plans.

Simmons Today

In an era when many women's colleges are faced with closing or becoming
coeducational in order to survive, Simmons has made several significant and
necessary transformations that enable it to remain open as a women's college.

It has gone from being a predominantly undergraduate to a predominantly graduate institution without losing its focus on the education of undergraduate women. It has changed its curricular emphasis to include a broader liberal arts education without sacrificing a practical orientation toward work. It has managed to diversify its student population, with a significant increase in minority and international representation, but still retain a general sense of commonality among students.

In the 1990s Simmons went through the same developments that have made other women's colleges obsolete: declining applications, falling academic standards, deficit spending, and low morale. However, with favorable demographic trends, an ability to attract endowment donations, good management, and a continuing pride in the education of women supported by the vast majority of faculty, Simmons successfully reversed the downward trends.

Indeed, in recent interviews, Simmons students noted that while they did not purposely choose Simmons because it was a women's college, they all appreciated that quality after being there. Without exception, they believed that it helped their sense of focus on future plans and their self-confidence. More than one student noted how she faced derision from friends for attending a women's college, but defended her decision with vehemence.[98] All felt very loyal to Simmons as a women's college.

Why, then, a women's college? Simmons not only offers students a woman-centered environment, with numerous role models and a proud history, but also creates a consciousness about women's positions and abilities in society. As one can see from Simmons's early history, a female student population does not necessarily result in faculty, administration, or students with a critical awareness of gender issues. Rather, this awareness comes with feminist or women-centered perspectives that pervade the institution from the classroom to the boardroom. With more than thirty core courses, the Women's Studies Department offers a major, a minor, and a graduate program entitled Gender/Cultural Studies; it draws about ten majors per year, most of them double majors.[99] The college also has a Feminist Union that promotes women's issues; the Alliance, which serves gay, lesbian, bisexual, and transgendered students; and a student-run Women's Center that provides space for and sponsors activities for women and offers "a good place to hang out."[100] In 1991 Simmons created the Simmons Institute for Leadership and Change, which "sponsors programs, activities, and resources that help initiate social change for women, raise women's issues to the state and national political level and reach out to [diverse] audiences."[101] With a faculty that brings gender awareness into the classroom, and the support of a variety of activist Simmons extra-curricular groups, Simmons has created the kinds of programs and centers that give voice and visibility to the concerns of women.

Notes

I would like to thank Claire Goodwin, Leah Laspina, and Jason Wood for their assistance during the research and writing of this chapter, as well as the University of Scranton for providing travel funds.

1. Quote from Richard B. Lyman Jr., phone interview by Susan L. Poulson Lincoln, Mass., January 11, 2004. In 1915, Simmons changed its name to Simmons College, omitting the word "female," a word commonly used to denote a women's institution in the Victorian era that seemed antiquated by the early twentieth century.
2. In the early 1960s, for example, Jewish and Protestant students were in roughly equal numbers, about 35 percent each; Catholic students were about 23 percent. Morris Keeton and Conrad Hilberry, *Struggle and Promise: A Future for Colleges* (New York: McGraw Hill, 1965), 128.
3. Kenneth L. Mark, *Delayed By Fire: Being the Early History of Simmons College (Concord, NH: Rumford Press, 1945),* 24.
4. Ibid.
5. The Simmons Corporation made LeFavour a member of its board at the same time that they elected him president.
6. Mark, *Delayed By Fire,* 28.
7. Ibid., 36.
8. www.wheelock.edu. Both colleges have predominantly women students: in 2003 Emmanuel adopted coeducation but still draws mostly women students, and Wheelock's curricular emphasis on education and social work attracts a disproportionate number of female students.
9. Mark, *Delayed By Fire,* 38–39.
10. Ibid., 161.
11. As late as 1917, the ACA refused to grant membership to Simmons graduates. However, in the late 1920s and early 1930s, Simmons became a member of the Association of American Universities, the New England Association of Schools and Colleges, and the American Council of Education. Mark, *Delayed By Fire,* 161.
12. Ibid., 30.
13. Ibid., 36.
14. Since Harvard's withdrawal in 1915 the school has been operated by Simmons.
15. Mark, *Delayed By Fire,* 128–31. Simmons College assumed the Prince School in 1918 but lost control over it for two years when Lucinda W. Prince, founder of the school, affiliated it with the School of Education of Harvard University. After two years, the school ended its affiliation with Harvard and returned to the control of Simmons. In 1926, Simmons College bought a mansion on the back of Beacon Hill, where the school remained for many years.
16. Simmons agreed that students at the Bouve-Boston School of Physical Education would be granted a Simmons College degree upon completion of a year of schooling at Simmons.
17. *A Brief History of Simmons College,* 4, www.simmons.edu.
18. Ibid.

19. More than two out of three students lived in the residences; the remainder commuted from the surrounding Boston area. *Simmons College Catalogue*, 1960–61, 31.

20. Richard B. Lyman Jr., telephone interview by author, Lincoln, Mass., January 11, 2004.

21. Kathleen Dunn, telephone interview by author, Lincoln, Mass., January 4, 2004.

22. *Simmons College Catalogue, 1960–61*, 31.

23. Ibid., 33.

24. Keeton and Hilberry, *Struggle and Promise*, 125. The authors used the scores determined by Alexander W. Astin in *Who Goes Where to College*, (Chicago: Science Research Associates, 1965).

25. Ibid., 123.

26. "Progress Report No. 2 on the Strengths and Weaknesses of a Simmons Education," *Simmons Review* 41, 2 (Winter 1960): 24–26.

27. "Women Can Cultivate the Capacity for Leadership," *Simmons Review* 42, 4 (Summer 1960): 1.

28. J. Garton Needham, "Does A Wom[a]n Face Special Conflicts As A Mother, Homemaker, Employee, Citizen?" *Simmons Review* 43, 1 (Fall 1960): 2.

29. "The Strengths and Weaknesses of a Simmons Education," *Simmons Review* 41, 1 (Fall 1959): 29.

30. Ibid.

31. Ibid., 31–32. Further, Needham writes: "They scoff at those who argue that working mothers lead to marital discord, to delinquent children, to the deterioration of the home. Perhaps this does happen, but not to them." 31–32.

32. *The Report of the President, 1964–5*, 2–5. Simmons College Archives (hereafter referred to as SCA).

33. In 1958, 31 percent of faculty members held a PhD By 1969, that number had risen to 45 percent.

34. The faculty unanimously endorsed the recommendations in a vote on the final report in January 1965 and the Alumnae Council also endorsed it. The self-study also spurred faculty activity. In 1964, the faculty voted to establish the Faculty Council, a standing committee charged to "lead, to educate, and to elicit opinion from the Faculty in order to promote in the Faculty a sharpened sense of its responsibilities to the College in general and to itself." Indeed, as the faculty became more involved in governance, the number of committees and subcommittees proliferated to the point, as a later report declared, "where no one knew what committees existed, or what their composition, terms of service, or even means of appointment were." Report on Simmons College Submitted to the Commission on Institutions of Higher Education New England Association of Colleges and Secondary Schools, Inc. by William E. Park, President, Simmons College, March 31, 1969. Section 3.3, SCA.

35. *The Report of the President, 1963–64*, 4.

36. Ibid., 5.

37. "Emerge: Dorothea Lunde Dix Scholars Program," promotional pamphlet, Simmons College, n.d., 4. Office of Dix Scholars Program.

38. *The Report of the President, 1963–64*, 4.

39. *Simmons College 1996–7 Fact Book*, Office of the Registrar, 16. SCA.

40. Lyman interview.
41. "Baccalaureate Is Dropped," *Simmons News,* March 2, 1961, 1.
42. *Simmons College Catalogue, 1962.*
43. "College Traditions Quietly Passing Away?" 23.
44. Faye Edwards and Ruth Lythcott. *Simmons News,* October 19, 1965,3
45. *The Report of the President, 1963–64,* 5.
46. "Katy Gibbs Offers Scholarship Aid," *Simmons News,* November 15, 1965, 4.
47. Elizabeth B. Rawlins, telephone interview by author, June 28, 2004.
48. *Simmons College Self-Report,* 1969, 1.8.
49. Letter from William J. Holmes, Simmons president, to the Simmons Community, *Simmons Janus,* April 2, 1971, 4. This financial aid program began in 1966.
50. *Simmons College Self-Report,* 1969, 1.12.
51. Rawlins interview.
52. "'Black Demands' Progress Report," *Simmons Janus,* October 29, 1970, 5.
53. "Black-Hispanic Organization Preserves Ethnic Traditions," *Simmons Janus,* October 24, 1980, 6.
54. Quote of Carol Leary, director of residence and task-force member. Mary Jo Foley, "Task force combats college racism," *Simmons Janus,* April 10, 1981, 1.
55. Elise Cohen, "Low Salary, Poor Advancement Await Women Here," *Simmons Janus,* April 9, 1971, 3.
56. "Singer Speaks on Birth Control," *Simmons Janus,* February 12, 1971,11.
57. "When Contraceptives Fail: Abortion," *Simmons Janus,* March 5, 1971, 11.
58. "Mister Simmons," *Simmons Voice,* April 26, 2001, 5.
59. "Celebrate Women's Month," *Simmons Janus,* October 10, 1980, 6.
60. "Participation in Traditions Waning," *Simmons Voice,* January 25, 2001, 1,7.
61. Editorial, *Simmons Janus,* March 5, 1971, 2.
62. "Report Finds Inequities in Simmons Faculty Pay and Status," *Simmons Janus,* April 9, 1971, 5.
63. Janet Cutler, "Theodore Calls for Strengthening of Female Self-Concepts," *Simmons Janus,* March 12, 1971, 15–16.
64. *Simmons College Catalogue, 1960–61,* 13; 1970–71, 217; *1980–81,* 107–9; *Simmons College Self-Study Report,* September 2000–2002, 28–29.
65. *Simmons College Catalogue, 1960–61,* 10; 1970–71, 217; *1980–81,* 106; *Simmons College Self-Study Report,* September 2000–2002, 28–29.
66. Margo McDermed, "Thesis Brings Instant Fame," *Simmons Janus,* March 12, 1971, 6.
67. Liz Sullivan, "A Decade of Achievement," *Simmons Review* 67, 2 (Spring 1985): 8.
68. Hennig quoted in ibid.
69. "Outgrowths: Management Development Programs," *Simmons Review* 67, 2 (Spring 1985): 4.
70. Ibid.
71. Founded in 1872, Garland initially offered women training in kindergarten teaching. In the early twentieth century, it completely transformed its mission to become a school for domestic education, altering its name in 1903 to the Garland School of Homemaking. After a twenty-year affiliation with the School of Education of Boston University, Garland became a junior college in 1947, offering associate in science degrees. The

college prospered during the 1930s and 1940s but then began to decline. Its last class, ninety-eight students, graduated in the spring of 1976. "Garland Junior College," College Archives, Simmons College, Boston.

72. Debra LaCava, "Simmons Sports Do Exist; Spring Schedules Outlined," *Simmons Janus,* April 16, 1976, 5.

73. *Memories of Simmons,* 1999–2000. Anonymous quotation from a collection of alumni memories for the 1999–2000 centennial celebration. SCA.

74. "Think about This," www.simmons.edu, under Campus life–Athletics, 1. (accessed June 4, 2004).

75. *Simmons College Self-Study Report,* September 1990, 42, Simmons College Archives, Lefavour Hall, Simmons College, Boston.

76. Ibid., 40–41.

77. Ibid., 42.

78. Stephen London, chair of Sociology Department, Simmons College, interview by author, Boston, September 22, 2003; Lyman interview.

79. *Simmons College Self-Study Report,* September 1990, 43, SCA.

80. Ibid., 20–21.

81. *Simmons College Self Study Report,* September 2000, 37, SCA.

82. Dan Cheever, Simmons College President, interview by Susan L. Poulson, September 22, 2003, Simmons College, Boston.

83. *Simmons College Self Study Report,* September 2000, 37, SCA.

84. *Simmons College Self-Study Report,* September 1990, 42, SCA.

85. *Simmons College Self-Study Report,* September 1990, 89, SCA.

86. However, as former associate dean Elizabeth Rawlins notes, the number of African American students at the undergraduate level has seemed to decline after expanding during the 1970s; many of the African American students at Simmons today are graduate students. Rawlins interview.

87. *1996–1997 Simmons College Fact Book.* Office of the Registrar, Simmons College, 14.

88. The "redefinition of minority" quote is from Elizabeth Rawlins, who asserts that while there are more minority students, Simmons is reaching out to fewer African American students at the undergraduate level. Elizabeth B. Rawlins, telephone interview by author, June 28, 2004.

89. *Simmons College Self-Study Report,* September 1990, 42, SCA.

90. Ibid.

91. "First Dean for Multicultural Affairs," *Simmons News,* September 28, 1995, 1.

92. *Microcosm,* 1985, 1990, 1995.

93. *Simmons College Self-Study Report,* September 2000, 57, SCA.

94. Ibid., September 1990, 96–97.

95. *Simmons College Report to the New England Association of Colleges and Secondary Schools, Inc.,* March 1969; *1980 Self-Evaluation Report of Simmons College,* October 1980; *Simmons College Self-Study Report,* September 1990; and *Simmons College Self-Study Report,* September 2000, all in SCA.

96. Without a strong central administration for many years, various parts of the college had developed in their own directions and operated as nearly independent entities.

By the late 1990s, for example, there were several variations of the mission statement in a variety of campus publications.

97. *Simmons College Self-Study Report*, September 2000, 3–4, SCA.

98. Student interviews.

99. Jill Taylor, chair, Department of Women's Studies, Simmons College, Boston, interview by author, Boston, September 22, 2003.

100. www.my.simmons.edu/campus-life/women (accessed June 15, 2004).

101. www.simmons.edu/silc (accessed June 14, 2004).

9

Spelman College

A Place All Their Own

Frances D. Graham and Susan L. Poulson

While many women's colleges have struggled to survive over the last forty years, Spelman College in Atlanta, Georgia, has flourished. Many women's colleges attracted needed students by opening graduate schools or continuing-education programs that serve adult students, but Spelman maintained its traditional orientation toward the African American undergraduate residential student. It has expanded its enrollment while raising admissions standards. There are several reasons for this upward trend: an urban location that attracts students who want the advantages of a big city; membership in a consortium that includes one of the few remaining all-male colleges, Morehouse College, whose adjacent campus provides for a rich social life; prudent financial management coupled with generous benefactors; and finally, a unique history and mission that integrate the realities of the lives of young black women into the curriculum and prepare these women for life after college.

Early Leadership

When the Atlanta Baptist Seminary for Girls (as Spelman was originally named) opened on April 11, 1881, it was the only private single-sex institution of higher education for black women. Its founders, Sophia B. Packard and Harriet E. Giles, were white schoolteachers and missionaries for the Women's American Baptist Home Missionary Society (WABHMS) in Boston, Massachusetts.[1] After seeing the struggles of black women during a mission trip to New Orleans, Packard and Giles decided to open a school for black women and girls so that they could take care of themselves and their families.[2]

The challenge of opening a school for black women in the Deep South after the Civil War was enormous. Even some members of the WABHMS thought Packard and Giles "too old to undertake such a work" and the proposal "too overwhelming."[3] Yet the pair persevered. Packard, an observer noted, was "a woman of powerful intellect and strong will, aggressive and energetic, with almost a masculine genius for business and capacity for leadership." She was "an excellent example of the type of stern, self-willed maiden woman that New England civilization took pride in producing." Although neither woman had a college degree, they were of the first generation of New England seminary-educated women; by nineteenth century standards, they were well qualified to teach, administer, and lead.[4]

The Atlanta Baptist Seminary for Girls opened as a Christian academy for women of all ages and at all educational levels.[5] The course offerings included various levels of reading, language, spelling, writing, vocal music, geography, arithmetic, Bible study, sewing, and cooking.[6] The first graduates, in 1887, were elementary and secondary students who became teachers, missionaries, or stay-at-home mothers.[7] By 1891, the number of students had grown from eleven to eight hundred. With the motto "Our Whole School for Christ," Packard and Giles infused Christian values into every aspect of the students' life.[8] The school's 1888 charter stated that the college was for "the establishment and maintenance of an Institution of learning for young colored women in which special attention is to be given to the formation of industrial habits and of Christian character."[9] Students were required to attend chapel twice daily, a nightly Bible study, Sunday service, and Sunday school.[10]

From its inception, Spelman relied upon aid from a variety of sources. A local black Baptist congregation, under the direction of Reverend Frank Quarrels, provided the basement of Friendship Baptist Church and the bare necessities to make certain the small space was as useful as possible.[11] Packard and Giles made constant appeals to northern philanthropists for help. In the 1880s they were lucky enough to acquire the patronage of one of the wealthiest individuals in the United States, John D. Rockefeller. A devout Baptist, Rockefeller responded to the appeals of Packard and Giles with generous and sustained contributions. For this, the school's name was changed in 1884 to honor Harvey Buel and Lucy Henry Spelman, the parents-in-law of John D. Rockefeller Sr.[12] In 1924, when the school wanted to emphasize its collegiate status, the name of the school became Spelman College.[13]

With the aid of such philanthropists, Spelman moved to its current site in Atlanta and began the development of a permanent physical plant. In February 1883 Spelman purchased nine acres of land and five buildings, called the Old Barracks because the union army had used them in the Civil War. During the next thirty-five years, Spelman built its core physical plant, erecting or refurbishing eight buildings on campus. In 1887 Rockefeller Hall was the first building dedicated, and Packard Hall was being built. In November 1901

Reynolds Cottage (the president's residence), MacVicar Hospital, Morgan Hall, and Morehouse Hall were all dedicated.[14] Spelman's growth rapidly surpassed that of most colleges founded ten years earlier. Today the college still sits on the same land and has more than thirty-two acres and twenty-six buildings.

Spelman began its transformation into a true college at the end of the nineteenth century. By 1886 Spelman added a Nurse Training program and graduated its first students from the Academic Department. Five years later, the Missionary Training Department and Teachers' Professional Department opened. In 1897 the College Department opened; it graduated its first class four years later, in 1901.[15]

Surviving the Jim Crow Years

The Spelman education—both its curriculum and its aim—was influenced by the Jim Crow system in the South. Even though Jim Crow norms entirely discredited black women's institutions, Spelman's administration never directly confronted the prejudicial system. As former Spelman faculty member Harry Lefever noted in his history of the civil rights movement in the 1960s and 1970s, Spelman expected its graduates to "live moral lives and . . . to serve others," yet they did not "challenge . . . the social injustices and inequities that existed in American society."[16]

Like many other historically black colleges and universities (HBCUs) Spelman vacillated between the vocational philosophy advanced by Booker T. Washington and the liberal arts ideal championed by W.E.B. Du Bois. Initially, Packard and Giles planned for a liberal arts institution and thus began with a Normal Department (to train teachers) and an Academic Department. However, Spelman also added an Industrial Department with courses in cooking, dressmaking, laundry, nursing, printing, and sewing. This vocational education, Giles made clear, would hold "a secondary place."[17]

Spelman also embodied the spirit of "race uplift": Through high academic and moral standards, it was the duty and obligation of black women to uplift their race. Black women at Spelman were concerned with improving both the state and the image of their people.[18] This ideology was much like the "true womanhood" ideal that encouraged white women to raise children to be strong, economically independent, and educated citizens. Black women were also expected to educate and raise their children to be successful citizens.[19] This philosophy of "race uplift" was evident in the college's first history, written twenty-five years after Spelman opened:

> [Spelman] aims to be the center and source of good influences, striving to ennoble and purify the lives of its individual pupils, to improve their homes, to permeate churches and Sunday-schools with an uplifting force, to supply the

public schools with competent teachers, and to enrich the whole life of the Negro race—industrial, social, religious, political—with higher ideals, better methods, and trained and qualified leaders. It seeks to educate the head, the hand, and the heart. . . . Spelman Seminary, therefore, educates for patriotism and tends to good citizenship. It endeavors to put its pupils into right relationship with Nature, with society, with God.[20]

This toleration of Jim Crow continued under the leadership of President Lucy Tapley, who served for eighteen years after Giles died in 1909.[21] Tapley first came to Spelman in 1890 as an English and arithmetic teacher and later held a variety of teaching and administrative positions. A descendent of two prominent New England fishing families, Tapley was known for her qualities "associated with high command": her "forcefulness, thoroughness, power of organization, confidence in her own judgment, [and] a superb sense of order."[22] While Packard and Giles had moved Spelman toward collegiate education, Tapley instead "stressed industrial education in industrial or house-wifely arts at the expense of intellectual training, and she seemed willing to tolerate southern mores." Tapley attracted additional funds from the Slater Foundation, which restricted use of its funds to developing the industrial course. Spelman was thus discouraged from becoming a fully collegiate institution. Some contemporaries believed that Tapley's insufficient educational credentials—she lacked a doctorate—meant that she was incapable of leading the school into the new era. Tapley even brought Jim Crow to campus, instituting a "white only" section for certain events at the school. Some challenged her decision to close the MacVicar hospital and criticized her lack of hiring black faculty and staff.[23]

Modernizing in the Mid–Twentieth Century: The Read Administration (1927–53)

During the presidency of Florence Matilda Read (1927–53), Spelman shed its vocational and precollegiate past and began the process of becoming the liberal arts institution that it is today.[24] In Read's first year, the board of trustees voted to discontinue the elementary school and directed Read to "develop a strong liberal arts college."[25] The curriculum was later transformed through the offering of more college-level courses, though not without the controversial classical-versus-technical debate. President Read established an endowment, which in 1927 was valued at more than $2 million.[26]

In 1929 Spelman expanded further and joined with Morehouse College and Atlanta University to form the Atlanta Consortium. This "Agreement of Affiliation" expanded in 1947 to include Morris Brown College, Clark College, and the Interdenominational Theological Center.[27] In sharing students, faculty, and facilities, these institutions—now known as the Atlanta University Center (AUC)—strengthened their academic quality. However, by 1947, Spelman, Morehouse, and Atlanta University were three of only seven HBCUs to meet requirements set by the Association of American Universities, and Spelman was one of only six HBCUs to receive an A rating from the Southern Association of Colleges and Schools.[28] Most notably, the AUC shared an interconnected social life that mixed students from various campuses, which helped to overcome some of the isolation students often felt on single-sex campuses.

The Civil Rights Era

The civil rights movement of the mid–twentieth century transformed Spelman. Whereas previous leaders avoided direct confrontation with segregation's norms, some faculty and students at Spelman now began to participate in direct action. Before the civil rights movement, Spelman administrators discouraged students from patronizing segregated businesses and public areas as much as possible; the insular and heavily regulated campus provided some protection from humiliation.

As Harry Lefever notes in his history of Spelman, the number of Spelman participants in the civil rights movement was small but significant. Lefever estimates that about 1 percent of students were actively involved and at most 4 percent were somewhat involved. Even fewer faculty participated: Three were arrested and only a few more were overtly supportive.[29] On March 9, 1960, the student presidents from each of the six institutions of the AUC published a full-page "Appeal for Human Rights" in several leading Atlanta newspapers. Over the next several years, students participated in civil rights protests, including sit-ins in Atlanta theaters and restaurants, kneel-ins in area white churches, freedom rides, the March on Washington, and Freedom Summer. One of those students, Ruby Doris Smith Robinson, was a full-time activist with the Student Non-Violent Coordinating Committee and was its executive secretary from 1966 until her death from cancer a year later. Some faculty publicly supported the movement. Professors Gloria Wade Bishop Gayles, Staughton Lynd, and Howard Zinn organized and trained protestors.

Spelman administrators had mixed reactions to the protests. Sometimes they publicly embraced the movement. Martin Luther King Jr., for example, whose grandmother, mother, and sister attended Spelman, was praised when he gave the annual Spelman Founders' Day address in 1960. Spelman president Manley and other AUC presidents helped organize a large integrated dinner in Atlanta when it was announced that King was to receive the Nobel Peace Prize. Yet the administration also discouraged Spelman students, warning them "to stay clear of any involvement with the movement."[30] In 1960 President Manley sent a letter to the parents of Spelman students, informing them that "the institution cannot accept responsibility for your daughter's participation in any of these demonstrations and the possible consequences."[31] When Spelman administrators suspended student Gwendolyn Zoharah Simmons for her repeated participation in protests, students from across the AUC rallied in her support until administrators relented and let Simmons stay, under strict probation.[32]

Spelman administrators also acted to restrain faculty involvement. In 1963, Spelman fired history professor Howard Zinn, who had encouraged student participation in protests. Despite his status as a tenured professor, his support from many Spelman students, and the finding by the American Association of University Professors that Spelman had violated his academic freedom, Zinn relocated to Boston University without a fight. English professor Gloria Wade Bishop Gayles was also fired for her participation, and Staughton Lind in the History Department resigned in protest. Similarly, Spelman administrators criticized student leaders for arranging a campus visit by Stokely Carmichael in 1966.[33] Lefever characterizes the administration's response to the civil rights movement as "ambivalent":

> A few administrators and faculty members were consistently supportive; another few were consistently hostile. Most, however, struggled with how to interpret their students' behavior and what they should do about it. At times, their responses were punitive and judgmental. At other times, even from the same individuals, the responses were supportive and encouraging. In some instances, administrators put students on probation and threatened to send them home, and yet at other times, those same administrators visited the students behind bars, provided them with books and reading materials, and worked for their release.[34]

Demands for More Student Freedom and Power

Spelman College, like many other colleges nationwide, was paternalistic toward students well into the 1960s, until forced by student rebellion to renounce the practice of in loco parentis, or parental supervision. In the early 1960s, for example, Spelman required that all students be in their rooms by 9 P.M., and any contact with male students was limited to heavily chaperoned "calling hours" in the late afternoon. Spelman discouraged visits to the city; only with written permission from the student's parents and from the hostess could a student leave. Students could attend movies, parties, and dances only in groups chaperoned by faculty.[35] Students were also required to rise early, clean their rooms, make their beds, and be subject to room inspection by a house mother; records of these personal activities were maintained in the same file as the academic activities.[36]

Regulation of student life extended to dress as well. In the early 1960s students were advised to wear "simple tailored dresses, skirts, sweaters, or blouses" with "low-heeled, comfortable shoes" to class; they would also need "dressy date dresses" for "teas, concerts, and informal dances." For formal dances, at least one evening gown was recommended, and for Founder's Day, they needed a white dress.[37] In 1963, "Tips for Campus Dress," given to first-year students, spelled out ways to "add to your charm as college young women." Ideal attire, the college advised, was "becoming and proportional to [a student's] figure." Students should avoid "the flashy showgirl look," clothes "that look like a second skin," and excessive makeup that makes the student "look like a member of the Barnum and Bailey Circus clown troupe." Jewelry "should always be worn with discretion."[38] In providing these guidelines, Spelman administrators fostered a middle-class sensibility in a well-educated student population. The Spelman ideal continued to reflect "race uplift," a woman capable of becoming a cultural role model in and out of the black community.

Students began to press for liberalization. In a 1963 meeting, "Liberty at Spelman College," held by Professor Howard Zinn and the Spelman Social Science Club, students expressed their frustration at the personal dress regulations, which, some asserted, removed "responsibility for personal decision making from the individual student . . . [and] distort[ed] and weaken[ed] a significant phase of the education process."[39] In 1969 Spelman students demanded "an end to compulsory regulations affecting campus dress, curfew, sign out, and destination designation."[40] Spelman College modified these policies later that year, ending the curfew for students who had parental permission.

Spelman also changed its policy on religious practices. Through the 1960s, students were required to attend chapel after breakfast on weekdays, a Thursday night prayer service, and Sunday school and service. Students were expected to "join in the singing, and listen attentively to the speaker"; excessive absences resulted in a lowered grade-point average.[41] In 1973 Spelman ended mandatory chapel attendance.

As the 1960s progressed, students demanded more say in decision making and more academic freedom on campus. Spelman stated, on the record, that it favored academic freedom and signed a document in 1969 with other AUC schools stating that they "endorse academic freedom—freedom to teach and freedom to learn; freedom to think, freedom to speak, freedom to write, and freedom to publish. These institutions also endorse citizenship freedoms including freedom of peaceful assembly, freedom of the press, and freedom to petition for redress of grievances."[42] In 1970 the first student and faculty representatives were added to the board of trustees.

Sex norms at Spelman were also traditional in the early 1960s. In 1963, the college held a conservative series of lectures and discussions titled "Sex on the Campus."[43] Spelman dean of students Naomi Chivers proclaimed in 1969 that she would expel any student who had an abortion.[44] However, in 1972,

Spelman received a grant from the Rockefeller Foundation and established a Family Planning Program to provide comprehensive contraceptive services on campus.[45]

Changes in the Curriculum

Even though the vast majority of Spelman students did not directly participate in protests, the civil rights movement made them increasingly aware of and impatient with the subordination of blacks in the United States. Students demanded that the Spelman curriculum become "relevant to black people."[46] The Eurocentric curriculum was outdated, students complained, and created an identity crisis.[47] A cartoon in the *Spelman Spotlight* portrayed a student next to questions such as "Why so much discussion about Negroes? African Americans? Black Power? Reconstruction?" Below the woman was "Italian Americans Read the History of Italy; Irish Americans Know the History of Ireland. . . . What Do We Know of African American History?"[48]

In response to pressure from a student group called the Ad Hoc Committee for a Black University, Spelman held a Speak Out in November 1968. Classes were cancelled and students, faculty, and administrators discussed in loco parentis regulations, as well as updating the curriculum to include more discussion of black Americans and non-Western issues. In 1969 student leaders from the institutions of the AUC called for several changes: that a black studies program be created and become part of the required courses in a discipline; that non-Western languages count toward any language requirement; and that the AUC invite "a noted scholar, author, or lecturer in Black Studies" to the convocation.[49]

Student activism in the 1970s continued to call for institutional change, particularly as it related to issues of identity.[50] In the fall of 1970, Spelman held a series of small group discussions, "New Directions for the Black Woman in the 1970s." Topics included "Women's Liberation," "The Drug Scene," "The New Morality," "The Career Woman," "The Woman in the Home," and "Some Aspects of the Male-Female Relationship." The focus, according to the sponsors, was on "the role of the black woman as she relates herself to some of the changing ideas in these areas."[51] As a result of student pressure for change, there were also several curricular developments. In 1970 the AUC began an Afro American studies program, and Spelman developed related courses. In 1971–72, for example, Spelman added the Sociology of Black Music, Police in the Black Community, Judeo-Christian Beginnings in Africa, and Black Religion.

Although students at Spelman varied in their political commitments and ideals, there was a growing militancy on the campus that responded to national and international events. In the fall of 1971, after the confrontation at the Attica prison in New York State, hundreds of students rallied in "solidarity with the slain brothers." Various speakers, including some from the Black Panther Party and the Pan-African Congress, spoke out. Students performed a skit, "The People's Tribune," which found New York governor Nelson Rockefeller guilty of first-degree murder and hanged him in effigy.[52]

By the mid-1970s, the pressure for change on campus seemed to have waned, but some students urged their sisters to be active. They worried that Spelman students were "more concern[ed] about the world as it exist[ed] at [that] moment, than about the way it might exist in the future or may have existed in the past."[53] In 1976, Greer Lauren Geiger characterized Spelman as having "'archaic stagnation' as regards the use of innovative renewed thought," with "certain teachers and departments . . . covered by a thick layer of dust and spider webs." Some students pressed for further change and challenged "present and future members of the Spelman student body to continue to be vocal and active in the shaping and direction of programs, activities, and regulations which affected their lives and their futures."[54] Some students came to campus with activist aspirations. One student found them

> bold, out-spoken, and quite confident, almost to the point of cocksureness. This is very evident among the freshmen as well as the seniors. They have brought to the college their attitudes and beliefs that they as black women were important; they know what they want, and they are going after what they believe is long overdue to black women academically, vocationally, and in their personal lives.[55]

Changes in Campus Media

In the 1960s the student and college media at Spelman were fairly conservative. The campus media entered the 1960s promoting a traditional ideal for the Spelman student. In the early 1960s, for example, one of the student newspapers, the *Spotlight,* featured Spelman students formally modeling spring fashions with such captions as "Calmness is An Asset" and "Charm is Thy Virtue."[56] In 1967 the *Spotlight* listed the names of senior women who were to get married after graduation, "a bond which sets them free to love and sacrifice and give and enhance some man's life with profound meaning and beauty."[57] As late as 1967, the *Spotlight* enthusiastically endorsed a visit by *Glamour* magazine to the Spelman campus to find "our best dressed girl." In addition to "neatness and self-assurance," the criteria included "good posture, a vibrant personality, and an awareness of style and fashion."[58]

After the mid-1960s, however, the campus media became less Eurocentric and began to celebrate African heritage. In the early 1960s, for example, the *Spotlight* highlighted travel opportunities to Europe for further study or for jobs. Beginning in the late 1960s, however, there was more coverage of Africa. In 1968, for example, the *Spotlight* featured an article on "Ghanian Dress Style."[59] In a campus lecture, "Negro Women—Torchbearers of Culture," Juanita Kidd

Stout, a common pleas court judge from Philadelphia, urged Spelman students to "attain a true picture of their heritage and not a fictionalized concept of it." In her extensive travels to Africa, she said, she had noted the importance of marriage and a strong family structure, as well as the respect that African children show their elders.[60] In the early 1970s the *Spotlight* began a regular feature, "Focus on Black Womanhood: Woman of the Month." In February 1972, for example, the focus was on Marian Wright Edelman, Spelman valedictorian of 1960, who became a well-known civil rights lawyer and, later, executive director of the Center of Law and Education at Harvard University.[61] By the mid-1970s, a majority of Spelman students sported Afros.

The campus media also reflected a growing political and social awareness among Spelman students. In a centennial history of Spelman, Beverly Guy-Sheftall and Jo Moore Stewart note that "college publications tended to ignore [protest] activities."[62] During the 1970s there was a noticeable growth in the campus media's coverage of black pride and consciousness. In the 1971 edition of *Reflections*, the Spelman yearbook, the editors prominently featured a new organization called Sisters in Blackness. Spelman celebrated black history month and a Black Arts Festival. Spelman and Morehouse students performed more plays by black authors.

Spelman began to seek a more distinct identity, with fewer ties to Morehouse. Throughout the 1960s the Spelman yearbooks referred to "Morehouse Men" and included pictures of Morehouse fraternity members. In 1970, however, there was no mention of the "Morehouse Men," and two years later the fraternity pictures were dropped from the yearbook. By 1975, Spelman began a tradition of "Mr. Blue and White" (Spelman's school colors), a contest in which Spelman students selected a male college student from the Atlanta consortium. More recently, Spelman ended the tradition of celebrating homecoming with Morehouse; the college began its own homecoming celebrations with its own queen.

The student push for more racial and social consciousness at Spelman was reflected in revisions to the "Statement of Purpose" in the early 1970s, which had seen little change since the 1930s, when more emphasis was placed on liberal arts education; in the 1970s, however, the statement reflected a greater social and political awareness:

> The College offers signal opportunities for leadership roles for Black women [and] . . . subscribes to the philosophy that free and unrestricted communication of all members of society is a sure approach to the achieving of democracy in personal and social relations. The institution believes that full participation of Blacks in American society is the only viable solution to social difficulties in this country. The college is aware that it exists in a multi-racial society and that this fact must be reflected in all facets of its operations and objectives.[63]

Members of Sisters in Blackness, a student organization begun in 1968 to promote black consciousness and social awareness on the campus and in the community and society at large. *Spelman College Archives.*

Controversy over the Selection of a President

The increasing desire for role models at Spelman led to controversy when the college selected a new president in 1977. Dr Albert E. Manley, chosen in the 1950s, had been the first black president of the college.[64] When he announced his retirement twenty years later, many at Spelman wanted the next president to be a black woman—the first in its history. However, "preference for a black female president was not expressed in the advertisement," Manley later recalled, and there was no indication how many of the 220 applicants were women. Three finalists were brought to campus to meet with students, faculty, administrators, and alumnae.[65] At some point the lines of communication broke down, and when Dr. Donald Stewart was selected, some students and alumnae were outraged. Several hundred students and a few faculty and staff members locked the board of trustees in the boardroom for more that twenty hours, prompting it to reconsider its appointment. However, after the board reaffirmed its decision, Stewart (1977–87) would become the last man to lead the institution.[66]

Students engage in an unsuccessful attempt in the spring of 1976 to change the decision of the board...t another man as president of the college by locking them in the boardroom for twenty hours. *Spelman College Archives.*

Stewart's tenure as president can best be described as quiet academic improvement. He spent the majority of his time building on the foundation of a liberal arts institution; developing an honors program and career-oriented minors such as management and organization, international studies, and computer and information science; and increasing the quality of incoming students.[67] Additionally, in 1987, Stewart added a significant science component to Spelman when NASA granted Spelman money for the Women in Science and Engineering Scholars Program, which would aim to increase the representation of minority women in those fields.[68]

The Influence of Feminism

The influence of the feminist movement on HBCUs was more muted than it was at predominantly white institutions because of the urgency instead to advance black Americans as a whole. Many black women did not identify with a movement that was largely initiated by, led by, and addressed to the needs of middle-class white women. In 1981, with the aid of a grant from the Charles Stewart Mott Foundation, Spelman opened the first HBCU women's center. The Women's Research and Resource Center (WRRC) had three major goals:

curricular development in women's studies, research on black women, and community outreach to women. The ambitions were global, with a particular attention to women in the African diaspora (133). Using a variety of grants, the WRRC made several attempts among the Spelman faculty to enhance the awareness of black women's issues. Since 1984 the WRRC has published *Sage: A Scholarly Journal on Black Women* (134). With another grant from the Charles Mott Foundation, Spelman endowed a chair in women's studies (135). More recently, former Spelman president Johnnetta Cole and WRRC director Beverly Guy-Sheftall have authored an astute reflection on gender in the black community, *Gender Talk: The Struggle for Women's Equality in African American Communities.*[69]

The Cole Years, 1987–97

When Johnnetta B. Cole assumed office in July 1987, Spelman got its first black woman president. Unlike Stewart, she received a warm greeting from the students, the alumnae, and the board of trustees. Already a well-known anthropologist and defender of women's rights, Cole spent a dynamic ten years in office. Spelman's student enrollment rose, its endowments increased, the physical plant enlarged, and the faculty population increased.

Spelman attracted much philanthropic attention during the Cole years. The 1992 donation of $37 million to the college by the DeWitt Wallace Reader's Digest Fund was the largest gift to a HBCU to date and now generates roughly $1 million in revenue and supports several scholarships. Camille O. Hanks Cosby and her husband, Bill Cosby, gave $20 million in honor of the appointment of Cole; the Camille O. Hanks Cosby Academic Center was dedicated in February 1996.

Under President Cole, the self-consciousness of the black women's college was reinforced. In 1979, for example, the college's "Statement of Purpose" was revised to include notable language: "As an outstanding historically black college for women, Spelman strives for academic excellence in liberal education. . . . Spelman has been and expects to continue to be a major resource for educating black women leaders." This statement also reflects some of the attention to issues beyond the campus, which Spelman students had called for since the 1960s. Through her speeches, her frequent meetings with students for breakfast, and "sister girl' chats on the lawn, President Cole tried to inspire students to higher standards. The college also sought to "instill in students both an appreciation for the multicultural communities of the world in which they live and a sense of responsibility for bringing about positive change in those communities."[70]

The Cole years also brought significant and sustained changes of the top administrative posts held by women. Whereas in 1960 and 1965, all the top administrators were men, in 1990, 1995, and 2000, all were women. (The pro-

Dr. Johnnetta Cole, who in 1987 became the first black woman president of Spelman, was generally regarded as very successful, as well as popular with students, during her ten years of service. *Spelman College Archives.*

gression ran from 0 women of 2 top administrators in 1960 and 1965 to 1 of 2 in 1970; 0 of 2 in 1975; 0 of 1 in 1980; and 2 of 2 in 1990, 1995, and 2000.)[71]

In her book *Conversations: Straight Talk with America's Sister President*, Cole explains that role modeling and creating a positive environment for young black women are central to Spelman's success: "Spelman women are not haunted on campus by racism and sexism, and as a result can turn their attention their studies." The campus is filled with role models, she writes; people do not assume "that Black folks don't like math and women cannot do science . . . [or] that women are just not as bright as men and will never understand economics as easily as men do. On the contrary, the assumption is that Spelman women will excel in all their studies." Since "the realties of African Americans and women are mainstreamed into the entire curriculum," Spelman provides a uniquely supportive environment. "It is as if a family," Cole writes, "indeed a community, comes to Spelman behind each student."[72]

Today's Students

In contrast to many other women's colleges that have seen their student populations decline, Spelman has steadily increased its enrollment during the past forty years; total students, only 532 in 1960, are almost 2,200 in 2004. (The increase has been consistent: 723 in 1965; 966 in 1970; 1,238 in 1975; 1,350 in 1980; 1,710 in 1990; 1,961 in 1995; and 2,127 in 2000.)[73]

Not only has Spelman increased enrollment, but also it has improved the academic qualifications of its students. Accepted applicants' SAT scores have increased more than 25 percent since the late 1960s; from an average of 772 in 1968 to an average of 1,059 in 2000. In the past decade, the average high school grade-point average of entering Spelman students has risen from 3.17 to 3.3.[74]

Since 1960 Spelman has exponentially increased its tuition, from $325 in 1960 to $9,660 in 2000. (The fees rose from $2,350 in 1980 to $3,500 in 1985; $5,400 in 1990; and $7,500 in 1995.)[75] The cost of a Spelman education is lower than those of its peers among private institutions in the Atlanta area but much higher than those of state universities (see Table 9.1). Morehouse and Agnes Scott, single-sex institutions located close by, cost about $10,000 and $20,000 more, respectively, than Spelman did in 2004, and the tuition of Emory, a co-educational private university, was more than twice Spelman's. On the other hand, the tuition of three state institutions in Georgia cost about $9,000 less.

Spelman's tuition falls about midway among HBCUs (see Table 9.2)—about the same as Xavier's in New Orleans and Dillard's in Louisiana and just a little lower than Lincoln University's in Pennsylvania. It is considerably higher than the tuition at Jackson State University in Mississippi, a public institution, but much lower than the tuition at Morehouse, Bennett, and Howard. Approximately 85 percent of Spelman students receive some form of financial aid.[76]

Rising Geographic Diversity

Usually, discussion of student population diversity indicates the racial mix among students. In this sense, Spelman is remarkably homogeneous: Students are 93 percent non-Hispanic black. However, Spelman has become more geographically diverse both in national and international terms. As Table 9.3 indicates, during the past forty years Spelman has drawn a more national and less localized population. In 2000, for example, 25 percent of the students hailed from five states outside the South: California, Illinois, New Jersey, New York, and Ohio.[77]

Spelman also participates in student exchanges with other campuses, particularly women's and former women's colleges. By the 1990s, these institutions included Babson, Connecticut, Grinnel, Haverford, Pomona, Vassar, Bryn Mawr, Mount Holyoke, Simmons, Smith, and Wellesley colleges and Ohio Wesleyan University.[78]

For the past fifty years, and with increasing momentum, Spelman has been expanding its study-abroad component by welcoming more international students, beginning in 1957, when one student received a scholarship to study

Table 9.1. Peer institutions in Georgia, 2004

	Student population	Type of Institution				Tuition in Dollars	
		Single sex	Coed	Public	Private	In state	Out of state
Agnes Scott College	1,000	x			x	33,000	33,000
Morehouse College	2,859	x			x	22,728	22,728
Spelman College	2,186	x			x	12,700	12,700
Emory	6,297		x		x	28,940	28,940
Georgia State	20,177		x	x		3,529	14,115
Georgia Tech	11,257		x	x		3,368	16,648
Univ. of Georgia	25,415		x	x		3,368	14,684

Sources: Web sites of individual institutions.

Table 9.2. Historically Black Colleges and Universities, 2004–5

	State	Student population	Type of Institution				Tuition in Dollars	
			Single sex	Coed	Public	Private	In state	Out of state
Spelman College	Ga.	2,186	x			x	12,700	12,700
Morehouse College	Ga.	2,859	x			x	22,728	22,728
Bennett College	N.C.	634	x			x	17,600	17,600
Dillard University	La	2,200		x		x	11,000	11,000
Howard University	D.C.	7,000		x		x	17,515	17,515
Xavier University	La	4,000		x		x	12,100	12,100
Jackson State Univ.	Miss.	6,315		x	x		3,612	5,864
Lincoln University	Pa.	2,000		x	x		14,186	18,224

Sources: Web sites of individual institutions.

Table 9.3. Spelman students' residence

	% Georgia (number)	% Southern (number)	% Non-Southern (number)	% Total (number)
1960	58	93	7	100
	(358)	(575)	(43)	(618)
1980	32	52	48	100
	(432)	(702)	(648)	(1,350)
2000	28	54	46	100
	(582)	(1,122)	(955)	(2,077)

Sources: Spelman College Bulletin, 1960–1; 1981–3; Fact Book, 2000–1.

overseas for a year. Since the 1960s Spelman students have participated in Operation Crossroads Africa. The college belongs to several study-abroad exchanges and since 1985 has conducted a monthlong summer program in Mexico.

Academic Clubs and Opportunities

The rising academic stature of Spelman is reflected in student activities. There are approximately nineteen honors and academic programs, ranging from Golden Key National Honor Society to Study Abroad, Freshman Studies, International Affairs, ROTC, and Continuing Education. In 1998, Spelman became one of only four HBCUs to be awarded a chapter of Phi Beta Kappa, the oldest and most prestigious honor society in the country. U.S. News and World Report in 2005 ranked Spelman as among the seventy-five best liberal arts colleges in the nation.[79]

Although Spelman abandoned compulsory religious attendance more than thirty years ago, there is still a strong religious presence on campus. More than thirteen student religious organizations support a variety of religious denominations. In 2002, the Lilly Foundation sought to strengthen the role of religion by granting Spelman $2 million for the Sisters Center for WISDOM, Women in Spiritual Discernment of Ministry. This religious presence, as well as a disapproval of homosexuality in the black community, may account for the relatively conservative climate against nonheterosexual students on campus, although they are supported by the administration.[80] There is one organization, Afrakete, that supports lesbian and bisexual students.[81]

Like many other women's colleges, Spelman has not placed much emphasis on athletics. When the Education Amendments Act passed in 1972, Title IX mandated that colleges and universities equitably fund men's and women's sports proportional to the gender representation in the study body. The act forced many coeducational institutions to dramatically increase spending on women's sports. One result has been a growing presence of women's sports across the nation. Women's colleges, however, were virtually unaffected due to the lack of student gender segregation. As a result, many women's colleges did not develop their athletic facilities or recruit talented women athletes as students. At Spelman, while there were physical education classes and intramural teams, there were relatively few intercollegiate teams. Recently, however, Spelman became a member of the Great South Conference and a provisional member of the National Collegiate Athletic Association, Division III. Spelman is also planning "new sports initiatives to upgrade and further develop the intercollegiate athletic and club sports programs."[82]

Today's Faculty and Board of Trustees

Since the 1960s Spelman has made great strides in improving the quality of the faculty. First, the faculty became more educated: from 1960 to 1975, the percentage of faculty who held a doctoral degree increased from 25 to 56 percent.[83] By 2003, 84 percent of the full-time faculty held PhDs or other terminal degrees.[84] Second, the college increased the pay of its faculty. In 1978, professors' pay fell below the national average, and 20 percent below peer institutions' payroll listings.[85] Today, income for faculty of various ranks falls in the top 30 percent of all comparable institutions.[86]

Third, like many HBCUs, Spelman made great strides in diversifying its staff to include Asians, Hispanics, and whites.[87] In 2004, 46 percent of the faculty at Spelman was black female, 11 percent white female, 4 percent Asian female, and 1 percent Hispanic female. Male faculty had a similar diversity: 18 percent were black male, 10 percent were white male, and Asian and Hispanic males each were 2 percent of the faculty. Ethnically, 64 percent of the faculty were black, 21 percent white, 6 percent Asian, and 3 percent Hispanic.[88] The Spelman College faculty is predominantly women, their percentage rising only slightly between 1975–76 (63 percent, or 57 of 90 faculty members) and 2004–5 (65 percent, or 102 of 156 faculty members).[89]

In the past forty years, Spelman has also transformed its board of trustees. In 1960 there was a slight preponderance of men, and by 1990, the number of women on the board had doubled; however, in 2000, more than half the board members were women. (The progression: 7 women of 16 members in 1960; 6 of 15 in 1965; 5 of 11 in 1970; 7 of 17 in 1975; 16 of 28 in 1985; 14 of 21 in 1990; 14 of 25 in 1995; and 12 of 23—fourteen black and nine white—in 2000.)[90]

New Demographic Challenges

Spelman intersects two subgroups in U.S. higher education: historically black colleges and universities, and women's colleges. These subgroups were founded for similar reasons: both sought to educate segments of the population that were subordinate and marginalized. Founders of these institutions were generally inspired to create educational opportunities for groups they considered underserved yet capable of tremendous contribution. Their education was often seen as a means to advance the social reputation of the subgroup, as well as to protect its members from the vagaries of an unfair society.

Until the middle of the twentieth century, these subdivisions held. Even though the vast majority of U.S. college students attended state coeducational colleges and universities, there were still restrictions and preferences that created a stable pool of applicants for these institutions. Blacks continued to be unwelcome in most southern nonblack institutions, and a large majority attended HBCUs, which are mostly located in southern states. High-status men's colleges along the Eastern seaboard continued to exclude women, enabling a mirror group of elite women's colleges to maintain their single-sex status.

Seismic changes in the landscape of higher education in the past half century have altered these niches, virtually eliminating the pool of applicants and putting these traditional subcategories under significant pressure to change their original mission. Following the *Brown v. Board of Education* decision and the civil rights movement, which eliminated restrictions on blacks attending southern institutions and enabled more to attend predominantly white institutions in the North, black students increasingly sought education outside the HBCUs. Recently, the HBCUs educate only 14 percent of all black students, although they graduate a higher percentage of their students than do non-HBCUs.[91] During the 1960s and 1970s, elite men's colleges began to admit women, luring away many women students who would presumably have otherwise attended elite women's colleges. Not surprisingly, these colleges faced not only the rising costs that all of higher education has felt, but also a declining pool of traditional applicants. Spelman, however, contradicts this trend. While many women's colleges and HBCUs have seen their enrollments and student qualifications fall, Spelman has seen its enrollment increase, the qualifications of its students continue to rise, and the institution becoming increasingly national and prestigious.

The evolution of Spelman has gone from having white women and men educating black women to black women educating black women. In the past forty years, Spelman has exhibited all the hallmarks of a successful college: It has increased its academic quality and population size; it has improved the quality of the faculty and the diversity of its offerings; it has improved its physical plant and its endowment; and it has received growing recognition as an excellent institution both within the black community and from outside. Along with these developments, Spelman has sharpened its focus on the realities of life for black women and designed a curriculum and institutional culture to propel them into positions of leadership and responsibility. This uniquely supportive environment, along with an attractive urban location in a consortium and prudent financial management, has enabled Spelman to expand upon the early foundation built during Jim Crow America.[92]

Notes

The authors would like to thank research assistants, archivists, and colleagues who generously contributed to this chapter, including Meredith Boniface, Beverly Guy-Sheftall, Leah Laspina, and Taronda Spencer. Susan Poulson also thanks the University of Scranton for partly funding her research.

1. Florence Matilda Read, *The Story of Spelman College* (Princeton, N.J.: Princeton University Press, 1961), 31.
2. Ibid., 32.
3. Ibid., 40, 36.
4. Original quote in Willard Rangers, *The Rise and Progress of Negro Colleges in Georgia, 1865–1949.* (Athens: University of Georgia Press, 1951), cited by Frances Graham, "The Founding of an All Black Female Seminary, Spelman, 1881–1927." PhD diss., University of Illinois, 1996, 91.
5. Adopted primarily from the *1992–93 Spelman College Bulletin* (with updates). See the Spelman home page for more information: www.spelman,edu/about/glance.html.
6. *Course of Study and Syllabus of Elementary and Secondary Work of Spelman Seminary,* 1911, 4–9, Spelman Archives, Women's Research and Resource Center, Spelman College, Atlanta (hereafter SA).
7. Beverly Guy-Sheftall and Jo Moore Stewart, *Spelman: A Centennial Celebration, 1881–1991* (Atlanta: Delmar Co., 1981), 31.
8. Albert E. Manley, *A Legacy Continues: The Manley Years at Spelman College, 1953–1976* (Lanham, Md.: University Press of America, 1995), 20.
9. Read, *Story of Spelman College,* 103.
10. Ibid.
11. Graham, *The Founding of an All Black Female Seminary,* 122; also in Guy-Sheftall, *Centennial Celebration,* 13.
12. Read, *Story of Spelman College,* 84–85.
13. The Spelmans were abolitionists who supported and aided slaves in their move toward freedom and migration to the North. The first name change occurred after John D. Rockefeller Sr. gave more than half the $17,500 needed to purchase the land the institution currently resides on (ibid.).
14. Ibid., 95.
15. Ibid.
16. Harry G. Lefever, *Undaunted By the Fight: Spelman College and the Civil Rights Movement, 1957–1967* (Macon, GA: Mercer University Press, 2005), 5.
17. Giles to Rev. T. J. Morgan, January 24, 1901, SA, cited in Lefever, *Undaunted,* 3.
18. Tera Hunter, "The Correct Thing: Charlotte Hawkins Brown and the Palmer Memorial

Institute," *Southern Exposure*. 11:51 (Sept./Oct. 1983), 37–42, cited by Johnetta Cross Brazzell, "Education As A Tool of Socialization: Agnes Scott Institute and Spelman Seminary, 1881–1910" PhD diss., University of Michigan, 1991, 2–3.

19. Ibid., 33.
20. *Historical Sketch of Spelman Seminary, 1881–1906*, 2–3, cited in *Spelman Self-Report*, 1979, 21. SA.
21. Ibid.
22. Quote of Claudia White Harreld, cited in Read, *Story of Spelman College*, 187.
23. Graham, *Founding*, 115.
24. While Packard and Giles had believed that a vocational education was appropriate for this population of women, they also thought that "educating the whole person" was most important. Manley, *A Legacy Continues*, 27–28.
25. Read, *Story of Spelman College*, 210.
26. Read, *Story of Spelman College*, 213–15
27. *Spelman Self-Report*, 1978, iii.
28. Ibid., iv.
29. Lefever notes that the number of faculty grew from thirty-eight full-time and seven part-time in 1957 to seventy-six full-time and eleven part-time ten years later. Lefever, *Undaunted*, preface.
30. Ibid., 183.
31. Letter from President Manley to parents of Spelman College Students, October 17, 1960, SA; Lefever, *Undaunted*, 61.
32. Lefever, *Undaunted*, 188.
33. Editorial, *Spelman Spotlight*, November 6, 1966, 2.
34. Lefever, *Undaunted*, 255–56.
35. Marian Pitts, "The Clothes Horse," *Spelman Spotlight*, May 4, 1960,4. See also Manley, *A Legacy Continues*, 20–21.
36. Letter to the editor, *Spelman Spotlight*, April 11, 1963.
37. *Spelman College Handbook, 1960–61*, 17–18.
38. Advice given by Gloria A. Knowles in "Tips for Campus Dress," *Spelman Spotlight*, September 11, 1963.
39. "Student-Faculty Confab Spurs Local Interest," *Spelman Spotlight*, April 11, 1963.
40. "Spelman College Speaks Out," *Spelman Messenger*, February 1969, 22.
41. Manley, *A Legacy Continues*, 20.
42. "Statement on Student Rights and Freedom," *Spelman Messenger*, February 1969, 23.
43. "College Sex Life Discussed: Mrs. Moreland First Speaker," *Spelman Spotlight*, October 17, 1963, 1.
44. "Unwed: Coed Faces Toughest Decision of Her Life," *Spelman Spotlight*, September–October 1969, 1.
45. *Spelman Self-Report*, 1990, 366.
46. Ibid.
47. Questions about the Eurocentrism of the curriculum surfaced in the 1966–67 school year. Marilyn A. Hunt, "The Identity Crisis on the College Campus," *Spelman Messenger*, February 1969, 9.
48. Untitled cartoon, *Spelman Spotlight*, January 1967, 2.

49. "AU Center Student Leaders Submit Strong Proposals," *Spelman Spotlight,* March–April 1969, 3.

50. Ibid.

51. LeConyea B. Butler, "New Directions for the Black Woman in the 1970s," *Spelman Messenger,* February 1971, 18–20.

52. "Attica Sparks Action in AU College Center," *Spelman Spotlight,* October 1971, 1.

53. "Spelman Students in the Seventies: A Pluralistic View," *Spelman Messenger,* Winter/Spring 1976, 2.

54. Greer Lauren Geiger, "A View of My Education," *Spelman Messenger,* Winter/Spring, 1976, 6.

55. Sadie S. Allen, "The Spelman Student 1976," *Spelman Messenger,* Winter/Spring 1976, 5.

56. "Pictures Speak for Spring Fashions," *Spelman Spotlight.* April 11, 1963, 4.

57. Ruth Elizabeth Baety, "Wedding Bells," *Spelman Spotlight,* March 1967, 6.

58. Jane Elaine Smith, "Our Glamour Girls," *Spelman Spotlight,* March 1967, 4.

59. "Ghanian Dress Style," *Spelman Spotlight,* December 19, 1968, 3.

60. Speech by Honorable Juanita Kidd Stout, November 20, 1971, reprinted in the *Spelman Messenger,* November 1970, 3–10.

61. Carolyn Woods, "Focus on Black Womanhood," *Spelman Spotlight,* February 1972, 10.

62. Guy-Sheftall and Stewart, *Centennial Celebration,* 79.

63. Spelman College Statement of Purpose, cited in the *1971–72 Bulletin, Spelman Self-Report,* 1990, 22.

64. *Spelman Self-Report,* 1978, iii.

65. Manley, *A Legacy Continues,* 95

66. Dr. Johnnetta B. Cole, 1987–97, the first black woman to be appointed president of Spelman; Dr. Audrey F. Manley, 1997–2002, the first alumna to be appointed president; and currently, Dr. Beverly D. Tatum, have each played a major role in continuing to lead Spelman and Spelman's students into the twenty-first century.

67. *Spelman Self-Report,* 1990, 70. Immediately succeeding citations of this source appear as page numbers in parentheses in the text.

68. The successful candidates also received a round-trip visit to a NASA site (ibid.,107).

69. Johnnetta Betsch Cole and Beverly Guy-Sheftall, *Gender Talk: The Struggle for Women's Equality in African American Communities* (New York: One World/Ballantine, 2003).

70. *Spelman Self-Report,* 1978, 13.

71. *Spelman College Bulletins,* 1960–61; 1964–65; 1970–71; 1975–76; 1985; 1990–91; 2000–2001.

72. Johnnetta B. Cole, *Conversations: Straight Talk with America's Sister President* (New York: Doubleday, 1992), 180, 181.

73. Office of Institutional Research, Spelman College; and U.S. Department of Education, National Center for Educational Statistics, "Reports on Enrollment, 1955–75," cited in Manley, *A Legacy Continues,* 70; *Spelman College Fact Book, 1997–98,* 2000–1, 2004–5. SA.

74. *Spelman College Fact Book, 2000–1.* SA.

75. *Spelman College Bulletins,* 1960, 1980, 1985, 1990, 1995; *Spelman College Fact Book,* 2000.

76. www.spelman.edu/about_us/glance, accessed June 29, 2005.

77. *Spelman College Fact Book, 2000*–1, 44–46.

78. *Spelman Self-Report,* 1990, 107.

79. www.spelman.edu, accessed June 30, 2005.

80. Dr. Myra N. Burnett, phone interview by Susan Poulson, January 26, 2005.

81. *Spelman College Fact Book, 2004–5.*

82. Ibid.

83. Manley, *A Legacy Continues,* 82.

84. www.spelman.edu/about_us/glance/ accessed June 29, 2005.

85. *Spelman Self-Report,* 1978, 247.

86. *Spelman College Fact Book, 2004–5.*

87. While administrators attempted to diversify the faculty, they mostly focused on increasing the number of white faculty on their campuses. Harold Wenglinsky, "Students at Historically Black Colleges and Universities: Their Aspirations and Accomplishments," Educational Testing Service, Princeton, NJ Policy Information Center, August 1997, 7.

88. *Spelman College Fact Book, 2004–5.*

89. Annual President's Report, 1975–76; *Spelman College Fact Book, 2004–5.* SA. Longitudinal statistics suggest that from 1997 to 2003 the faculty was fairly equal not only by race and gender but also in terms of rank, degrees, salary, and tenure status.

90. *Spelman College Bulletins,* 1960–61, 1964–65, 1970–71, 1975–76, 1985–86, 1990–91, 1995–96, 2000–2001.

91. Peter Schmidt, "Affirmative Action Has Failed to Integrate Colleges, Report Says," *Chronicle of Higher Education,* January 17, 2003, p. A-20.

92. As Dr. Audrey Forbes Manley, the seventh president of the college, has noted: "Spelman College exists today because of the collective sacrifices, wisdom, strengths, challenges and successes of its forbears." *Blueprint for the Future,* Spelman College Strategic Plan 2010. SA.

10

"Trust and Dare"

Adaptations and Innovation at the College of Notre Dame

Dorothy M. Brown and Eileen O'Dea, SSND

Reviewing the programs of the College of Notre Dame of Maryland in 1960, a visiting team from the Commission on Higher Education of the Middle States Association began its report with a most unsixties introduction. It noted that "the quiet dignity of the College and its community of Sisters, the seriousness of purpose in instruction, and the loyalty of the lay faculty are striking." The report reiterated the "quiet dignity" phrase in a section on students, declaring: "The quiet dignity of the students reflects the distinctive virtues of gracious living apparent everywhere on the campus."[1] It was in every sense the quiet before the storm.

In the next four decades, Notre Dame made the crucial decision to remain primarily a women's college, initiated a strategy of curricular innovation and risk taking that assured its survival, and affirmed its mission and tradition of meeting the needs of the underserved. Its creative leaders lived the words of the founder of their religious congregation of the School Sisters of Notre Dame: "Trust and dare."[2]

The Beginnings

Founded in 1873 as a Collegiate Institute in Baltimore, the College of Notre Dame of Maryland received its charter from the State of Maryland in 1896. Authorized to award undergraduate and graduate degrees, in 1899 it became the first Catholic college for women in the United States to award the AB degree. The founding congregation, the School Sisters of Notre Dame (SSND), had sent its first missionary sisters from Munich, Germany, to the United States in 1847. With motherhouses in Baltimore and Milwaukee, the congregation rapidly expanded and became known for its effective teaching in elementary and secondary schools in dioceses up and down the east coast and in the Midwest. By 1925 its College of Notre Dame was among the first wave of colleges and universities to receive regional accreditation from the Middle States Association, having one hundred students, the requisite minimum. While Notre Dame was initially primarily a residential college, the economic depression of the 1930s brought increasing numbers of commuter students. By the 1960s the day students outnumbered the residents. Like the pioneering colleges for women, Mt. Holyoke, Vassar, Wellesley, and Bryn Mawr, Notre Dame grounded its programs in the liberal arts and sought no quarter from men's or coed universities. The goal was always quality.[3] At Notre Dame, not surprisingly, a distinctive strength was teaching.

Surveys of Notre Dame's graduates indicated a good number who became teachers and many who pursued further education. In 1959 a survey of 550 alumnae found 61 percent married; 50 percent had elected further study after the AB; 16 percent had received graduate or professional degrees. The greatest number (272) were teachers, followed by those in science research, in business, and in social work. In their comments, alumnae repeatedly credited their education for providing a sense of independence, confidence, faith, and values. One observed: "I can only say that I am intellectually curious. I do not think I shall ever know enough"[4]

Changing Dynamics: Notre Dame and the State

Notre Dame shared in the educational ferment, reforms, and expansion of the late 1950s and 1960s. Two developments in particular enabled the college to gain the outside funding needed for further expansion. The first, generally cited as disincorporation, altered the nature of governance at Notre Dame. In 1957 the college was incorporated as an independent educational institution in the state of Maryland, transferring administrative authority and financial responsibility from the SSND community to the board of trustees. Its all-SSND membership was augmented with two laypersons. The president and board would now seek funds from the federal government and the state of Maryland, as well as foundations.

Notre Dame had an ambitious five-year plan for 1958–63. A new science building and chapel and expansion of the faculty were goals.[5] Additionally, as the preparatory and lower schools moved from the Charles Street campus to Baltimore County, the college's signature tower building, Gibbons Hall, had to be renovated for college classrooms and administration. Although the board approved the new building projects, the president, Sister Margaret Mary O'Connell, also sought the approval not only of the SSND provincial but also of the mother general in Rome.[6]

A second development that enabled Notre Dame and other sectarian colleges to receive government funding was a lengthy battle in the courts. The question of institutional autonomy and the church affiliation of the College of Notre Dame was formally addressed in the Maryland courts in *The Horace Mann League v. J. Millard Tawes* (1964). The Horace Mann League, an association of public school administrators and advocates, sought an injunction to halt awarding funds to Notre Dame and other sectarian colleges, arguing that the plaintiffs were being taxed for a religious and nonpublic purpose and that the funding violated the First Amendment of the Constitution.[7] In the summer of 1966, the Maryland Court of Appeals ruled for the plaintiffs, stating that the "ethos that permeated these institutions made it impossible to differentiate between the religious and secular aspects of their operations." State aid, the court ruled, was unconstitutional. The decision stood, as the U.S. Supreme Court refused to review the case.[8] Still, Notre Dame moved forward and secured a loan agreement with the U.S. commissioner of education for the Knott science building in January 1966. It was dedicated and ready for students in 1967.

Five years after *Mann*, in *Tilton v. Richardson* in 1971, the U.S. Supreme Court ruled that aid for construction to church-related colleges did not violate the "no establishment" clause if certain criteria were met: that aid was given for a secular purpose, that the primary effect of the aid was neither to advance nor hinder religion, and that the program did not entail "excessive entanglement" of government with religious bodies.[9] Subsequently, presidents from the Maryland Independent College and University Association journeyed to Annapolis and successfully convinced Governor Marvin Mandel to support state funds for private institutions, stressing the cost to the state if it had to absorb and educate the students from those institutions. The legislature appropriated $2 million a year to be apportioned among the twenty-four private colleges and universities.[10]

The ACLU and Americans United for Separation of Church and State (looking for a test of *Tilton*) quickly filed suit in *Roemer v. Board of Public Works* (1972) for an injunction blocking any award of Maryland funds to church-affiliated colleges. The federal district court panel ruled two to one for the state, arguing that the institutions were "substantially autonomous." In 1976, the Supreme Court in a five-to-four vote affirmed the decision that the Maryland statute did not violate the "no establishment" clause of the First Amendment. The College of Notre Dame of Maryland and the other sectarian colleges named in *Roemer*, the Court found, respected academic freedom and were "not pervasively sectarian."[11] One historian concluded: "It is probably no exaggeration to say that the Roemer decision made the difference between life and death for many church-related institutions."[12]

New Challenges: Exploring Federation

The years between *Mann* and *Roemer* in 1964 and 1976 were tumultuous for the nation and U.S. higher education. Campuses responded to protests over racial and economic injustice, over the war in Vietnam, over the gender gap, over relevance in curricula, over lack of voice in institutional governance. It was "movement" time for civil rights, youth, women, and peace. Catholic colleges and universities also responded to the changes proposed in documents of the Second Vatican Council. Women's colleges confronted decisions by all-male universities like Yale and Georgetown to become coeducational institutions. All this occurred in the context of changing economic and demographic realities: the stagflation of the 1970s and the end of the baby boom. For a Catholic women's college like Notre Dame of Maryland, it proved a time of enormous challenge and change.

In the tumultuous year of 1968, with the nation and Baltimore rocked by assassinations and race riots, Notre Dame's president for eighteen years, Sister Margaret Mary, submitted her letter of resignation to the board. Her successor, Sister Mary Elissa McGuire, an associate professor of economics with known acumen in investing, seemed a logical choice to board members (and quite a few members of the faculty) to deal with financial challenges. Appointed acting president in the summer of 1968, Sister Elissa had certainly not sought the office and always insisted on the "acting" in her title. Yet decisions made during her three years in office, in particular the decision to stay the course as a women's college, proved crucial for the identity and future direction of Notre Dame.[13]

One of the greatest challenges facing the new leadership was declining enrollment in the college. In the fall of 1968 Notre Dame's full-time enrollment stood at 731 students in its traditional day program, the fifth year the total exceeded seven hundred, and the last. Its Catholic college neighbors in north Baltimore, Loyola College, founded by the Jesuits (enrollment of about eight hundred men) and Mount Saint Agnes, established by the Sisters of Mercy (enrollment of about four hundred women), also faced declining enrollments. Mount Saint Agnes, however, was in dire financial straits. As early as the spring of 1967, Loyola's president, Joseph Sellinger, S.J., asked Father William Kelly, a Jesuit newly appointed as academic vice president with a track record as a troubleshooter, to explore possible tricollege cooperation. Father Kelly approached Notre Dame's academic dean, Sister Bridget Marie Engelmeyer, to discuss a possible merger.[14] Mount Saint Agnes could no longer continue alone. Some action, he believed, was imperative.

The presidents of Loyola, Notre Dame, and St. Agnes appointed a Tri-College Coordinating Committee, chaired by Kelly, to explore the various options for their institutions. Mount Saint Agnes's representatives spoke for a merger, while Loyola and Notre Dame favored more cooperation in developing the strengths of each college. Notre Dame department chairs took the lead in arranging meetings with their counterparts at the other two colleges. At Kelly's suggestion, Loyola and Mount Saint Agnes arranged to be visited by the same Middle States evaluating team in 1969.[15] The team, while evaluating the separate strengths and challenges of each institution, also considered the potential for cooperation.

Both colleges received reaccreditation from the Middle States Commission on Higher Education, but the team report, in considering cooperation, contained a sobering observation. "The central question," the team concluded, "is not whether and how they can improve their programs, but whether they can survive another decade." Mount Saint Agnes's recently appointed lay president, John H. Ford, wrote to Lawrence Cardinal Shehan concurring with the team's concern. The total enrollment was fewer than four hundred, the deficit was $200,000, and the Sisters of Mercy had announced that they could not provide any funds. Ford concluded: "To summarize my convictions about Mt. St. Agnes College, I would have to say the position is nothing less than perilous." "Unless," he continued, "there be decisive and timely steps taken to, in some manner, unify the efforts of the three Catholic colleges of Baltimore, I believe it quite appropriate to question the eventual survival of any of them." When a Middle States team visited Notre Dame in February 1970, its report gently added to the pressure for cooperation, observing: "Notre Dame has an opportunity to provide insights for all of higher education in the way that it responds to the cooperative framework with Loyola and Mt. St. Agnes."[16]

One month later, the Tri-College Committee of administrators and faculty recommended that the three colleges be federated by September 1971, although "federation" was left undefined.[17] The committee asserted that a liberal arts college should have at least a thousand students and "that neither Mount Saint Agnes nor Notre Dame can in the foreseeable future achieve alone a student population range of 800–1000." Federation, they argued, would have several advantages in securing grants and loans and financial aid resources.

Loyola's board responded positively to the recommendation for federation. In April 1970, it passed a resolution stating: "In the interest of continuing high quality higher education under Catholic auspices in the Baltimore metropolitan area, the Board of Trustees of Loyola College is committed to joining our two sister institutions, the College of Notre Dame of Maryland and Mount Saint Agnes College, in a federation." The board proposed that the operations of Loyola and Mount Saint Agnes be brought together on Loyola's campus by September 1971. The board of Mount Saint Agnes also supported federation and passed a similar resolution at its May meeting.[18]

Notre Dame, however, was not ready to support federation. Its board deferred acting on a federation proposal pending Sister Bridget Marie's consultation with the faculty. (She found they were for cooperation but not a merger.) Notre Dame proposed instead that the three colleges continue efforts to increase their level of cooperation. At a special board meeting on July 13, 1970, Sister Kathleen Feeley, soon to be selected by the board as president-elect, suggested specific areas that might be explored for economy and efficiency. They included plant maintenance, telephone service, security, purchasing, counseling, and placement. During 1970–71, she suggested, departmental chairs of the three colleges could work out cooperation "department by department." The co-institutional proposal saw "dedicated women and men working together to maintain quality higher education under Catholic auspices, . . . facilitating greater academic and social interaction among the students, thus providing a unique campus atmosphere." The bottom line was: "At the present time Notre Dame is not in favor of a complete merger into one institution but it does not rule out the possibility at some future time." Trustee Thomas Larkin, reviewing the proposal, noted that in business mergers it was "essential that the top administrative echelon of each institution desire a merger." Larkin did not perceive trust as "the prevailing atmosphere" at the colleges. The board voted acceptance of the proposal with the one dissenting vote of Henry Knott, who

Sr. Kathleen Feeley, SSND, President, CND, responsible for the creation of the Weekend College, Continuing Education, graduate programs, and the Renaissance Institute. *Archives of the College of Notre Dame. Date unknown.*

argued that the question ought to be what was best for Catholic higher education in Baltimore—not for any individual college. While he preferred a merger,
Knott voted finally to support the Notre Dame co-institutional proposal.[19]

Sister Elissa, however, and the board of trustees were clear that Notre Dame
had to be creative in charting a future course for itself. Sister Elissa asked Sister
Kathleen Feeley to assume the leadership of a broad-based community discussion on identity and direction. The project was appropriately titled Quest.

Quest, the reflective process under the direction of Sister Kathleen, convened in September 1970. In a "day of dialogue" members from various constituencies of the college discussed a range of possibilities for the future direction of
the college. More than 150 gathered, including seven of eleven members of the
board of trustees; fifty-five faculty; thirty-eight alumnae, parents, and friends;
sixty students; and all members of the administration. Sister Kathleen remembered that "everybody turned out and worked well." The Quest participants
considered a variety of options: to continue the present limited exchange of
students while remaining independent of any structural alliance with Loyola
and Mount Saint Agnes; to consider a federation and its gains and losses; to
examine gains and losses in a merger and in co-institutional cooperation. At
the end of the day, the overwhelming sentiment was to cooperate but not to
merge. Two consensus decisions emerged: a pledge to work co-institutionally
with Loyola–Mount Saint Agnes to achieve the advantages possible through
academic cooperation, and a recommitment to women's education.

The student newspapers, *Columns* at Notre Dame and the *Greyhound* at
Loyola, had been following the merger-cooperation talks closely. After the
Notre Dame decision, a *Greyhound* editorial asserted that the "pigheadedness"
of Notre Dame administrators had doomed the merger. It suggested that the
student governments and newspapers of each college organize to press for a
merger from the ground up. A flurry of front-page responses in *Columns* heatedly took issue with the "pigheadedness" allegation. Notre Dame's decision,
Columns editors reported, had come only after broad community participation
and discussion.[20]

In September 1970, as Notre Dame affirmed its decision not to merge,
Mount Saint Agnes and Loyola announced their decision to merge and to
become coeducational in the fall of 1971. Appearing on a local television news
program, Father Sellinger, joined by the acting president of Mount Saint Agnes
(then Elizabeth Geen), informed the Baltimore public of the merger, announcing that there would be one college, named Loyola College, and that he would
be its president.

Exploring Interinstitutional Cooperation:
Notre Dame and Loyola

While Notre Dame turned away from a merger, it did work with Loyola to create a joint library. In 1967 the administrations and boards of the two colleges agreed to create a new independent corporation, the Loyola–Notre Dame Library. Notre Dame provided 90 percent of the land (in lieu of some capital funds); the colleges agreed to a 50–50 percentage funding for construction and insurance; other shared costs would be based on enrollments and usage. The new facility had the capacity to hold 300,000 volumes, doubling the combined shelf space of Loyola and Notre Dame. In the board of trustees' discussion at its special July 1970 meeting, board member George Constable set out the factors converging to force a decision on the library: Notre Dame's declining enrollment and thus financial difficulty, the impending merger of Loyola and Mount Saint Agnes into one collegiate administration, and the impetus of the government loan subsidy for the library. Sister Elissa reminded the board that originally, "when Notre Dame entered into the cooperative agreement it was with the understanding that Loyola would not go coed." Notre Dame, she reported, had "made a statement to the effect that we expect Loyola to remain a men's college." At the September 1970 Notre Dame board meeting, Sister Elissa bridled at a suggestion that Notre Dame, which had some room vacancies, should open its dormitories for neighboring institutions. "Notre Dame," she asserted "should not become a service station."[21]

Five years later when Loyola wanted to purchase ten acres of land adjacent to the joint library, the Notre Dame board unanimously agreed not to sell. Board member Sister Paula asked: "What businessman would ever listen to a suggestion that he surrender part of his building or facilities to his chief competitor in order that the competitor might function more effectively?" Sister Kathleen at the December board meeting observed that given the recent history, Notre Dame would only be willing to lease land "if we could both turn over a page which would obliterate the suspicion, loss of faith and rivalry which events of the past had engendered." In 1977 Loyola renewed the request, having secured a donor willing to pay $50,000 an acre for the ten acres. In a letter to Sister Kathleen, Henry Knott advised her to accept the offer: "The refusal to do this, in my humble judgment, would irreparably damage your image in the community, since you have no need of it." The offer was rejected.[22]

Innovation and Expansion:
Continuing Education and Weekend College

Sister Kathleen observed that after these decisive events she and the college never looked back. Beginning her presidency in the fall of 1971, she was acutely aware of the critical need for enrollment and revenue.[23] The college had to grow.

Left to right: Sr. Margaret Mary, SSND, president, College of Notre Dame; Rev. Joseph Sellinger, SJ, president of Loyola College; and Henry J. Knott, CND board member were involved in discussions of cooperative relations with Loyola College in 1971. *Archives of the College of Notre Dame.*

Sister Kathleen's first initiative was to expand the number of students with a new continuing-education program. Notre Dame hired alumna Mary Lu McNeal, someone who would be aware of the anxiety, and sometimes fear, some older women faced as they returned to the classroom. McNeal had earned an MA and returned to Notre Dame in the early 1950s as personnel director and instructor in political science; she had then taken time out to raise her family.

The Continuing Education program enabled many middle-aged women like those shown here to return to college. *Archives of the College of Notre Dame. Date unknown.*

Sister Kathleen sent her to Mundelein College in Chicago to study its successful continuing-education program. McNeal then consulted with administrators at George Washington University and contracted to have members of their faculty come to Notre Dame to offer their Developing New Horizons, a successful program of guidance and counseling for adult women. The board approved $10,000 for start-up funds in 1972. McNeal began on a part-time basis with a part-time secretary. To market the program, she planned conferences, sometimes jointly developed with Goucher College and Essex Community College, designed to bring women to the campus to discuss issues and ideas. City councilwoman Barbara Mikulski and political activist Mary Pat Clarke were supportive and encouraged women to consider the opportunities available at the college.

Two hundred and three women enrolled in the first continuing education courses in the 1972–73 sessions. McNeal interviewed each one. Most were in their forties or fifties. "The intent," McNeal noted, "was to provide a welcoming environment where an older student could be assimilated gradually into the academic community." McNeal remembered the arrival of one alumna with her four children, one a baby in her arms, and no money. She advised her to take courses in a community college (for the low tuition) and then to come to Notre Dame. Students could prepare a portfolio to be evaluated for credit or waivers and use the College Level Examination Program (CLEP). Regular faculty did the advising. For the first courses, which were offered only for the continuing-education students, McNeal attracted some of the best teachers. While there was early resistance by some faculty, word soon spread that the adult women were wonderful assets in the classroom. As more women entered the program, they were integrated into regular day courses. Enrollment and tuition revenue rose.[24] But it was not enough.

Notre Dame administrators next explored the possibility of a graduate program. In 1973 Sister Mary Oliver Hudon became an assistant professor of education and was given a special presidential assignment to investigate the feasibility of graduate programs for Notre Dame. Sister Oliver began by interviewing department chairs. It was not a promising start. They were generally adamant against graduate programs, fearing they would weaken the undergraduate curricula and the commitment to teaching. Meanwhile, Sister Kathleen witnessed the opening of the pioneering, innovative weekend college program of Mundelein College. She had seen the future and, as she phrased it, "took the ball and ran."[25]

Returning to Notre Dame, she told Sister Oliver to stop working on graduate issues and to begin developing a weekend college program. Sister Oliver, like McNeal, was dispatched to Mundelein. The Mundelein director advised her that the key to success was to select influential faculty and get them interested. They would sell it. There were major hurdles to surmount. Faculty, concerned with the compression of courses, raised the issue of time and credit hours. Sister Oliver countered that adult students did more work on their own outside the classroom. The content of their courses could be delivered, but in a different mode. Weekend College would admit adult women and men, and the admission of men proved a significant point of concern and contention. After a series of meetings and focus groups, the weekend college proposal still had a "tough ride" with the curriculum committee. Nevertheless, it went forward with a mandate from Sister Kathleen.[26]

Although there had been no formal feasibility study or external scan, Sister Oliver and Sister Kathleen were aware that a number of other Maryland colleges were considering weekend degree programs. They determined to be the first. The telegenic Sister Mary Oliver appeared on local TV to promote the new weekend college. Radio ads and posters on the backs of buses announced the program. An article in the *Baltimore Sun,* December 4, 1974, set out the details. Weekend College was "for working adults who have always wanted to go to college, but couldn't." Students would enroll in courses that met every third week for fifteen weeks. Concentrations were in business, communications, and interpersonal dynamics, all grounded in the liberal arts. Classes began on Friday evening and were offered through Sunday morning. Residence-hall rooms were available to women and men on a limited basis. The program opened in January 1975 with eighty-one students—sixty women and twenty-one men.[27]

As the director of Weekend College, Sister Oliver, like McNeal in Continuing Education, offered highly personalized assistance. She interviewed each student who matriculated. She found that many of the women had worked to support their husbands' educations and interrupted their own; others had hit a glass ceiling at work; others, after separation or divorce, were seeking credentials. The men usually had managerial jobs but lacked credentials.[28]

Like Continuing Education, Weekend College had a lean administration, consisting of Sister Oliver and one full-time secretary. Start-up funds were modest, with the board agreeing to the transfer of $14,500 from quasi-endowment. Faculty provided the advising. Sister Oliver was available every weekend for advising, troubleshooting, coffee making, or envelope stuffing.

The academic concept was of one faculty teaching in all of Notre Dame's programs. At the beginning, the Weekend College courses were offered by faculty who volunteered. (Continuing Education worried that their "cream" would be skimmed off by the new entity.) Eventually, letters of appointment and contract renewals stated that faculty could be expected to teach in any of the programs of the college.

In its first twenty years of existence, the Weekend College grew rapidly and became a central component of Notre Dame. In the spring semester of 1977, 141 students enrolled in weekend college programs, 386 for the academic year. Two years later, responding to a request from four local Catholic hospitals who had closed their RN education programs, Weekend College launched a BS in nursing. It was the first program at Notre Dame offered only in Weekend College, but, as Sister Oliver stated, Notre Dame believed it could contribute to Catholic health care in Baltimore. It was an entirely new area for the college, but one clearly grounded in its mission. It met Sister Kathleen's test for program development. "Always," she said, "keep your eye on what women need. Notre

Dame works to empower women."[29] In 1986 the Middle States team, while urging the faculty and administration to continue to monitor the Weekend College programs to ensure that they were "comparable with the high quality of those taught in the traditional schedule," concluded: "The success that the College of Notre Dame has experienced in its Weekend College program cannot be overstated."[30] There were 909 students enrolled in the Weekend College in the fall semester of 1985; ten years later in the fall semester, there were 1,778.[31] By comparison, in the fall of 1985, there were 481 full-time students enrolled in the day program of the women's college; in 1995, there were 615.

The report of the 1980 visiting team from the Middle States Association had echoed the 1960 team on the "quiet dignity" evident in campus culture. They found that "permeating the life of Notre Dame is a sense of cheerfulness, ease and calm; life seems gracious and whole and unhurried by the effects of fragmentation present in so many institutions today." "Notre Dame," the report continued, "has a long and important tradition in higher education, yet it may best be described at this moment as being endowed with potential, and potential could be construed as a plus or minus." The "key question" faced by the college was fiscal stability. Planning was imperative.[32]

Sister Kathleen continued her strategy of developing new programs. In 1983 a program in English as a Second Language was launched to prepare international students for admission to U.S. colleges, including Notre Dame. SANDALS, Summer at Notre Dame: Academic Leadership Skills, was also established in 1977, a summer program for less-privileged girls in Baltimore who, again, would be better prepared to elect college. The Morrissy Honors Program was instituted in 1982 for the best students. Notre Dame administrators also sought to attract students from local community colleges.

Optimistically, the Long Range Planning Committee set a goal of one thousand full-time women students in the day program. When the 1980 Middle States team arrived, the goal was not in sight. Recognizing the significant turnover in the Admissions Office, the team recommended revising the goal realistically downward, engaging an experienced professional as admissions director, and providing her with support and consultants to assist in realizing enrollment objectives. It suggested working for better articulation with the community colleges for direct transfer programs. The team report concluded, however, that it was clear that Notre Dame students in all of the college programs were "happy about attending Notre Dame; they like the College and are articulately enthusiastic about it."[33]

Adaptation and Innovation: Graduate Education

Sister Oliver, who had so successfully launched and directed the Weekend College, was appointed academic dean in 1978. One of her first important charges from Sister Kathleen was to return to a consideration of graduate studies. A feasibility study and long-range plan were completed in 1982. Both supported the development of graduate programs. At its May meeting in 1983, the board of trustees heard the report of Sister Oliver, who asserted that graduate programs would meet the need for diversification, enhance the undergraduate program, and meet a demand identified in market studies. Surveys of students and graduates of the Weekend College found that many wished to continue their education at Notre Dame. Proposed were two MA programs, a master of administrative sciences, with specializations in human-resource management and health-care administration, and an MA in education with concentrations in instructional leadership and mathematics education. Both would be offered through the Weekend College format.[34] Approved by the Maryland State Board of Higher Education in May 1984, Notre Dame initiated its MA in administrative sciences, admitting sixty-six women and men in the fall semester. By the spring of 1985, a faculty group was developing a proposal for a new MA in liberal studies.[35] This was followed in 1988 by an MA in adulthood and aging. The 1986 Middle States team report had urged the college to "be cautious" about adding graduate programs. Reviewing Notre Dame's required five-year Periodic Review Report in 1992, another Middle States committee observed it was not immediately evident what caution has been exercised when adding these programs.[36] Graduate enrollments for the fall 1991 semester totaled 343.[37]

The major expansion of the graduate division occurred in the 1990s in education. Sister Kathleen, who actively recruited SSNDs for administrative or faculty positions, brought Sister Sharon Slear to Notre Dame to create graduate programs in education, building on the college's strong undergraduate record and reputation in education. Notre Dame had approved an undergraduate Accelerated Certificate in Teaching Program in 1987 (ACT). Sister Sharon and the faculty developed a fifteen-credit graduate certificate program in curriculum and instruction in 1989, followed by an MA in leadership in teaching in 1992 and, two years later, by a master of arts in teaching (MAT). Partnership agreements were completed with the Departments of Education of Baltimore City and Baltimore County. Courses were offered at centers in Harford and Anne Arundel counties and in southern Maryland. Graduate enrollments in the education programs exceeded one thousand in the fall of 2000. In 2002, graduate and undergraduate programs in education were reviewed and received National Council for the Accreditation of Teacher Education (NCATE) accreditation. In 2004, the Maryland Higher Education Commission approved a PhD program in instructional leadership for changing populations.[38]

Adaptation and Innovation: "55 and Better"

Meanwhile, Notre Dame initiated a program for those "55 and better" in the Baltimore community. Sister Kathleen turned again to Mary Lu McNeal, who had so successfully launched adult education, for a new adult initiative. McNeal did her homework. Attending a conference on adult programming in Washington, she heard of the experiences at Harvard, Northwestern, and Berkeley. The program director at the University of Rochester advised her that starting a program for adults was like "starting a locomotive and then getting out of the way as it roared down the track." McNeal surveyed programs at Johns Hopkins and American University to avoid duplication. She visited church groups and women's clubs. Through community outreach, she identified and invited interested women and men to Notre Dame to share their ideas on curriculum (noncredit offerings) and administration.

In 1989 the Renaissance Institute was launched. While Mary Lu McNeal was the part-time director (again with a part-time secretary), the Renaissance Institute followed a self-governing model. Members paid an annual fee to join and selected its nine-member council. McNeal was helped in recruiting by an Elderhostel mailing list, but also remembered going "anywhere and everywhere to talk about it." After a reception in May, the institute was launched with fifteen courses. Essentially they embodied Sister Kathleen's vision that the Renaissance Institute should have academic, spiritual, and social components. Volunteer

The Renaissance Institute has brought older students back into the classroom. *Archives of the College of Notre Dame.*

faculty, generally from the membership or recently retired from the college, were not paid. A tutor from St. John's College in Annapolis met with faculty and coordinators on working with adults in tutoring programs. By 1992 the Renaissance Institute received national recognition for its programming and innovation.[39] While it did not expand enrollment or tuition income, it did meet a need that Sister Kathleen perceived in the Baltimore community, and had the potential to expand the outreach of the college into new communities and possibly to attract new donors.

An Institution with Many Facets

Notre Dame was sustaining itself through curricular innovation and emphasizing a traditional strength in its student-centered programs. In addition to the traditional undergraduate college for women, Continuing Education, the Weekend College, expanding graduate programs, the English Language Institute, and the Renaissance Institute, the college added a Child's Place, a preschool program, in 1985 and a Women's Institute, a noncredit program for women in the community, in 1991. Sister Kathleen, the academic dean observed, believed that if you weren't doing anything new, you weren't doing anything.[40]

Given the multifaceted growth of Notre Dame, the college confronted questions of mission. It revised its mission statement in February 1977, trenchantly stating: "The Mission of the College of Notre Dame of Maryland is to provide, primarily for women, a liberal arts education in the context of the Judeo-Christian tradition."[41] The Middle States team that visited Notre Dame in 1986, however, strongly recommended "that the College review its mission statement to be certain it reflects Notre Dame at this time, including its graduate programs, men in some programs, career preparation within a strong liberal arts tradition, community centeredness, globally concerned orientation and sensitive awareness to individual needs." Yet at the same time, the team agreed that "in a world of conflicting and often dubious values, the College of Notre Dame's commitment to values is admirable." Sister Delia Dowling, the academic dean, saw the college's mission, as interpreted and expanded by Sister Kathleen, as inclusive, adding diverse populations, while remaining grounded in the essentials: Notre Dame was Catholic, committed to the liberal arts, and primarily for women.[42]

Faculty and Student Issues

The exponential growth of the Weekend College and graduate programs did place a strain on faculty and students. While the 1986 Middle States team had found an "enthusiastic, optimistic, enviable esprit de corps evident among the Notre Dame faculty," it also saw a faculty that was overextended. No faculty member, the team asserted, should teach more than five days a week. The administration had to recognize the different demands of graduate teaching and preparation and advising as it determined a full-time faculty load. An earlier Middle States team had commented on the talented and "sacrificial" service of the faculty.

Notre Dame responded by raising faculty salaries and addressing the financial challenge posed by the decline in women religious. The SSND faculty members had comprised a "living endowment" of the college through their "contributed services." The estimated value of their donated services in 1990 was $330,099. With the decline in vocations experienced by all religious communities and in anticipation of reduced reliance on SSNDs, the Notre Dame board planned to absorb the loss of those services and also began to pay the religious faculty at the same salary scale as their lay colleagues. While the administration and board had set a salary target in 1980 of reaching the 60th percentile of the Class II B AAUP salary standard for faculty, that was not achieved for the senior ranks until 1991.[43] The AAUP annual listing of faculty salaries found Notre Dame continuing to lag behind its Maryland neighbors in this area.[44]

In the student area, the recruitment, enrollment, and retention of eighteen- to twenty-one-year-old women in the traditional day program needed sustained attention. When Loyola opened in the fall of 1971 as a coed institution, full-time enrollment at Notre Dame dropped from 617 to 549 students. In 1975, when the enrollment had dipped to 509 in the day program, the Budget Committee of the board of trustees reported a sense of "deep concern," stating: "Student enrollment, which is the life blood of the college, had declined drastically. Since income depends chiefly upon student enrollment, it seems logical to expect that if this source of income declines, there should be a parallel curtailment in expenditures, if we hope to operate on an even keel."[45] To attract more students, the director of admissions successfully lobbied for more scholarship funds in the budget, particularly for National Merit students, and won increased financial support for her office.[46] Sister Kathleen, convinced that Notre Dame's product was "right" but the "selling is wrong," tried a series of admissions directors.

One variable in recruiting and retention is always the quality of student life. As Notre Dame and Loyola were discussing cooperation in 1970, Notre Dame's students were pressing for parietals. In a letter to the parents of resident students in March 1970, the chair of the student parietal committee explained that "parietal refers to male visitors being allowed in girls' rooms at certain specified times." There was, the letter declared, inadequate lounge space. Parietals would not only allow visits in a more relaxed atmosphere but also give students the opportunity to demonstrate that they could accept responsibilities. The students had surveyed policies at comparable institutions. Their internal student survey showed overwhelming support for parietals on Saturday and Sunday afternoons. (Only twenty-two parents responded to the student letter;

fourteen were against parietals.) Two members of the board did meet with the students. At its September 1970 meeting, the board passed a resolution that "no male visitors be permitted in the girls' rooms at any time."

The issue did not die. Three years later, student resident leaders met Sister Kathleen in an open forum to discuss parietals again. The board, after a flurry of letters pro and con from students, faculty, and administrators, appointed a committee chaired by Sister Kathleen to consider the student request. In the summer, the head of the Parents and Friends organization sent a letter to parents asking for a response, stating: "We are interested in preserving the principles and moral stability of the oldest, Catholic all girls college in America." In all caps, she urged, "TAKE A LONG LOOK AT THE RESULT OF PARIETALS IN OTHER CATHOLIC INSTITUTIONS." One parent heatedly wrote: "Most parents do not wish to pay for education that includes dormitory training in seduction, promiscuity, and prostitution."

Meanwhile, Sister Kathleen was not only confronting this parental outburst, but also facing determined students who were threatening to ignore restrictions. She warned that violators would be brought before the Committee on Student Affairs and could face immediate suspension. "Decisions," she insisted, "must be made according to principle, not pressure." Forwarding a packet of materials on parietals to the academic dean, she wrote: "Speaking personally, it is draining psychic energy out of me, and I am almost at the end of my supply." Parietals and the students eventually won the day and fulfilled the dean's prediction that, once approved, the hours for visitation would be expanded. In all the turmoil of the 1960s and early 1970s, parietals was the issue that most aroused the student voice at Notre Dame.[47] It was the issue that marked the most significant transformation of residence life on women's campuses since the 1920s.

In 1982, Mary Laverty, with her doctorate in the field of higher education and with student affairs experience at Saint Mary's, Indiana, was appointed the first lay dean of students after a national search. Laverty found a rich tradition and good foundation of services to build on. She chose a wellness model, encompassing physical, spiritual, emotional, and cultural aspects.

Under Laverty's leadership, the college strengthened career planning and initiated a black-student mentoring program. A new Student Activities Office instituted International Week. An intercampus program board organized events with Goucher, Towson, Loyola, and Johns Hopkins. When a new computer lab replaced the student pub, Laverty worked to establish a social center. Called the Charles Street Connection, it provided a center on the weekends and a place to eat and gather during the day. Recognizing that renovation and expansion of the gym facilities in LeClerc Hall were imperative since the current space did not meet NCAA specifications for intercollegiate competition, Laverty won administrative and board support for a new sports complex.[48] The facility was one of the major priorities in the Capital Campaign, Second Spring, launched in 1979. By the 1990s, as Title IX enhanced the opportunities and visibility of women in sports, Notre Dame fielded varsity teams in NCAA Division III competition in basketball, field hockey, lacrosse, soccer, swimming, tennis, and volleyball. It became one of the most highly successful competitors in the Atlantic Women's Colleges Conference.

Lafferty's successors in student affairs developed programs consonant with the SSND mission to develop women "who can transform the world." A Certificate in Leadership and Social Change rigorously combined academic courses and service, culminating in a capstone seminar with a student-designed plan and then action to address a social issue.

An on-campus social challenge for Catholic campuses with the emerging gay rights movement was how to be supportive of their gay and lesbian students and to respect the diversity of their faculties. Support but not advocacy was the general Catholic college practice toward gay and lesbian groups, and was the practice at Notre Dame for the Lesbian and Friends group and an "ally" program of lesbian faculty.[49]

Raising Money

Securing the financial resources to support quality educational programs at Notre Dame was a continuing major challenge. Sister Kathleen's central strategy was program expansion to increase enrollments and revenues with new populations, while sustaining the core women's four-year college. The strategy kept the Notre Dame budget in the black throughout the 1980s. Like all college presidents, she was also energetic in seeking additional resources, working with the Maryland Independent College and University Association to secure state funding for each Maryland student educated and a state program of capital funds available to the colleges on a regular, rotating basis.

To further enhance fund-raising efforts, the board approved the appointment of a director of development in 1973 to identify individual donors, develop grant proposals, and initiate capital campaigns. An SSND colleague in the Development Office remembered Sister Kathleen's keen disappointment each time she failed to convince a donor to support the college. Sister Kathleen remembered innocent beginnings, noting: "I think I thought people would give money to nuns."[50]

The board further aided fund-raising by providing Notre Dame leadership with strategy, wealthy connections, and individual donations. Board members Bernard Trueschler, the president of the Baltimore Gas and Electric Company, and Francis X. Knott of the Arundel Corporation provided key leadership for the Second Spring campaign. (Trueschler named Sister Kathleen to the BG&E Board, which gave her good connections with the Baltimore business community.) The Second Spring Campaign targeted the renovation of LeClerc Hall and Economy Hall for a computer center, renovation of Gibbons, Theresa, and Mary Meletia halls, as well as endowment for scholarships and faculty salaries.[51] The Marion Burk Knott Sports Complex was the most tangible, immediate evidence of its success.[52] At the end of the capital campaigns of the 1970s and early 1980s, the market value of the endowment had increased from $2.7 to $12.5 million.

Notre Dame's Evolving Identity

Notre Dame continued to explore possible ways to cooperate with its neighbor, Loyola. In 1981 Loyola and Notre Dame, funded by the Ford Foundation, contracted for a study on potential cooperation. Loyola's goal, the study concluded, was clearly merger; Notre Dame remained open to "cooperative efforts which would be educationally enriching and cost effective." On the other hand, Notre Dame was interested in exploring the possibility of building a joint student center on its property. The following year, a joint Loyola/Notre Dame Trustee Committee recommended that both colleges share their long-range plans. A subcommittee would be appointed to identify areas for cooperation.[53]

Yet the strategic plans of the two colleges in the 1980s and 1990s show that the colleges, each faithful to their mission, were moving farther apart rather than closer together. While both developed and expanded graduate programs and established satellite campuses, Loyola College increasingly stressed selectivity of students and research faculty. It introduced programs in art and music rather than send its students to the established programs at Notre Dame. Conversely, Notre Dame developed its business, nursing, and other professional programs while sustaining its long commitment to the liberal arts.

Notre Dame stressed accessibility and opportunity, as it had since its founding, and its commitment to the education of women. In the 1980s and 1990s, that access and opportunity were hallmarks of its programs for the adult learner and an increasingly diverse undergraduate population. Notre Dame administrators cited a National Institute of Education report on rising admissions standards which found that as institutions controlled their "inputs" they paid insufficient attention to their outputs. The academic dean, Sister Oliver, commented that "colleges that admit only the brightest students can take little pride in producing bright students." The challenge, she believed, was to take students who have the potential to succeed and prosper in Notre Dame's environment. Comparing Notre Dame to colleges like Loyola, which marketed their admissions as "highly competitive," Sister Oliver concluded: "We have a different way of approaching human potential and I don't feel ashamed of that fact. . . . We've taken the harder road."[54] The college's commitment to and care for the individual, a hallmark in each of its programs, produced a good record of "outputs" of competent, successful graduates.

In 1992, Sister Rosemarie Nassif became the college's ninth president. She had earned her PhD in physical chemistry from Catholic University. Like Sister Kathleen, she received an American Council of Education internship to prepare for her new responsibilities. She found in Notre Dame an essentially healthy institution. Sound financial aid policies were in place. An extended capital campaign, "Creating the Future," had achieved its ambitious goal of $14 million. In the academic area, with good leadership in admissions, the traditional women's college enrollments had increased. In the fall semester of 1991–92, there were 552 students in the day college; Continuing Education enrolled 212 students; Weekend College enrollments for the fall totaled 1,517, while graduate students (before the major growth in education programs) numbered 344. A Middle States Committee reviewing the college's five-year "Periodic Review Report" in 1992 found that the general studies program of the women's college had been strengthened and that the Weekend College and graduate programs were having a significant impact. In fact, the committee report concluded, "without them the College might not exist to offer its excellent Day program."[55]

Faculty grew over time in connection with the increasing number and size of the college's programs. In 1981–82, there were 63 full-time faculty and 42 adjuncts. By 1992–93, there were 7 more full-time faculty for a total of 70, and the adjuncts had more than doubled, to 94. In 1999 full-time faculty had grown to 81, of whom 55, or 68 percent, were women (and 5 percent were minorities); these numbers were approximately the same in 2004: 79 full-time faculty, of whom 53, or 67 percent, were women.[56]

Plans and Change

Sister Rosemarie moved on a series of fronts in planning. R. M. Stern Architects was chosen to develop the campus master plan for facilities, buildings, and grounds. Campbell and Associates advised on potential goals for the next capital campaign, suggesting $30 million was feasible. KPMG Peat Marwick consultants prepared an organizational assessment. An information technology assessment was completed by another consultant. Faculty, administration, and the board developed a new strategic plan and a Vision Statement for 1996–2001. The vision, as the college began its second century in 1996, was to become "A Learning Community of Excellence for the 21st Century Woman."[57]

Seemingly, a great deal of groundwork for action was in place. Yet the pace had been rapid, and suggested changes, particularly to move to a vice-presidential model administratively and a divisional model academically, evoked major concerns from faculty and student leadership. They pressed for more

involvement in these decisions and more discussion before any implementation. With the president's announcements that both the popular academic dean
and dean of students had submitted their resignations in the fall of 1995, these
concerns increased. Sister Rosemarie reported to the board that the resignations
had "created a sense of tension and turbulence on campus." The leaders of the
Faculty Senate and student government asked to meet with board members.
Their questions centered on the administrative and academic models and the
resignations. In February 1996, Sister Rosemarie announced that she would
step down in June, at the end of the centennial year of the Catholic women's
college, "simply because it was the right thing to do."[58] Sister Rosemarie met
with faculty, staff, and students. She spoke of planning, the increase in enrollments, and financial stability. The *Baltimore Sun* cited her statement that her
priority would be "to strengthen the mission of the College . . . as we chart our
second century."[59]

When a Middle States evaluation team arrived a year later, in March 1997,
they found the Notre Dame infrastructure sturdy and the college essentially in
good health in spite of these sweeping administrative changes. Like its predecessors, this team recommended attention to the college's mission statement.
The team report observed that when faculty talked of the college, they were
generally speaking of the traditional women's college. Notre Dame needed to
see itself whole and allocate its resources accordingly.[60] The team supported
a recommendation from the college's self-study that "the incoming President
should initiate and monitor a major community dialogue to explore and develop a common understanding of the relationships between the mission of the
College and the growth and diversity of the College." The report concluded by
asserting its confidence in the college's sense of its vitality, identity, and mission.
The new leadership had a unique opportunity to focus on a "New Moment."

Transition to Lay Leadership and Affirmation of the Mission

Notre Dame, like almost all other Catholic institutions, has recently appointed
more laypeople to important leadership roles as the numbers of women religious and priests continue to decline. In 1997 there were only eleven SSNDs
in a full-time faculty of seventy-five. While the chair of the board of trustees
was the provincial leader of the School Sisters of Notre Dame and members
of the congregation were also board members, the only SSND member of the
administration was Sister Eileen O'Dea, the vice president for institutional
planning.[61]

In April 1996, when the board elected as interim president an alumna,
Dorothy M. Brown, a professor of history at Georgetown University, member
of the Commission on Higher Education of the Middle States Association, and
former faculty member at Notre Dame, she became the first lay president at

Notre Dame. At the fall 1996 orientation assembly for first-year students and their parents, Brown was introduced as the interim president, followed by the acting dean, a professor of physics from Notre Dame's faculty, and the dean of students, who had been in her position for two weeks. A parent remarked with surprise, "Why, they are all new!"

In their search for a new president, the board of trustees engaged a search firm and determined that candidates could be members of the School Sisters of Notre Dame or laypeople. Their choice was Mary Pat Seurkamp, another layperson. Educated at Webster College in Missouri, then a Catholic college for women, Seurkamp had completed her doctorate in higher education at the State University of New York at Buffalo. She had served in a range of administrative positions at St. John Fisher College in Rochester, both in the academic and student affairs areas.

Like Sister Kathleen and all her predecessors, Seurkamp faced the challenges of securing the resources to support quality academic programs and of articulating, and rearticulating, the college's mission in a time of rapid change. Working with the board, she successfully completed a capital campaign of $20 million and then extended the goal to $30 million. In 2001 the market value of the endowment stood at $36 million. As she worked with faculty, students, and board members to develop a new strategic plan, she also pressed for a new mission statement. As the first permanent lay president, Seurkamp was committed to building on the vision and values of the founding congregation of the School Sisters of Notre Dame.

After extensive discussions with faculty, staff, and board members, the board approved a new mission statement in May 2002. It incorporated three goals from the SSND mission document. While the college statement retains women, liberal arts, academic excellence, and the Catholic tradition as anchors, it is broadened to encompass the changed reality of new populations and programs:

> The College of Notre Dame of Maryland educates women as leaders to transform the world. Embracing the vision of the founders, the School Sisters of Notre Dame, the College provides a liberal arts education in the Catholic tradition. Distinctive undergraduate and graduate programs challenge women and men to strive for intellectual and professional excellence, to build inclusive communities, to engage in service to others, and to promote social responsibility.[62]

Notre Dame had moved decisively, rapidly, and successfully to meet the challenges facing a Catholic women's college. In many ways, its choices and actions during the last halfcentury had modeled the words of the foundress of the SSNDs as she sent her sisters on mission—"Trust and dare." That faith and daring are no less needed for the future.

Notes

1.   *Report to Trustees, Administration, Faculty, and Students of College of Notre Dame of Maryland by An Evaluation Team, Representing the Commission on Higher Education of Middle States Association of Colleges and Schools, 1960* (hereafter Middle States Report). College of Notre Dame of Maryland Archives, (hereafter CND Archives).

2.   See *Collected Letters of Mother M. Theresa Gerhardinger, School Sister of Notre Dame,* ed. Sr. M. Hester Valentine, SSND (Winona, Minn.: St. Mary's College Press, 1977).

3.   For Collegiate Institute see Bridget Marie Engelmeyer, SSND, *Sister Ildephonsa Wegman: Footnote to Legend* (Baltimore: College of Notre Dame of Maryland, 1996). See also Sister David Cameron, *Notre Dame of Maryland 1895–1945* (New York: Declan X. McMullen Co., 1947) and Debra M. Franklin, ed., *The Heritage We Claim: College of Notre Dame of Maryland, 1896–1996.* (Baltimore: College of Notre Dame of Maryland, 1996). Mary Oates is completing a new history of the college. For context on founding Notre Dame and other Catholic women's colleges, see Kathleen A. Mahoney, "American Catholic Colleges for Women: Historical Origins," and Thomas M. Landy, "The Colleges in Context," in Tracy Schier and Cynthia Russett, eds., *Catholic Women's Colleges in America* (Baltimore: Johns Hopkins University Press, 2002).

4.   Outcomes Survey of Alumnae 1947–1959, Self-Study for Middle States 1960 visit; 653 questionnaires were sent with an 84 percent return rate. Some respondents listed more than one occupation.

5.   For notes on the general meeting of the board, March 1959, and the report of Rev. Edward V. Stanford, OSA, February 1962, an administrative consultant, see Sister Bridget Marie Engelmeyer files, 1961–62, CND Archives. The board formerly was composed of the SSND president, academic dean, treasurer, provincial, and superior. The consultant suggested developing an auxiliary board from the business community to aid in fund-raising. The board did approve hiring a professional for development. The college actually put in place a two-tiered board, with a corporation of SSND members who had to approve any sale or transfer of property. The college student newspaper, *Columns,* reported that Sister Margaret Mary received official approval from the SSND mother general the same day Governor J. Millard Tawes signed the bill for the $750,000 Maryland grant, April 18, 1962.

6.   Board of Trustees Minutes, January 11 and February 28, 1966, Minutes Book #2, CND Archives. Sister Frederick Mary interview with Sister Margaret Mary O'Connell, 1989, CND Archives.

7.   The Maryland legislature had appropriated $750,000 for a new science building if the college raised matching funds by January 1964.

8.   The exhibits presented to the court of appeals are in the papers of the Financial Officer, CND Archives. Also the court record, In the Court of Appeals of Maryland, September term, 1965, No. 356: *The Horace Mann League of the United States of America, Inc., et. al, appellants v Board of Public Works of Maryland et. al., Appellees,* testimony of Sister Margaret Mary and Sister Maura, I, 440–96 and 53–33. Cardinal Shehan recommended William Marbury as the attorney for the Catholic colleges. Included in Notre Dame's exhibit was a circular rendering of its programs and objectives. The outer circle included as an objective: "to train young women who will be not only able, but determined to fulfill their mission as Catholic leaders in the various walks of life."

There was also the statement: "The life of a student at Notre Dame is surrounded and permeated with the spirit of faith. Young women are encouraged to grow intimate with their Creator, that they may choose to employ their talents in bringing about the world order He has planned." See also Franklin, *The Heritage We Claim*, 32; Nicholas Varga, *Baltimore's Loyola, Loyola's Baltimore, 1851–1986* (Baltimore: Maryland Historical Society, 1990), 443. The other four institutions were Loyola College, Saint Joseph's, Mt. St. Mary's, and Western Maryland College. For the federal loan see Board of Trustees Minutes, January 1966, Minute Book #2, CND Archives.

9. Charles H. Wilson Jr., *Tilton v Richardson: The Search for Sectarianism in Education* (Washington: Association of American Colleges, 1971). Wilson described the atmosphere at the *Mann* hearings as "hostile" (45). See John A. Crowl, "High Court Upholds Grants by U.S. for Construction on Catholic Campuses," *Chronicle of Higher Education*, July 5, 1971: 1,8. See also *Lemon v Kurtzman*, 40 US 602 (1971).

10. Maryland moved to a new formula for state aid based on enrollments, which almost doubled the amount available for private colleges. Varga, *Baltimore's Loyola*, 490–91.

11. Ibid., 490, 501–11. Maryland annually appropriated funds for private colleges and universities in block grants set at 15 percent of funding for state institutions. In 1976, Notre Dame received $90,000 from this program.

12. Ibid., 511. See also Alice Gallin, O.S.U., *Negotiating Identity: Catholic Higher Education Since 1960* (Notre Dame, Ind.: University of Notre Dame Press, 2000), 36–39, for implications for Catholic colleges and universities of *Mann* and *Roemer.*

13. Board of Trustees Minutes, July 4, 1968, Minute Book #2, CND Archives.

14. Ibid., June 28, 1967, Minute Book #2, CND Archives.

15. See Varga, *Baltimore's Loyola*, 452–64.

16. Ibid. Varga cites Kelly's initiative to develop grant proposals jointly for federal funding under Title III for developing institutions. John H. Ford to Lawrence Cardinal Shehan, D.D., January 8, 1970, in Minute Book #2, CND Archives. Notre Dame's academic dean, Sister Bridget Marie, argued against forwarding the joint evaluations for the presidents as a recommendation. She had consulted with her faculty and found they were for cooperation but not a merger. The Coordinating Committee did work for a common calendar and catalogue. *Report to the Faculty, Administration, Trustees of the College of Notre Dame of Maryland by the Visiting Team of the Middle States Commission*, February 1970 (hereafter *Middle States Report*).

17. Kelly had urged that the college consider federation in 1968. The appointment of Ford slowed down the process, as the new president asked for time to assess the situation.

18. *Assumptions and Recommendations of the Tri-College Study Committee*, March 24, 1970; Resolution of the Board of Trustees of Loyola, April 25, 1970; Resolution of the Board of Trustees of Mount Saint Agnes, May 26, 1970, in Minute Book #2, CND Archives.

19. Board of Trustees Special Meeting Minutes, July 13, 1970, Minute Book #2, CND Archives.

20. See "Response to The Greyhound Concerning Merger: A Triple View," *Columns*, November 16, 1970. The only joint student activity was the short-lived creation of a

newspaper, *Twain,* which died after two issues. Its editors had accepted an advertisement from a clinic that provided counseling on abortion.

21. Board of Trustees Minutes, July 13 and September 23, 1970, Minute Book #2, CND Archives.

22. Ibid., April 25, November 14, and December 17, 1975, Minute Book #4, CND Archives. At the November 14 meeting, the academic dean, Sister Bridget Marie, pointed out that "Loyola needs us, and that the only thing Notre Dame could get from Loyola would be a coed atmosphere."

23. The 1970 Middle States team report noted that the Notre Dame administration was "acutely conscious" of the financial challenges. *Middle States Report,* 1970, CND Archives.

24. Mary Lu McNeal, interview by authors, Baltimore, June 13, 2003; enrollment figures, Office of Institutional Research, CND. The highest enrollment in the continuing education program was 703 in the academic year 1993–94. Minutes of the Board of Trustees, February 25, 1972, Minute Book #3, CND Archives.

25. Sister Kathleen Feeley, interview by authors, Baltimore, June 16, 2003.

26. Sister Mary Oliver Hudon, phone interview by Dorothy Brown, July 15, 2003. Kathleen Feeley, interview by authors, Baltimore, June 13, 2003. See Kathleen Feeley, December 19, 1974, to Board of Trustees, Minute Book #3, CND Archives.

27. In a tongue-in-cheek article, December 3, 1976, *Columns* reported the creation of Midnight College. Courses ran from midnight until the early morning. Sister Dracula Marie was the director of the program.

28. Hudon interview; Kathleen Feeley to Board of Trustees, November 7, 1974, Minute Book #4, CND Archives.

29. Sister Mary Oliver Hudon, interview by Dorothy Brown, Baltimore, July 15, 2003; Feeley interview, June 16, 2003. Sister Mary Oliver noted that the four hospitals were not satisfied with the nurses who had earned an AA at the community colleges. The cost of the BS would have been prohibitive in the traditional day program. It was, she observed, "a tough program to get going" but was accredited by the National League of Nursing on the second try.

30. *Middle States Reports,* 1980 and 1986, CND Archives.

31. Enrollment figures from the Office of Institutional Planning. In 1985 women comprised 95 percent of the enrollment; in 1995, 88 percent. The 1995–96 totals include 527 students in the Accelerated Certificate in Teaching introduced in 1987. Gallin, *Negotiating Identity,* 49–51, notes the growth of the part-time adult learner in Catholic colleges and universities in the 1970s and 1980s.

32. *Middle States Report,* 1980, CND Archives.

33. Ibid. Kathleen Feeley reported to the board at its September 25, 1980, meeting that she believed Notre Dame could grow to about eight hundred full-time students in its day program.

34. Board of Trustees Minutes, May 19, 1983, Minute Book #5, CND Archives.

35. Notre Dame had to overcome the opposition of two Maryland colleges and demonstrate to them and to the State Board of Higher Education that the new degree programs did not duplicate other programs available to Maryland residents. See Board of Trustees Minutes, November 10, 1983, January 19 and May 17, 1984, and May 16, 1985, Minute Book #5, CND Archives.

36. Middle States Committee response to Periodic Review Report, College of Notre Dame of Maryland, 1992, CND Archives.

37. Full-time faculty grew from sixty-three in 1981–82 to seventy in 1992–93; the major growth in faculty was in the number of adjuncts, which increased from forty-two to ninety-four in those years. The student-faculty ratios were 12:1 and 14:1. The percentage of full-time faculty with the doctorate increased from 45 percent to 61 percent in 1992–93, and to 70 percent in 2000–2001. Of the 343 graduate students in 1991, 85 percent were women.

38. Sister Sharon Slear, PhD, Boston College, had experience as a secondary school administrator. As chair of the Education Department of Notre Dame, she more than answered Kathleen Feeley's call to develop programs. The NCATE approval was achieved in 2002. At that time, students in education comprised 80 percent of the graduate enrollments. The Weekend College degree program in nursing had also offered course work at off-campus locations in Frederick and Prince George's counties in 1998 and 1999.

39. McNeal interview.

40. Sister Delia Dowling, interview by authors, Baltimore, June 23, 2003.

41. Mission Statement approved by the Board of Trustees, February 25, 1977, Minute Book #4, NDC Archives.

42. *Middle States Report,* 1986; Dowling interview.

43. In 1981, the board of trustees moved its goal from the 40th percentile to the 60th percentile. In 1990–91, it had achieved 91 percent of the goal. Board of Trustees Minutes, March 21, 1991. The SSND contribution to be absorbed in the budget was approximately $300,000.

44. See *Middle States Report,* 1986 and 1980, CND Archives. A faculty study of salaries, "Up by Our Boot Straps," in 1976 concluded that the longer faculty served at Notre Dame, the more disadvantaged they became. The Faculty Senate urged increasing salaries from 10 percent to 25 percent (Board of Trustees minutes, December 10, 1976, and March 21, 1991, Minute Book #5, CND Archives); statistics on the contributed services and endowment from the Office of Institutional Planning. Surveys of faculty in a 2001 Higher Education Research Institute/University of California at Los Angeles (HERI/UCLA) study found 92.3 percent of faculty respondents reported overall job satisfaction. Stress factors were time pressure and teaching load. Only 29.7 percent agreed that faculty were rewarded for being good teachers.

45. Memo to Kathleen Feeley and the Board of Trustees from the Budget Committee, Board of Trustees Minutes, April 18, 1975, Minute Book #4, CND Archives. Also in April, Loyola College asked to purchase ten acres of land for a new athletic facility, a request Notre Dame refused.

46. Board of Trustees Minutes, September 5, 1975, and February 25 and September 8, 1977, Minute Book #4, CND Archives.

47. See the file on parietals in the Office of Student Affairs papers, CND Archives, for letters, surveys, clippings, and resolutions. In 1972, the administration agreed to parietals on an experimental basis on Saturday and Sunday afternoons. This was not approved by the board and thus the pressure in 1973. Today male visitors to the college may be in the dormitory "common areas" at all times, but neither they nor female visitors may sleep in these areas. See the *College of Notre Dame of Maryland 2004–2005 Student Handbook,* available online www:ndm.edu.

48. Sister Patricia McLaughlin, June 13, 2003, and Mary Laverty Funke, June 16, 2003, interviews by authors, Baltimore. Surveys of students consistently showed strengths in teaching, individual attention, and desire for more social programming. See, for example, Quest 77 reported in *Columns*, November 3, 1977. Lacrosse was introduced in March 1978. .

49. Data provided by the vice president for student development, June 9, 2004. A "Social Norms Statement" was drafted in May 2004.

50. Feeley interview, June 16, 2003.

51. Board of Trustees Minutes, December 10, 1976, and December 10, 1977, Minute Book #2. Notre Dame did seek and secure several small grants to support faculty development; see, for example, Board of Trustees Minutes, September 17, 1976, Minute Book #4, CND Archives. Notre Dame also participated in the Independent College Fund of Maryland, in which the presidents of four-year liberal arts colleges collaboratively fund-raised. In 1980, Notre Dame's share of this effort was $40,000. Board of Trustees Minutes, October 1, 1981, Minute Book #5, CND Archives.

52. See "Trustees Approve Construction of Sports and Activities Center," *Columns*, May 26, 1988.

53. Henry Knott to Kathleen Feeley, in Board of Trustees Minutes, September 8, 1977. See also Board of Trustees Minutes, December 14, 1979; October 1 and December 10, 1981; and March 24, 1983, Minute Book #5, CND Archives. In April 1985 Notre Dame's chief financial officer floated the idea of Notre Dame's building a parking garage and leasing it to Loyola for revenue. Loyola rejected the concept, discovering that its students and faculty were loath to walk the distance to the Loyola campus. See "Parking proposal offered to Loyola," *Columns*, April 9 and "Loyola rejects parking proposal," September 10, 1987.

54. Sister Mary Oliver cited in "Study sets guidelines for schools—how does CND measure up?" *Columns*, February 28, 1985. Faculty member Jeanne Stevenson agreed, commenting: "I will match a good student here against a good student at Loyola any day." Students, she insisted, developed their potential at Notre Dame and were not lost in the shuffle. The differences in the philosophies of Notre Dame and Loyola are also reflected in their costs, with Notre Dame being less expensive and hence more accessible to women from low- and moderate-income families. In 2004–5, tuition and fees at Notre Dame were $20,300, and room and board was $7,800; the comparable costs at Loyola were $27,450 and $8,830. See usnews.com, America's Best Colleges.

55. Enrollment statistics from the Office of Institutional Planning, CND. See *Middle States Report*, 1992, CND Archives. The board of trustees in 1999 comprised eleven women and fourteen men; 4 percent were members of minorities. In 2004, there were twenty women and eight men on the board with 10 percent minority membership. In 1999, 25 percent of the full-time students in the Women's College were minority students; in 2004, 26 percent.

56. The board of trustees in 1999 had twenty-five members; eleven were women (44 percent), and 4 percent were minorities. By 2004, the board had twenty-eight members, twenty of whom (71 percent) were women, and 10 percent were minorities. The students include a larger percent of minorities: 25 percent of the Women's College in 1999 and 26 percent in 2004.

57. Strategic Plan, 1996–2001, and Vision Statement, Office of Institutional Planning, CND Archives. The four strategic goals were: Connect a strong liberal core of studies with twenty-first-century professional opportunities; develop a learning community that embraces holistic education; promote excellence in teaching and learning by increasing technological resources; increase fiscal strength through the development of revenue resources and effective financial planning and management.

58. February 29, 1996, the Baltimore *Sun* in a front-page story "Notre Dame's President to Leave," reported: "The president of the College of Notre Dame of Maryland startled her campus yesterday by saying she would step down in June, at the end of the centennial year of the Catholic women's school, simply because it was the right time to do so."

59. Board of Trustees Minutes, November 16, 1995, Minute Book #5, CND Archives. Six student leaders addressed the board. The president of the Faculty Senate explained that the restructuring process had divided the college. "Nassif steps down," *Columns*, March 4, 1996, covers the meetings. Sister Rosemarie became director of a small foundation in Baltimore before being selected president of Holy Names College in Oakland, California.

60. See *Report of the Visiting Evaluation Team of the Middle States Association,* March 1996, CND Archives.

61. Statistics from the Office of Institutional Planning. In 2001–2, there were eighty-eight full-time faculty; thirteen were SSNDs. In September, Sister Eileen O'Dea assumed new responsibilities as vice president for mission.

62. Mission Statement approved by the Board of Trustees in 2002, CND Archives.

Case Studies of Affiliated Women's Colleges

The case studies in Part Four review three colleges affiliated with larger prestigious coeducational universities: Barnard College at Columbia University, and Girton and Newnham colleges at Cambridge University. These studies show that men's colleges adopting coeducation (or coresidency in Cambridge) places tremendous pressure on the women's colleges to sustain their academic standing. In one case, Girton College at Cambridge, administrators decided to admit men because its single-sex status combined with a somewhat distant location would not attract the kind of students they sought.

In Chapter 11, Andrea Walton describes the prodigious efforts to establish Barnard College in the late nineteenth century and the similarly prodigious efforts by Barnard to retain its single-sex status a century later. The decision by Columbia University to admit women to its College of Arts and Sciences in 1983 resulted in a brief decline in applicants at Barnard, as some had predicted. However, beginning in the 1990s applications to Barnard have risen, making it even more selective than before coeducation at Columbia. Walton attributes Barnard's success to instituting curricula reform, improving the physical plant, tapping synergies and competition in the new Barnard-Columbia relationship, articulating Barnard's contribution to the university, and supporting female identity and greater inclusiveness in Barnard's single-sex environment.

For comparative purposes, this section includes a study of two colleges that were established in the nineteenth century as women's colleges at Cambridge University. In Chapter 12, Leslie Miller-Bernal finds some dynamics in British higher education similar to those seen in previous chapters on U.S. colleges. As long as the relatively few (and therefore very talented) women were funneled into Girton and Newnham, then the only two women's colleges at Cambridge, the academic achievements of its students and the reputation of the colleges were relatively high. Once all the men's colleges at Cambridge became coresidential in the 1970s and 1980s, many of the talented women students chose to attend the more prestigious formerly men's colleges. Handicapped by a location distant from the center of the city that made it more isolated and less desirable in the eyes of some, Girton decided to admit men in 1979. Newnham, with a more convenient location, has retained its single-sex status. Both colleges, however, have seen their academic standings fall from their levels before the recent coeducation movement.

11

Rekindling a Legacy
Barnard College Remains a Women's College

Andrea Walton

In 1888 a determined twenty-four-year-old New Yorker, Annie Nathan Meyer, sent a thought-provoking and now famous letter to the *Nation* on the subject of higher education for the women of New York City. Meyer raised two important concerns: first, the growing number of women in New York City who, given the limited opportunities for advanced study nearby, faced the dilemma of either leaving home to pursue a collegiate education or foregoing their dream of higher studies; and second, the inadequacies of New York City's only provision for women's liberal arts education, Columbia University's Collegiate Course for Women.[1] Established in 1883, the Collegiate Course was a product of Columbia's intractable opposition to coeducation—a measured response to a petition signed by more than 1,400 citizens (among them, clubwomen, civic reformers, prominent doctors, lawyers, financiers, and even former U.S. presidents) calling for Columbia to provide for women's education. Meyer drew particular attention to the arrangements already in place for women to study at two preeminent universities that were known for their deep attachment to the all-male traditions of higher education, Harvard and Cambridge.[2]

As Meyer noted, Harvard's Annex provided women with lectures by Harvard professors but refused to certify their hard-won learning. Columbia's Collegiate Course, in contrast, granted degrees to the women who passed a set of examinations on the prescribed syllabus Columbia men followed but offered women no instruction or guidance in their studies. Beyond comparing their situation to women's lot in other cities, the women of New York City and their supporters pressed on to campaign for a full-fledged collegiate experience for women. Convinced that women in New York City needed an annex if they were ever to benefit from the full-fledged liberal arts education that was available to Columbia men, Meyer spearheaded a fund-raising campaign to establish a female coordinate college at Columbia University. An educational "experiment" to provide women with a Columbia education through coordination, Barnard College, funded only by a small group of civic-minded subscribers (each paying fifty dollars a year for four years), opened its doors and welcomed its first twenty-two students in 1889.

In the century that followed, Barnard College came to prosper within Columbia University's structure, becoming a place where women excelled as administrators, trustees, scholars, and students, despite the challenges inherent in collegiate coordination with a male-dominated, research-oriented institution. And Columbia, while keeping women at a distance, also benefited substantially as a university from the presence of Barnard College—a women's college with its own faculty, endowment, and board of trustees—within its wide-ranging configuration of academic units. By the 1970s, however, coordinate relations between Barnard and Columbia were less sanguine and the future of Barnard-Columbia collaboration less certain.[3]

After a contentious decade of negotiations concerning a possible merger between the two institutions—an idea that faced considerable resistance from Barnard students, faculty, alumnae, trustees, and administrators—the leaders of Barnard and Columbia agreed that Columbia College would become coeducational and Barnard College would retain its all-female character and coordinate affiliation with the university. In September 1983 history was made as the first young women admitted to Columbia College, members of the class of 1987, arrived at the university's main gate at 116th Street, just across Broadway (one of upper Manhattan's major thoroughfares) from its longtime neighbor, all-female Barnard College. This is "a breakthrough," one of the new "coeds" proudly told a cluster of photographers and reporters waiting anxiously to cover the arrival of 229-year-old Columbia College's first group of female "freshmen" and transfer students.[4]

In considering the major turning points and noteworthy pioneers in the history of women's higher education in the United States, one readily thinks of the contributions of late nineteenth-century reformers and college founders like Annie Nathan Meyer. Also frequently acknowledged are the women who broke gender barriers and integrated the country's most prestigious and traditional all-male institutions during the second wave of coeducation, which swept the country beginning in the 1960s and saw the advent of coeducation at Ivy League institutions, including Columbia College, and the nation's military academies. But women's advances in higher education in the post–World War II era have involved struggles not included in the familiar story of women's fight for access to men's education. Women faculty members, trustees, administrators, and students have fought to preserve their own institutions. In considering the case of women's education at Columbia University, it is important to remember the story of the women who, even as Columbia College adopted coeducation in 1983, continued to see value and purposefulness in Barnard's all-female tradition. Not only were Barnard's leaders able to resist what they regarded as an ill-advised merger with Columbia, but they were also able to negotiate a new era in coordinate relations and to capitalize on Barnard's place within Columbia University, even after the advent of coeducation at Columbia College.[5]

This chapter focuses on the challenges and achievements of the women who were stewards of Barnard's legacy and who contributed to the re-invigoration of Barnard's all-female mission in the twentieth century, especially in the post-1960s era when women's colleges experienced tremendous pressures.

A Tradition of Independence within a Coordinate Structure

Even before the founding of Barnard College in 1889, the story of women at Columbia stood apart from the experience of other women's annexes and independent women's colleges in the Northeast in a number of significant ways. First among them was the advantage that undergraduate and graduate women at Columbia University have always earned a Columbia degree for their scholastic achievements. Another notable difference was in the nature of the coordinate relationship between Barnard College and Columbia University. Signed in 1900, Barnard's agreement of university affiliation provided the women's coordinate with voting representation on the University Council and, of paramount importance, guaranteed the basis of Barnard's institutional integrity and identity, namely, the right to maintain its own endowment and board of trustees and to hire its own faculty, open to men and women. Over the years, the leadership that women brought to Barnard's executive office–titled the deanship from 1889 to 1953 and thereafter the presidency—and to the college's board of trustees mirrored the college's commitment to training female leaders.[6] At the same time, Barnard developed a system of faculty exchanges with Columbia's departments of arts and sciences that enhanced the ability of both institutions to attract talented faculty and hence to expand and diversify curricular offerings readily and economically. Reinforcing the ties established between Barnard and Columbia through such exchanges, Barnard succeeded in establishing its own new campus very early, in 1897, across from Columbia's impressive cluster of McKim, Mead, and White buildings in Morningside Heights (upper Manhattan).[7]

With the possible exception of Wellesley, Barnard was distinctive among the Seven Sisters for its tradition of female executive leadership. Under its early deans, especially Dean Virginia Crocheron Gildersleeve, a Barnard College alumna and Columbia PhD, Barnard grew beyond a local institution for New York City women into a formidable liberal arts college for women and a leader in women's education. Moreover, through the years, the partnership between

Barnard's deans and Columbia's presidents fostered mutually beneficial ties that were an integral part of realizing a particular type of liberal arts experience for women. By mitigating the internal and external pressures for coeducation, Barnard helped to preserve Columbia College's all-male character until 1983 and contributed to the university's capabilities in research and teaching.[8]

Changes in Barnard's Mission over Time

In its early years, especially before the 1900 coordinate agreement, Barnard College carried the burden of proving itself and demonstrating that women were intellectually capable students and scholars. Its mission was to provide women with a Columbia education that showed that in educational terms, Barnard was Columbia.[9] Dean Ella Weed (1889–94) anchored Barnard's academic strength and built its standing within the university by imitating men's education. The next dean, Emily James Smith Putnam (1894–1900), helped to develop multi-layered ties to Columbia. Strengthening the power and image of the office of dean after Laura Gill's somewhat contentious tenure (1901–7), Dean Virginia Crocheron Gildersleeve (1911–47) began to forge Barnard's distinctiveness (what she once described as the college's "own particular bent") by infusing Barnard's rigorous academics with real-world politics and feminism.[10]

In the years immediately following World War II, educators at Barnard, like faculty and administrators elsewhere, grappled with a number of new challenges in preparing their students in a world of changing gender expectations and social structures.[11] Barnard educators focused on the question of what was the "best" type of education for women. Millicent McIntosh, who headed Barnard from 1947 to 1962, and who was dean when the title of Barnard's chief executive was changed to "president" in 1953, was a Barnard trustee, former headmistress of Manhattan's all-female Brearley School, the holder of a PhD in literature from Johns Hopkins, and the mother of five.[12]

Under McIntosh three things happened. First, Barnard welcomed a new era in women's higher education with a new type of executive leader, a woman scholar-administrator who was married and had children. Second, the college undertook a revisioning of its undergraduate curriculum and, to some extent, began to reconsider the college's obligation to its undergraduate students. Third, and hardly least important, Barnard undertook closer collaboration with Columbia in the areas of instruction and residential life. If in retrospect McIntosh's message was socially conservative or offered Barnard students what one historian has described as "mixed signals" concerning the balance of family and career ambitions,[13] her views also reflected a Deweyan concern with fusing theory and practice and, in terms of women's education specifically, a concern with narrowing the divide between a woman's formal higher studies and her postcollege life. As McIntosh outlined:

The peculiar opportunity as well as the problem of the independent college for women lies in developing a curriculum which is flexible enough to educate both scholars who will go forward to professional and graduate schools and young women who marry either during or soon after their college career. This curriculum must also train an individual to be adaptable enough to change from one role to the other, or to combine the two. The understanding of this opportunity and the meeting of this challenge provide the main justification for the women's college as an entity apart from men's institutions.[14]

The limited archival records and source materials available from McIntosh's years at Barnard College's helm suggest that administrators at least discussed whether Barnard might address its financial problems, including the need to offer more competitive faculty salaries, through a Barnard-Columbia merger.[15] The level of serious consideration given to this proposition is unclear. What is clear, however, is that McIntosh helped forge greater cooperation between Barnard and Columbia and that she firmly believed such actions would not "necessarily mean a loss of integrity or independence" for Barnard College.[16] In 1948, only the Music Department offered joint courses between Barnard and Columbia. During McIntosh's tenure, cross-campus departmental collaboration in mathematics, physics, and religion soon followed. In 1952 a new intercorporate agreement allowed for Barnard-Columbia cross-registration and ten years later, in 1962, joint classes were introduced.[17] Since Barnard's founding its students had benefited from access to Columbia's vast library and faculty resources, while Barnard's all-female campus life provided women with the ample opportunities and emphasis on personal growth for which the nation's leading independent women's liberal arts colleges had earned distinction. In the absence of traditional gender constraints and competition with men, Barnard students had ample opportunities to hone their leadership skills in student government (an early Barnard tradition), to excel in athletics, to oversee student publications (such as the *Barnard Bear*), and to shape the character and direction of campus organizations.

This new stage in Barnard-Columbia relations after World War II changed gender relations. Men and women mixed more on campus—in classrooms and on the dance floor, for instance. Some new collaborations between male and female undergraduate student groups developed, for example, in dramatics, and women had opportunities to participate in and even assume leadership roles in such Columbia-sponsored activities as the daily student newspaper, the *Columbia Spectator*. Over the years, the resulting collaborations enlarged rather than diminished the range of opportunities for women. In addition, the measure of de facto coeducation achieved through collaboration, and the growing female enrollments in Columbia's graduate program (and growing number of female doctorates), while not challenging the ideological bedrock of Columbia University's longstanding gender discriminatory practices and

Barnard women and Columbia men in the 1960s, when Columbia was still all-male, on the walkway through Barnard's campus, with historic Milbank Hall in the background. *Barnard College Archives.*

policies, did at least help expose a generation of Columbia faculty men to co-educational classrooms and to the experience of teaching academically gifted women.[18]

That said, closer Barnard-Columbia ties and the prospects of closer ties were not unproblematic. By the time Barnard celebrated its seventy-fifth anniversary in 1964, the appeal of women's colleges had declined and the pressures affecting the decision making of research universities had intensified and become increasingly complex. Millicent McIntosh's successor, Rosemary Park (1962–67), former president of Connecticut College, was keenly aware of these dynamics and hence urged the Barnard College trustees to be vigilant about Barnard's place within Columbia University. Like a number of Barnard alumnae, Park hoped Barnard College would consider the "advisability of closer identification with Columbia" in light of Radcliffe's gradual "surrender of its separate academic identity" to Harvard in the early 1960s, which, in Park's estimate, did not necessarily advance the status of women at the university.[19]

Pressures for Merger

Protracted discussions concerning a possible Barnard-Columbia merger and the related coeducation debates raged at Columbia in the 1970s and 1980s. The issues were inevitably seen in the context of historic Barnard-Columbia ties, the advent of coeducation in formerly male bastions (especially the Ivy League), and the growing fiscal challenges for universities to maintain top-notch research faculty and facilities and for small liberal arts colleges, especially single-sex institutions, to maintain competitive applicant pools. In all, the Columbia-Barnard discussions were a testimony to how national developments in higher education and the currents of change outside Columbia's gates had significantly changed institutional priorities and perspectives vis-à-vis coeducation at Columbia. The negotiations also revealed how Columbia's leaders (all men, save for a few women trustees) and Barnard's leaders (a combination of women and men in administration and on the board of trustees) envisioned the future, both for their individual campuses and for the relations between the two campuses.

Socially conservative and status-conscious Columbia had ferociously opposed coeducation in the 1880s. Faced with demographic challenges, formidable deficits, and staunch competition from the newly coeducational Ivies and formerly all-male selective liberal arts colleges in the Northeast, it now saw coeducation as a fiscal and social imperative. Moreover, from Columbia's perspective, the timeline for achieving coeducation could be expedited through a merger with its all-female coordinate, Barnard.[20] Columbia advanced its proposal for a merger based on the tacit assumption that, as one newspaper account bluntly stated, "Barnard would not survive if Columbia began admitting women."[21]

Columbia was not alone in thinking that a merger made sense for both Columbia and Barnard. Indeed, certain members of the Barnard College board of trustees were sympathetic to a merger with Columbia. But, there were also a number of Barnard trustees, including alumnae such as Eleanor Elliott and Helene Kaplan, whose championing of Barnard's autonomy reflected both the institutional drive toward self-preservation and skepticism about the possibility of an equitable Barnard-Columbia union. In addition, a number of Barnard's faculty questioned whether Columbia men were prepared to integrate women students and faculty most fully and equitably into the intellectual and social life on campus.

The merger debate pitted an eager Columbia and a reluctant Barnard against each other and strained intrauniversity ties. Some members of the university viewed admission to Columbia as the first step in breaking down the gendered barriers of the "old boys' club," while others were less sanguine about the possibilities of achieving gender equity within the structure and culture of established male-dominated institutions such as Columbia.[22] As one Barnard student leader observed: "Women still face prejudice subtle and overt. . . . A woman must prove her worth by making it in a man's world. Coeducation as it commonly exists today is essentially that."[23] Barnard trustees and faculty fought to preserve Barnard's excellence in liberal arts teaching and its record of mentoring female students.

Barnard trustees were instrumental in protecting Barnard's interests at the negotiating table with Columbia. Some Barnard College faculty used Barnard's history to underscore the significance of the merger talks and their possible outcomes for Barnard College and for women's education at Columbia University. Annette Kar Baxter, an alumna (class of 1947) and professor of American studies at Barnard, was one of the most outspoken and articulate voices of caution. "What advantages to Columbia University might be lost if Barnard's independent board of trustees, its faculty and its curriculum were to be expunged?" she asked a committee of Barnard and Columbia trustees.[24] From Baxter's vantage point, and indeed that of many Barnard supporters, too many proponents of a swift merger had geared their energies toward solving Columbia's fiscal difficulties. They had underestimated or failed to acknowledge the distinctive role that Barnard had long played in the university and, moreover, what long-term changes might be brought by an ill-considered or poorly implemented merger. Baxter and similar-minded Barnard faculty members and students voiced their concern that Barnard's "distinctiveness" might be lost "in the bargain."[25]

It was, in fact, Barnard's distinctiveness that through the years of coordination contributed to Columbia University's own growing reputation as a multifaceted university and as a producer of female PhD holders.[26] Barnard could point to the accomplishments of its women faculty and alumnae within the academy and in the professions and other spheres of public life. One recalls, for example, that Barnard's own Dean Virginia Gildersleeve had been the only woman to serve on the committee to establish the United Nations charter at the end of World War II. For most of Barnard's existence, its identity has been shaped, on the one hand, by women's history and gender expectations in the larger society and, on the other hand, by Columbia's male exclusiveness. But the 1970s brought a new rationale for women's colleges and advocacy on their behalf. New studies in female/feminist psychology and the baccalaureate origins of high achievers and profiles of the alumnae of women's colleges (studies such as those undertaken by Elizabeth Tidball and the Women's College Coalition) suggested the efficacy of an all-female environment in promoting women's intellectual achievement.[27]

It was not surprising that Barnard College, with its strong tradition of women presidents and high-ranking female administrators, a tradition of a gender-mixed faculty and board of trustees, and an active alumnae association, enjoyed an impressive number of physicians, scientists, prize-winning writers and artists, and doctorates in the ranks of its graduates[28] (see Tables 11.1 and 11.2).

Internal Critiques of Campus Culture:
Race and Feminism

Barnard's identity was itself contested in the decade or so leading up to the negotiations with Columbia. The small, teaching-oriented liberal arts for women was struggling to define its future relationship to Columbia, a top-tier, male-dominated research university, at the same time that it was also changing in response to two major internal critiques of its campus culture.

The first critique centered on race. While in the late 1960s many white, middle-class Barnard students focused their attention on Barnard's control over their personal lives through parietal rules and dress codes and on the college's efforts to strengthen ties with Columbia, Barnard's African American students, voicing their concerns about racism on campus, demanded a housing unit open only to African American students, ethnic meal selections in the college cafeteria, and greater voice in curricular policy making.[29] The second critique centered on Barnard's curriculum, in particular, an effort to infuse the emergent area of women's studies and the concerns of the women's movement into the college's intellectual life. Some regarded Barnard as a women's college still shrouded in the "climate of unexpectation" of the 1950s and ambivalent about the women's movement outside its gates.[30] One Barnard faculty member later observed: "For years, any reminder that this was a women's college made many people here very uneasy." She continued: "The prevalent view was not only that no women's college could be as good as a top men's school, but also that any institution that admitted that women might have special educational needs was somehow an embarrassment."[31]

Although there was some ambivalence on Barnard's campus about the proper relationship between feminism and Barnard's mission, Barnard's president, Martha Petersen, who was appointed as successor to Rosemary Park in 1967 (and served until 1975), set up a task force to consider the meaning of the feminist movement for the college and the education it provided.[32] Catharine Stimpson, "a young, charismatic" English professor with a "sense of the importance of feminism and its place within the academy," chaired the committee.[33] The outcome of the meetings was a plan for a women's center, with a founding belief "that women can live and work in dignity, autonomy, and equality."[34] As Jane S. Gould, Barnard class of 1939 and the first permanent director of the Barnard Center for Research on Women, later wrote: "We were a mixed group . . . but with a shared conviction that Barnard should do more than it had always done. A 'superior education' for women should offer more than admission to a still discriminatory, white-male tradition."[35] Inspired by the intellectual foundation that the committee had laid out for the new center, alumna trustee and committee member Eleanor Elliott secured the funding. She persuaded the family of the late trustee and alumna Helen Rogers Reid (class of 1903) to use the income from Reid's bequest to found the women's center. The sugges-

Table 11.1. Female Representation in Governance at Barnard, 1945–2005

	Elected female trustees	% Female board members	Highest- ranking woman trustee	Top executive (% women)
1945–46	9	38	Vice-chair	Virginia Gildersleeve, dean (100)
1950–51	11	50	Chair	Millicent MacIntosh, dean (67)
1955–56	12	50	Chair	Millicent MacIntosh, president (67)
1960–61	12	50	Clerk	Millicent MacIntosh, president (67)
1965–66	12	55	Clerk	Rosemary Park, president (75)
1970–71	15	58	Clerk	Martha Petersen, president (75)
1975–76	15	56	Chair, clerk	Martha Petersen, president (67)
1980–81	15	54	Vice chair	Ellen V. Futter, acting president (67)
1985–86	17	55	Chair and co–vice chair	Ellen V. Futter, president (67)
1990–1991	17	50	Chair and 2 of 3 vice-chairs	Ellen V. Futter, president (67)
1995–1996	23	66	Chair, vice chair, honorary vice-chair	Judith Shapiro, president (71)
2000–2001	24	63	Chair, vice-chairs	Judith Shapiro, president (56)
2004–2005	24	71	Chair, vice-chair	Judith Shapiro, president (67)

Source: Barnard College Announcements, 1945–46 to 2004–5.

tion resonated with the Reid family, as Helen Rogers Reid had been an ardent suffragist, the first female chair of Barnard's board of trustees, in 1947, and a supporter of such innovations at Barnard as a policy of maternity leave.[36]

At its founding in 1971, the women's center was the physical home for the study of women on Barnard's campus, and the only space singularly devoted to advancing equity for women within Columbia University. Over the years as women studies was institutionalized, the center posed a challenge to the culture of the women's college and to the pedagogy and academic culture of

Table 11.2. Women faculty at Barnard, 1997–2004

	Full-time		Part-time	
	Total	% women	Total	% women
1997	168	58	108	67
1998	174	57	107	67
1999	172	57	90	71
2000	174	58	117	66
2001	183	58	110	69
2002	185	60	107	73
2003	186	59	107	68
2004	183	57	113	70

Source: www.barnard.edu/opir/faculty/women.html. Permission to cite, Yenny Anderson, OPIR, Barnard College.

the masculine academy. As Gould later noted: "Despite the tensions between the principles of feminism and those of the institution, we were able to build a solid women's center which became an accepted feminist presence both on the Barnard-Columbia campus and in the bigger community."[37] In 1975 a lectureship was established, with a commitment to an equitable representation of scholars of color among the invitees. Three years later women's studies became an official program.

A New Phase in the Barnard-Columbia Coordination: The Early 1970s

Barnard and Columbia had failed by early 1972 to reach a shared vision of the possibility of coeducation through merger. Instead, the colleges agreed to a policy of open registration and cross-billing for their students. Barnard also secured a promise that Columbia College would not admit women.[38] Thus Barnard retained the benefits of its standing within the university and guarded its competitive advantage vis à vis independent women's colleges. However, since at the time nearly twice as many Barnard students as Columbia College students typically cross-registered, the agreement caused Barnard to assume a new, sizable financial obligation. Barnard was also now required to give Columbia a majority representation on ad hoc tenure committees (three to two).[39] Still, the agreement safeguarded many aspects of Barnard's independence as a women's college. Whereas Radcliffe College's new relationship to Harvard University, signed in 1970, had ceded much of the female coordinate's affairs to Harvard, and had become known as the "nonmerger merger," Barnard's new relationship to Columbia, which allowed for open access, was conceptualized, at least in official rhetoric, as "integration without assimilation."[40]

Barnard administrators and faculty comprehended fully that the new policy of "open access," albeit a necessary step, had the potential to undermine Barnard's identity. As one Barnard faculty member put it: "If many courses in the University were approved for the Barnard general requirement, the sole Barnard-taught and -designed course required of all students would be [Freshman] English. The result was a serious concern about Barnard's 'identity.'"[41]

The faculty member went on to voice a concern, widely held on Barnard's campus, about whether Barnard, given the new agreement, would stand back and allow itself to be defined mainly in comparison to Columbia or whether Barnard would define itself and sharpen its identity: "Is there anything in Barnard's curriculum which makes it a distinctive part of the University? Or is Barnard simply the undergraduate college at Columbia University which admits women and where you do not have to take Humanities and Contemporary Civilization courses required in Columbia College?"[42]

Resistance to Continuing Pressures for Merger or "Unification": The Mid-1970s

The question of identity that preoccupied Barnard leaders and faculty was suddenly eclipsed in the winter of academic year 1975–76 by concern about Barnard's imminent survival. Barnard was surprised to learn that the Columbia College faculty had voted in November 1975 to move toward coeducation on its own and admit women.[43] Although the Columbia trustees rejected their faculty's position out of consideration for Barnard College, it was clear that Columbia's president William J. McGill saw the existing Barnard-Columbia coordinate relationship as inequitable and untenable—in his words, "partially parasitical."[44] In the spring of 1976, McGill informed Barnard's president, Jacqueline Mattfeld (who succeeded Martha Peterson), that he wanted "unification" of the two administrations and faculties by 1985.[45]

The impasse between McGill and Mattfeld stiffened the resolve of Barnard trustees and faculty to preserve their college's legacy. Confident that Barnard had "a machinery more committed to a women's education than Columbia by itself ever could have," Barnard leaders asserted that not only was Barnard far from being parasitical, it actually contributed diversity to Columbia's configuration of academic units.[46] From Barnard's vantage point, the two institutions were "able to provide a more rich and diverse undergraduate experience for their respective student bodies by enabling them to have unimpeded access to the resources . . . provided by an affiliated institution of *comparable academic standards and contrasting character* and educational style" (emphasis added).[47]

Barnard's trustees reaffirmed the college's historical mission in May 1976. They continued to see Barnard as dedicated to "the provision of undergraduate education of the highest quality in an environment which is particularly sensitive to the intellectual and personal needs of its students and in which women's abilities and aspirations flourish through their full representation and participation in that college as scholars, scientists, artists, teachers, students and administrators."[48] As Dorothy Denburg (an alumna, class of 1970, and current dean of Barnard College) discusses in her study of curricular change at Barnard, the goals outlined in 1976 were not remarkably different from what Dean Emily James Smith Putnam in 1898 had described as Barnard's mission: to imbue students with the "knowledge of life that shall enable them to bear themselves steadily and wisely in a time of changing conditions."[49]

Barnard's leaders' views of the college's future competitiveness were buoyed not only by their sense of institutional history and their attachment to the college's historic mission. Trustees and administrators also carefully studied the educational environment to determine whether the college would be able to weather coeducation at Columbia. Between 1976 and 1978, President Mattfeld and Barnard officials conducted a survey of women in newly coeducational Ivy League institutions and the applicant pool of female high school students. They also undertook a comparative analysis of teaching loads and salaries in Barnard's peer institutions. Contrary to the belief held strongly in certain parts of the university community that Barnard would close its doors and cease to exist if Columbia turned coeducational, survey data and alumnae sentiment indicated that with careful planning Barnard could have a viable future. A poll conducted for Barnard College by Louis Harris and Associates in the spring of 1977 showed "overwhelming agreement" among various stakeholders (current students and alumnae, trustees, faculty, and administrators) "that Barnard is committed equally to its status as an autonomous college for women and to a continuing affiliation with Columbia University."[50]

The challenge for Barnard's leaders was to find a compromise with Columbia and to develop as a university-affiliated women's college. The intricate web of intracollegiate and departmental relations that had coalesced over decades of successful coordination made a severing of Barnard and Columbia's coordinate ties difficult. Yet differences in curriculum, deadlines, credit systems, and fee structures between Barnard and Columbia all posed certain impediments to a merger, as did, in certain respects, the personalities involved in decision making and the timing of administrative changes at the two institutions.[51] The heightened tensions between Barnard and Columbia and the impasse in merger negotiations led to Mattfeld's forced resignation at Barnard in 1980. McGill's departure from the Columbia presidency soon thereafter created an opportunity for a fresh start in Barnard-Columbia discussions of the future of coordination and the possibilities of coeducation. Columbia's new president was Michael

Sovern, former dean of the Columbia Law School; Barnard's new president was Ellen Futter, a Columbia-trained lawyer (JD 1974), Barnard alumna (class of 1971), and Barnard trustee known for her pro-Barnard's independence stance. Together they explored ways to achieve what was termed "de facto" coeducation, through such outlets as greater cooperation in residence life and dining halls and plans for greater cross-registration.[52]

A New Dynamic within Coordination:
Columbia Goes Coed and Barnard Stays Single Sex

By the end of 1981, many issues had been resolved, but no workable solution for a Barnard-Columbia merger had been reached. A Columbia committee headed by Professor Ronald Breslow studied the impact on women's colleges when nearby men's institutions turned coeducational. When the Breslow Committee concluded that Barnard College would not be hurt if Columbia were to accept women, university officials decided that no barrier remained: Columbia College must go coeducational.[53] All other Ivy League institutions by this time admitted women, and the social and fiscal pressures and incentives for Columbia to do so were formidable.[54] Facing a daunting deficit that by the late 1970s exceeded $87 million, Columbia had already dipped into its endowment. College leaders understood the reality of its dwindling male applicant pool and increased competition for outstanding students.[55]

In an ironic twist, Columbia and Barnard reversed their nineteenth-century stances. Columbia had then stalwartly opposed coeducation but now viewed its all-male status as "anachronistic." Barnard, on the other hand, had been an institution built as an "experiment" in response to women's exclusion at Columbia but now regarded its historic all-female mission as gaining new relevance and urgency.[56] But Barnard College's future, given the major changes at Columbia, remained uncertain. Though able to avoid what it regarded as an inequitable merger, the college still faced the challenge of maintaining its viability and navigating its path. One problem was finances. Barnard's budget was in relatively good shape, but its endowment, as Table 11.3 shows, was the smallest of the Seven Sisters' and dwarfed by Columbia's. With an eye on assuring Barnard's competitive future as a women's college, Barnard trustees launched a capital campaign in 1980 to raise $20 million, earmarking the funds for two areas of crucial need: the long-overdue renovation of campus buildings and the augmenting of Barnard's endowment (especially to meet the growing need for student aid). The idea of maintaining Barnard's independence within Columbia University appealed to a number of alumnae donors and friends of the college. By May 1982 pledges totaled $8 million, and by the campaign's conclusion in 1985 the college had surpassed its fund-raising goal by $2 million.[57]

When Columbia's president Sovern and Barnard's president Futter realized they could not negotiate what Columbia saw as a suitable level of de facto coeducation through collaboration, the administrators moved forward to broker a new coordinate agreement—a compromise—that appeared both to meet Columbia's priorities and to address their shared concerns over Barnard's survival.[58] Subject to review in seven years, the 1982 agreement ended Barnard's nearly century-long monopoly over women's baccalaureate education as Columbia University's women's coordinate by allowing Columbia College to admit women in the fall of 1983. But the new coordinate agreement also reaffirmed Barnard's standing within the university and the value of Barnard-Columbia coordinate ties for both parties. Under the agreement, Barnard retained its university affiliation and obtained more independence in academic matters, including, of paramount importance, control over its tenure process.[59] This aspect of Barnard's governance—so crucial to Barnard College's integrity and autonomy as an academic institution and to its identity as a selective, teaching-oriented liberal

Table 11.3. Endowments of Barnard and peer institutions

Seven Sisters	1980–81	2003–4
Barnard	25,880,000	144,152,000
Radcliffe	40,347,000	n/a
Bryn Mawr	55,521,000	478,452,000
Mt. Holyoke	61,449,000	397,464,000
Vassar	104,834,000	608,261,000
Smith	129,126,000	924,464,000
Wellesley	133,192,000	1,179,988,000
Other peer (COFHE) institutions:		
Trinity	—	363,654,000
Carleton	—	511,200,000
Wesleyan	—	517,631,000
Oberlin	—	593,742,000
Amherst	—	993,417,000
Swarthmore	—	1,080,026,000
Pomona	—	1,149,720,000
Williams	—	1,229,516,000

Sources: 1980–81 data, results of the 1981 NACUBO Comparative Performance Study and Investment Questionnaire; 2003–4 data, results of the 2004 NACUBO Endowment Study.
Note: Barnard lists the endowment of its selective "peer" institutions on its Web site; see www.barnard.columbia.edu/opir/endowmnt/endow1.html.

college within a research university—had been a point of contention between Barnard and Columbia since the early 1970s. More than a few Barnard faculty had become alarmed by cases where a Barnard candidate's tenure bid had been endorsed by Barnard's dean only to be denied later at the university level. Such cases raised concerns among Barnard faculty that Barnard College's staffing needs and system of peer review were routinely subordinated to Columbia's research and graduate education priorities.

Notwithstanding any ground that Barnard preserved or gained under the 1982 coordinate agreement with Columbia, Barnard was indeed left in a precarious position. Like other women's colleges whose fate had been shaped by the coeducation decisions of nearby men's institutions, Barnard faced the uncertainty of what impact the new admission policy at Columbia would have on Barnard's enrollments and selectivity. Rising to the demands of the moment, President Futter projected unwavering confidence as she announced the new Barnard-Columbia agreement, touting the long-awaited agreement as "a tremendous triumph." She continued: "It is the first time in the history of Barnard that we have entered into a new relationship with Columbia and not given up any new autonomy. . . . For the first time we can look forward to a long-term stable relationship with Columbia without the sword of possible merger hanging over our head."[60]

The Immediate Impact of the 1982 Barnard-Columbia Agreement

The 1982 Barnard-Columbia agreement, which brought the admission of women at Columbia College in the fall of 1983, marked a new era in Barnard-Columbia coordinate arrangements and in women's education at Columbia University as a whole. Beginning in 1983, the two traditional collegiate units of Columbia University, Barnard College and Columbia College, offered academically talented female students two distinct choices.[61] Women could opt to attend Columbia and be modern-day pioneers in Ivy League coeducation, similar to the first women "coeds" at Princeton or Yale. Women's other option was to attend Barnard, a small university-affiliated liberal arts college for women, and accept the challenges of being part of a women's institution that was reaffirming the value of its single-sex tradition.[62]

The benefits of the coeducation decision for Columbia College were immediately clear: In the first year of coeducation, applications to Columbia College were up 56 percent. Moreover, while admitting what was then the largest class in its history, Columbia also improved traditional measures of quality in its applicant pool (SAT scores and class rankings) and obtained an entering class that was 45 percent female, the highest percentage of first-year women in the Ivy League. Barnard, in contrast, experienced a drop in applications when

Columbia admitted women, just as some naysayers had forewarned. This drop represented a change from the four years preceding the new Barnard-Columbia coordinate agreement (1978 to 1982), when Barnard's applications had risen 51 percent.[63] Of the 126 females accepted at both Columbia and Barnard, 8 matriculated at Barnard; 78 entered Columbia; and the 40 others attended elsewhere. Also, nine of the twenty-six transfer students accepted at Columbia were transfers from Barnard.[64] But soon Barnard's admissions reflected what Barnard officials had counted on: the college's resiliency and the appeal of an elite women's collegiate education—especially the unique environment that Barnard offered as a small women's liberal arts college affiliated with a top-tier university.[65] Not only did Barnard's enrollments start rising in the 1990s, but also its applications increased. The college was able to retain its small liberal arts character and be even more selective, accepting only about 40 rather than 45 to 50 percent of applicants (see Table 11.4).[66]

For Columbia College, the introduction of coeducation called for certain immediate changes on campus. It needed, for example, to comply with Title IX guidelines, to establish new health facilities and counseling services for women, and to renovate lavatories and residence halls. Columbia addressed some of these logistical needs quickly by relying on its time-tested relationship with Barnard and on services already established for Barnard women. Interestingly, some undergraduates recognized the limitations of Columbia's approach. As the editors of the *Columbia Spectator* warned: "It takes a lot more than admitting women for a school to lose its identity as a male bastion."[67] Early coeducation at Columbia did not involve a sustained discussion of the campus climate for women (for example, there was only a committee on women's studies) or a revisiting of Columbia's traditional mission, classroom pedagogies, hiring, or definition of excellence. Indeed, the women who arrived at Columbia's gates in the early years of coeducation entered an academic world much the same as generations of men before them.

Women's interests in attending newly coeducational Columbia were motivated by two basic considerations. For those new female matriculants who were conscious of women's less than equal status in the academy, this opportunity to attend Columbia allowed them to be part of a historic "breakthrough" at one of the country's last all-male institutions of higher education.[68] For others who perceived their admission at Columbia in more individualistic terms, this was the chance to embrace tradition, to garner the cachet of an Ivy League degree, and to attend the selective undergraduate college that best fit their intellectual aspirations. Regardless of how women viewed themselves, however, the university would see them in gendered terms—as women, Columbia's new coeds. However, if the presence of these female Columbians inevitably created some new challenges, if some changes were slow, and if there were some pockets of resistance, one important attitudinal barrier had weakened considerably: In the

Table 11.4. Barnard enrollment, 1940–2004

	Total
1940	983
1945	1,240
1950	1,112
1955	1,227
1960	1,455
1965	1,767
1970	1,949
1975	1,926
1980	2,491
1985	2,136
1990	2,123
1995	2,278
2000	2,290
2004	2,287

Sources: For 1940–1960 (the 1939–40 year and so on, annual registrar's report, provided by Jocelyn Wilk, University Archives, Columbia University; 1965, 1970, 1975, 1980, 1985, and 1990, New York State Education Department Office of Research and Information Systems Annual Fall Enrollment Survey; 1995, 2000, and 2004, www.barnard.edu/opir/students/enrolls.html, accessed August 24, 2004. Chart prepared by Melanie Rago, Indiana University.

nineteenth century women had been excluded and asked to prove their intellectual mettle, whereas now women students were recruited and recognized as helping to enhance Columbia's competitiveness.

Reinvigoration of First-Year and General Education

As the essays in this volume consider, the pressures for coeducation were considerable in the 1960s and 1970s. Even elite single-sex institutions such as Barnard and its reference group of selective northeastern women's colleges, which up until this point had remained rather insulated from market pressures and popular trends, were compelled to reassess their viability and the merits of a new admissions policy. In comparison to the situation of the independent Seven Sisters, Barnard's situation as a liberal arts college for women was complicated, as was Radcliffe's at Harvard and Pembroke's at Brown, by the legacy and politics of its coordinate relationship to a research university. But the crucial difference in Barnard's case was that Barnard had historically maintained its own faculty—a source of stability, identity, and leverage, which neither Pembroke nor Radcliffe, which relied on faculty from their respective universities, enjoyed. This unique strength had been integral to Barnard's ability to forge its identity within Columbia University and helps explain why Barnard—unlike Radcliffe, for example—did not necessarily see coordination as an arrangement to "escape from."[69] Moreover, by the time of the second coeducation debates at Columbia University in the 1970s and 1980s, women comprised approximately half of Barnard's faculty, and the sense of the college's historic mission and ties to the university were sufficiently strong as to be taken seriously by both parties at the Barnard-Columbia negotiating table. By contrast, by the early 1970s Pembroke had folded into Brown, and Radcliffe, having ceded much of its internal decision making to Harvard, had become what many regarded as merely a "paper college."[70]

   After the Barnard-Columbia negotiations ended with the decision that Columbia College would admit women directly beginning in the fall of 1983, Barnard administrators began to direct their energies to crafting a plan for Barnard's future. As one Barnard faculty member recollecting the curriculum reforms of 1983 described:

> Once Columbia had become coeducational it destroyed forever Barnard's monopoly on women who wanted to go to college here on Morningside Heights. Some had wanted to go to Barnard because Barnard was Barnard and some had wanted to go because Barnard was across the street from Columbia and integrated with it. On that latter group of people we would certainly no longer have the monopoly. . . . With all of the external change that was going on, Barnard had to go back and ask itself "Is our identity clear in academic terms?"[71]

   Barnard had to consider possible ways to distinguish itself from peer women's colleges, on one hand, and from its neighbor and longtime collaborator—now also competitor—Columbia College, on the other hand. In actuality, Barnard had been considering its options for a while. For example, a 1976 consultants' report had posed three possible strategies for Barnard to pursue in relation to Columbia University.[72] One path was to encourage more research on women (this would be the option, for instance, that President Jill Ker Conway tried at Smith) or to become an institute for advanced study (as Radcliffe ultimately did). Another option was to emphasize women's continuing education, as was the case at Sarah Lawrence beginning in the 1960s. A third option was to develop ties with other educational agencies and institutions in the metropolitan area.[73]

   In the end, Barnard forged its own path, true to its historic roots and legacy but responsive to the new demands on the rising generation of college women. Although Barnard did seek to enrich its curriculum by entering into certain new collaborations (such as approving a new degree in music with Juilliard), Barnard mainly pursued the strategy of curricular accentuation and differentiation. The 1983 reforms focused on re-invigorating the first-year of studies and the general education experience.[74] More than being the college within Columbia University that had a female-only admission policy, Barnard cultivated its supportive yet challenging teaching-oriented environment as a small liberal arts college. It also became the unit within Columbia University that self-consciously studied and promoted an understanding of gender as central to its mission.[75] As such, Barnard faculty and administrators' energies built upon Barnard's tradition of providing a rigorous liberal arts education for women that was attuned to the reality of women's lives. They welcomed the task of updating the curriculum, programming, and campus policies in order to better prepare women for leadership roles and for the demands of their intellectual and social lives after college.

This sharpening of Barnard's identity and mission was, in large part, the product of a concerted reform effort approved by the Barnard faculty on February 7, 1983.[76] To be sure, Barnard had previously attempted curricular reforms, but circumstances earlier had hindered the process, particularly the anxiety that Barnard would be "submerged into Columbia."[77] By contrast, once Barnard's institutional future was clearer, the Barnard College faculty could galvanize around change. As Barnard professor Bernice Segal recalled: "It was quite clear that we were not going to be engulfed by Columbia. They had gone coed—that was their worst threat and now we were going to deal with that situation but we were not going to be nonexistent. We were going to try and be viable and actually it was a very different mood. . . . The attitude was, 'It is not going to come to nothing—we are going to have curriculum change.'"[78] The question remained, though, What curriculum would reflect the values embedded in Barnard's founding mission—to allow women to demonstrate their intellect by providing them an education comparable to Columbia's—while enabling Barnard to navigate a new era in relations with Columbia University and to solidify its leadership in women's higher education at a time of formidable challenges and opportunities?

A Coordinate of Coeducational Columbia

Only twenty years have passed since the advent of coeducation at Columbia College and, concomitantly, the beginnings of a new era in Barnard's history. Thus, the long-term impact of these changes and their meaning for women's education at Barnard College remain to be discerned. The challenges for Barnard in the post-1983 era appear to fall into five broad, related areas: enhancing its competitiveness through curricular reform and campus building, negotiating the competition between Barnard and Columbia and their students, tapping new synergies in Barnard-Columbia coordination (e.g., athletics, women's studies), articulating Barnard's contribution to a coeducational Columbia (what I refer to as a new complementarianism), and searching for ways to support female identity and greater inclusiveness in Barnard's single-sex environment.

Within the roster of highly selective women's colleges, Barnard offers its students the unique combination of the benefits of a small, teaching-oriented liberal arts college along with access to the resources of a top-tier research university, and the vast intellectual and cultural attractions and employment possibilities of a major cosmopolitan setting. Indeed, the rhetoric that New York City is Barnard's laboratory, a theme that Barnard College administrators promoted early in the college's history, has assumed a new saliency as Barnard has striven to distinguish itself among other selective colleges in what had become an "academic buyer's market." One 1983 college-fair recruitment slogan, for example, proclaimed proudly that Barnard offers students "A Slice of the Big Apple."[79] Emphasizing the opportunities to be found in New York City, in addition to touting Barnard's Ivy League university connection, has been a way to differentiate Barnard from competing women's colleges located in more bucolic or small-town settings. But if the metropolitan setting and ties to a research university have helped Barnard find its niche among women's colleges, what has helped to distinguish Barnard in the eyes of any prospective female applicant from its neighbor directly across the street—coeducational Columbia College?

The answer to this crucial question involved a careful consideration of Barnard's curriculum and campus climate. To its credit, after resisting a merger with Columbia College, an autonomous but affiliated Barnard College neither fell into imitating Columbia College nor hesitated to tackle the serious question of how Barnard must change with the times in order to continue to attract top-caliber students and to preserve its standing as one of the foremost producers of female leaders. One early outcome of Barnard's self-study was the decision to strengthen its liberal arts curriculum by bolstering requirements in mathematics, quantitative reasoning, and science.[80] This step allowed Barnard to be counted among the country's most highly selective women's colleges, like Smith and Bryn Mawr, which were designing curricular reforms to prepare women more effectively for an increasingly complex and technological age and which aimed to help further women's advance into high-profile, traditionally male-dominated professions.[81]

Barnard's curricular reforms showed Barnard's currency with national education debates in the early 1980s. Indeed, the changes at Barnard not only came at a pivotal new era in Barnard-Columbia relations and a crucial time for women's colleges as a distinctive group, but also coincided with a period of scrutiny and intense self-examination by colleges and universities more generally. Institutions of higher learning across the nation sought new ways to improve their quality and to produce graduates who were better prepared for new economic and political realities. In a reaction to the curricular freedom that had developed during the student activism of the 1960s and 1970s, colleges began to reconsider the aims and purposes of the undergraduate curriculum, especially general education requirements.[82] Columbia retained its commitment to humanism, with its major nod to the currents of reform in the 1970s and 1980s being the introduction of coeducation. By contrast, Barnard retained its female-only admissions policy but updated its curriculum. The "new" curriculum at Barnard emphasized interdisciplinary work, honors study, a required literary seminar (with an emphasis on writing), and first-year seminars (which brought first-year students into contact with senior faculty).[83] The choices that the Barnard faculty made accentuated their college's longstanding strengths and solidified an orientation for Barnard that stood in strong contrast to Columbia's core approach and its famous Western civilization survey. Such change, President Ellen Futter told the Barnard faculty, "sharpens our identity."[84]

Barnard-Columbia's coordinate structure had always constrained but also facilitated Barnard's ability to capitalize on its university ties while developing a separate identity as a women's college. This marketable characteristic was used in the post-1983 era to further distinguish Barnard from competitors in the areas of its traditional strengths (such as teaching), to capitalize on its unique resources (its faculty of scholar-teachers, university affiliation, and urban setting), and to address certain areas related to women's education that were not necessarily accentuated in coeducational settings. The major aim was to provide women interested in the university with a choice: education at an institution of "comparable academic standards and contrasting character and educational style."[85]

Curricular reforms required considerable financial resources and alumnae and donor support, in addition to the commitment of Barnard faculty and administrators. Barnard had since its founding subscription struggled to articulate its financial needs to the donor community. While, as Table 11.3 shows, Barnard's alumnae giving and endowment have always been low compared to those of the other Seven Sisters, the 1980s onward brought greater opportunities for fund-raising among Barnard alumnae.[86] In the period from 1972 to 1984, for example, the number of Barnard alumnae increased from 14,000 to 21,400, or nearly 53 percent, but the donations rose much more—from $359,000 to $960,000, or 167 percent.[87] A fund-raising campaign held from 1990 to 2000 raised $162.9 million and enabled the college to engage in many initiatives, including improving student aid, building a new residence hall, and establishing five faculty chairs.[88] Even with this success, Barnard has had less ample financial resources than its competitors have and thus feels the weight of rising costs—for example, salaries in the urban setting—associated with maintaining its competitiveness.[89]

One particularly crucial area where Barnard has directed attention in the past two decades is financial aid.[90] Such support was needed to continue to assure quality by attracting a talented and diverse applicant pool and to make a Barnard education accessible, given its substantial sticker price. In 1984–85, the academic year after Barnard began to compete with a coeducational Columbia College, Barnard was the fifth most expensive undergraduate institution in the United States, with a complete student budget for study and living costs estimated at $15,759.[91] The college remains expensive. In 2002–3, tuition and fees at Barnard were $26,528 and room-and-board fees totaled $10,462. Today, approximately 56 percent of Barnard students receive "some amount of aid," and 17 percent of the college's operating budget is devoted to aid.[92] This allocation of resources and the school's recruitment efforts through summer programs and high school visits have enabled Barnard to offer its students the enriching experience of a diverse campus.[93] In 2004 Barnard's 2,297 students included women from across the United States and forty other countries, and minority students comprise almost one-third of the undergraduates.[94] Asians, representing 17 percent of students, constitute the largest group of students of color.[95] Together, African American, Native American, and Latina students represent 13 percent of students.[96]

In addition to changes in its curriculum and degree requirements and greater commitment to diversity among its student population, Barnard undertook changes in campus and cocurricular life. For the first time in its history, Barnard has become nearly fully residential.[97] In the college's early decades, Barnard's lack of residential facilities had, like the pull of the city, constrained the rise of college spirit at the institution, but overall had decided benefits for the urban coordinate college. The costs associated with maintaining residence halls were avoided, but equally important, Barnard's identity as a commuting school had another advantage—having students return home each evening helped soften some of the resistance among New York City's socially conservative elites to the idea of sending their daughters to college. Today Barnard's residence halls enhance Barnard's attractiveness to prospective students. A fully residential campus was key in Barnard's effort to address frequently expressed parental concerns about the safety of its urban campus while capitalizing on the considerable intellectual, cultural, and educational advantages of the urban setting. Further, the expansion of residential facilities has aided Barnard's efforts to recruit and retain a more diverse, national, and even international student population. Moreover, the expansion of residential facilities has meant that Barnard could, in line with national trends in higher education, offer the range of services and programming that prospective students—including those from New York City itself—were increasingly considering in their selection of an undergraduate institution.[98]

The building of an eighteen-story residence hall at the corner of 116th and Broadway in the mid-1980s, financed in part with a loan from the New York State Dormitory Authority, provided a quadrangle effect and was heralded as a "significant symbolic statement" of "vitality and renewal."[99] According to architect James Stewart Polshek, dean of Columbia's Graduate School of Architecture, the design effectively captured "the ascendancy of Barnard and its power and confidence as an institution with an identity distinct from that of Columbia."[100] In retrospect, by 1989, its centennial year, Barnard not only represented a metropolitan option among elite women's colleges but also, equally important, had been able to enhance the distinctiveness of its collegiate culture and to accentuate its particular vision of undergraduate education within Columbia University.

Competition and Comparisons: Women's Differing Experiences at Barnard and Columbia

By the 1990s most observers agreed that coeducation at Columbia was not going to lead, inevitability, to the demise of Barnard. In 1994 (a decade into the era of coeducation at Columbia and Barnard's new agreement with Columbia), regular-admission applicants to Barnard totaled 2,734, of whom 55.2 percent were admitted, and by 2004, 4,380 applicants, of whom 1,201, or 27.4 percent, were admitted—making Barnard one of the nation's most competitive women's colleges.[101]

The women who helped integrate Columbia College in the 1980s encountered curiosity, high expectations, much anticipation, and a new spirit of competition between two longtime collaborators, Barnard and Columbia. A *New York Times* reporter interviewing Columbia new "coeds" upon their arrival probed their reasons for selecting Columbia. Some of the 357 female first-year students had rejected single-sex education in their college selection process; "Enough of all girls," one enthusiastic "coed" announced. Some, but certainly not all, were buoyed by the spirit of the women's movement and the sense of being part of a "breakthrough" for women. Some deemed their choice of Columbia College as "only fitting," because Columbia was the alma mater of a father, brother, or other male relative. For others, though, the decision to enroll at Columbia actually meant a departure from family tradition, as in the case of one young Columbia College woman who elected not to enroll at her mother's alma mater, Barnard, because "a Columbia degree will have more prestige in the long run."[102]

More difficult to capture than the reasons underlying their college choice is how well Columbia's new "coeds" were integrated into the campus life at Columbia. Although levels of de facto undergraduate coeducation had been reached through cross-registration on Columbia's campus since the 1960s, and nearly 84 percent of incoming Columbia students in the class of 1987 supported coeducation, the concept of a female Columbian was nonetheless something that needed to enter into the consciousness of longtime Columbia professors.[103] Like the women who pioneered coeducational experiments in the nineteenth century, Columbia's early women felt themselves singled out for attention. "At first, when a professor in one of my classes would discuss something he would talk to the room, and then look back to the women," reflected Linda Mischel, CC '87, on her experiences in the Columbia classroom. The sense of novelty or in some instances resistance associated with the switch to coeducation did not keep women, many of whom had been outstanding leaders during their high school years, from engaging in Columbia's campus organizations and attaining leadership roles in the coeducational setting. "Over the past two years it has become very clear that the people who are most active in student organizations on campus, whether political or social, are women," Alex Navab, president of the Columbia College students told a reporter from the *New York Times* on the eve of graduation in May of 1987. He noted that women held about three-quarters of campus leadership positions. Women also competed and excelled in the classroom, earning top honors as valedictorian and salutorian of the first coeducational graduating class (both honorees were daughters of Columbia faculty members).[104]

Far less public fanfare greeted the women who, choosing a single-sex tradition, entered Barnard College in the fall of 1983. Many were attracted by the accessibility of the faculty, the intimacy of the liberal arts setting, the "chance to experiment" without getting "lost in a huge institution," and the strengths of Barnard's curriculum and opportunities for independent and interdisciplinary study.[105] More insight about the impact of the 1982 agreement on Barnard and its students came a year after Columbia admitted women, in a December 1984 article appearing in the *New York Times* entitled "Barnard Savors Its Independence." The article highlighted President Ellen Futter's view of then recently implemented curricular reforms at Barnard and her vision of the future for Barnard College; it also discussed how the presence of under-graduate women on both campuses had, along with greater opportunities and choices for women, given rise to new types of intrainstitutional rivalries and stereotypes. In particular, the profile described how the presence of women at both Barnard and Columbia drew comparisons and a sense of competition that shaped undergraduate women's experience within the university.

The comments of Mark Simon, president of the Student Admissions Committee at the time of Columbia's first coeducational entering class, captured one view shared by many in the university community during these early years of coeducation: "The women who now choose Barnard are making that choice because they think they'll thrive in an all-female environment, not be hindered by men. Columbia women, on the other hand, are not afraid to compete."[106] As the article noted, however, there was a contrasting view of Barnard women. This view was voiced adamantly by President Ellen Futter, who instead of focusing on women's competition with men characterized Barnard women as talented women who were benefiting from the advances of earlier generations of women but were now facing the new self-imposed and cultural pressures of being "superwomen." In Futter's view, the notion that an all-female environment was any less rigorous than a coeducational one was specious. Rigor and excellence in higher education need not be predicated on direct competition with men, she argued; what matters is maintaining an engaging environment for learning that allows women to excel. In her eyes, Barnard was a place where "women are neither ignored nor coddled. They are simply taken seriously and respected."[107] Christine Royer, director of admissions, similarly held that "a women's college is not just a building or a campus, it's an attitude. Here everyone just assumes that a woman can do everything and be everything she wants to do and be."[108] This climate of high expectations for students has been integral to Barnard's noteworthy record of graduating high-achieving women.[109] Part of Barnard's success, both historically and especially after the advent of coeducation at Columbia College, has been the large percentage of women faculty and the commitment of faculty women and men who find a selective women's liberal arts college such as Barnard a challenging and rewarding milieu for a scholar-teacher.[110]

Since Columbia College became coeducational in 1983, Barnard-Columbia relations have been complicated. Intrauniversity rivalry manifests itself in student publications, where opinion pieces and commentaries concerning Barnard-Columbia relations compare, or even caricaturize, the two colleges and their student populations. Many of the myths and stereotypes focus on women. Some musings concern intellectual life, for example, whether the colleges are equally rigorous, which college is "best," and whether Barnard is a "fallback" for women and a "back door" to a Columbia education. Other stereotypes and preoccupations concern social life, for example, whether Barnard is a lesbian haven (a charge that, historically, critics have leveled against all-female colleges); whether Barnard students should have "swipe access" at Columbia's residence halls, or whether instead certain boundaries between the two neighboring colleges should be maintained; whether Barnard women are less committed to scholastic pursuits than to their marriage prospects; and whether Barnard and Columbia women are romantic rivals in dating and partnering with Columbia men.[111]

New Synergies between Barnard and Columbia

If new types of competition have shaped recent Barnard-Columbia dynamics, Barnard-Columbia coordination in the postcoeducation era has also benefited from new collaborations and synergies. Interestingly, in the era of the new Barnard-Columbia agreement and undergraduate coeducation at Columbia College, athletics—an arena that had previously delineated the separate worlds of Columbia men and Barnard women—became one arena where institutional boundaries became blurred. Barnard and Columbia female undergraduates can now, at least in theory, unite as teammates rather than as competitors. The establishment of a consortium in 1983 (the outcome of six months of negotiations), approved by the National Collegiate Athletic Association, made it possible for Columbia to face the staffing and budgetary challenges of compliance with Title IX and for Barnard-Columbia women to compete in nine Division I varsity sports (Barnard-Columbia currently compete in fourteen).[112] "It is an extracurricular function that does not go to the heart of the academic program (at Barnard), which makes it a particularly attractive area for cooperation for both Barnard and Columbia."[113] While opening new opportunities and making possible the "intelligent use of limited space," the collaboration has involved trade-offs. For example, while in return for its budgetary contribution Barnard does work with Columbia in hiring and other administrative decisions that affect the stature of the Athletic Department, Barnard women no longer claim the Barnard bear as their mascot. The uniforms of all women's teams at Columbia University display the Columbia lion.

In an effort to advance friendship among the university's undergraduate women, a small group of women students at Columbia and Barnard resurrected a tradition that had not found favor at Barnard College earlier in the century—the sorority. Sororities (then called fraternities) were banned in 1915 because then-dean Gildersleeve and student government leaders believed them to be divisive.[114] With coeducation on the horizon, the idea of a sorority was resurrected. Planned in the spring of 1983, the Columbia University chapter of Alpha Phi welcomed its first pledges the following fall, drew its inaugural membership equally from women at Barnard and women at Columbia's School of Engineering, and then gained some members from Columbia College.[115] Part of the sorority's founding mission was to "dispel the myths about the other side of the street."[116]

As in the past, Barnard and Columbia have benefited in the post-1982 era of coordinate relations from sharing resources and developing complementary strengths. For example, Barnard offers the course work in teacher preparation, dance, and theatre, and Columbia offers computer science and the visual arts.[117] Most notably, reflecting the influence of the women's movement and a renewed interest in the effectiveness of women's colleges, Barnard has promoted itself as a place within Columbia University that focuses on the study of gender and the study of women. Carefully situating itself to support women across the university and yet not be perceived as a safety valve that might lessen pressure on Columbia to promote equity in its staffing, departments, and faculty ranks, Barnard's Center for Research on Women has become a bridge between Barnard College and coeducational Columbia College. Barnard has had a Women's Studies Department since 1988. In 2005–6, the Women's Studies Department has a roster of six faculty, including two Mellon postdoctoral fellows, ten affiliated full-time faculty, and five visiting and adjunct faculty.[118]

Columbia, in response both to its changing student population and to the sway of new intellectual paradigms in the academy, eventually introduced gender study into its curriculum. Currently, Columbia undergraduates can earn a degree in women's and gender studies, a major offered in conjunction with Barnard. Columbia's Institute for Research on Women and Gender was founded in 1987, with literary scholar Carolyn Heilbrun (Columbia PhD 1959) as its director until 1989. The institute, which sponsors a graduate certificate program and has attracted renowned feminist scholars to Columbia's faculty—among them, for instance, literary scholar Gayatri Chakravorty Spivak, historian Alice Kessler-Harris, and anthropologist Lila Abu-Lughod—is the self-described "locus of interdisciplinary feminist scholarship and teaching at Columbia University."[119]

A New Complementarianism

Barnard's current president, Judith Shapiro, is an articulate spokesperson for the college. Inaugurated in October 1994, Shapiro, former provost at Bryn Mawr and an anthropologist with expertise in the cross-cultural study of gender, ushered in Barnard's second decade under the new coordinate agreement with Columbia with such reflections as these in her address, on the role of women's colleges:

> In a society that favors men over women men's institutions operate to preserve privilege, while women's institutions challenge privilege and attempt to expand access to the good things of life. Thus, the rationales for man's institutions and for women's are not parallel. . . . The significant contributions of women's colleges lie not only in what they do for women, but also in what they do for professional and collegial relationships between women and men. . . . Why do we need a women's college to help move this progress forward? Because women have the most compelling interest in it. And a women's college—a Barnard—is a center of energy for mobilizing and expanding that interest. . . . Barnard has a pivotal role to play in Columbia's project of achieving true coeducation.[120]

Having until 1983 exerted a monopoly over traditional-aged women's undergraduate education at the university, Barnard now stands as a distinctive choice for women students. As a women's liberal arts college within a great research university, Barnard represents what one faculty member described as "the best place [in the academic world] for a woman to be. You have Barnard with its single-minded commitment to gender studies and you have the resources of Columbia. . . . If you are a woman, you have a lot of choice."[121] And yet, as friends of Barnard College are quick to note, Barnard's value as an academic unit within Columbia University today extends beyond the question of college choice. Upon assuming office, President Shapiro opened a new chapter in the college's history by underscoring that Barnard is not merely a female alternative to coeducational Columbia College: Barnard's identity and excellence as a liberal arts college rests in offering a distinctive environment for teaching and learning—an environment where men and women comprise about equal numbers among trustees, the higher levels of administration, and faculty. As such, whereas Barnard was born of women's exclusion from Columbia in the 1880s, and Barnard's early leaders sought to bolster their college's standing by emulating Columbia College, Barnard today brings a unique contribution to Columbia University and to women's education more generally—a successful model of coeducation at work. Barnard College, as President Shapiro and others have argued, is an integral part of achieving a fully coeducational Columbia.[122]

Toward Greater Inclusiveness

The "four critical" years of college are crucial in shaping a student's values, self-understanding, and aspirations.[123] Until the 1980s, discussion of the challenges for Barnard women, and the modern women's college, generally focused on such well-documented tensions as combining marriage, family, and career and hence reflected traditional heterosexual assumptions.

In the 1980s a number of student groups, among them the Lesbian Alliance, the Columbia Gay and Lesbian Alliance, and Labia, began to agitate for greater tolerance for sexual diversity on campus. In 1988 Barnard became one of the earliest colleges to offer a lesbian literature course.[124] Still, for some students, change on Barnard's campus has been too incremental. In 1998 a controversy surrounded a Barnard recruitment brochure that (in a section on "alumnae achievements") specifically noted that Barnard graduates are likely to marry and have children. Shannon T. Herbert, president of Lesbians and Bisexuals in Action at Barnard, was among those who spoke out against the brochure, seeing its emphasis on a traditional view of female identity and success as a defensive, image-preserving strategy on the college's part. "There is a stigma attached to women's colleges," Herbert argued. "A stereotype that they produce unshaven, unmanageable, unruly women, or women who become lesbians." In responding to criticisms of the brochure, President Shapiro clarified the college's intentions: "The real message we want to send is that women can have it all."[125]

Today Smith College is perhaps the women's college most recognized for affirming sexual diversity among its students. It offers women two lesbian houses, a gender-neutral student code, and a transgendered policy for residential halls. Although by comparison Barnard seems to lag in campus consciousness and debate of issues related to sexual orientation and transgendered students, the discussion of such subjects, according to a spring 2004 *Columbia Spectator* article, appears to be "gaining traction."[126] In commenting on Barnard's policies and perspectives, Suzanne Trimel, director of public affairs at Barnard, told the *Spectator:* "If a student began here as a woman and then wanted to change her gender, does that mean we would kick her out of college? No, it doesn't. We are a sensitive and caring community. That said, the question has not arisen. To the best of our knowledge, no Barnard student has changed gender."[127]

It seems likely, based on Barnard's past support for women's and gender issues (demonstrated by such initiatives as the Barnard Center for Research on Women), that the college will consider the growing recognition of challenges facing transgendered students as administrators review policies and explore ways to better meet the needs of all Barnard students. Members of the Barnard community recognize that although Barnard's campus is affirming of women, further work remains in moving toward the goal of an equitable and inclusive college experience. "There is still not gender parity in the regular curriculum," observed Janet Jakobsen, current director the Barnard Center for Research on Women, on the occasion of the center's thirtieth anniversary in 2001. That said, the engagement with women's issues on Barnard's campus is strong and vibrant, and an important aspect of how the college projects itself to prospective students: "As a college for women, Barnard embraces its responsibility to address issues of gender in all their complexity and urgency, and is committed to an integrated curriculum that recognizes the importance of gender in all forms of endeavor."[128]

So, what does the future hold for Barnard College? On one level, Barnard's future will be linked inevitably with the continued vitality of selective women's colleges and with the ability of its leaders to be effective planners and fundraisers who are committed to assuring access and excellence at the college. On another level, Barnard's future will continue to be shaped by its proximity to Columbia and the nature of their coordinate relationship. In the post-1983 era, Barnard has had to grapple with fundamental questions of purpose and identity. What is the need for a women's college at Columbia University once Columbia College adopted coeducation? What is the need for a women's college when the gender barriers to entry at the nation's colleges are gone and legal mandates call for gender equity?

Barnard forged a strong identity as a women's college early in its history, while capitalizing on its university ties and thereby achieving distinction among university coordinates. At the same time, Columbia has also continued to benefit from its coordinate ties with Barnard. In 1998, Barnard and Columbia negotiated a new coordinate agreement, signed with little public fanfare, to extend the terms of their most recent agreement (1989) for another ten years, with a provision that allows for a five-year extension. In addition, a committee of trustees meets semiannually to review Barnard-Columbia ties, which are governed by a series of detailed agreements that cover the finances and logistics of collaboration and the sharing of resources.

In the post-1983 years, Barnard has flourished, not because the college changed in any fundamental way but rather because the faculty, trustees, and administrators accentuated the college's historical strengths and connected them to new circumstances. Barnard continues to maintain its tradition of female trusteeship and executive leadership and its independent faculty with a strong women's presence.[156] Today the women's college is a successful coordinate not of a male college but of a coeducational one. Yet Barnard leaders today remain mindful of their college's legacy. Barnard College is uniquely situated to compete both with selective all-female and coeducational independent liberal arts colleges and with its longtime neighbor and coordinate partner, Columbia.[129] In 2000 Barnard received four thousand applications for 550 places, making it the most exclusive women's college in the country.[130] Annie Nathan Meyer, who rose to the challenges of her generation, would most likely be proud of where the Barnard "experiment" is today. She would appreciate what the college's recent generation of leaders has achieved as pioneers of women's liberal arts education and, indeed, as "pioneers of true coeducation."[131]

Notes

1. Annie Nathan Meyer's January 26, 1888, letter to the *Nation* is reprinted in her retrospective *Barnard Beginnings* (Boston: Houghton Mifflin, 1938), 167–74.

2. For information about Girton College, Cambridge University, see Chapter 12 in this volume.

3. Andrea Walton, "The Dynamics of Mission and Market in the Coeducation Debates at Columbia University in 1889 and 1983," *History of Education* 31 (November 2002): 589–610.

4. Quoted in Lisa Belkin, "First Coed Class Enters Columbia College," *New York Times,* August 30, 1983.

5. For a discussion of the leadership displayed by Barnard administration and trustees, see Janet Fern Alperstein, "The Influence of Boards of Trustees, Senior Administrators and Faculty on the Decision of Women's Colleges to Remain Single-Sex in the 1980s" (PhD diss., Columbia University, 2001).

6. The title of Barnard's executive head was changed from "dean" to "president" primarily to raise public consciousness of Barnard's fund-raising needs apart from Columbia's

and to enhance Barnard's competitiveness in fund-raising compared to that of the other Seven Sisters (all of which were led by presidents).

7. Helen Lefkowitz Horowitz, *Alma Mater: Design and Experience in the Women's Colleges from Their Nineteenth Century Beginnings to the 1930s* (New York: Alfred A. Knopf, 1995), 134–42.

8. Andrea Walton, "Achieving a Voice and Institutionalizing a Vision: The Barnard Deanship at Columbia University, 1889–1947," *Historical Studies in Education/Revue d'Histoire de l'Education* 13 (Fall 2001): 113–46.

9. Ella Weed to Silas Brownell, October 28, 1890, Barnard College Archives, Woolman Library, Barnard College, New York. See also Meyer, *Barnard Beginnings,* 46, and Walton, "Achieving a Voice."

10. Barnard dean, *Annual Report, 1946–47,* as quoted in Dorothy U. Denburg, "Curriculum Change: A Case Study in Successful Innovation" (EdD diss., Teachers College, Columbia University, 1986), 78. See also Walton, "Achieving a Voice."

11. For a discussion of women's education in the 1950s, see Mirra Komarovsky, *Women in the Modern World: Their Education and Their Dilemmas* (Boston: Little, Brown, 1953); Paula Fass, *Outside In: Minorities and the Transformation of American Education* (New York: Oxford University Press, 1989); and Andrea Walton, "Signs for the Future: Educators Consider the Female Student," paper presented at the annual meeting of the American Educational Research Association, April 27, 2000, New Orleans.

12. McIntosh was the first mother to hold Barnard's executive position. Emily James Smith Putnam had secured trustee approval to remain dean after her marriage in 1899 but resigned upon her pregnancy a year later, knowing beforehand the weight of trustee opinion against combining motherhood and the deanship. See "Reminiscences of Millicent McIntosh," Columbia University Oral History Research Office Collection, Columbia University, New York City.

13. Rosalind Rosenberg, "'The Woman Question' at Columbia: From John Burgess to Judith Shapiro," beatl.barnard.columbia.edu/cuhistory/archives/Rosenberg/woman_question. htm. Professor Rosenberg's *Changing the Subject: The History of Women at Columbia* (New York: Columbia University Press, 2004) appeared as this essay was in its final stages of preparation and hence its insights could not be addressed or incorporated here.

14. Barnard Dean's *Annual Report,* 1952–53, 3; Denburg, "Curriculum Change," 105.

15. Barnard Dean's *Annual Report,* 1950–51.

16. Barnard College, *A History of Barnard College* (New York: Barnard College, 1964), 99.

17. Alperstein, "Influence of Boards of Trustees," 53.

18. For data about Columbia's female doctorate production, see Rosalind Rosenberg, "Continuing the Woman Question: John W. Burgess to Judith Shapiro," *beatl.barnard. columbia.edu/cuhistory/archives/Rosenberg/woman2.htm.* For Barnard's effectiveness in graduating future holders of doctorates, also see the Franklin and Marshall Study (1998), www.barnard.edu/opir/students/fm_study.html

19. Quoted in Annette Kar Baxter, "The College's Leading Women and Their Roles," *Barnard Magazine* 53 (1964): 36. See also Minutes of the Barnard Faculty, February 19, 1964, Columbia University Archives, Low Library, Columbia University, New York City (hereafter CUA); Patricia A. Sullivan, "Rosemary Park: A Study of Educational Leadership during the Revolutionary Decades" (PhD diss., Boston College, 1982), 147–60; and Barnard dean's *Annual Report,* 1962–64. For a discussion of Radcliffe, see Dorothy

Elia Howells, *A Century to Celebrate: Radcliffe College, 1879–1979* (Cambridge, MA: Radcliffe College, 1978).

20. For a more extensive discussion of the coeducation deliberations at Columbia, see Walton, "Dynamics of Mission and Market."

21. Quoted in Alperstein, "Influence of Boards of Trustees," 61. See also "Columbia College Is Scored on Coeds," *New York Times*, November 30, 1975.

22. See Robert Freedman to the Barnard-Columbia Trustees Committee, December 13, 1970; and Barnard-Columbia [B-C]Trustees Committee Transcript, April 12, 1971, 10, 67, CUA. See also Minutes of the Barnard College Trustees, December 3, 1969, CUA. For background on the general debate about how best to educate women, see Jill Ker Conway, "Coeducation and Women's Studies: Two Approaches to the Question of Women's Place in the Contemporary University," *Daedalus* 103 (1974): 239.

23. B-C Trustees Committee Transcript, April 11, 1971, 54, CUA. See also Walton, "Dynamics of Mission and Market."

24. B-C Trustees Committee Transcript, May 12, 1971, 55, CUA.

25. Ibid, 53.

26. See note 19.

27. M. Elizabeth Tidball and Vera Kistiaskowsky, "Baccalaureate Origins of American Scientists and Scholars," *Science* 193 (August 1976): 646–52; and Tidball, "Of Men and Research: The Dominant Themes in American Higher Education Include neither Teaching nor Women," *Journal of Higher Education* 47 (July–August 1976): 373–89.

28. For research on the effectiveness of women's colleges, see Lisa Wolf-Wendel, "Research Issues on Women's Colleges," in *A Closer Look at Women's Colleges*, July 1999, accessed October 22, 2004, at *www.ed.gov/pubs/WomensCollege/chap3fin.html*; and M. Elizabeth Tidball, *Taking Women Seriously: Lessons and Legacies for Educating the Majority* (Phoenix: Orynx Press, 1999).

29. "Barnard Students Demand Expanded Negro Recruiting," *New York Times*, February 25, 1969, and "Barnard Head Asks Patience By Blacks," *New York Times*, March 4, 1969.

30. Radcliffe's Mary Bunting drew national attention to this problem. See www.news.harvard.edu/gazette/1998/01.29/MaryBunting-Smi.html.

31. Quoted in Linda Greenhouse, "Barnard: A Time of Self-Analysis," *New York Times*, January 16, 1974, 72.

32. Peterson's inauguration in the winter of 1968 coincided with the Columbia student protest against the university's central administration, as well as with a campus maelstrom over the case of Barnard student Linda LeClair, who drew attention in the national press as Barnard College officials attempted to respond to her violation of housing policies (she hid from Barnard officials that she was living off campus with her Columbia College boyfriend).

33. Jane S. Gould, *Juggling: A Memoir of Work, Family, and Feminism* (New York: Feminist Press, 1997), 142.

34. Ibid. See also Jane S. Gould, "Women's Centers as Agents of Change," in Carol S. Pearson, Donna Shavlik, and Judith G. Touchton, *Educating the Majority: Women Challenge Tradition in Higher Education* (New York: American Council on Education/Macmillan, 1989), 219–29.

35. Jane S. Gould, "Personal Reflections on Building a Women's Center in a Women's College," *Women's Studies Quarterly* 12 (Spring 1984): 6.

36. Remarks by Eleanor Elliott, "Anniversary Celebration for the Center for Research on Women Commemorates the Center's Place in History," November 9, 2001, available at www.barnard.columbia.edu/new/news/news111901b.html.

37. Gould, "Personal Reflections," 4.

38. For the terms of Barnard-Columbia 1973 Agreement, see Edward B. Fiske, "Columbia Plans to Take Women in Beginning in '83; Columbia College to Admit Women in the Fall of 1983," *New York Times*, January 23, 1982, 26. For a general discussion of the 1973 and 1982 Barnard-Columbia intercorporate agreements, see Walton, "Dynamics of Mission and Market."

39. Greenhouse, "Barnard ."

40. Columbia University and Barnard College, 1973, 26–34, as quoted in Alperstein, "Influence of Boards of Trustees," 57. For Radcliffe, see Howells, *A Century to Celebrate*; and Laurel Thatcher Ulrich, ed., *Yards and Gates: Gender in Harvard and Radcliffe History* (New York: Palgrave Macmillan, 2004).

41. Quoted in Denburg, "Curriculum Change," 117.

42. Ibid.

43. "Columbia Bars Plan to Admit Women," December 14, 1975, *New York Times*, 67; "Columbia Is Scored on Coeds."

44. McGill quoted in "Columbia College Is Scored on Coeds," 61.

45. Edward B. Fiske, "Barnard and Columbia in Merger Struggle," *New York Times*, May 30, 1976; Fiske, "Columbia Asks Barnard for Rise in Coeducation," *New York Times*, May 27, 1976.

46. "Columbia Is Scored on Coeds."

47. Barnard College Trustees, 1976, 1, in Alperstein, "Influence of Boards of Trustees," 65.

48. Quoted in Denburg, "Curriculum Change," 79.

49. Quoted in ibid., 79.

50. Quoted in Alperstein, "Influence of Boards of Trustees," 55.

51. Ibid, 74–75. See also Robert A. McCaughey, *Stand Columbia: A History of Columbia University in the City of New York* (New York: Columbia University Press, 2003).

52. Edward B. Fiske, "Acting Head Chosen by Barnard Trustees for Post of President," *New York Times*, May 7, 1981; and Fiske, "Columbia Plans to Take Women Beginning in '83," *New York Times*, January 1, 1982.

53. Edward B. Fiske, "Columbia Unit Delays Decision on Coeducation," *New York Times*, December 21, 1981.

54. For example, some Princeton alumni were vociferous in their opposition to coeducation. See the Horton Collection, Mudd Library, Princeton University, Princeton, New Jersey. Wabash (Indiana), Hampton Sydney (Virginia), and Morehouse (Georgia) were the remaining nonreligiously affiliated men's liberal arts colleges.

55. Alperstein, "Influence of Boards of Trustees," 90.

56. Walton, "Dynamics of Mission and Market"; Fiske, "Columbia Asks Barnard for Rise" and "Columbia Unit Delays Decision"; Gene I. Maeroff, "The All-Male College Vanishing," *New York Times*, August 21, 1984.

57. Walton, "Dynamics of Mission and Market." I would like to thank Donald Glassman, Barnard College archivist, and Penny Van Amburg, director of development communications, for information regarding the capital campaign. See also Mattfeld's "Without

Peer," as noted in Alperstein, "Influence of Boards of Trustees," 84–85, and consult www.barnard.edu/giving.

58. Before Sovern assumed the Columbia presidency, a report by a faculty committee led by Columbia chemist Ronald Breslow had provided some evidence (based on the histories of other all-female institutions) that Barnard would remain viable in the event of coeducation at Columbia. As Breslow, in reflecting on his committee's report twenty years later, noted: "The main thing our report achieved was to give a good rational argument that we could become coed and not destroy Barnard." Quoted in Ciel Hunter, "Panel Reflects on Twenty Years of Coeducation," *Columbia Spectator,* March 5, 2004.

59. At the time, Barnard enrolled 2,500 students and Columbia had 2,900. The average SAT total score for Barnard students was 1,225 combined, while the average score for Columbia College students was 1,270 combined. See "Barnard and Columbia College At a Glance," *New York Times,* January 23, 1982.

60. Fiske, "Columbia Plans."

61. Women might also pursue a degree through the School of General Studies (for non-traditional adult students) or the Fu Foundation School of Engineering.

62. Mandeville, "Women and the Ivies," *Columbia: The Magazine of Columbia University,* 8/2 (1982): 12–20; Marcia Synott, "A Friendly Rivalry: Yale and Princeton Universities Pursue Parallel Paths to Coeducation," in Leslie Miller-Bernal and Susan L. Poulson, eds., *Going Coed: Women's Experiences in Formerly Men's Colleges and Universities: 1950–2000* (Nashville: Vanderbilt University Press, 2004), 111–50; and S. Daley, "Barnard Adjusts to Competition with Columbia," *New York Times,* August 8, 1983.

63. Alperstein, "Influence of Boards of Trustees," 90. See also "Barnard and Columbia College at a Glance."

64. For data, see Belkin, "First Coed Class."

65. Georgia Dullea, "Barnard Savors Its Independence," *New York Times,* December 2, 1984.

66. For admissions information on Barnard, see articles in *Barnard Bulletin,* for example, "New Recruitment Strategies Help Maintain Barnard's Acceptance Rate," April 29, 1991; Sophia Sapozhnikov, "Barnard's Number of Applications Skyrockets," November 19, 1997.

67. Quoted in Alice Boone's retrospective "*Spectator* Fans the Flames in Conflicted BC-CC Relationship," *Columbia Spectator,* December 22, 2001; and Greenhouse, "Barnard."

68. Belkin, "First Coed Class."

69. The phrase is Radcliffe president Mary Bunting's in describing her perspective on Harvard-Radcliffe coordination to leaders of Princeton in the late 1960s, quoted in Synnott, "A Friendly Rivalry," 115.

70. Annette Kar Baxter, "On Women's Colleges," *New York Times,* November 5, 1979; Carole Leland, *Men and Women Learning Together: A Study of College Students in the Late 70s: Report of the Brown Project,* Brown University, April 1980 (mimeograph); and Polly Welts Kaufmann, ed., *The Search for Equity: Women at Brown University, 1991–1981* (Hanover: Brown University, 1991)

71. Quoted in Denburg, "Curriculum Change," 147.

72. Alperstein, "Influence of Boards of Trustees," 69–70.

73. For Smith, see Auden D. Thomas, "From Vision to Action: Jill Conway at Smith College" (PhD diss., Indiana University, 2004). For Radcliffe, see Thatcher, *Yards and Gates;* and for Sarah Lawrence, see Linda Eisenmann, "Brokering Old and New Philanthropic Traditions: Women's Continuing Education in the Cold War Era," in Andrea Walton, ed., *Women and Philanthropy in Education* (Bloomington: Indiana University Press, 2005), 148–66. Sarah Lawrence opted to admit men in 1968, but the percentage of male students has remained low.

74. Denburg, "Curriculum Change," esp. 128, 141.

75. For Barnard's mission statement, see *www.barnard.edu/about/mission/html.*

76. Denberg, "Curriculum Change," 127.

77. Quoted in ibid, 146. My discussion here relies on Denburg's study.

78. Ibid.

79. D. C. Denison, "Selling College in a Buyer's Market," *New York Times,* April 10, 1983.

80. Edward B. Fiske, "Barnard Shifting Curriculum to Give Math More Emphasis," *New York Times,* February 27, 1983. Today, Barnard students are required to take course work in nine ways of knowing: reason and value, social analysis, historical studies, cultures in comparison, laboratory science, quantitative and deductive reasoning, language, literature, visual and performing arts. There is also a two-term physical education requirement. See *www.barnard.edu/academics/cur.html.*

81. Edward B. Fiske, "Coeducation at Columbia: A Double Perspective on Single-Sex Schools," *New York Times,* February 1, 1982.

82. Edward B. Fiske, "Wave of Curriculum Changes Sweeping American Colleges," *New York Times,* March 10, 1985; Fiske, "Changes Sweeping Universities' Curriculums," *New York Times;* April 12, 1987; and Fiske, "Core Studies Gain Ground at Colleges," *New York Times,* April 17, 1989.

83. Barnard had in fact been a pioneer in interdisciplinary studies, having introduced a program in American studies in 1939. This modern push toward interdisciplinarity at Barnard built upon this tradition but also reflected a curricular trend in U.S. colleges and universities in the 1980s. See also Fiske, "Core Studies Gain Ground."

84. Futter quoted in Dullea, "Barnard Savors."

85. Barnard College Trustees, 1976, 1, in Alperstein, "Influence of Boards of Trustees," 65.

86. Potential donors, including foundations, often mistakenly assumed that Barnard shared in Columbia's wealth. As mentioned earlier, the title of Barnard's executive officer was changed from dean to president in 1953 in part to enhance Barnard's visibility to potential donors.

87. These data are for the period 1972 to 1984. See Edward B. Fiske, "College Alumni are Sending Record Donations to Alma Maters," *New York Times,* February 14, 1984.

88. Penny Van Amburg to author, February 4, 2005.

89. www.barnard.edu/giving.

90. For information on the Barnard Campaign, see beatl.barnard.columbia.edu.

91. Barnard belonged to a tier of expensive and prestigious institutions in which less than a thousand dollars separated the "most expensive" university, Massachusetts Institute of Technology ($16,130), from the tenth costliest, Sarah Lawrence College ($15,180). Although its costs were not significantly less than Barnard's, Columbia was not among

the country's ten most expensive institutions in 1984. To understand the elite nature of Barnard and Columbia's reference group, it is useful to note that in 1984 the average cost of tuition, room, and board at a public college was $4,881, while the cost of attending a private college was $9,022. See Gene I. Maeroff, "College Costs Up, but Rate Slows," *New York Times*, August 14, 1984.

92. Data retrieved February 7, 2006 at www.barnard.edu/about/facts.html.

93. Ibid. For a discussion of the increasingly diverse applicant pool at Barnard, see Lisa Szymanski, "More Applicants Means Higher Selectivity for Barnard Class of '02," *Columbia Spectator*, March 2,1998.

94. Sixty-six percent of Barnard students are from outside New York State. Students from New England represent 12 percent of the college; students from the South, 7 percent; and students from the Midwest and Southwest, 9 percent. Data retrieved February 7, 2006 from www.barnard.edu/about/facts.html.

95. Ibid. At most women's colleges African Americans form the largest minority. See Beverly Guy-Sheftell, "Diversity and Women's Colleges," in "A Closer Look."

96. See www.barnard.edu/about/facts.html. Barnard still faces the challenge of diversifying its faculty to be more reflective of its students and of the broader society. Scholars of color comprise only 14 percent of the college's faculty. See www.barnard.edu/about/facts.html#enrollment, accessed June 20, 2005.

97. Today nine out of ten Barnard students live on campus.

98. Georgia Dullea, "More City Students Choose Dormitory Life," *New York Times*, November 11, 1986. For the rise of the student as client, see John Hardin Best, "The Revolution of Markets and Management: Toward a History of American Higher Education since 1945," *History of Education Quarterly* 28 (Summer 1988): 177–91; and Martin Trow, "American Higher Education: Past, Present, and Future," *Educational Researcher* 17 (April 1988): 13–23.

99. Larry Rohter, "Nearing 100, Barnard Plans 18-Story Dormitory Tower," *New York Times*, October 25, 1986.

100. Ibid.

101. For data, see "Barnard Applicants: Summary of Statistics, 1994–2004," retrieved February 7, 2006, at www.barnard.edu/opir/admissns/applic.html. During this span, the median SAT scores for students admitted to Barnard rose from 580 to 660 and from 610 to 650 in verbal and math, respectively.

102. Belkin, "First Coed Class."

103. Hunter, "Panel Reflects."

104. Ibid.

105. Dullea, "Barnard Savors."

106. Belkin, "First Coed Class."

107. Dullea, "Barnard Savors."

108. Belkin, "First Coed Class."

109. In the period 1920–95, Barnard rankings were: All Sciences (6), Life Sciences (9), Psychology (2), and Chemistry (71). In recent decades, even given greater competition, Barnard has remained distinctive. Its rankings are: All Sciences (11), Life Sciences (13), Psychology (2), and Chemistry (109). See the Franklin and Marshall Study, 1998, www.barnard.edu/opir/students/fm_study.html.

110. Important background information on trends in Barnard faculty hiring and promotion and in the characteristics of Barnard faculty from 1900 to 1974 is found in Robert A. McCaughey, "A Statistical Portrait of the Barnard Faculty, 1900–1974" (Department of History, Barnard College, Columbia University, 1975). Barnard's Web site offers more recent data.

111. See, for example, from the *Barnard Bulletin:* Cathy Webster, "CC Woman Misunderstood," October 1, 1986; letter from the editor, March 8, 2000; Nicole Bufario, "Finale to the Women's College Debate," October 9, 2000; Rebecca Krevosky, "West Side (of Broadway) Pride," February 21, 2001; and Christy Thornton, "Barnard Students Not a Bunch of Columbia Rejects," March 8, 2002. From the *Columbia Spectator,* see Ciel Hunter, "Has Coeducation Changed Columbia?" September 15, 2003; Emmanuelle St. Jean, "Columbia-Barnard Relationship Benefits All," September 16, 2003; Isolde Raftery, "Why Can't Barnard Students Swipe into Columbia Dorms?" March 1, 2004; and "End Residential Segregation: Current Housing Rules at Columbia and Barnard Are Too Strict," staff editorial, March 25, 2004.

112. Barnard is the only women's college competing in Division I. The Seven Sisters compete in Division III. Dave Rubel, Jared Gollob, and John Zimmerman, "Athletics Face Biggest Changes," *Columbia Spectator,* January 23, 1982. See Mita Millick, "The Women Athlete at Barnard: Does She Exist?" *Barnard Bulletin,* November 26, 1997.

113. Mary M. Witherell, "Barnard and Columbia Form Athletic Consortium," *Barnard Bulletin,* March 2, 1983. See also "Columbia and Barnard Agree on Joint Athletic Program," *Barnard Bulletin,* November 2, 1983.

114. Amy Clyde, "Alpha Phi: Pledging Diversity and Sisterhood," *Barnard Bulletin.* November 2. 1983.

115. "Columbia Gets Its First Sorority Chapter, and 40 Are Initiated," *New York Times.* September 24, 1984.

116. Ibid. See also Marisa Brahms and Nicole Trepicchio, "Lions Don't Hang Out with Bears, Oh My!" *Barnard Bulletin,* March 5, 1997. Columbia University's chapter of Alpha Phi closed in 1998. Barnard women are eligible to join the four National Panhellenic sororities that Columbia University currently has on campus—Alpha Chi Omega, Delta Gamma, Kappa Alpha Theta, and Sigma Delta Tau—as well as one coeducational society, Alpha Delta Phi. See www.studentaffairs.columbia.edu.

117. See www.barnard.edu/opir/relation.html.

118. See www.barnard.columbia.edu/wmstud.html.

119. See www.columbia.edu/cu/irwg/frame_history_b.html and www.columbia.edu/cu/irwag/programs/main/one/index.html.

120. Judith Shapiro, Barnard College Inaugural Address, 27 October 1994, Available at www.barnard.edu/president/inaug.html

121. Quoted in Ciel Hunter, "Has Coeducation Changed Columbia?" *Columbia Spectator,* September 15, 2003.

122. Shapiro, "Role of Women's Colleges."

123. Alexander W. Astin, *Four Critical Years* (San Francisco: Jossey-Bass, 1977).

124. Quoted in Carrie Stewart, "Lesbians Lack On-Campus Support," *Barnard Bulletin,* February 1, 1988.

125. Karen W. Arenson, "Barnard Students Will Stick with Ms.," *New York Times,* December

8, 1998. For a stinging critique of the Barnard administration's response to the concerns of lesbian students, see Laura Schlessinger, "On . . . Lesbian and Gay Activists and Biological Errors," Gay and Lesbian Alliance Against Defamation Web page, www.glaad.org/publications/resource_doc_detail.php?id=2855, accessed November 14, 2004.

126. "Code Covers Transgendered," *Washington Times*, June 16, 2003; Isolde Raftery, "Can a Man Attend Barnard College," *Columbia Spectator*, November 17, 2003; and Fred A. Bernstein, "On Campus, Rethinking Biology 101," *New York Times*, March 7, 2004.

127. Quoted in Bernstein, "On Campus."

128. Quoted in Karen Arenson, "Women Studies Center Is 30," *New York Times*, November 7, 2001. See "Requirements for the Liberal Arts Degree," www.barnard.edu/academics/cur.html.

129. As Table 11.2 shows, women account for more than half of Barnard's current faculty. This compares to the national average of 34 percent. See www.barnard.edu/about/facts.htm/.

130. See Women and the Academy, beatl.barnard.columbia.edu/learn/timelines/women.htm.

131. Shapiro, Inaugural Address. See also Rosenberg, "Continuing 'The Woman Question'" and Nancy J. McVickers, "Reflecting on Women, Coeducation, and Cultural Change," at www.yale.edu/wff/gendermatters/pdf/GM_McVickers.pdf.

12

Cambridge University's Two Oldest Women's Colleges, Girton and Newnham

Leslie Miller-Bernal

For more than five hundred years, Cambridge University educated only men. In the mid–nineteenth century, people concerned with furthering women's higher education organized two colleges for women. Colleges of the university do not award degrees, however, and it was not until after World War II that the university granted women degrees. Girton was Cambridge's first residential women's college, although when it opened in 1869, it was actually located in Hitchin, a town about twenty-six miles outside the city of Cambridge, where it remained until 1872. Newnham was Cambridge's second women's college, but as its promotional literature notes, when it opened it 1871, it was the first women's college located within the city. While Girton and Newnham shared many characteristics for the first century of their existence, they reacted differently when men's colleges of Cambridge University began to admit women students in the early 1970s. Girton admitted men undergraduates in 1979, making it a "mixed" or "coresidential" college, whereas Newnham remained a women's college with only women "fellows."[1]

This chapter focuses on two issues: why Girton became a mixed college while Newnham remained single sex, and what the consequences of these different decisions have been for the colleges' functioning and for their women students. My basic argument is that even at an elite "collegiate university" like Cambridge, the transition of men's colleges to coresidential colleges has had major effects on women's colleges.[2] These effects may not be as dramatic as they have been for autonomous women's colleges in the United States, but the recent coeducational movement nonetheless has created challenges for both Girton and Newnham.

Before Women Became Full Members of the University

Girton College owes its existence to the determination, persistence, and organizational skills of Emily Davies (1830–1921), the daughter and sister of clerical schoolmasters. Davies herself had been educated only at home, and like others at the time, she realized that the lack of education impeded women's advancement. Davies worked on women's causes with a group of like-minded people, some of whom gave her financial support when she decided to establish a women's college. The wealthy and unconventional artist Barbara Leigh Smith Bodichon (1827–91) made the largest individual financial contribution, giving one thousand pounds to the initial fundraising, ten times more than the next-highest contributors listed in the original prospectus.[3] She is frequently referred to as a "co-founder" of Girton.[4]

Emily Davies is known for her unwavering commitment to two principles. The first was that women should be educated in a place geographically separate from men to avoid even the suggestion of impropriety. When Girton moved in 1872 from its original location to its present one, it was still two and a half miles from Cambridge.[5] Davies's second principle was that women should have the same entrance procedures, course of study, and exams as men students had. Davies's first success was her three-year campaign to convince Cambridge authorities to allow girls to take the same admissions exams as boys, the Cambridge Local Examination. For Davies, "difference" meant "lower," and she intended to fight "the prejudice and assumption of the inherent inferiority of women's intellectual capacity . . . in an unambiguous fashion."[6]

One of Davies's male allies, Henry Sidgwick, a fellow of Trinity College, had a different view about the form that women's education should take. As a Cambridge insider, Sidgwick had been active in seeking reform of men's admissions and tripos (honors) exams. He therefore did not favor putting women through the examinations that men took, since he saw them as inappropriate for all students. In 1871, while the first women students at the college organized by Emily Davies were still residing twenty-six miles outside Cambridge, Henry Sidgwick "took the bold step" of renting a house in Cambridge for women to hear "special lectures for women" or take a "special examination" for women. A school founder and educational reformer from the north of England, Anne Jemima Clough, agreed to preside over these women students. Thus began Newnham College.[7]

In their early years, Girton and Newnham colleges differed as a result of the influence of their founders' philosophies. Henry Sidgwick had a "freer and more elastic" approach to women's higher education than did Emily Davies.[8] He allowed students to attend Newnham even if they did not intend to take the final examinations that for men students led to degrees. He also encouraged Newnham students who were working toward a tripos to negotiate timetables with their teachers that took into account how well their previous education had prepared them for this work.[9]

Emily Davies insisted that Girton students take the same exams as men students and that they finish their work within the time period allotted for men. Given many women students' inferior preparation for university-level work, such requirements caused a great deal of strain. Since women students did not have even the guaranteed right to take the tripos, Girton students had to prepare for exams that they could not be certain they would be allowed to take.[10]

A campaign to get the university to open the tripos exams to women began in 1880. Sidgwick and Davies joined the campaign, but their philosophical differences prevented them from working together. In 1881 the University Senate voted 366 to 32 to grant women the right to take the tripos examinations. Since women would still not receive degrees, Cambridge had created a new category: "a graduate without a degree."[11] And yet, women students felt this to be a very important step, as is vividly conveyed in a letter of a Newnham student to her sisters:

> I am writing to you now in the interval of awful suspense, for I am so excited I really cannot work. In less than an hour the voting takes place. . . . [later] Hurrah! We have won! . . . When women get the Degrees (for this is only the thin end of the wedge) it will be nothing to this. We all feel it is the great crisis in the history of women's colleges.[12]

Women's integration into Cambridge University did not progress rapidly or smoothly. Although they had the right after 1881 to take the tripos examinations, women still needed to obtain permission from faculty to attend lectures or laboratory classes.[13] A Newnham student of the time later wrote about how women students felt they were at the university "on sufferance," with "no status as undergraduates." She was aware that "many members of the University disapproved of women's colleges," which made the authorities of the two women's colleges encourage their students to "be as unobtrusive as possible" and discourage them from participating in "the life of the University."[14]

Despite their marginal position, some of the early women students achieved outstanding exam results. In 1880, for example, a Girton student, Charlotte Angas Scott, tied with a man student for the eighth-highest grade in the mathematics tripos. When Agnata Ramsay of Girton was the only student at the university to obtain a first in the classics tripos of 1887, Emily Davies decided that women had proved they were willing and capable of studying the same curriculum as men and that therefore it was time to request that they receive degrees.[15] Sidgwick, who had a great deal of influence in Cambridge affairs, did not at first agree, however, and ultimately the Council of the University

Senate let the matter drop.[16] In 1890 a Newnham student, Philippa Fawcett, received one of the highest possible honors: Her tripos results placed her above the Senior Wrangler, the top man in mathematics.[17] But all these results were unofficial; no matter how great their academic success, women were given only certificates indicating that they had studied at Cambridge, not degrees.

In the 1890s women came to the university better prepared, since girls' secondary schooling had been "transformed."[18] Particularly in the new girls' public (that is, elite private) schools, where by the early 1890s about two-thirds of Oxbridge women students had been educated, girls received advanced instruction from increasingly qualified teachers.[19] As a result, students' academic programs at Newnham and Girton became quite similar. In 1897 Henry Sidgwick agreed with Emily Davies that the time had come to try to convince Cambridge University to award women degrees, as London University and Manchester University already did. The day of the vote in the Cambridge University Senate was riotous. Special trains brought university graduates to Cambridge for the specific purpose of enabling them to vote against the measure. Undergraduates' sentiments were "whipped up" to frenzy; they constructed effigies of Newnham and Girton students, putting one on a bicycle that they hung from an upper window of the Senate House; they built a huge bonfire with some placards and college railings; and they stormed the gates of Newnham College. The measure was soundly defeated, 1,713 to 662.[20]

The issue of women's membership in the university surfaced again at the conclusion of World War I, a time of many social changes, including ones "particularly significant for the affairs of women." Perhaps most notable was the parliamentary bill of 1918 that enfranchised married women over age thirty.[21] The war had had a devastating effect on Cambridge's and Oxford's finances, so for the first time, these two universities sought state help.[22] Women and their allies saw this as an opportunity to get governmental backing for their attempts to receive equal treatment. Oxford voted to give women degrees in 1920, but rather than encouraging Cambridge to do likewise, university officials used Oxford's "capitulation" as an argument to keep Cambridge single sex.[23] Women at Girton and Newnham lobbied members of the University Senate to be made full members of the university and thereby to receive degrees, but in 1920 the measure was defeated, 904 to 712.[24] Women, their allies, and larger public opinion saw this as a temporary situation, since all the other universities in the British Isles by that time awarded women degrees and teaching posts. Cambridge people immediately began to prepare a compromise position, namely that women should be accepted as full members of the university but their numbers limited. The senate voted again in 1921, but still women were defeated, this time accompanied by a mass demonstration of men students who chanted, "We won't have women," and after the vote, stormed and destroyed part of the gate of Newnham.[25]

The lack of membership in the university did not affect just women students. In fact, given the increasing number of college activities that women participated in and the decline in chaperonage, many women students felt happy with their college life. But the same was not true for women fellows (also called "dons"), who were barred from participation in university governance even on matters affecting their employment, and who were very restricted in their use of the main library and research facilities. As one perceptive Newnham alumna wrote about the situation when she was a student in 1922:

> As women students we were accepted, even if sometimes considered rather odd. We were treated courteously at lectures, by lecturer and audience alike. We could join most of the University societies. We were hardly conscious of such disabilities as still existed. . . . It was not until later that I realized how hardly a position so favorable to the students might bear upon the women dons, many of whom were undertaking a lot of University work but were ineligible for any University appointments.[26]

During the 1920s, some changes did occur that improved the situation for women students and fellows. In 1923 women students were finally given the formal right to instruction in the university and in laboratories. At the same time, the university limited the number of women receiving university instruction to five hundred. Women also were granted "titular degrees," which meant that they could put such initials as "BA" after their names, but they still did not receive an official degree at the Senate House, nor could they proceed to a master's degree. In 1926 women academics became eligible for appointments to the university; of 183 new university lectureships appointed, 11, or 6 percent, went to women. Women academics continued to feel "distinctive and subordinate," however. They could not participate in university governance nor vote in the senate. The mistress of Girton College and the principal of Newnham College (the colleges' heads) were able to attend university functions by "courtesy" rather than right and were "lumped together with wives on such occasion." Women fellows were even forbidden to wear academic robes and resorted to using hats to designate their status.[27]

When women obtained full membership in Cambridge University in December 1947, the issue had become so noncontroversial that the resolution was unopposed. By delaying its implementation slightly, the (then) queen, later the queen mother, became the recipient of the first degree bestowed by Cambridge on a woman, an honorary doctor of laws, which some commentators believe gave the October 1948 event appropriate "ceremony and respect."[28] Not until 1960 did members of Newnham College and their allies get the quota on women students at the university removed, however, and it took five more years to lift the ban on mixed-sex colleges.[29]

Women's Position at Cambridge When Coresidency Began

By 1972, when the first three men's colleges of Cambridge University started to admit women undergraduates, Newnham and Girton were well-established, if relatively poor, colleges for women. Their students often received high marks in the tripos exams, making the colleges academically competitive with the best men's colleges. While there were differences between the two colleges, perhaps particularly in their public images, they shared the important characteristic of having been the only way women students could attend this very prestigious university.

In the early and mid-1970s, women were still a minority of undergraduate and graduate students at all British universities, but they were an even smaller minority at Cambridge. In 1975–76 women nationwide were 35 percent of undergraduates, whereas at Cambridge they were only 17 percent.[30] Probably reflecting the public image of Cambridge as mainly for men, highly qualified young women were less likely than highly qualified young men to apply for admission: 8.3 percent of such women compared to 13.7 percent of such men applied to Cambridge in 1973.[31]

The faculty of Cambridge University in the early 1970s was also predominantly men. In 1973 women were slightly less than 5 percent of the teaching staff, and the fellows were mostly in the women's colleges. These figures for Cambridge were again about half those for universities across the rest of Britain. In 1975 Cambridge appointed its first woman vice chancellor (the real head of the university, in contrast to the figurehead chancellor), Dame Alice Rosemary Murray, something it did not do again until 2003.[32]

The social movements of the 1960s and early 1970s affecting student life in the United States were also evident in Cambridge, at both the men and women's colleges. Students protested parietal hours and any other signs of in loco parentis; they sought to have student representation on college committees and more say in decisions affecting college life. Students allied themselves with progressive political movements in their communities, nation, and even other countries.[33] The "Robbins Report," published in 1963 by the national government, put pressure on all British universities to expand to meet the increased demand for higher education and the need for a better-educated labor force. Colleges in Cambridge began to place more emphasis on outreach to maintained or state schools (what Americans call public schools) rather than just receiving students from the elite public and independent schools (what Americans call private or prep schools).[34] They also recognized the need to enroll more women students, a position reinforced in 1973 by a government position paper, "Equal Opportunities for Men and Women."[35]

Women's issues began to receive more attention among Cambridge University students in the 1960s and 1970s. Early signs included the revival of the women's boat race against Oxford, dubbed the contest of the Amazons, in 1964, and the election of the first woman president of the prestigious Cambridge Union (the university debating society) in 1967.[36] Germaine Greer, a well-known feminist and author of *The Female Eunuch,* debated the conservative columnist William F. Buckley Jr. at the Cambridge Union in 1972. Greer commented that she had become aware of "sexual tensions" in the university when she had studied there in the late 1960s. Although she was taunted as a lesbian, the house supported the women's liberation movement by a vote of 546 to 156.[37] Just two years later, a woman president of the Cambridge (University) Student Union described as an "ardent supporter of Women's Lib" resigned from her position because those who had supported her were themselves defeated. In an interview for the university student newspaper, she talked about the difficulties she had had as a woman, with the "male/female dominance problem" becoming "red-hot" in tense situations.[38] During the 1970s both Newnham and Girton Colleges had feminist groups. The Scarlet Women, based at Newnham but open to "sisters" from anywhere, described itself as "pledged to oppose anything at all which smacks of male domination."[39] Girton had a feminist reading group, and its undergraduates subscribed to the feminist magazine, *Spare Rib,* at least for a trial period.[40]

During the approximately one hundred years during which women students studied at Cambridge only in their own colleges, older men's colleges were much wealthier than the women's colleges. Ruth Cohen, a principal of Newnham, noted in 1971 that women's colleges had much greater teaching expenses than men's colleges did. Since very few of their women fellows were also university teaching officers, as many fellows of men's colleges were, the college, rather than the university, had to pay their salaries. Cohen also noted that this expense was the reason that, while the number of students at Newnham had risen from about 230 in 1920 to about 370 in 1971, the number of official fellows had risen only from eighteen to twenty-two. The next principal of Newnham, Jean Floud, made these same points and added that women's colleges of the past had coped in part by underpaying their fellows. "This has never been just and it is no longer expedient," she said at a 1973 meeting of alumnae. "Our Fellows must be paid at market rates, for we cannot risk any decline in the quality of our Fellowship."[41] In a ranking of Cambridge's twenty-four colleges in 1975 on the money each received from investments for the twelve months ending June 30, 1974, Girton was fourteenth from the top, with £75,144; Newnham was twenty-first, with £21,438. By comparison, the richest college, the much older men's college, Trinity, had more than ten times these amounts—£974,000. Both Girton and Newnham depended more on internal income from fees; Girton ranked eighth of the twenty-four colleges and Newnham, tenth.[42] In 1974 the mistress of Girton called inflation one of the college's "outstanding problems" and said that "retrenchments" were "inevitable."[43]

A major difference between Girton and Newnham, particularly from the perspective of students, has always been location. The historic buildings of Girton (those built after the move from Hitchin in 1872) are two and a half miles outside Cambridge. In 1969 the college built another campus closer to the center of town, Wolfson Court, but it houses a minority of undergraduates and is generally not as popular as the older campus. Few students have cars (first-year students are not allowed to), and parking within the city is difficult, so most Girton students cycle into town. Newnham, on the other hand, is much more centrally located—very close to some of the academic departments where lectures take place, and not far from the older, prestigious formerly men's colleges such as Trinity, Clare, and Kings. Although it is never easy to tell how stereotypes develop, it may be that these differing locations contributed to the images of Girton students being clearer as well as less flattering than those of Newnham students. Fewer students at other colleges go to Girton, which means that images of its students and college life are not as easily contradicted by reality.

In any case, by the late 1960s, Girton women students had a reputation for being intellectual and sporty. A 1957 graduate who visited her old college in 1969 and then wrote about her impressions for the *Sunday Times Magazine* described the image of Girtonians as "bespectacled and dowdy earnestness, sturdy cyclist's calves, a solid devotion to hockey and abstract causes." The image was persistent, too, she noted; in 1967 a college society was formed called "Society for the Metamorphosis of the Girton Image."[44] Another article in the popular press at about the same time reported that the (male) author heard from men students that Girton "girls" were more often talked about than taken out because they were seen as "excessively intellectual and inordinately ugly." Even the mistress of Girton recognized the stereotype of Girton as a "lay nunnery"; she asked that the photos accompanying the article include men to disprove this common belief.[45] Students were aware of these stereotypes, of course. An informal student publication at Girton began an article about a hockey team by mentioning the college's reputation as "blue-stockinged, jolly hockey-sticks, pass-along-the-wing-girls-that's-the-sort-of-thing." Geographic isolation may have not only contributed to such images but also fostered a need to develop college life. In 1973 Girton students boasted that their college was the only women's college to have a bar, the center of drinking and social life at many colleges.[46]

Newnham College students, in contrast, seem to have been subject to fewer stereotypes in the years before coresidence began in the men's colleges. One older Newnhamite recalled an atmosphere of "freedom, flexibility and tranquility" that she believed still characterized the college in the early 1970s.[47] Newnham's students, who included such famous names as A. S. Byatt, Margaret Drabble, Rosalind Franklin, Germaine Greer, Dorothy Hodgkin, and Sylvia

Plath, were generally seen as somewhat more trendy, less conventional than Girton students. Such views may have had a historical basis. As a writer to the *Times* noted, early Newnham students were very radical, even though they had tea on the lawn. They talked of socialism, anarchism, and unorthodox sexual morality.[48] Newnham authorities in the early 1970s seemed to believe that their college was still like this. In 1973 at a dinner for the retiring principal, Ruth Cohen, the vice principal of Newham said that "unconventionality" had "always" characterized the college. The retiring principal fit in with this tradition, the vice principal continued, as she had "strong and radical views on many subjects."[49] Newnham was not unconventional in all ways, however. A woman research fellow at Girton in 2003 recalled that her mother, who had been a student at Newnham in the mid-1920s, was thrown out of Newnham for getting married; that experience "scarred her for life," according to her daughter.[50] In the 1970s, the College Council regularly discussed and voted on whether students who married could continue their studies, an issue that fellows at Girton also voted on.

The Beginnings of Coresidency

Although women fellows and women students still experienced discrimination in the late 1960s, their colleges had some advantages within the Cambridge system. Women students all went to one of the three women's colleges (from 1954 on, not only Newnham and Girton but also New Hall). Similarly, all women fellows who taught at the university were at one of these three colleges. Thus Newnham, Girton, and New Hall were guaranteed the best of the small number of women who applied to Cambridge and also the best of the women academics.[51]

Three men's colleges—Churchill, Clare, and Kings—announced in the late 1960s that they were going to admit women students in 1972 and thereby become coresidential. It did not take long for people at the women's colleges to recognize what this would mean for them. A senior tutor at Girton later explained, "The prospect of fierce competition for the crème de la crème of academic women brought painfully home to us how spoilt the three women's colleges had always been."[52] The mistress of Girton put it more simply: "We had lost our monopoly."[53] Women students might prefer to go to the older and more prestigious men's colleges in the center of town, perhaps particularly if they were interested in the sciences. Women academics might choose to become fellows at these richer colleges. In recognition of such issues, representatives of the three men's colleges began to meet with representatives of the three women's colleges beginning in February 1969. While everyone agreed that "the men's colleges would not want to take large numbers of the ablest candidates from the women's Colleges, or to make it difficult for them to fill places in science subjects," it was not as easy to decide how to coordinate admissions procedures.[54] All that these meetings ultimately achieved was a "non-binding agreement to phase the men's colleges' lemming-like rush towards the sea of co-residence."[55]

Members of Girton believed that due to their college's relatively remote location, they had the most to lose from men's colleges becoming coresidential. Beginning in late 1969, discussions about the future "began in earnest." While members recognized the proud role Girton had played in women's higher education, they felt "haunted" by "the specter of a severe decline in the college's academic standing."[56] The governing body decided by the necessary two-thirds vote to apply to Privy Council for an enabling statute, which would allow the college to become mixed quickly, by taking a simple vote, if it felt the need. When the statutes changed in 1971, college members did not think they were in any way "committing" themselves "one way or the other."[57]

Newnham initially reacted with more confidence and equanimity than Girton did to the men's colleges becoming mixed. The principal, Ruth Cohen, reported that people at Newnham were "pretty la-di-dah" about the effect on Newnham's admissions because they believed that there was enough talent for all the colleges.[58] She said she welcomed mixed colleges since they were the only way of getting a substantial increase in the number of women students at Cambridge.[59] In the view of one reporter, the principal demonstrated that the "suffragette spirits lives on," as she asserted that Newnham would not admit men until "far more women" were "guaranteed places at Cambridge."[60] In speaking at a centenary luncheon, the principal did admit that men's colleges being coresidential would mean that Newnham would be in competition for the "ablest girls who want to come to Cambridge as students," but she added that Newnham people did not "see this as a threat" to their "position."[61] Nonetheless, by 1973 fellows and students at Newnham were discussing coresidence. Students prepared for an "extraordinary meeting" to discuss this issue by noting some facts: Only 12 percent of students admitted to the university were women, and women of higher caliber were turned away, whereas men students of a lower standard gained "easy admittance."[62] Students and fellows voted to remain a women's college, but then and when they next voted in 1977, the vote was close and contentious. In fact, the discussion created so much divisiveness that the college placed a moratorium on discussion for several years.

Newnham officials sounded somewhat less confident two years after the first men's colleges went mixed. As a fellow who was at Newnham at the time recalled, anxiety focused on two major issues: the quality of students, since there was the assumption of a "finite pool," and recruitment of fellows, particularly in the sciences.[63] When the principal, Jean Floud, gave a talk to alumnae, she mentioned that applications from women to Cambridge University were "distinctly sluggish." Given the need for the university to maintain its standing as a center of scientific excellence, and given that "too few" women wanted to study science, the position of women's colleges was "vulnerable." More men's colleges were becoming mixed, so women in science were "diverted" from women's colleges to coresidential ones. And yet, Principal Floud noted, Newnham was still in a "position of strength." She favored encouraging more women to apply to Cambridge and limiting the number of mixed colleges.[64]

Girton's Decision to Admit Men

In early 1976 Girton's College Council decided to admit men in stages: first as fellows and graduate students in 1977, and then as undergraduates in 1979.[65] Given the change in the college's statutes five years earlier that permitted coresidency, the decision needed only a simple majority. The vote was not unanimous, however; about one-third of the college fellows opposed the change.[66] While one might expect that fellows who had been at Girton for a long time wished to preserve it as a women's college, it was actually senior fellows who tended to be most in favor of becoming coresidential. According to the recollections of various fellows who were present at the time, these senior women made forceful arguments about the lack of an alternative. Girton was having trouble with undergraduate admissions, as applications had dropped by about one-fifth.[67] More students were coming through the "pool," a group of applicants who did not get selected by their first-choice colleges.[68] In this way students were indicating their preference for mixed-sex colleges. The college was having particular trouble in finding enough women student scientists, and Girton did not want to specialize in the arts. Fellows in favor of the change used Emily Davies's legacy as a justification for becoming mixed: Whatever men's colleges did, Emily Davies had believed, Girton should do. Now men's colleges were becoming coresidential, and so Girton needed to as well. Also, given that Girton was the first residential women's college, fellows argued that it was fitting for it to become the first women's college to go mixed. Younger fellows were naturally most concerned about their careers and so they tended to be the most worried about becoming coresidential and facing competition from men fellows. But those who lost the vote did so with "excellent grace" and worked with "as much enthusiasm as those who won" at making coresidence a success. As one fellow expressed it, they behaved like "good Girtonians."[69]

Girton students were not told about the decision to admit men until November 27, 1976, at an open meeting of graduate and undergraduate students. The new mistress, Brenda Ryman, told the students that the governing body had voted three weeks earlier to become coresidential.[70] Outraged, the JCR (Junior Common Room, which means the undergraduate members of the college) invited the mistress to an open meeting, during which they expressed their strong displeasure at not having been consulted about coresidency. They noted that students at all other colleges except Christ's had had the chance to voice their opinions before the vote of the governing body. The mistress explained that although the governing body had no desire "to conceal anything from the students," the formulation of future college policy was "somewhat different from everyday college affairs in which students were undoubtedly consulted." She pointed to the drop in Girton applications after the men's colleges admitted women; in other words, about the same number of women were being distributed among a greater number of colleges. Students at the open meeting remained upset that the issue of coresidence had not even been on the agenda of the College Council, on which their student representative sat. They passed a motion by twenty-eight to seven (with four abstentions): "The JCR disapproves of not being consulted about co-residence in Girton."[71]

While Girton students complained about being excluded from discussions of coresidency, this did not mean that they disapproved of the college's admission of men. At the same JCR open meeting, another motion was proposed: "The JCR disapproves of co-residence in Girton." The proposer, Rachel Moore, expressed concerns about three issues: that the first male applicants would be "somewhat undesirable"; that coresidency would isolate Girton even more, as students' social life would become increasingly focused on the college rather than the university; and that students would lose the "choice" of single-sex or mixed-sex colleges. The mistress disagreed that male applicants would be "undesirable" and reiterated that the college had to be "realistic" and face the fact that female applicants to Cambridge were "certainly not keeping pace with the number of places becoming available to women in the university." She added that Girton, with its "principal disadvantage" of distance from town, had three choices: "It could become a 'specialist' college of some sort, it could close down, or it could go co-residential." The motion of disapproval of coresidency was soundly defeated, nineteen to three (six abstentions).[72]

Although most Girton undergraduates appear to have favored coresidency, the student newsletter, *True Grit*, published five letters on the subject, four of them negative. The arguments in the letters were generally sophisticated and revealed that students knew about developments in other colleges and also about implications of a new law, the Sex Discrimination Act. For example, one student used the writings of Simone de Beauvoir to examine women's "rejection of women's institutions" like Girton. She argued that "if women themselves considered the female of equal worth to the male, they would not seek so disproportionately to be token females in a man's establishment, when they already have their own." Another student who declared that she was "wholeheartedly in favor of co-residence in all Cambridge colleges" nonetheless did not favor Girton's decision at this time because the university was not at all close to the national average of a 40 percent "intake" of women.[73]

Some of the students who expressed their opinions on coresidence in *True*

Grit referred to what other students or the larger public thought of Girton and Cambridge University. This was true of students who opposed coresidence, as well as the one student who favored it. Rachel Moore, who proposed the JCR motion condemning coresidence, wrote that she felt "very ashamed" of her college. She realized that "most of the students in Cambridge assume that this is a student decision, as it would be in their colleges, and they are finding the idea of a sex-starved Girton most amusing." M.C., who had used Simone de Beauvoir's writings in her opposition to coresidence, also wrote about how the mistress's action of "presenting a potentially progressive policy in an unreasonable way" was thereby "perpetuating" Girton's "reputation for being traditional and set in its ways." She contrasted what had happened at Girton with the consultation on coresidence that had occurred at Newnham. The one student who favored coresidence said she did so because "times have changed" so that Girton now had trouble "attracting applicants of the 'right caliber'" and also because coresidence produces a more "natural" and "happier" environment. She thought that the coresidence decision would "endear" applicants to the "first women's college to break with the past" who otherwise would be "put off this university by its more backward aspects."[74]

Planning for the transition to coresidence began early in the spring term of 1977. For four months, subcommittees of the committee charged with the planning studied four topics: arrangements for graduate students, living arrangements, sports facilities, and common-room facilities. As the mistress had promised when she announced the coresidence decision, undergraduates participated on the three subcommittees relevant to their college lives, and graduate students participated in the fourth. The subcommittees' reports of May 1977 recommended upgrading facilities at Girton, arguing that they had to be made "as complete and attractive as possible" if Girton were to become "a really successful coresidential college." For example, they wanted party rooms for dancing and drinking, a bar complex with table tennis, and a darts room nearby. Sports facilities received a great deal of attention. As the senior tutor said: "Good sports facilities are an important attraction to many able young men. . . . We are convinced that if we advertise ourselves as a coresidential college we must live up fully to that image."[75] The changes recommended in living arrangements did not cost as much. The undergraduates on the planning subcommittees insisted that Girton had to have "the courage of its convictions."[76] They wanted mixed-sex corridors, bath and washroom facilities, and lavatories. To preserve modesty, doors were fitted that went from the floor to the ceilings. Similarly, the subcommittee recommended new cubicle curtains for the changing areas around the college's swimming pool that would be "adequately secured at the sides (to avoid horse-play!)." Committee members also discussed ways to preserve students' choice of single-sex groupings, whether in single-sex enclaves in the residence halls or in having a tutor of the same sex.[77]

Women's and Men's Experiences
since Girton Became Coresidential

Fifty-seven men undergraduates entered Girton in October 1979, making them slightly more than one-third of the entering class of 167 students.[78] Neither all the men nor all the women students were prepared for being at a newly mixed college. Some of the men had not applied to Girton but rather had been picked up from the "pool." Some of the new women students were unaware that they were going to a college that would have men students. And yet, most people recall that the transition went quite smoothly, despite certain "tensions" due to some "girls" in their second and third years having been opposed to coresidence.[79] The men students in the early years developed solidarity from being a minority; they felt as if they were pioneers and were "very proud" of being different.[80] One man who did apply directly to Girton two years after it became mixed, because his low grades in his previous academic work led him to try a college that he had been told would be easier to get into, said that the standing joke at the time was that all men students at Girton were either wimps or fascists. The men students tried to disprove these images by creating an active drinking society.[81]

Men undergraduates involved themselves in the student government (JCR) from the start, and the spending patterns of the JCR began to reflect their interests. At the first JCR open meeting where men students were present, for example, a man student proposed, and another seconded, the motion that the JCR spend £180 (about $250) for eight rugby balls for the sole use of the newly formed Girton College Rugby Club. The motion passed unanimously, with one abstention. Fifteen hundred pounds were also allocated to the Boat Club; as the woman proposer said, the club was having difficulty borrowing boats "this year" since other colleges now saw the newly mixed Girton "as competition."[82] At the next meeting, men proposed and seconded a motion for spending £800 on disco equipment. This proposal did not pass unanimously. Although some students argued that a disco would benefit Girton's social life, others expressed concern "especially about the expense at a time when money was short." This motion passed, nonetheless: twenty-five to four, with ten abstentions. During this time, the JCR continued to vote to spend some of its money on social causes, for example, £50 to a telephone crisis service and another £50 for the Cambridge Pregnancy Advisory Group.[83]

Reactions to the physical as well as social changes at Girton varied. Some women students resented the fact that after all the years that they had put up with inferior facilities, now that men students were members of the college, they had improvements like new squash courts.[84] Fellows talked about the atmosphere being less studious, which might seem like a criticism, but which some fellows believed was more "normal."[85] A fellow who had been a graduate student at Girton in the 1960s said that while the college used to be "prim" and "old-maidish," with students trying for perfection, it had a more relaxed atmosphere after it became mixed.[86] A student who had been at Girton in the 1960s and returned for a visit thought the college seemed "more lively," but she asked, "Will the easy-going atmosphere still breed the eccentrics of yester-year?"[87] The senior tutor, who had been involved in planning for the transition, was enthused: "There is a new spirit in the air in College at present, the sense of a new beginning, or a more vital future. Long may it last."[88]

Girton had little trouble attracting male applicants. In fact, women were a minority of new students between 1983, four years after men undergraduates were first admitted, and 1993. (The percentage of men for sample years: 35% in 1979; 45%, 1980; about 60%, 1983 and 1986; 53%, 1984; 51%, 1989; 55%, 1992; 54%, 1993; 49%, 1994; 42%, 1995; 49%, 1996; and 51%, 2000.)[89] Girton's popularity with men, perhaps due to the perception that it would be an easier college to get accepted by, is indicated by the numbers applying directly to Girton rather than coming from the "pool." In 1989 a substantially greater number of men (254) than women (214) applicants listed Girton as their first preference.[90] The imbalance in admissions did create concern. Students raised the issue of discrimination against women and ethnic minorities in 1990, when women were only 38 percent of entering students.[91] The college's 1992 admissions report discussed how Girton needed "to attract more female applicants from all backgrounds."[92]

Girton became mixed at the fellowship and graduate levels two years before men undergraduates entered. In 1977 eight men were appointed as research fellows; other men with teaching duties at Girton without the title of fellow were then given that status. Thus by the first year of full coresidence, there were twelve men fellows, of whom seven chose to live at the college.[93] Girton also ensured that there would be at least one male tutor (a fellow who gives advice and counseling) before men undergraduates arrived. The first male tutor appointed, John Marks, was a man of "mature years" and a physician. According to the senior tutor of the time, Marks was "guaranteed to still the wildest parental imaginings about women students and male moral tutors!"[94] The number of male fellows increased so that by the early 1990s, Girton had about an equal number of men and women fellows. (For select years, percentages of male fellows and teaching officers were: 27%, 1979; 29%, 1980; 38%, 1987; 47%, 1992; 48%, 1996; and 46%, 2002.)[95]

Interviews with men and women fellows reveal a high degree of satisfaction with being affiliated with Girton. Over and over again, fellows said that Girton is a friendly, unstuffy, egalitarian, informal, "remarkably collegial," inclusive, family-friendly, and relaxed college. Several fellows also commented that Girton is more feminist than other colleges, having kept the best parts of a women's college atmosphere. A few noted with satisfaction that the current vice mistress is a man, but the title has remained the same. Many fellows praised the "balance" that Girton has achieved in terms of students' and fellows' gender. Those fellows who have been associated with other Cambridge colleges or have a spouse who is a fellow elsewhere often said that conversations among fellows at Girton are more interesting. Fellows listen to each other, sit in large circles rather than in exclusive groups, and talk about subjects that include but are not limited to intellectual concerns. While disagreements naturally arise, the college identity seems to be one in which people get along and do not form factions that will not speak to each other.[96] One fellow observed that the most unexpected result of becoming a mixed college was that men fellows are interested in women's rights and in encouraging women students.[97]

Although fellows are very positive about Girton today, some expressed worries about the future. Girton is not a rich college and so may have trouble offering "perks" like child care, job sharing, good computing facilities, and inexpensive housing, which may be necessary to attract young academics to a noncentral college.[98] Some fellows fear that the closeness among fellows may be lost due to Girton's large size.[99] Many fellows commented on the arts-science divide, although some said that it was actually less than at other colleges because people from all disciplines talk to each other. A practical issue is that fellows in the sciences need to be near their labs, which means that they cannot take the time to come to Girton for lunch. If scientists eat at Girton, it is usually at Wolfson Court, a separate, more modern campus closer to the center of town that houses some students, mainly graduate and law students. The result is that arts fellows know each other better and tend to see scientists only on formal occasions.[100] A couple of fellows worried about keeping the gender balance among fellows, since many of the most senior fellows are women and will be retiring soon.[101]

Academics at Girton since Men's Colleges Became Coresidential

Men's colleges' transition to coresidency has affected their academic standing as well as that of women's colleges. Most people believe that men's colleges admitted women not out of their concern with equal opportunities for women but to improve their colleges' academic performance by enrolling gifted women. Becoming coresidential was important to men's colleges for attracting the best men students too.[102] By continuing to attract highly qualified men and adding top women, the formerly men's colleges have in general moved up the tripos-league standings.

Women's colleges have suffered as a result. Since former men's colleges were able to "skim" the "academic cream" of women students, women's colleges' academic rankings declined.[103] Girton's standing in the Tompkins League of tripos results has gone from one of the top colleges to one of the lowest. In

1972, before Girton became mixed, Girton ranked third among the twenty-four colleges then in the league table.[104] By 1979, a lower proportion of Girton women than all women in university received firsts; a year later Girton women scored close to all women at the university, but Girton men did considerably worse.[105] In the mid-1990s Girton's mistress talked about trying to improve exam results. She commended students for achieving twenty-eight firsts in their finals and for having "moved 5 places up the Tompkins Table" but commented that they "still" had "too long a tail, which drags us down."[106] In more recent years, Girton's standing has usually hovered around the bottom third of Cambridge's colleges, but in 2004, it fell eight places, to twenty-fifth.[107]

While the ranking of colleges is popular among prospective students and teachers as a way of assessing Cambridge's colleges, many better informed people criticize the Tompkins Table. The criticisms are generally aimed at explaining why differences between men and women are the result not of their abilities but of the exams themselves. When the proportion of women at the university was much lower, so that the women who attended tended to be particularly gifted, women's colleges fared well. But now differences between men and women are more apparent.[108]

One criticism of the Tompkins Table is that it magnifies differences between colleges, when in actuality, the scores of those at the bottom are quite close to those at the top. The ranks are computed by the following formula: five points are given for a first, the highest grade; three for a II(1); two for a II(2); and one for a third, the lowest passing grade. Thus firsts receive disproportionate weight. For several reasons, women students are generally less likely than men to be awarded firsts: Women tend to study arts subjects, in which firsts are less commonly given, and women do not take risks in their essays—their answers are not "assertive" or dismissive of other points of view, sometimes called "the Cambridge answer"—a style that is rewarded most highly in the tripos exams. This bias in exam grading has been noted for at least a decade. In 1994, for example, Girton students passed a motion noting that "university wide, women get fewer 1sts than men" reflecting a "difference in the academic, and social, experience of women at the University." The JCR went on record as supporting "the efforts being made by the women's campaign and working parties in the university to address the causes of and possible solutions to the gender deficit in higher education."[109] In the early part of the twenty-first century, Cambridge University seems to have started to address this issue. A committee charged with studying gender biases in academic assessment issued a report that discussed the "gender gap" and how it varied by subject. The vice chancellor of Cambridge University welcomed the report and said that it provided "tangible goals" for rectifying "women's academic underachievement."[110]

Regardless of the flaws of the Tompkins tables, Girton fellows and students of Girton are aware of the low ranking of the college and frequently comment on it. One fellow explained the college's rank by saying that to achieve more firsts, students need to "meet up with" more students who are on their way to achieving firsts. Also, Girton would need to have "main" or "core" fellows who can gear students to exams in the way that happens at some other colleges. This fellow, himself a graduate of Girton, was not very bothered about this issue, however, as he believes Girton students "do get a good, well-rounded education."[111] Students sometimes expressed concern about Girton's rank, especially when they thought about its effect on how people at other colleges regarded them, but at other times, they defended Girton's more relaxed, happy atmosphere. As one student who came to Girton in 1980 said, he was not a very academic student, so Girton's social atmosphere was "spot on" for what he needed.[112] Another former student argued that it was not the most academically successful students who did the best later on in life, but people who have well-rounded experiences of

Dr. Julia Riley, a member of the Girton faculty, supervises two physical science students in 1999, twenty years after male students were admitted to the college. At Cambridge University college fellows often use their own comfortable college rooms for supervisions, a key way students receive instruction. *Photo by Neville Taylor for the 1999 Girton College Prospectus. Reproduced by permission of The Mistress and Fellows, Girton College, Cambridge.*

the type that Girton offered.[113] JCR Committee members have gone on record as being against restrictions (on the use of the college bar and playing music, for example) that they feared fellows might impose on them in an attempt to improve Girton's position in the academic league tables. "It was generally felt on committee that we like the relaxed atmosphere of Girton," they noted.[114]

While students in some years have applauded Girton's "relaxed" atmosphere, in other years they have worried about academic achievement.[115] In October 1998 the JCR Committee discussed a report from the College Council that showed exam results and their slight fall from the previous year, including more thirds. Although committee members wondered about female underachievement, they were reassured that it was less than at most other colleges.[116]

Many students report having received an excellent education at Girton. One student who studied archeology and anthropology from 1995 to 1998 said that "academically" Girton was "amazing." She mentioned how she benefited from a one-to-one tutorial each week.[117] Students often said that they learned a lot from fellows and from other students; they commented on the breadth of opinions to which they were exposed and the invigorating discussions that took place. Occasionally students mentioned that they felt they would have received better supervisions in a richer college. One man who studied English literature, for example, said that until his third year, he had been in large groups of ten students, whereas in other colleges he would have received more one-on-one instruction.[118] A science student said that his supervisors were often recent graduates, cheaper for the college but perhaps not the best for his studies.[119]

Fellows vary in their views of whether men or women students dominate academically. Their perspectives may be related to their disciplines. For example, in economics there are almost always more women than men students, and the president of the Joan Robinson Society is usually a woman student.[120] Men students seem to do better in the technical subjects in economics, but women students do better in applied topics, according to a fellow.[121] Two science fellows said that women students are usually hardworking, perhaps to a degree that is detrimental to their well-being; men students, on the other hand, can be "maddening" in their lack of preparation for supervisions, yet at the same time they are "risk takers."[122] One law fellow noted that some men dominate in groups, but not invariably. She has noticed that while occasionally a man will talk so much during supervision that others are shut out, women almost never do this.[123]

Some fellows talked about changes over time in student qualities. One said that there had been more problems in the early years of being a mixed college because they chose "posh" men from the pool, and Girton is "not very good at posh boys." Another fellow said that the fellows used to have the "naïve view" that women needed encouragement, men some "beating around the ears," but it is no longer true, if it ever was. And yet this same fellow noted that it is more difficult to convince men students that it is "cool" to discuss academic work.[124]

Finances of Girton

Many people at Girton believe that the main problem the college faces for the future is adequate finances. Mistresses have commented on monetary difficulties for at least thirty years, calling Girton a "poor" or "very poor" college. In 1974, the mistress discussed three "outstanding problems" facing the college: the effects of inflation, new road plans for motorways, and moves for coresidence in the university.[125] In the 1990s Girton found itself having to pay about £2.5 million for its new buildings at Wolfson Court at the same time it was renovating buildings at the old site and the government cut back financial support for higher education.[126] These difficulties led Girton to appoint a director of development in 1993.

Currently Girton has about a £30 million endowment, putting it in the bottom middle of Cambridge colleges. The director of development described the particular challenges of fund-raising at Girton. Not only is it a former women's college, and women tend to be poorer and hence not able to give as much as men, but also, since it became mixed, some potential donors believe that it has lost its "raison d'être." Fund-raising usually "plays" to history, but this is more complicated since Girton became mixed. One argument is that founder Emily Davies was a pragmatic person who would have made the same decision about admitting men. Davies was also concerned that women have the same educational opportunities as men, a goal that Girton continues to be committed to.[127]

Fellows and students recognize problems that stem from Girton's tight budget. While students are mostly very happy with the education they received and the facilities that were available to them, many believed that facilities would have been better had Girton been as rich as some other colleges they visited. Students noted in particular that sports facilities, the boat club, and computers could have been improved.[128]

Fellows mentioned a wide range of problems that stemmed from insufficient money, from difficulties in being able to compete successfully with other colleges for outstanding women students and university fellows, to undermining goodwill in the college community when all expenditures have to be justified.[129] More funding is particularly important now that government support is being cut while expectations about what colleges will offer are rising.[130]

Student Life at Girton

Girton's location, while usually perceived as having a negative effect on applications, appears to contribute to students' satisfaction with and loyalty to the college. Almost every student interviewed mentioned the intense, close friendships they developed because they made Girton, not university activities, the center of their college life. Many said that they remained in touch with Girtonians; for some, even ten or fifteen years after leaving college, their best friends continue to be people they met at college. One woman who was at Girton between 1981 and 1984 said that she "adored" Girton because she belonged to a "real community" where she formed "long-lasting friendships" and felt she was in a safe environment, a "very caring place."[131] A few students, men as well as women, mentioned that the spatial layout of Girton contributed to their friendships. Rather than student rooms arranged along staircases, as is true for most of the older Cambridge colleges, Girton's rooms are along corridors. Students have to pass each others' rooms and get to know more students that way.[132]

A question important to this study is the position of women since Girton admitted men undergraduates. Given women's leadership opportunities in women's colleges, it is relevant to ask whether they continue to hold their share of leadership positions in mixed colleges. One quantitative measure is the percentage of JCR presidents who have been women. Of twenty-five JCR presidents since 1980 (omitting one whose first name was gender neutral, so the gender could not be determined, but counting one man who had to leave college due to bad grades), nine have been women (36 percent). While women have not always been 50 percent of Girton's students since 1980, they have averaged much higher than 36 percent. Looking at women's share of the presidency by decades, five of ten presidents between 1980 and 1989 were women; four of eleven between 1990 and 1999; and none of the four presidents between 2000 and 2003. The trend appears to be in the direction of male dominance. Some of the other officers of the JCR have also tended to fall into gender stereotypical roles. Treasurers, for example, have mostly been men; in fact only five of twenty-three treasurers, or 22 percent, were women between 1981 and 2003. Perhaps indicative of a new trend, two of four treasurers between 2000 and 2003 were women. Secretaries, not surprisingly, have more often been women; of seventeen recorded between 1982 and 2003 whose gender could be determined by first name, three were men (82 percent women). The last male secretary was elected in 1996.[133]

One other quantitative indicator of power sharing between women and men undergraduates is the gender of students who proposed motions at open meetings of the JCR. A sample of every fifth meeting, broken down into four intervals, showed that right after men were admitted to Girton, between 1979 and 1981, women proposed the vast majority of motions—19 of 24 (79 percent). From then on, however, women have proposed a minority of motions: 14 of 42 (33 percent) between 1982 and 1989; 20 of 45 (44 percent) between 1990 and 1993; and 7 of 17 (41 percent) between 1994 and 1999. In contrast to the trend with the presidency of the JCR, however, these figures do not seem to indicate increasing male dominance. It is also important to note that women's underrepresentation is remarked upon. In 1992 JCR Committee members (comprised of the officers of JCR) acknowledged women's lack of involvement, saying that they needed to "encourage first years and more women to get involved in the JCR!"[134]

Some but not all motions that Girton students propose at JCR meetings match stereotypical gender-role expectations. In May 1990, for example, a woman proposed (and another woman seconded) affiliating with an organization concerned with survivors of sexual abuse. On the other hand, sometimes women proposed motions on international issues; at that same meeting, for instance, a woman proposed giving the maximum amount possible under JCR rules to an Afghanistan aid appeal. Similarly, while men often proposed motions on subjects concerned with their own interests, such as one in December 1986 for the renovation of the cellar for a pool table, they sometimes proposed motions that do not fit stereotypical notions so clearly, for example, one in January 1990 for a donation for students to travel to a conference on illiteracy.[135]

In general, most students are aware of Girton's history as the first women's residential college in England. During interviews, women often said how proud they were to be a part of that history. Men students indicated some awareness of the history and even occasionally mentioned their pride in it, but women and men said that they thought the history was more important to women. The many paintings of women on the walls in the college reminded students of this history (and surprised students visiting from other colleges).[136] While it is not possible to know whether issues connected to women came up more often at Girton than at colleges with an all-male history, students were aware that Girton's past made women's issues particularly relevant. In 1986, for example, a student who was pressing college authorities to give a substantial sum to a county organization concerned with the training and retraining of women cited Girton's "unique and historic position in women's education" as a fact that made such a contribution appropriate.[137] Students often said that one of the characteristics of Girton they liked best was its "balance" of women and men. Of course, not everyone saw the college as balanced. One man who was JCR president in the early 1990s complained of what he felt was a "feminist slant" in some of his supervisions in English literature. This man also believed that some of the college's financial problems were the result of choosing a woman for bursar rather than "the most highly qualified individual."[138]

Girton continues to recognize women's special needs. For women who want to live separately, there is a women's corridor. Classes in self-defense have also been organized, and women receive rape alarms.[139] Students themselves have recognized the importance of women-only events such as a women's lunch.[140]

In 1987 the JCR went on record as concerned with the "appalling deficiency of child care" at the university and how that constituted discrimination against women. They asked for reassurances from Girton authorities that no one would be denied admission due to child-care responsibilities.[141] Although abortion does not get unanimous support at Girton, students in 1991 voted to give money to an organization that brought Irish women who wanted abortions to England.[142] Girton has had a sexual harassment policy since 1992 modeled after the university's, and in 1997 students decided that they should include a sexual harassment policy in their own constitution.[143] In 1998 Girton had an exhibition that celebrated fifty years of women receiving Cambridge degrees; one night a week was reserved for women only to visit it.[144] Women students inform each other, by announcements at JCR meetings, posters on bulletin boards, and flyers in their mail boxes, of workshops, support groups, and talks on such issues as eating disorders, date rape, Take Back the Night marches, and sexual abuse. Very often students have voted to support such campaigns by financial donations.[145]

Members of Girton pride themselves on being part of a liberal, tolerant, inclusive community. Students have voiced concern, for example, when the proportion of students coming from state schools was low.[146] They have joined other colleges in trying to increase the proportion of ethnic and racial minorities at the university; in 2002 only about 13 percent of students admitted to the university were ethnic minorities, with most of these being Asians.[147] While most former students who were interviewed said that they thought Girton was quite a comfortable place for those in the minority, others admitted that they were not sure and recalled that Muslim and black students generally kept to themselves. One minority group that no one thought felt excluded and that in fact some people found too vocal were the religious Christians. A few students recalled instances when the "God squad," as they are sometimes called, made unwelcome advances.[148]

The situation for gay and lesbian students appears to be mixed. In some ways, Girton students seem aware and supportive of gay and lesbian issues, at least since the 1990s and, according to some former students, even earlier. Besides supporting and contributing money when the university sponsored a lesbian and gay awareness week in 1990, the JCR Committee decided in 1994 that it needed a "lesbigay" representative. The first person who came forward to take this new position was a first-year student who was not himself gay; two years later, the committee decided that they needed a woman lesbigay officer as well, "to make them approachable to all."[149] The following year they also took action to boycott goods produced by Philip Morris since that company sponsored Jesse Helms's election campaigns, and Jesse Helms had blocked materials he thought would promote homosexuality.[150] In 1998 students decided to participate in a "white ribbon campaign" to call attention to the problem of lesbigay suicide.[151] Yet while some former students said they knew gay or lesbian students who were open about their sexuality, several recalled friends who had not felt comfortable exploring their sexuality until after they left Girton.[152] As recently as 2000, a spate of "lesbigay abuses" occurred at Girton; the JCR said it was determined to sort out the problem "ASAP."[153]

Student life is undoubtedly different from what it was before Girton became a coresidential college. In recent years alcohol consumption, vomiting, and damages to the physical plant are problems that the community often discusses.[154] While it is not possible to know how much these problems are due to men's presence, and how much to changing mores of the student culture, most people believe that men students are guilty of the worst excesses. It is similarly difficult to know if the greater emphasis on social life and the reduced emphasis on academic work are due entirely to the presence of men. One ironic consequence of a less intellectual atmosphere is the greater stress experienced around exam time. But despite these typical kinds of problems, Girton students still report feeling that their college is less traditional and more balanced than other colleges. As one former woman student said, when she visited other colleges, she was "gob-smacked" at the truth of the stereotypes of public [i.e., elite private] school students. This was not an experience she had at Girton.[155]

Developments at Newnham since the Mid-1970s

Newnham College has changed less than Girton has since the mid-1970s, on the surface at least. It is still a women's college with all women fellows. And yet it too has had to adapt to the increasing popularity of mixed-sex colleges. Despite its good location, beautiful buildings and grounds, historic importance for the higher education of women, generally satisfied students, and many notable alumnae, Newnham continues to face problems in admissions, in relative academic standing, and in finding fellows for certain academic subjects.

The issue of becoming a coresidential college has been discussed "at least three times" at Newnham.[156] Unlike those at Girton, Newnham college authorities did consult with students each time. In the autumn of 1976, the principal talked to the JCR and explained that fellows had been discussing "the future development of the college" for over two years. She talked about the effect of men's colleges' move to coresidence but stressed that there was no reason Newnham had to go mixed, even when the opportunities for men and women were equal. To ascertain the views of undergraduates, she asked all students to answer a questionnaire.[157] The results of this poll split the students practically down the middle, with 52 percent favoring coresidence, a margin that was judged to be "insignificant."[158] To prevent further agitation and conflict, the college put a five-year moratorium on discussion of coresidence. And yet in 1980 Principal Jean Floud remarked during a fund-raising talk that Newnham might not stay single-sex "forever." She wanted Newnham to have the facilities to be in a position to "make a smooth transition to a new identity" if ever "a time should come when the educational needs of women can best be met in the context of a mixed college."[159] A more recent poll of students, in the late 1980s or early 1990s, found that they were "very much in favor of remaining all-women."[160] Fellows remain divided about coresidence, with such strong feelings on each side that they are generally reluctant to discuss the issue.

Arguments in favor of a single-sex college are similar to those made in the United States. Historically, women's colleges provided practically the only access to higher education for women and were the only places that hired women academics. Even after men's colleges of Cambridge University admitted women, their numbers were so low that women's colleges remained important for the overall numbers of women students and academics. Women's colleges are also considered more supportive of their students, providing an environment in which they feel safe and comfortable. In part this means that their women students are predicted to perform better academically, particularly in subjects that are not traditional for women to study, such as physics and mathematics, but it also refers more broadly to their learning leadership skills through top positions in student government and other college clubs. A fellow who has studied the history of women's higher education, Gillian Sutherland, argued that being a women's college makes it easier to do what Newnham historically has done well: take teaching and caring for students extremely seriously, not just while the women are students but as a lifetime point of reference; and educate women politically by being "a very democratic institution."[161] Other fellows believe women's colleges are necessary to preserve choice; some women want to reside only with members of their own sex, or their religion or culture may mandate single-sex residential accommodations. Cambridge University may not need three women's colleges as it has now (besides Newnham, New Hall, and Lucy Cavendish, the latter for women over twenty-five), but preserving one women's college is essential for meeting these students' needs.[162]

Not everyone at Newnham accepts the arguments in favor of women's colleges. Students who came to Newnham through the pool usually did not intend to come to a women's college (unless possibly they applied to New Hall and did not get in). At least at first, these women tend not to see the need for a single-sex environment; some do come to like Newnham very much, however. Some fellows or college teaching officers also believe that women's colleges are no longer necessary. They point to the academic success of women generally and to the lack of difference in a positive direction between the exam results of Newnham students and other women at the university.[163]

Academics at Newnham

Men's colleges becoming mixed and taking the academic "cream" of women students has affected Newnham, as it has Girton. In Newnham's case, the results are striking because the college ranking had been so high. In 1972 and 1973, for example, Newnham ranked first of twenty-three colleges in the proportion of students who got firsts or II(1)s; in 1974 and 1975, it ranked third and second, respectively. But since the late 1970s, Newnham has generally not fared well, although there have been some exceptions. In 1978 Newnham ranked thirteenth, or about midway among twenty-five colleges, in the proportion of students who achieved firsts or II(1)s, but in 1988 it was at the bottom of the Tompkins League. More precise comparisons show that in many years, a lower proportion of Newnham students than women at the university achieves firsts or II(1)s. For example, in 1991, 40.2 percent of Newnham women achieved

As one of three all-women colleges of Cambridge University, Newnham College is believed to be particularly attractive to women whose cultural traditions favor separation between young men and women. *Photo by N. Christie, 2006.*

firsts or II(1)s, in comparison to 46.2 percent of all women at the university. In 1990 and 1992, Newnham did well in the Tompkins League, ranking sixth. A decade later, however, Newnham was at the very bottom of the table for four consecutive years, 1999–2002.[164] In 2004 Newnham improved remarkably and earned the accolade of "the fastest improving [college] in the university for academic performance" by moving from twenty-first to thirteenth in the Tompkins league table.[165] In 2005, however, Newnham had returned to the twenty-first position.

While Newnham's officials have been disappointed when the college's students did not achieve very good academic results, they do recognize the limitations of judging success according to the Tompkins League table. The senior tutor pointed out that there was not a great difference between colleges at the top and those at the bottom. Another fellow also criticized the exams themselves as requiring women to learn to behave like men.[166] The principal emphasized that the league tables use exam results from all three years; Newnham students start out low but achieve much better in their third year.[167] Moreover, Newnham has almost always been able to point to some successes: In 2002, for example, there were twelve more firsts than in 2001, and five were top firsts. When arts were separated from the sciences, Newnham went from twenty-second among colleges in 2001 to eleventh in 2002. Such achievements made it "difficult," the senior tutor wrote, "not to experience outlandish pride."[168] When trying to account for why Newnham students did not do better overall, the senior tutor mentioned young women's problems of confidence and motivation. A university study found that twice as many women as men reported their courses to be "extremely stressful."[169] While these facts help in understanding women's exam performances, they still do not explain why students at Newnham often did not do better than women at other colleges of Cambridge University, a fact that fellows who favor Newnham becoming coresidential noted.

One reason officials at Newnham worry about students' exam results, even though they are critical of the exams themselves, as well as of the Tompkins League table, is that they affect the public's perception of the college.[170] Being seen as a less academically rigorous college can result in teachers at secondary schools thinking that their top female students should try for another college. Newnham students are sensitive to the image of their college as not very academic; several mentioned that this was one of the common views held by students at other colleges.[171] Newnham continues to try to improve its standing by such initiatives as intensive prep programs for first-year students.[172]

Newnham's difficulties with applications contribute to the issues of academic performance and how Newnham is perceived. Newnham gets fewer direct applications than it used to; one secondary source said in 1979 that Newnham's applications had dropped by almost one-half, at the same time that New Hall's and Girton's fell by one-fifth, although the time period was not clearly specified.[173] In some years, applications have gone up; for example, in both 1988 and in 1992, the admissions tutors reported increases, attributed in part to the greater proportion of women applying to the university overall.[174] And yet in 1992, 40 percent of Newnham's students came from the pool (students who did not get selected by their first-choice colleges).[175] In 2001 the admissions tutor reported that applications to Newnham had gone up, while applications to the university were down by 11 percent. Nonetheless, she noted that Newnham still needed to obtain "many more direct applications to the College" and find "new ways to attract the brightest and the best, whatever their background."[176] In recent years, Newnham has obtained about 25 to 35 percent of its students from the pool, as estimated by a fellow who was the admissions tutor from 1997 to 2000.[177]

While not everyone associated with Newnham has negative views about obtaining large proportions of students from the pool, many do. One college teaching officer said that some of his best students come from the pool.[178] Students report that they are aware, at least when they first arrive at college, of who has come from the pool and who has applied directly. Students who did not apply directly to Newnham generally want that known; they apparently think that this reduces the "stigma" of being associated with a women's college.[179] Some students and fellows say that while young women will apply to Newnham despite its being a women's college, there are few who will apply *because* it is a single-sex institution. Exceptions seem to be primarily Muslims, students from China, and lesbians, according to students.[180] A former admissions tutor said that such facilities as state-of-the-art gyms and special art rooms are important for "tipping the balance" in making interested students decide to apply. Newnham has created from former laboratories a performing arts room that students described as very nice, even though few students use it.[181] This former admissions tutor also created "open days" for fifteen-year-old girls; by having such young girls visit Newnham, the admissions tutor had hoped to dispel "their prejudice" against women's colleges. She reported feeling "frustrated" that despite all her work, young women "still wanted to apply to mixed colleges."[182]

Finances at Newnham

Like Girton and other women's colleges in England and elsewhere, Newnham is relatively poor. It has been successful at fund-raising, however, so that while it is still not a rich college, its wealth is above the median of Cambridge colleges, which means it is expected to contribute to, rather than receive from, a college fund intended to make colleges a bit more equal.

In 1977 Newnham was still poor enough to be one of six colleges that received aid from the colleges' Fund Committee. A comparison of Newnham with the men's college Caius showed that while the two were roughly similar in size and had similar incomes from fees, dues, and charges, Caius's income from private sources was several times higher than Newnham's.[183] By 1980 Newnham had launched an appeal with alumnae to raise £875,000. Former "members" gave over £250,000, which the principal called "amazing," given their overall "quite modest salaries."[184] By the time Newnham formally launched its development campaign in 1987, with a goal of £10 million, it had already raised £700,000. Prince Philip, then chancellor of Cambridge University, gave a "special message of support" for the appeal, saying that while "all the colleges have their particular characteristics . . . Newnham is rather a special case." Its "enviable academic reputation," Prince Philip continued, requires "a major investment in buildings, facilities, and teaching appointments."[185]

A new principal, Onora O'Neill, appointed in 1993, credited her predecessor with achieving "financial consolidation." That, in addition to good tripos results, put Newnham in a "confident mood."[186] In 1999 the principal described Newnham as "one of the better-off colleges," required to give funds to support the poorest colleges. Its total income from endowment was then £1,400,000.[187] Newnham continued its fund-raising efforts, launching a "20/10 campaign" with a goal of £20 million within the decade, or by 2010. The principal pointed out that beginning in 2000, colleges no longer received public funds in the form of fees for students. Since undergraduate grants had ended, many students were going into debt to finance their education. Cambridge University and the colleges needed to spend more money to provide them with financial assistance.[188]

As at Girton, most Newnham fellows who were interviewed saw financial issues as one of the college's greatest challenges for the future. Several noted the connection between finances and improving the college's academic standing, another of their concerns. As one fellow said, having money enables colleges to be academically ambitious and radical.[189]

Fellows at Newnham

Newnham not only has all women students, but all women fellows as well. The two do not necessarily go hand-in-hand—-the other women's college of Cambridge University that has traditional-aged undergraduates, New Hall, has men fellows—-but Newnham's statutes mandate all women fellows. Newnham has considered changing its statutes to allow men to become fellows. The last time a vote was taken, it was one shy of the two-thirds majority needed. Had Germanie Greer been able to attend the meeting, it would have been two votes under. Some science fellows resigned, and the subject of men fellows is now taboo.[190]

Several problems result from having an all-women fellowship. Especially in the past, when there were few women university teaching officers (UTOs),

Newnham had little chance of appointing UTOs as fellows. An advantage to a college of having fellows who are UTOs is that the university pays most of the fellow's salary, saving the college a great deal of money. Another problem Newnham has faced is getting fellows in such fields as physics and mathematics, and yet today's women students are more likely to study these subjects. Newnham has dealt with this problem by sharing fellows with some other colleges or appointing men as college teaching officers (CTOs), who have most of the responsibilities of fellows but cannot participate in college governance.

Men CTOs vary in their reactions to their status. A couple said that they thought that if Newnham were legally challenged, the male CTO distinction would not hold up in court. Formerly, male CTOs were not allowed even to sit on committees. Today most such differences have been abolished, but CTOs still cannot sit on the governing body (with the exception of the bursar) nor call themselves fellows. The male bursar, who in most colleges would be a fellow, has a vote on the council but not on the governing body, even if the issue being discussed is the same, what one male CTO called "silliness." While some male CTOs are happy to be relieved of most committee responsibilities, one said he occasionally found it irritating to receive a note saying: "The Fellows would like to invite you to dinner." Yet all male CTOs said that fellows treated them as equals and were friendly and welcoming.[191]

Another issue concerning the fellowship that Newnham faces is the paucity of senior fellows. One fellow who has been at Newnham only six years says that she is already considered senior. A longtime fellow said that all less-endowed colleges are scrambling for senior posts, but at a women's college, there is an "extra twist" since they all have to be women. Young academics are in an insecure position, with the result that there is a great deal of mobility. Thus Newnham fellows no longer have shared criteria about how to do things but rather have to "work" at common understandings. Perhaps this is one reason why some male CTOs and some fellows said that they did not think that Newnham made it clear in what ways being a women's college was distinctive. The discrimination women face in promotions at the university contributes to mobility too. A few years ago twelve women left Cambridge because they had been offered prestigious "chairs" at other universities and perhaps also because the "vast increase in bureaucracy" makes university teaching unattractive.[192]

Student Life at Newnham

In contrast to students at Girton, Newnham students are very involved in university, as distinct from college, activities. They are proud of their "outward-looking" stance, at the same time that they have a strong Newnham identity. In part Newnham students' involvement in university organizations is a result of their need to "work" at a social life that involves men. But even a lesbian student who was a member of Newbiles, Newnham's LBGT (lesbian, bi-sexual, gay, and transgender) society, was very involved in several university societies. This is not to say that Newnham students are not involved in college activities, however. They are, and report being satisfied with the range of activities that the college sponsors, including a very strong sports program, but they are also well known for their participation in university affairs.

The image of Newnham College and its students appears to be different now that virtually all colleges are coresidential. Rather than the "trendy" image of pre-coresidential years, Newnham students report that students at other colleges think of them all as lesbians, vegetarians, or perhaps both. They are also well known for their involvement in left-wing causes.[193] Another image, one that many students find upsetting, is that they all were "pooled" to Newnham and, related to this, that the college is not academically strong. Several students mentioned that Newnham students are not seen as radically feminist, as are students at the other, newer women's college, New Hall. And yet Newnham students are involved in feminist groups and sometimes comment on sexism in the university at large.[194]

Newnham does seem to be a comfortable college for lesbians. Partly this is a result of its left-wing orientation that includes, as one student said, being quite feminist, antiracist, and antihomophobic.[195] One third-year student, a lesbian, said that had she been at another college, she probably would not have had a girlfriend, as she has had at Newnham. Even if she were on an all-women corridor or staircase, she would have known that men were nearby and not felt as safe.[196] While heterosexual students seemed comfortable with a visible lesbian presence at their college and only mildly irritated by the college's reputation for lesbianism, one student said that she thought it "strange" that all the officers of the JCR were lesbians. Whether or not she was correct about this, it was an indication of what other students also said: Lesbians are a central or inner group at Newnham.[197]

Students describe several groups at Newnham that have very different beliefs or lifestyles. Besides lesbians, students mentioned ethnic and religious minorities who believe in the segregation of men and women, religious Christians, and students involved in drinking societies.[198] Despite the marked differences among these groups, and the existence of some antagonism between them, Newnham students say that they have a strong sense of a college community. They appreciate the college's democratic ethos or that students who come from elite schools are not "privileged." Students refer to the wonderful mix of students and how much they learn from other women who have very different backgrounds from themselves. They also believe that the friendships they form with other students at their college are particularly intense. Several students said that they thought female friendships at women's colleges are closer than those that develop at mixed colleges.[199]

Students, and some fellows, occasionally raise the issue of how Newnham's atmosphere might be different if the college were coresidential.[200] One fear is that it would become a less balanced college than it is now. Current students appreciate the college's concern with the "whole" person and the emphasis on being "rounded" individuals who need to both work and play.[201] Two seemingly opposite views emerge with how academics would be different if Newnham had men students. One is that Newnham would be a more relaxed place. Several students and some fellows thought that students might not work quite as hard or get so "hysterical" at exam times if men students were around who would be generally less anxious.[202] The contrasting opinion was that Newnham students were relaxed and did not work as hard as they would if they were in direct competition with men students. Not only did some Newnham fellows believe this, but a fellow at Girton who had done supervisions at Newnham said that she thought Newnham women were "unrealistic" about the amount of work they needed to do.[203] One way that these apparently differing views might be partly reconciled is what one retired fellow said: Newnham students are generally relaxed and less competitive than men students, but just before exams, they get very tense since they do not feel as if they have worked hard enough all term.[204]

Conclusions

This study of Cambridge University's two oldest women's colleges shows how greatly they were affected when men's colleges became coresidential. While officials at both women's colleges welcomed the admission of women to men's colleges of the university as a way of increasing access for women to this elite institution, they also recognized that no longer would Girton and Newnham be guaranteed all the best women students and academics. They had no choice but to compete with the older and richer formerly men's colleges, but they did so by different methods.

Girton College, already handicapped by its noncentral location, chose to admit men, first as fellows and graduate students, then as undergraduates. Although not all fellows believed this was the best decision, they accepted it. Admitting men had a major effect on the college's academic standing. Especially in the early years of coresidence, Girton's men students tended to be either those from the pool who had not been selected by men's colleges or men who applied because they thought they would have an easier time being accepted at a formerly women's college. At the same time, the academically strongest women tended to apply to formerly men's colleges since they were the most prestigious. These two trends combined to make Girton's academic standing plummet. Twenty-two years after becoming coresidential, Girton's rank had improved somewhat, to around sixteenth or seventeenth of twenty-four Cambridge colleges in the league table for exam results, but in 2004 and 2005, its rank sank to the bottom or next to the last.

Newnham College, with its good location and excellent students, chose to remain all women, although the decision created a significant degree of acrimony. Remaining all women did not prevent its academic ranking from falling in the same way that Girton's did, since the academically strongest women were no longer applying to Newnham, either. In fact, Newnham's academic standing became particularly low recently, at the very bottom or one or two away from the bottom of the league table. Although it improved dramatically in 2004 to the thirteenth rank (of twenty-five), in 2005 it fell again to twenty-first. As at Girton, though, even in its worst years, some Newnham students were very successful in their exams, and most members of the university, at least, recognize the antifemale bias of the league tables. Moreover, at both Newnham and Girton, students tend to improve academically between their first and final year, what is called "value-added." Ranks of colleges along this dimension find Newnham and Girton at or close to the top.[205] What is evident, however, is that fewer British women today want to attend a women's college. Newnham takes a quarter or more of its students from the pool, which contributes to its reputation as an "easy" college for women students to be accepted by and consequently, to the view that it is not academically strong. And yet the great prestige that comes from attending Cambridge University, in whatever college, means that Newnham does not have trouble admitting its desired number of students, about four hundred undergraduates. The differences among colleges may be important to Cambridge insiders, but to the larger world, it is attending Cambridge University that is impressive.

As a result of becoming coresidential, Girton's atmosphere changed quite dramatically and, most people seem to believe, generally for the better. It is a less serious college now and more lively. As predicted, the college has become more isolated as student's intense social life has become centered at the college. While many college activities have a good mix of men and women, male dominance has appeared in a few aspects of the student government. For a brief time, Girton admitted more men than women students, but today the gender of its students, as well as its fellowship, is well balanced. Fellows report that they like the college atmosphere very much, contrasting it with the more male-dominant, less friendly environments in formerly men's colleges. Students also enjoy Girton, as revealed in a 2002 quality-of-life survey at the university: Undergraduates who ended up a college that was not their first choice were asked if, given the choice again, they would elect to come. Slightly more than three-quarters of students at Girton said yes, the highest score of any Cambridge college.[206]

Newnham's atmosphere may have changed less than Girton's, but having quite a large proportion of students from the pool means that many students really wanted to be at a mixed college. Some of these students, however, come to appreciate over time how supportive the college is for women, perhaps particularly for those studying subjects not traditional for women, such as physics, mathematics, or chemistry. Newnham's reputation may have changed more than its actual atmosphere has, as students report that students at other colleges think that all Newnham students are politically radical, not academically strong, and lesbians. Newnham's undergraduates may be some of the most diverse of the university since the college is a place where ethnic and religious groups who believe in separating men and women will send their daughters, and also a college that is comfortable for lesbians.

Newnham comes across as a more unsettled college than Girton in that many people believe that it will inevitably have to admit men. Even if it does not, it seems that the issue arises periodically and causes conflict each time. Having an all-women fellowship creates as many or more problems as an all-women student population. Newnham's difficulty in competing successfully with other colleges for women fellows, particularly in fields such as mathematics in which women have historically been underrepresented, has led to such awkward solutions as having male college teaching officers.

In some ways this study shows how two women's colleges made different but reasonably successful adaptations to a major challenge. Newnham and Girton are each building substantial additions to their libraries; both have improved their financial standing through fund-raising. Members of both colleges believe that their college has a better, more egalitarian atmosphere than formerly men's colleges.

Similar to the situation in the United States, but more extreme, single-sex higher education is disappearing in England. All the men's colleges of Cambridge and Oxford (the two collegiate universities) have admitted women, and the last remaining women's college at Oxford, St. Hilda's, recently voted to admit men. In addition to one women's college for mature women, Lucy Cavendish, Cambridge has two women's colleges for traditional-aged undergraduates, Newnham and New Hall. The latter has had a mixed-sex fellowship for several years, however, which many people believe is a step toward becoming a thoroughly mixed college.[207] Considering all the colleges of Oxford and Cambridge, including those that are specialized (for mature students, for example, or for postgraduates), today only three of seventy (thirty-one at Cambridge and thirty-nine at Oxford) are not coresidential.

From a U.S. perspective, where students at women's colleges have usually been entirely separate from men academically and socially, it might seem that students at women's colleges in the Oxbridge federated system have the best of both worlds. The larger university is coeducational; men and women students attend classes together, frequently have supervisions together, and participate in many university clubs together.[208] Being at a women's college provides women undergraduates with a space that they can claim as their own. And yet this is not how prospective students see women's colleges at Cambridge. They still see them as anachronistic and as making it more difficult to have an active social life that includes men. To date it appears that no amount of publicizing the benefits of single-sex colleges or introducing girls at a young age to a beautiful college like Newnham convinces many of them that they want to attend a women's college.

Notes

I wish to thank Professor Bruce Leslie at Brockport State College and Dr. Diana Lipton, Newnham College, both of whom read and provided me with thoughtful comments on an earlier draft of this chapter. I have benefited from their expertise, but of course, any mistakes are entirely my own. I would also like to thank those who helped me obtain access to needed information, including Dame Marilyn Strathern, mistress of Girton; Kate Perry, wonderful Girton archivist and friend; and Anne Thomson, archivist at Newnham. I appreciate the many people who in interviews enabled me to learn about these two colleges, and those who helped me with obtaining photographs, particularly Kirsten Edbrooke and Francisca Malaree in Girton's Development Office.

For interviews, the following codes have been used, with consecutive numbers differentiating individuals: NF=Newnham fellow (all women), current or retired; NMTO=Newnham male college teaching officer; NS=Newnham student, present or past; GFF=Girton female fellow, current or retired; GMF=Girton male fellow (all current); GFS=Girton female student, past or present; GMS=Girton male student (all past).

1. Fellows (regular or teaching fellows) are essentially the teaching staff of Cambridge colleges. They have college rooms and in fact may live in college, at least part-time; they frequently eat in college; they sit on many college committees, have the right to vote at meetings of the governing body, and supervise students in tutorials. Fellows may or may not be university teaching officers as well, but even if they are not, they will be part of university departments' faculties, often with offices in those buildings, too.

2. Cambridge University, like Oxford, is a "collegiate university," which means it has a federated structure comprised of two parts: independent but not degree-granting colleges, and a university. All students are admitted to a college of the university, where they live and usually have most of their tutorials (supervisions) from college fellows. Each college has a student government body (confusingly called JCR for Junior Common Room) and many activities (sports, clubs, and special events) for their students. At the same time, students attend lectures at the university and may choose to participate in university clubs, probably the most prestigious of which are sports like rowing, the Union (the debating society), and the Cambridge Union of Students. The degree to which Cambridge is "elite" is well demonstrated by the proportion of students who have received three grades of A in the exams that qualify them for university: 90 percent of those accepted to Cambridge versus 11 percent of students accepted by all universi-

ties in the United Kingdom in 2001. See *Cambridge University Reporter,* Special No. 7, 2003.

3. W. B. Hodgson, *Education of Girls, Employment of Women, Two Lectures,* 2nd ed. (London: Trubbner, 1869), appendix.

4. M. C. Bradbrook, *"That Infidel Place": A Short History of Girton College, 1869–1969* (Cambridge: Girton College, 1984/1969), 22.

5. Davies chose the original location of Hitchin when she was unsure whether the college for women would be affiliated with Cambridge, Oxford, or London. Rita McWilliams Tullberg, *Women at Cambridge* (Cambridge: Cambridge University Press, 1998), 31.

6. Ibid., 13–22, 34.

7. Ibid., 37. Although the first residence for Newnham students was in the city of Cambridge, it was not in its present location. In 1875 thirty students, a principal, and a resident lecturer moved into the first building of the present site. Ibid., 54.

8. Sara Payne, "Newnham Centenary," *Cambridge Evening News,* October 1, 1971, 13–15, Scrapbook #1, Newnham College Archives, Cambridge University, Cambridge, England (hereafter NCA).

9. Gillian Sutherland, "Introduction to the Revised Edition," in Tullberg, *Women at Cambridge,* xii.

10. Tullberg, *Women at Cambridge,* 48–50.

11. Ibid., 65, 68. See Paul R. Deslandes, "Culture of Masculinity in Oxbridge Undergraduate Life, 1850–1920," *History of Education Quarterly* 42 (2002): 544–78, for a discussion of the increasing importance of the tripos exams at the same time that women became more integrated into Cambridge and Oxford.

12. E. A. Andrews, "Hurrah! We Have Won!" in Ann Phillips, ed., *A Newnham Anthology* (Cambridge: Newnham College, 1979), 17–19.

13. Tullberg, *Women at Cambridge,* 69.

14. C. Crowther (Kenyon), "Women on Sufferance," in Phillips, *A Newnham Anthology,* 37–39.

15. Cambridge degrees and exams are classified as firsts (the highest grade), second class (divided into II.1 and II.2), and third class. Some disciplines have finer ranks for firsts; for example, the top first in mathematics is distinguished as the "Senior Wrangler."

16. See Tullberg's discussion of the complex politics behind this decision in *Women at Cambridge,* chap. 6, "1887: The Damp Squid," 69–82.

17. Interestingly, Girton students felt they were academically disadvantaged by Emily Davies's insistence that they follow the same procedures as men students. Rather than being able to concentrate on reading and studying for their tripos exams, as Newnham students could, Girton students had to study for a more general exam called the Previous or, more informally, the Little Go, at the same time they were preparing for the tripos. Most women students had not had schooling that prepared them well for the subjects covered in the Previous.

18. Sutherland, "Introduction," xii–xiii.

19. Joyce Senders Pedersen, *The Reform of Girls' Secondary and Higher Education in Victorian England* (New York: Garland Press, 1987), 177–91, 353.

20. Tullberg, *Women at Cambridge,* 116. See a Girton student's description of the day's events in Bradbrook, "'That Infidel Place,'" 98–99.

21. Ibid., 122–23.

22. Elisabeth Leedham-Green, *A Concise History of the University of Cambridge* (Cambridge: Cambridge University Press, 1996), 191.

23. Tullberg, *Women at Cambridge*, 129. Janet Howarth makes the same point, writing that Cambridge "did acquire a certain competitive edge by being more anti-female," in "The Transformation of an Elite? Women and Higher Education since 1900." Transcript of the day's proceedings, September 24, 1998, 29, personal loan of Dr. Gillian Sutherland.

24. Tullberg, *Women at Cambridge*, 152.

25. Ibid., 165.

26. E.M.R. Russell-Smith, "The Art of Theorising," in Phillips, *A Newnham Anthology*, 155–58.

27. Tullberg, *Women at Cambridge*, 174–78. See also Gillian Sutherland, "'Nasty Forward Minxes': Cambridge and the Higher Education of Women," in *The Transformation of an Elite? Women and Higher Education since 1900*, papers presented at a one-day conference at the University of Cambridge to mark the fiftieth anniversary of women's full membership in the university, September 24 1998, 85–98. On the subject of women academics' use of hats to denote their status, see M. E. Grimshaw, "Sunday Nights in Kennedy," in Phillips, *A Newnham Anthology*, 165–67.

28. Tullberg, *Women at Cambridge*, 183.

29. The university retained the right to limit the number of women students at the university, even though it did not have that power for men. This changed in 1987 when the university adopted a formal policy of equal opportunities. Ibid., 187.

30. *Cambridge University Reporter*, 1980–81, no.16, Student Numbers, provides the Cambridge figures; Sara Payne presents the national comparisons in "Memories of Cycles and Chaperones," *Times*, October 4, 1971, Scrapbook #1, NCA.

31. *Times Higher Educational Supplement* [*THES*], November 1, 1974, Scrapbook #1, NCA.

32. "Forty Years On . . ." The CUWAG Report on the Numbers and Status of Academic Women in the University of Cambridge, September 1988, Girton College Archives, Cambridge University, Cambridge, England (hereafter GCA). Gill Sutherland, Review of Rita McWilliams Tullberg's *Women at Cambridge*, *THES*, October 10, 1975, Scrapbook #1, NCA. The first woman vice chancellor, Dr. Rosemary Murray, had been the head of another women's college at Cambridge, New Hall, which opened in 1954.

33. See the minutes of the JCR meetings at Girton, which provide an excellent record of student concerns. In 1973, for example, Girton students voted at one open meeting to donate ten pounds to the Anti-Discrimination against Women Campaign in Cambridge and to request that the Girton College Council "give every encouragement to co-residential colleges to admit more women and to male colleges to admit women as fellows and undergraduates." Students also discussed education in various African countries and the disinvestment movement (removing investments from South Africa). Minutes of the JCR Open Meetings, November 13, 1976, GCA.

34. In the mid-1970s, 66 percent of Cambridge University men students and 73 percent of women students came from the middle class, percentages that were considerably higher than the average for British universities. See Peter Wilby, "Finance-the-Ritz Conundrum," *THES*, October 14, 1977, Scrapbook #1, NCA.

35. 1973 *Newsletter from the Mistress, Girton Review*, GCA.

36. *Times,* March 13, 1973. The woman was a Newnham student. Scrapbook #1, NCA.

37. *Cambridge Evening News,* November 4, 1972, Scrapbook #1, NCA.

38. Articles about Jill Lewis, *THES,* April 26, 1974, and *Stop Press with Varsity,* May 18, 1974, Scrapbook #1, NCA.

39. *Cambridge Evening News,* October 28, 1972, Scrapbook #1, NCA. A year earlier, an article in the *Times* called the Scarlet Women a "women's lib cell." Sara Payne, "Memories of Cycles and Chaperones," *Times,* October 4, 1971, Scrapbook #1, NCA.

40. At the same meeting, the JCR voted unanimously to subscribe to *Spare Rib,* a feminist magazine, for a trial period. Minutes of JCR Open Meetings, February 11, 1976, GCA.

41. Ruth Cohen's remarks can be found in her notes for a talk at a centenary lunch on September 30, 1971, Scrapbook #1, NCA; Jean Floud's speech at the Annual General Meeting of the Roll on October 27, 1973, is found in the 1974 Newnham College Roll Letter, NCA.

42. "Finances of Cambridge Colleges Under Scrutiny," *Cambridge Evening News,* March 10, 1975, Scrapbook #1, NCA.

43. *Newsletter from the Mistress,* 1974, GCA.

44. Susanne Puddefoot, "Light Blue Stockings," *Sunday Times Magazine,* March 30, 1969, 24–29, GCA. Puddefoot's article also points out that while Girton's location may be scoffed at for its "protective apartheid," it is good for study. Moreover, the college has fostered "the ideal of marriage as well as the growth of true minds."

45. Michael Wynn Jones, "The Girls of Girton," *Nova,* February 1968, GCA.

46. *True Grit* student newsletter. The article about hockey comes from an undated issue that appears to be November or December 1975. The information about the bar comes from issue 3, November 22, 1973, GCA.

47. Sara Payne, "Newnham Centenary," *Cambridge Evening News,* Oct 1, 1971, 13–15, Scrapbook #1, NCA.

48. Philip Venning, letter to the *Times,* October 13, 1971, Scrapbook #1, NCA.

49. 1973 Newnham College Roll Letter, NCA.

50. GFF12, taped interview by the author, Girton College, March 24, 2003.

51. All three women's colleges had only women as fellows. While this does not have to be the case, it is the most common pattern and has been viewed as an important way to guarantee jobs for women academics.

52. Melveen McKendrick, speech on coresidence, January 19, 1980, GCA.

53. Muriel Bradbrook, transcript of an interview by Charles Larkum and Kate Perry, September 22, 1992, GCA.

54. Admission Committee II, Preliminary discussions on admission of women to men's colleges, February 27, 1969, GCA.

55. McKendrick, speech on coresidence.

56. Ibid.

57. Ibid.

58. Richard Bourne, "No Freak-out at Newnham," *Guardian,* October 1, 1971, Scrapbook #1, NCA. On the other hand, the senior tutor at Girton at the time claimed that at all three women's colleges, their "graceful cooperation and brave faces hid very real misgivings." McKendrick, speech on coresidence.

59. Payne, "Memories of Cycles and Chaperones."

60. Bourne, "No Freak-out at Newnham."

61. Ruth Cohen, Notes for a talk at lunch on September 30, 1971, Scrapbook #1, NCA.

62. Student pamphlet, "Next to None." n.d. (1973, based on content), Scrapbook #1, NCA.

63. NF3, interview by the author, tape recorded, Newnham College, March 26, 2003.

64. 1975 Newnham College Roll Letter, 22–23, NCA.

65. According to the mistress at the time, Muriel Bradbrook, the decision was made "in effect" in early 1976, although the actual vote was "recorded" a few weeks after the arrival of a new mistress, Brenda Ryman, in the autumn of 1976. See Muriel Bradbrook, handwritten note on Somerville College's (Oxford) decision to admit men, 1992, GCA.

66. Bradbrook interview transcript.

67. Diana Geddes, "A Woman's Place is in the College," *Education*, May 25, 1979, GCA.

68. Students applying to Cambridge who do not get into the college of their choice are put into the "pool" as possible students for another college. The most desirable colleges get fewer students from the pool. When Girton started taking many applicants from the pool, this meant that virtually all of them had tried to get into one of the newly mixed, formerly men's colleges (the only exceptions being students who might have applied to Newnham or New Hall).

69. McKendrick, speech on coresidence; Bradbrook, handwritten note; Bradbrook interview transcript; taped interviews by the author with GFF4, March 17, 2003; GFF8, March 13, 2003; and GFF5, May 28, 2003, GCA.

70. This was technically true, but the decision had really been made earlier. See preceding note. The new mistress did inform a smaller group of students, those in the student government or JCR Committee, the previous day, November 26, 1976.

71. Minutes of the JCR Open Meeting, December 2, 1976, GCA.

72. Ibid.

73. *True Grit*, November 1976, GCA.

74. Ibid.

75. McKendrick, speech on coresidence, GCA.

76. Ibid.

77. Coresidence planning, box GCAC, GCA.

78. Kate Perry, Girton archivist, personal e-mail communication, August 19, 2003. This is the number recorded in the tutorial matriculation list. The senior tutor, Malveena McKendrick, reported that 58 men students entered, and other sources claim 53 men. McKendrick said that she was pleased with the breakdown between arts and sciences: 95 men and women students came to study an arts subject, while 72 came for science. McKendrick, speech on coresidence, GCA.

79. GFF1, taped interview by the author, March 10, 2003. Dr. M.E.J. Hughes also talks about how, to undergraduates like herself who were at Girton at the time, the transition seemed "to go very smoothly." Later, as a fellow of a men's college beginning to admit women, she realized how much work has to go on "behind the scenes" for it to appear an easy transition. Speech at Old Girtonians (OGs) dinner, 1993, GCA.

80. GMS5, phone interview by the author, April 22, 2003, GCA.

81. GMF2, taped interview by the author, April 4, 2003, GCA.

82. JCR Open Meeting, October 15, 1979, GCA.

83. JCR Open Meetings, January 21 and February 4, 1980, GCA. Donations to groups and agencies in the larger community were subject to a monetary limit of fifty pounds.

84. Stephen Kenyon, "Leap Year at Girton," GCA; GFF5, taped interview by the author, May 28, 2003, GCA.

85. GMF3, taped interview by the author, February 5, 2003, GCA. A woman student who came to Girton in 1981 also commented that academics were "poor relations" in comparison to academics at other colleges. GFS4, phone interview by the author, April 23, 2003, GCA.

86. GFF9, taped interview by the author, March 5, 2003, GCA.

87. Glenys Roberts, "University Challenge," *Express Woman*, n.d. (1981), GCA.

88. McKendrick, speech on coresidence, GCA.

89. *Newsletter from the Mistress*, 1979; *Guardian*, February 22, 1983, GCA; *Girton College Newsletters*, 1980, 1987, 1990, 1993, 1994, 1996, GCA; 2001/2002 Report on Admissions, covering 1989–95, 2000–2002, GCA.

90. Report on Admissions, Notes on Applications, 1989/90 entry, GCA.

91. JCR Open Meetings, October 17, 1990, GCA.

92. *Girton College Newsletter*, 1992, Admissions Report, GCA.

93. McKendrick, speech on coresidence, GCA.

94. Ibid.

95. *Girton College Newsletters*, 1979–2002, GCA.

96. Comments made by the following fellows during interviews by the author: GFF1, GFF5, GFF9, GFF10, GMF1, GMF2, GMF3, GMF4, GCA.

97. GFF10, taped interview by the author, April 2, 2003, GCA.

98. GFF2, taped interview by the author, March 13, 2001; GFF3, taped interview by the author, March 21, 2003, GCA. The director of development mentioned that one fundraising goal is for child care for fellows and students. The college is trying to build a nursery at Wolfson Court. GFF7, taped interview by the author, March 7, 2003, GCA.

99. GFF3, GFF8, taped interviews by the author, 2003, GCA.

100. GFF2, GFF4, GFF5, GFF10, GMF4, taped interviews by the author, 2003, GCA.

101. GMF4, GFF10, taped interviews by the author, April 2, 2003, GCA.

102. McKendrick, speech on coresidence. The anecdote that the senior tutor used as evidence for this point came from an experience her husband had while interviewing an applicant to the men's college with which he was affiliated. The applicant asked about coresidency plans, and when McKendrick's husband said that such plans did not exist, the applicant said he would go elsewhere because he would not dream of "going to a college that excludes half the human race."

103. 1994 Letter from Mistress, *Girton College Newsletter*, GCA.

104. Letters, *Guardian*, March 27, 1973, GCA.

105. In 1979, 8.1 percent of Girton women received firsts, compared to 8.7 percent of all women in the university; 31.3 percent of Girton women received II(1)s vs. 35.1 percent of all women in the university. In 1980, Girton men were slightly ahead of all men in the university in their proportion of firsts (16.3 percent vs. 14.5 percent) but much worse in II(1)s (20.4 vs. 31.4 percent); Girton women were slightly below all women on firsts and very slightly above on II(1)s. *Girton College Newsletter*, 1979 and 1980, GCA.

106. 1994 Letter from the Mistress, *Girton College Newsletter*, GCA.

107. In 1999 Girton was 21 of 24; in 2000, 18 of 24; in 2001, 17 of 24. Sarah Cassidy, "Christ's College Holds on to Top Slot at Cambridge," *Independent,* July 30, 2001; John O'Leary, "Oxbridge Opens Up," *Times,* May 16, 2001, electronic access. Girton's position in the 2004 exam results' league table is mentioned in Richard Garner, "Women's College Climbs Cambridge League," *Independent,* July 12, 2004, education.independent.co.uk/news/story.jsp?story=540101, accessed August 12, 2004. The mistress of Girton was naturally disappointed by this result but attributed it in part to the women's colleges, Newnham and New Hall, being given the first opportunity to select women applicants from the pool. Private communication, August 5, 2004.

108. Some people who have been at Cambridge a long time also say that in the past, women's colleges and Kings, which has a reputation as a left-wing college, were the only ones that cared about exam results. Most colleges generally cared more about sports and students' "character," although some were concerned about exam results in particular subjects in which they had a reputation for excellence.

109. JCR Open Meeting, November 11, 1994, GCA.

110. Ekaterina Krylova, "Women's Troubles," *Cambridge Student,* February 13, 2003.

111. GMF2, taped interview by the author, April 4, 2003, GCA.

112. GMS5, phone interview by the author, April 22, 2003, GCA.

113. GFS4, phone interview by the author, April 23, 2003, GCA.

114. JCR Committee meeting, November 21, 1993, GCA.

115. Ibid., October 27, 1996, GCA.

116. Ibid., October 25, 1998, GCA.

117. GFS2, phone interview by the author, March 17, 2003, GCA.

118. GMS6, phone interview by the author, May 1, 2003, GCA.

119. GMS1, phone interview by the author, May 23, 2003, GCA.

120. Joan Robinson, one of the most famous economists of the twentieth century who, in the opinion of many people, should have been awarded the Nobel Prize, was an undergraduate and graduate student at Girton, hence the name of the student organization.

121. GMF3 interview.

122. GFF2, GFF5 interviews.

123. GFF3 interview.

124. GFF4 and GFF10 interviews.

125. Muriel Bradbrook, *Newsletter from the Mistress,* 1974, 3, GCA.

126. *Girton College Newsletter,* 1993, GCA.

127. GFF7 interview.

128. GMS1, GMS6, GFS2 phone interviews; GMS4, taped interview by the author, March 4, 2003, GCA.

129. GFF4 and GMF2 interviews.

130. GFF1 interview.

131. GFS3 interview.

132. GMS1, phone interview by the author, May 23, 2003, GCA.

133. JCR Committee Minutes, 1980–2003.

134. JCR Committee meeting, April 29, 1992, GCA.

135. JCR Open Meetings, May 7, 1990, December 4, 1986, January 29, 1990, GCA.

136. GFS2, GFS3, GFS5, GMS1, GMS3, GMS2, GMS4, GMS5, GMS6, interviews by the author, spring 2003, GCA.

137. JCR Open Meeting, May 5, 1986, GCA.

138. GMS6 interview.

139. See JCR Open Meeting, February 7, 1991, GCA, for a discussion of self-defense classes. Students noted that men's classes could be arranged if there was interest in them.

140. See JCR Committee, November 28, 1998, when students commented that while it might have been better if men, too, had seen a video on domestic violence, women-only events were important.

141. JCR Open Meeting, February 23, 1987, GCA.

142. Ibid., October 21, 1991, GCA.

143. Ibid., January 21, 1992, and JCR Committee meeting, May 4, 1997, GCA.

144. JCR Committee meeting, January 18, 1998, GCA.

145. See, for example, JCR Open Meeting, November 14 1990, where students voted to give thirty pounds to the "No Means No" campaign.

146. JCR Open Meeting, February 23, 1987, GCA. Only 14 of 172 entering students were coming from state schools that year.

147. Of 3,137 students accepted by Cambridge in 2002, 12 were black Caribbeans, 11 were black Africans, 2 were "black other," 112 were Indian, 27 were Pakistani, 10 were Bangladeshi, 72 were Chinese, 55 were "Asian other," and 110 were "other." *Cambridge University Reporter,* Special No. 7, table 5, 2003.

148. GMS4, GMS5 interviews.

149. JCR Open Meeting, January 29, 1990, and JCR Committee meetings, January 23, and October 2, 1994, and October 13, 1996, GCA.

150. JCR Open Meeting, January 23, 1991, GCA. Another reason students objected to Philip Morris's support of Jesse Helms was his racial slurs against a black political rival.

151. JCR Committee, October 18, 1998, GCA.

152. GFS2, GFS3, GMS1 interviews, spring 2003.

153. JCR Committee, October 15, 2000, GCA.

154. See, for example, JCR Committee meeting, February 21, 1993, on concern about student behavior over a weekend, including vomit in bathroom showers. Minutes from the January 16, 1994, committee meeting mention that students were being assessed over 1,100 pounds for damages, mostly for cleaning up vomit. Minutes from March 7, 1999, mention that a formal hall was banned due to "record bad behavior" and make practical suggestions for the future, including having starters on the table when people arrive so that they would be less likely to drink on an empty stomach.

155. GFS2, phone interview by the author, March 17, 2003, GCA.

156. NF3, recorded interview by the author, March 26, 2003, NCA.

157. JCR Committee, November 24, 1976, 1970–1979 box, NCA.

158. Peter Wilby, "Finance-the-Ritz Conundrum," *THES,* October 14, 1977; Caroline Leuw, "Seven Down, Seven to Go," November 3, 1979, *Stop Press with Varsity,* Scrapbook #1, NCA.

159. John Gaskell, "Problems Facing an All-Women's College," *Cambridge Evening News,* March 5, 1980, Scrapbook #1, NCA.

160. NF3, recorded interview by the author, March 26, 2003, NCA. College papers are sealed

for thirty years. It is thus not possible at this time to get more precise information about these later votes.

161. Ibid.

162. NF2, taped interview by the author, March 20, 2003; NF1, taped interview by the author, April 29, 2003, NCA.

163. Interviews with a variety of students and fellows by the author, NCA.

164. Information about the Tompkins League rankings and proportions of II(1)s come from Newnham College Roll Letters and articles found in scrapbooks, NCA.

165. Garner, "Women's College Climbs Cambridge League."

166. NF3 interview.

167. Stuart Martindale, "News Features: Why Don't Girls Come First?" *Varsity,* December 10, 2001, www.varsity.co.uk

168. Senior Tutor's Report, 2002, Newnham College Cambridge, Roll Letter, NCA.

169. Senior Tutor's Report, 2001, NCA.

170. Senior Tutor's Report, 2000, NCA.

171. NS8, phone interview by the author, June 6, 2003; NS1, taped interview by the author, April 3, 2003; NS6, taped interview by the author, February 21, 2003, NCA.

172. Senior Tutor's Report, 2000.

173. Diana Geddes, "A Woman's Place is in the College," *Education,* May 25, 1979, GCA.

174. Newnham College Roll Letters, 1988 and 1992, NCA.

175. Fiona Maddocks, "Women Only, and Wanting to Keep it That Way," *The Independent,* March 9, 1992, Newnham scrapbook #2, NCA.

176. Letter from the Admissions Tutor, Lisa Kendall, 2001, Newnham College Roll Letter, NCA.

177. NF1 interview.

178. NMT01, taped interview by the author, May 28, 2003, NCA.

179. NS9, taped interview by the author, February 21, 2003, NCA.

180. NS8 taped interview by the author, February 21, 2003, NCA; NMT01 interview.

181. NF1 interview; NS4, taped interview by the author, February 14, 2003.

182. NF1 interview; Newnham College Cambridge Roll Letter, Admissions Report, 2000, NCA.

183. Peter Wilby, "Finance-the-Ritz Conundrum," *THES,* October 14, 1977, Scrapbook #1, NCA.

184. John Gaskell, "Problems Facing an All-Women's College," *Cambridge Evening News,* March 5, 1980, Scrapbook #1, NCA.

185. "Newnham Has a Great Appeal." *Cambridge Evening News,* November 23, 1987, Scrapbook #2, NCA.

186. Summary of Dr. O'Neill's speech, 1993, 16–17, Newnham College Roll Letter, NCA.

187. Letter from the Principal, 1999, Newnham College Roll Letter, NCA.

188. Newnham College Roll Letter, 2000 and 2001, NCA.

189. NF3 interview.

190. NMT01 interview. See also the article in the *Cambridge Evening News,* "Newnham May Let In Men as Fellows," January 15, 1990, Scrapbook #2, NCA. The 1989–90 Newnham yearbook has a photo of students demonstrating against the admission of male fellows, NCA.

191. NMT03, NMT01, taped interviews by the author, May 28, 2003; NMT02, taped interview by the author, May 8, 2003, NCA.

192. NF3 interview.

193. One student said that she would rather be thought of as a lesbian than a communist.

194. See, for example, a letter of a Newnham student, Jennifer Wallace, in *Stop Press*, May 8, 1987, in which she talks about how "male dominated and androcentric" the sports coverage was in that student newspaper. Scrapbook #2, NCA.

195. NS4 interview.

196. NS7, taped interview by the author, March 4, 2003, NCA.

197. NS8 interview, as well as NS3 and NS5.

198. Drinking societies seem to exist at all Cambridge colleges, whether or not they are officially recognized. Students allude to them and their practices, such as students dressed in their underwear or gowns going to forty college doors and drinking a vodka at each door. According to some students, both male and female drinking societies are very popular.

199. NS4, NS9 interviews.

200. Perhaps one issue that would not have been raised if the fellowship were mixed is the appropriateness of a transsexual fellow. In 1997 Newnham received national attention because a famous fellow at that time, Germaine Greer, used an "essentialist" feminist argument in opposing the appointment of a former man physicist. Ironically Dr. Rachel Padman had not encountered problems during her PhD program at St. John's, then an all-male college of the university, even though it was during that time that she had her surgery. Germaine Greer's opposition was not successful, it should be noted; Dr. Padman remains a fellow of Newnham. See Phil Baty, "The Essential Guide to Sexuality," *THES*, July 18, 1997.

201. NS1 interview.

202. NS8, NMT02, and NMT03 interviews.

203. GFF8 and NF1 interviews.

204. NF2 interview.

205. Letter from the Mistress, *Girton College Newsletter*, 2002, GCA.

206. Ibid.

207. The Cambridge University student newspaper reported in March 2004, that the JCR at New Hall passed a motion to admit male students, with students arguing that to remain a women's college was "retarding rather than advancing the rights of women in Cambridge." The president, however, argued against the motion, citing evidence from the United States that women achieve more if they attend single-sex colleges. See Charlotte Forbes, "New Boys, New Hall?" *Varsity*, March 5, 2004, www.varsity. co.uk/article_1.asp?category=3anddoc=22550andid=15563andid=13720, accessed July 7, 2004.

208. A woman who had graduated from Wellesley and then attended Newnham as an affiliated student remarked on how different the two institutions were. As she said, Newnham did not seem so distinct from a coeducational institution. NS2, taped interview by the author at Hamilton College, N.Y., July 10, 2003, NCA.

PART **V**

Conclusions

13

The State of Women's Colleges Today

Leslie Miller-Bernal and Susan L. Poulson

The major challenge for women's colleges today is the firmly entrenched norm of coeducation that exists at all levels of our educational system, from primary school to higher education. Most people in the United States today do not think of single-sex education as an option. They barely think of women's or men's colleges at all, and when they do, they associate them with the past when men's and women's spheres were more separate in all aspects of life. Such beliefs create a self-fulfilling prophecy. If high school girls see women's colleges as an anachronism and will not even consider attending one, in the marketplace of higher education, this means that women's colleges face severe enrollment problems, sometimes closing or becoming coeducational, thus making single-sex education even less an option than it was previously. Today there are fewer than 60 women's colleges, whereas in 1960 there were 233, and as recently as 1986, there were 90 (see Appendix 2).

Despite their rarity, many women who have attended or otherwise been associated with women's colleges see them as particularly valuable. Not only does research continue to demonstrate that alumnae of women's colleges fare better educationally and occupationally than do alumnae of coeducational colleges, but while they are students, women who attend women's colleges report feeling "empowered" in ways they never have before.[1] Elite women's colleges are rated among the nation's top liberal arts colleges. In 2005, *U.S. News* ranked Wellesley 4, Smith 13, Bryn Mawr 21, Mount Holyoke 24, Scripps 26, and Barnard 29. Six women's colleges among the top thirty is impressive, especially considering how few women's colleges there are.

And yet the challenge of coeducation has meant that most surviving women's colleges have changed tremendously. Few, less than 20 percent, are able to function like the elite colleges among them. No longer are most what they once were—liberal arts colleges serving traditional-aged residential students. Instead the majority of women's colleges have adapted to changes in the marketplace by changing their curriculum, altering the ways they enroll students, and reaching out to different, often less academically prepared, population groups. They have changed in so many ways that their alumnae sometimes see them as different colleges.[2]

Factors Affecting How Women's Colleges Adapt to the Challenge of Coeducation

One question we raised in Chapter One about women's colleges is whether they have been successful in meeting the challenges of the larger cultural environment that increasingly favors coeducation. Our answer is, overall, yes, but in so doing they have usually needed to change, sometimes in dramatic ways. The case studies in *Challenged by Coeducation* have demonstrated the diversity among women's colleges and the principal ways they have survived. Which adaptations colleges have made are affected by a variety of factors including location, historical prestige, wealth, and particular subcultures served.

Location

Urban women's colleges usually have a variety of adaptations available to them that rural or suburban colleges do not. This is ironic, as founders of many women's colleges deliberately chose rural areas since they believed students' health would be protected by fresh air and exercise. Today many young women prefer urban areas since they are more conducive to an active, stimulating social life. To widen students' academic as well as social opportunities, some urban women's colleges have established links with other institutions, such as Spelman's membership in the Atlanta Consortium and Simmons's involvement with the six Colleges of the Fenway. Urban women's colleges also can appeal to older students who wish to attend college in the evening on a part-time basis. Similarly, graduate programs can be established that offer advanced degrees to adult workers. Graduate programs by law must be coeducational, so these women's colleges do enroll men as well as women. Mills College's undergraduate enrollment has declined over time, but its graduate school has continued to expand. Texas Woman's University is similar to Mills in offering graduate degrees; it also has a large contingent of part-time students. Both colleges also have a high percentage of transfer students.

Another aspect of a college's location is how close it is to a men's or, more usually, a coeducational college. The few women's colleges that are in close proximity to other colleges can advertise themselves as providing students with both a single-sex and a coeducational environment—a "best of both worlds" scenario. Barnard benefits from being across the street from a major research university that is also one of the prestigious Ivy League institutions, Columbia University. In fact, Barnard is part of the university, even though it has its own faculty, president, and board of trustees. Newnham College of Cambridge University is similar, although in its case, it is one of twenty-five colleges of the university; it is located very close to academic buildings where lectures are held and is also quite close to some of the formerly all-male prestigious colleges such as Trinity, Pembroke, and Kings. Spelman is contiguous to all-male Morehouse. Examples of other women's colleges not included in this book that benefit from this type of location are Scripps, which is one of the Claremont Colleges cluster; College of St. Benedict in Minnesota, which has a cooperative relationship with all-male St. John's, six miles away; and Bryn Mawr, which is very close to Haverford.

Historical Prestige

Prestige has a variety of benefits, including the ability to choose from highly qualified applicants, many of whom come from privileged families, and large donations from wealthy alumnae and foundations willing to support successful institutions. Barnard and Vassar are among the elite of women's colleges, both having been designated in the 1920s as two of the Seven Sisters. Girton and Newnham are similar in being part of Cambridge University, one of the most prestigious universities in the world. It is interesting that Barnard and Newnham have remained all women, but Vassar and Girton have both admitted men. An obvious, if partial, explanation is the location of Vassar and Girton—farther from men's or coeducational colleges than Barnard and Newnham are. Even with their better locations, though, Barnard and Newnham have been challenged by the demands of coeducation. Barnard has resisted Columbia's attempts to merge, and today it is doing well in terms of applications and enrollments of strong students, but earlier it faced financial and enrollment difficulties. As part of Cambridge University, Newnham does not have difficulty enrolling students, but it does find it hard to obtain students who want to be at a women's college. This problem affects the prestige of Newnham in the internal hierarchy of Cambridge colleges, which in turn leads to periodic pressure from some of its affiliated academics to admit men.

Wealth

Wealth makes it more likely that an institution can remain a traditional women's college. The college can use its resources to enhance its facilities and keep up with technological developments and students' expectations for comfort and beauty. Although wealth is often associated with a college's prestige, it has an independent effect too. Among the Seven Sisters, for example, Wellesley seems the most secure, in large part due to its very high endowment (over a billion dollars in the beginning of the twenty-first century). Spelman has benefited from large donations, including most famously in 1988, $20 million from Bill and Camille Cosby, the largest gift given to a historically black college, a record surpassed in 1992 when Spelman received $37 million from a fund set up by DeWitt Wallace, a founder of *Reader's Digest*.[3] Even some of the colleges that have ultimately admitted men, Wheaton and Wells, for example, had sufficient endowments not to face this wrenching change earlier. Especially at Wells, the endowment was for a long time used to support students who could not have afforded to attend otherwise. While most colleges follow this practice to some extent, Wells did it for such a high percentage of its students and for so much of their tuition costs that college personnel referred to the practice as "buying students."

Another form of wealth that frequently is not acknowledged is the non-remunerated labor of women religious (commonly referred to as nuns) at Catholic women's colleges. Both Mundelein and College of Notre Dame are excellent examples of the ability of Catholic colleges to initiate innovative programs by counting on long hours of unpaid work. This form of wealth is declining, however, as fewer women enter the religious life and Catholic colleges' faculties are recruited from among virtually the same group of academics that secular colleges employ.

Ties to a Particular Subculture

Groups that are outside the cultural mainstream sometimes have established their own educational institutions. In fact, this is one of the main reasons that women's colleges originated—so that women could receive higher education when most colleges were closed to them. When Catholics were discriminated against, they established their own colleges, first for men and then later for women. Catholic women's colleges benefited from having nuns as faculty whose work was not remunerated and from having guaranteed students—young Catholic women. As Catholics have become part of the mainstream of U.S. life and Catholics' religious practices have come to resemble those of other Christians, Catholic women's colleges have had to search for other groups who could benefit from their educational programs. Colleges like Notre Dame, Maryland, and Trinity University (formerly college), Washington, D.C., among many others, have done a remarkable job of reaching out to underserved populations. Their students today are frequently racial and ethnic minorities, older women, and single mothers (and women who fit all such categories). They have established innovative programs like weekend colleges that are often open to men too. Thus while many Catholic women's colleges have been able to survive, they no longer resemble the kind of colleges they used to be and often, in fact, have mostly non-Catholic students.

Historically black colleges and universities (HBCUs) are similar to Catholic colleges in appealing to a particular subculture. In contrast to Catholic institutions, however, most black colleges were coeducational from the start. Like secular institutions in the Midwest, black colleges found it more expedient to educate women and men together. A few black single-sex institutions were established, however, with Spelman being the most famous of the women's colleges. While the majority of black Americans no longer attend HBCUs since predominantly white institutions have opened up to all racial and ethnic groups, black colleges still fulfill important functions in the black community. They accept promising students who would not be admitted to other institutions that rely more on standardized test scores, and they support students in ways that less welcoming, predominantly white colleges do not. Thus Spelman with its good reputation, long history, fortuitous location, and relatively large endowment has continued to attract mostly young black women.

A Major Response to the Challenge of Coeducation: Becoming Coeducational

It is ironic to label the admission of men to women's colleges as becoming "coeducational," since "coed" was originally a derogatory term applied to women at formerly men's institutions. Nonetheless, this is how the larger public and many colleges themselves refer to the transition from being a women's college to a college for women and men. The transitions to coeducation covered in the case studies of *Challenged by Coeducation* span four decades since the 1960s. This was the era during which virtually all men's colleges became coeducational and the number of women's colleges declined dramatically. The transitions themselves differ in terms of the reasons why they occurred and students' reactions to admitting men. These variations in turn reflect changes in higher education and, more particularly, developments at most traditional (i.e., residential liberal arts) women's colleges. In general, students' resistance to the admission of men has increased over time as they have come to recognize the rarity and advantages of women-only educational environments. They also have learned tactics from other protests, particularly the one at Mills; at the same time, trustees and administrators have also been able to prepare for students' expected outrage.

When Vassar College decided to admit men in 1969, a majority of students and faculty approved of coeducation. Few people at the time thought about discrimination against women. After all, the second wave women's movement had hardly begun. The term "sexism" was just being coined; sexual harassment policies and rape crisis centers did not yet exist. In the educational arena, M. Elizabeth Tidball had not yet published her pioneering studies that demonstrated the long-term benefits of attending women's colleges, nor had the term "chilly climate" been used to describe typical coeducational environments.

Vassar authorities appear to have decided to admit men as a response to the cultural focus on integration and in order not to lose the college's strongest students to the elite, previously all-male colleges like Yale and Princeton. While some Vassar students did not like the idea of giving up the college's identity as a women's college, they did not engage in sustained protest.

The situation at Girton College of Cambridge University was not that different from Vassar's in terms of students' lack of resistance to the admission of men. Girton was the first women's college to be established at either Cambridge or Oxford, and in 1979 it became the first to admit men undergraduates. Students protested at not being consulted, as students at men's colleges of the university had been about the admission of women, but their protest was confined to a meeting and to writing about their feelings in a student publication. Girton students even voted, after the fact, to support the decision itself. Fellows (academics) of the college were split in their feelings about the decision to become coresidential. In general, senior fellows supported the decision more than junior fellows did. Longer association with Girton seemed to have convinced senior fellows that there was no other way of keeping their college attractive to applicants.

When Wheaton College announced in 1987 that it was considering becoming a coeducational institution, major protests erupted. By then, awareness of discrimination against women in higher education was more advanced. Wheaton itself had been promoting a "gender-balanced" curriculum as a way of infusing feminist ideals into all academic programs. But administrators and trustees were concerned about falling applications, which they attributed to an irreversible decline of interest in women's colleges. The college's president also argued that with the rise of opportunities for women, separatism was no longer beneficial; instead, men needed to learn to work with powerful women. Nonetheless, students and alumnae, fearful that their college's focus on women would be lost, vehemently protested the coeducation announcement. Faculty voted to condemn the process by which the decision had been made, and a group of alumnae filed a lawsuit to recover money they had donated during a recent capital campaign for Wheaton as a women's college.

The most famous protest over a women college's decision to admit men occurred at Mills in 1990. Again trustees were motivated by a fall in undergraduate enrollments and the seemingly irreversible tide of coeducation. Students' blockades of buildings, their strike, their tenacity, the publicity their protest received, and the promises of students, faculty, and their allies to assist in enrollment efforts, all led trustees to change their minds within two weeks. The trustees' reversal was met with joy even though it was a conditional reversal: Undergraduate enrollments were to meet certain targets; the endowment was to increase to a certain level, and so on. These targets were not all met, however; goals have been subsequently modified as the college seeks to sustain itself through its graduate program and other initiatives.

The fierce resistance to Texas Women's University's becoming fully co-educational in 1994 may be surprising since for TWU as a public institution, this change was mandated. The university's board of regents was attempting to control a development they believed to be inevitable due to recent court cases stipulating that other public institutions (all-male Citadel and Virginia Military Institute) had to admit all qualified applicants. Earlier, in 1972, students had accepted federal requirements that TWU open its Institute of Health Sciences to men, with their only resistance being attempts to establish women-only student organizations. But in 1994 TWU students responded angrily to the regents' ruling that the institution could not remain all women in its General Division. Like students at Wells about a decade later, they were inspired by Mills students' ability to persuade Mills's trustees to change their minds about admitting men. The protests at TWU included graffiti, sit-ins, vigils, and a tent city; students raised money and garnered support by effective use of publicity. TWU protestors also filed a class-action lawsuit claiming that the regents had not followed legal requirements when making their decision. Nonetheless, the courts upheld the regents, citing the Equal Protection Clause of the Fourteenth Amendment, but stated that TWU could remain a university for women in terms of its curriculum and atmosphere.

The vehemence of protest over a women's college becoming coeducational continues. Even before Wells College trustees announced their decision to admit men students in the fall of 2005, students had organized to try to influence them to keep the college all women. Students had long been told about the advantages of women's colleges. Lesbian, bisexual, and a few transgendered students felt particularly threatened by the idea of men on campus. And yet, given the dire straits of the college in terms of its low enrollments and budget deficits, and given the other options that had been tried but not succeeded, some people believed that the trustees, many of whom were alumnae, had been slow to face the inevitability of opening up Wells to men. The trustees may also have been reluctant, knowing the protest that would ensue. Once they made the announcement in the fall of 2004, students took over a building, stopped attending classes, erected a tent city, arranged for local as well as national publicity, and used the Internet to organize and obtain support from alumnae and parents. Inspired by the example of Mills, Wells protestors believed that they could reverse the decision. Of course, not only students but also administrators and trustees had learned from previous protests. Despite a lawsuit filed by parents, which did not receive a favorable court hearing, Wells College continued on its path of admitting men while promising students that it would remember its mission and remain committed to its diversity goals.

With the exception of TWU, where change was imposed or about to be mandated, each of these four women's colleges (Vassar, Girton, Wheaton, and Wells) has chosen to admit men students. Choice is a slippery concept, however. Unless one accepts the motto that has sometimes surfaced in campus protests over the admission of men—"Better dead than coed"—it may be that there really was no alternative for these colleges. Women's colleges like Trinity in Burlington, Vermont, Mount Vernon in Washington, D.C., and Mundelein in Chicago, no longer exist as independent entities. Even if the four formerly women's colleges focused on in this book could have survived as single-sex institutions, they might have had to make other changes, as Mills and the College of Notre Dame have, that they would find unacceptable—establishing or enlarging graduate degree programs, developing a preprofessional or applied curriculum, opening evening divisions at which students study part-time, and perhaps becoming less selective. It is debatable, of course, whether even these changes would have succeeded at campuses in relatively isolated locations, particularly Wheaton and Wells.

The recent upsurge in coeducation occurred relatively quickly for men's colleges. Within a space of less than fifteen years, between 1969 and 1983, virtually all the men's colleges in the United States admitted women. For women's colleges, the corresponding phase has been more protracted; in fact, it is still ongoing. From some perspectives, this is surprising. In general, men's colleges were richer and so did not need women students as much as poorer women's colleges needed to expand their enrollments. The increasingly sophisticated protests over the admission of men students to women's colleges provide an answer to this apparent puzzle. Women students and their allies, bolstered by the women's movement and the research indicating the benefits of women-only spaces, have come to understand more clearly what they might lose if their colleges admitted men. They were also heartened by the success of protests at Mills in reversing an institutional decision. In other words, most people associated with women's colleges, particularly since the 1980s, have seen the transition to a coeducational institution as having definite drawbacks. Typically the decision to admit men, especially in the last two decades, has been made only when there seemed to be no alternatives.

In recent years, the proportion of men students among undergraduates has declined. Today only about 44 percent of undergraduates are men. This means that women's colleges that have recently opened their doors to men will find it more difficult to recruit them than did colleges like Vassar that became coeducational more than thirty-five years ago. Since the underrepresentation of men is greater among blacks and Hispanics, becoming a diverse coeducational college today is particularly challenging.

Characteristics of Formerly Women's Colleges

An important question we raised in Chapter One is whether formerly women's colleges are distinctly different from other coeducational colleges. Specifically we have been concerned to determine whether formerly women's colleges have lived up to the promise of coeducation by creating gender-equal environments. According to six former presidents of women's colleges that admitted men, who after a meeting in 2000 at the Mellon Foundation wrote about their colleges' experiences, their institutions are more gender equal than others (see Appendix 1). On the face of it, this would seem likely for several reasons. First, formerly women's colleges have a history that has celebrated women and their achievements. Not only is this history available in written form, but it is usually physically manifest in female iconography around campus. Second, unlike formerly men's colleges, formerly women's colleges have not had fraternities and football, two ways male dominance has often been expressed and solidified. Third, formerly women's colleges have remained predominantly female, with a high percentage of women in top administrative posts and faculty, including senior faculty, and a high percentage of women students, usually between 60 and 75 percent, even many years after becoming coeducational.[4]

In terms of campus leadership after men are admitted, the evidence is more mixed. Wheaton and Vassar seem to have a good representation of women students in key positions, with the exception being, perhaps, the president of student government. At Girton, Cambridge University, not only has the president tended to be a man student, but so have treasurers, while women are usually the secretaries. It is interesting that students at Wells are aware of this possibility and have vowed that when men are admitted, they are not going to let a male-dominant pattern emerge.

More difficult yet is the issue of male dominance in classroom discussions. Few researchers have examined whether men are more likely to dominate classes at formerly women's colleges, as studies have shown they typically do in other coeducational institutions.[5] Vassar is one college where classroom dynamics have been studied, and the picture that emerged was complicated. The proportion of women to men in a class, the subject matter, and the gender of the professor, all affected who talked the most.

Formerly women's colleges vary among themselves, of course. Some, like Wheaton and Vassar, have committed themselves to gender equity and have attempted to devise mechanisms for preserving their legacy. Similarly, TWU has strengthened its mission statement and instituted a women's studies requirement. But formerly women's colleges not studied here, perhaps ones that have never made women's issues a central focus of their institution, may not be more gender equal than other coeducational colleges. Clearly it takes effort and vigilance to ensure that an institution keeps gender equity issues in mind as new programs and policies develop.

Not only do formerly women's colleges vary among themselves, but so do their women students. Probably all predominantly white colleges could do a better job of incorporating and supporting racial minorities.[6] There are reasons to be concerned about diversity when a women's college admits men, thereby making gender its central focus. It is telling that at Wheaton College, the proportion of white students increased after men were admitted even though more minority faculty were appointed. Wheaton's new black scholar-musician president, however, has announced that he plans to make diversity a central concern of his administration. Another group of students who need attention are gay (lesbian and homosexual), bisexual, and transgendered women and men. Women's colleges have in recent years become known for their support of people with various sexual identities and genders. Given the many studies indicating that, in general, women are less homophobic than men, the atmosphere for gay, bisexual, and transgendered students has to be carefully monitored when a women's college admits men.[7] At Girton College, for example, despite the continued existence of student officers for gay men and lesbians, a few antigay incidents have occurred.

The Future

Will all women's colleges disappear? Will formerly women's colleges be able to maintain their commitment to gender equity? These are difficult, yet intriguing, questions. Today it seems that strong women's colleges like the remaining Seven Sisters (Wellesley, Smith, Mount Holyoke, Barnard, and Bryn Mawr), Agnes Scott, Spelman, and Simmons may continue indefinitely. Whether at some point they decide that they can still be faithful to their missions with men students, however, is less certain. In other words, even if enrollments and finances do not create difficulties for them, these colleges may eventually conclude that there is no longer sufficient reason for them to maintain their women-only student populations.

The ability of formerly women's colleges to promote gender equity over the long term would seem to depend in part on the culture at large. Colleges, after all, are not immune to social developments. In the 1950s, for example, before the second wave of the women's movement, women's colleges were not particularly feminist institutions. While they had more women on their faculty than did coeducational colleges, and their women students developed leadership skills as the heads of student organizations, marriage and motherhood, not careers, were emphasized. At least in part the recent feminist rationale for women's colleges came about as people searched for a raison d'être once women could attend virtually any college or university in the country.

The case studies of *Challenged by Coeducation*, particularly of those women's colleges that have admitted men, suggest mechanisms for developing and perpetuating gender equity. Given the tendency for colleges to establish short-lived initiatives, mechanisms need to be institutionalized if they are to last. What follows is a short list of suggestions based on what other colleges, most of them discussed in this book, have done:

Curriculum

Women's studies is now an established discipline that should be supported at all colleges but perhaps particularly at formerly women's colleges. Some institutions have developed a specialty in the newly emerging field of queer studies too. While the idea of including gender issues throughout the curriculum has been popular at times, for example, at Wheaton and TWU in the 1980s, most institutions have found it necessary to focus such studies in a specialized department, usually called Women's Studies but sometimes labeled Gender Studies. TWU has made a course in women's studies part of its general requirements; Wells College is considering doing the same. Such a requirement can ensure that the centrality of gender to higher education and other institutional spheres gets at least some academic attention during a student's college years.

Just as men's colleges assumed that their curricula did not need adjustment when women entered their institutions, most women's colleges assume the same. With the passage of time, however, students' preferences may change the amount of emphasis particular disciplines receive. So far, however, formerly women's colleges—including TWU, which historically has had a curriculum shaped around fields that mostly women enter—have not altered their academic programs in any particular ways.

Campus Life and Environment

Traditions are important to students. Ceremonies celebrating the founding and history of each women's college need to be continued when men become students, as they help remind people of the institution's original vision and cultural importance. Wells College, for instance, has recently revived the tradition of standing outside in a circle at the end of the convocation that opens the fall semester; all community members "pass the flame" of knowledge by lighting each other's candles and then sing the alma mater. Continuing this ceremony will be one way of connecting the "new" Wells with the former, all-women Wells.

All-women events and spaces should be considered. A well-funded, attractively housed women's resource center can provide women students with continued leadership opportunities as they develop libraries, organize conferences and symposia, and invite guests to campus to speak on topics that concern them, for example, eating disorders or acquaintance rape. Many colleges also retain campus clubs organized by and for special groups of women, for instance, a black women's society, and continue the option of women-only dorms. Women's special needs for safety should be acknowledged as they have at Girton by distributing rape alarms and offering self-defense classes. Events that are particularly relevant to women can reserve special times for women only. During a week's exhibition to celebrate fifty years of women getting Cambridge University degrees, for example, one evening at Girton was specified women-only.

Sports for women need continued support and expansion. A frequent complaint of women at institutions where men are admitted is that only then are sports facilities improved. It may be inevitable that as colleges seek to attract men and anticipate larger enrollments and better finances, they enhance their physical plants. And yet women need to have concrete reassurance that the improvements are for them too. Renovating women's locker rooms, for example, might well be undertaken at the same time that ones for men are established. The addition of new women's sports teams when teams for men are getting under way should also be considered.

In general, colleges should continue to celebrate women's lives, visually and in college publications, since women have been their historical focus. To make themselves welcoming to men students, some formerly women's colleges have succumbed to the temptation to appear to be a "regular" coeducational college. An examination of college Web sites, for example, reveals variation in how obvious colleges' histories as women's colleges are. Wheaton College makes its history clear in the common "about [the college]" section; in the second paragraph it mentions that it was founded as a female seminary and that it was a women's institution for 150 years before becoming coeducational. In its overall description of athletics, it has a photo of women playing soccer. In contrast, Goucher College, which admitted men at about the same time as Wheaton, makes its history as a women's college harder to see. Under "Welcome," for example, the Goucher Web site mentions that the college has been open to "people" since 1885. TWU's mission statement, easy to reach under its "about" section, states clearly that it "empowers and affirms the full development of students, primarily women."

Personnel

A commitment to gender equity requires that colleges pay attention to gender ratios. With the exception of Girton College at Cambridge University, gender ratio among students has not been a problem—men do not become anywhere near the majority of students at formerly women's colleges. But gender ratios among faculty, administrators, and trustees need to be monitored as colleges attempt to meet the needs of their new men students. Moreover, it is not just numbers that matter. A commitment to equity requires careful hiring and conscious attempts to socialize new community members to the college's ethos. While many of the current generation of faculty and administrators have matured during a period of feminist consciousness, this may not continue to be the case. Materials for transmitting information about the college's history, goals, and concerns about equity would be useful to develop. In addition, periodic workshops, perhaps as part of new faculty's orientation, should contain instruction about "chilly climate" issues—how to recognize and deal with male dominance in the classroom.

As the foregoing considerations indicate, placing gender equity concerns at the forefront of any institution, in combination with commitments to diversity of race, sexual identity, and social class, requires work. Formerly women's colleges are well placed to contribute to this meritocratic ideal, but faculty, administrators, and students need to be vigilant if they are to be successful in preventing male dominance and other forms of inequity from resurfacing.

Notes

1. See the summary of this literature in Leslie Miller-Bernal, *Separate by Degree: Women Students' Experiences in Single-Sex and Coeducational Colleges* (New York: Peter Lang, 2000), esp. chap. 7.

2. See Burton Bollage, "True to Their Roots—Catholic Women's Colleges, Appealing to a New Student Population, Rediscover Their Mission of Serving the Under Served," *Chronicle of Higher Education*, March 25, 2005, chronicle.com/weekly/v51/i29/29a02601.htm, for a description of changes at Trinity University in Washington, D.C., once considered "almost" a Seven Sisters college and now serving primarily black older women, most of whom are not Catholic and attend part-time in the evenings since they also are employed. A group of alumnae tried unsuccessfully in the mid-1990s to force Trinity back to its traditional mode by cutting off donations.

3. Julie L. Nicklin, "Fund Gives Spelman College Stock Valued at $37-Million," *Chronicle of Higher Education*, May 13, 1992, chronicle.com/prm/che-data/articles.dir/articles-38.dir/issue-36.dir/36a03201.htm, accessed July 10, 2005.

4. The exception to this is Girton at Cambridge University, where men students have predominated in some years for the reasons discussed in Chapter 12 and mainly to do with the overwhelming prestige of being at Cambridge in any college.

5. For examples of studies that show male dominance in classrooms, see David A. Karp and William C. Yoels, "The College Classroom: Some Observations on the Meanings of Student Participation," *Sociology and Social Research* 60 (1975): 421–39; and Sarah Hall Sternglanz and Shirley Lyberger-Ficek, "Sex Differences in Student-Teacher Interactions in the College Classroom," *Sex Roles* 3 (1977): 345–52. A study conducted at Vassar that does not show these results is Anne Constantinople, Randolph Cornelius, and Janet Gray, "The Chilly Climate: Fact or Artifact?" *Journal of Higher Education* 59 (1988): 527–50.

6. A recent study, unfortunately not dated, makes the point that minority students have not fared as well as white students at women's colleges. They report fewer interactions with faculty and less interpersonal support, and consequently are not as satisfied as white students. See Paul D. Umbach, Jillian L. Kinzie, Auden D. Thomas, Megan M.

Palmer, and George D. Kuh, "Women Students at Coeducational and Women's Colleges: How Do Their Experiences Compare?" National Survey of Student Engagement, Indiana University Center for Postsecondary Research.

7. Some studies on the greater homophobia of men include Sheela Raja and Joseph P. Stokes, "Assessing Attitudes toward Lesbians and Gay Men: The Modern Homophobia Scale," *International Journal of Sexuality and Gender Studies* 3 (1998): 113–34; Gregory M. Herek, "Heterosexuals' Attitudes toward Bisexual Men and Women in the United States," *Journal of Sex Research* 39 (2002): 264–74.

APPENDIX 1

Statement of Six Past Presidents of Formerly Women's Colleges, 2000

Exceptional Coed Colleges:
A New Model for Gender Equality

Background

In April 2000, Mary Patterson McPherson, Vice President of the Andrew W. Mellon Foundation, convened a meeting of presidents of selective women's colleges that had gone coed. The informal luncheon conversation was held at the Foundation offices in New York on April 5 to discuss current issues that were of interest to all of us. Dale Marshall had suggested to Pat that such a meeting would be useful knowing that she regularly convened gatherings of educators to reflect on shared concerns.

All of our colleges had gone coed 10 to 30 years earlier. We discussed what we had learned about creating a campus culture of gender equality for both men and women. We thought the lessons would be helpful to a wider range of institutions as they strive to become more hospitable to women and minorities.

As we talked about how the admission of men had changed our campus cultures, we were struck by how similar the changes were on all of our campuses. It was clear that what has emerged is a new model of gender equality, a third way that retains many of the empowering features for women of women's colleges but that also socializes men and women to respect each other as equals.

After the meeting in New York, the women college presidents decided to follow up by writing about the conversation at Mellon. We wrote the brief summary that follows to increase understanding of the value of the changes that have occurred. We also wanted to inspire other types of schools to learn from our experiences.

Frances Fergusson, President Vassar College, 1986–2006
Claire Gaudiani, President Connecticut College, 1988–2001
Dale Rogers Marshall, President Wheaton College, 1992–2004
Judith Jolley Mohraz, President Goucher College, 1994–2000
Michele Tolela Myers, President Sarah Lawrence College, 1998–
Jamiene S. Studeley, President Skidmore College, 1999–2003

Higher education is about nothing if not about opening doors and our colleges—six formerly all-women's liberal arts colleges—are experts at opening doors. With the founding of these institutions, women embarked on lives women had never imagined before. A century later, we began opening our doors to men, and the colleges that set the standard for women's education began setting a new standard for coeducation where both men and women are equal partners in learning and where there is no chilly climate for either women or men. In the past year, a number of our colleges have marked significant anniversary milestones as coeducational institutions, an appropriate time to celebrate our successes and reflect on the lessons for higher education.

Time has made it clear that the decision to become coeducational has worked extremely well for Connecticut College, Goucher, Sarah Lawrence, Skidmore, Vassar and Wheaton. We are all significantly stronger institutions today than at the time of our highly publicized, and in some cases loudly protested, transformations. Our gender ratios are close to those of most other coeducational institutions, including those which were formerly all men. Our application numbers are strong—in many cases at an all-time high, with SAT scores and other quantifiable quality measures higher than they've ever been. Importantly, our schools offer a model of gender equality that is different from any other type of institution and that can provide lessons about the face of the future, lessons about how to become more inclusive without losing traditional values.

The Coed Controversy

The decisions to go coed were not easy ones. Alumnae can still remember where they were when they heard the news. Many mobilized to protest the decision; others rallied to the defense, feeling that coeducation was long overdue.

Trustees felt the weight of responsibility for their institutions' futures. The demographic picture showed declining numbers of female high school graduates expressing interest in women's colleges. Sarah Lawrence made its decision in 1968, Vassar and Connecticut in 1969. The coincident decision by men's colleges, including Harvard, Princeton, and Yale, to admit women created a dramatic domino effect. While some women's colleges decided to remain single sex, others saw the issue as one of survival.

In some cases trustees considered merging with men's colleges and relocating campuses. In others, they considered the extreme action of abandoning the undergraduate, residential liberal-arts mission for non-traditional and vocational revenue-generating programs. Long and intense study and discussion, sometimes using very participative processes, led to the conclusion in all of our cases that the best option for our long-term well-being was that of coeducation—but on our own terms, as mistresses of our own houses. Skidmore admitted men in the early 70's, and Goucher and Wheaton in the late 80's, having learned from the earlier experiences.

The Coed Success

The overriding fear of the opponents of coeducation was that once men were admitted, they would dominate the classroom and the campus and diminish the supportive culture which enabled women to become strong and independent. Many thought the schools would lose their distinctiveness, their whole rationale for being. Many had difficulty conceptualizing a culture that would be equally welcoming to and supportive of both women and men.

These fears were intensified as faculty and staff consciously worked to make their campuses welcoming to men. Advocates for women's equality had long been critical of the approach of men's colleges to admitting women, saying that "you can't just add women and stir." They meant it was not fair to admit women without making accommodations to women's needs. Our six colleges, each in its own way, were committed to taking affirmative actions to recruit men and make accommodations that would be welcoming to men. For example, when Connecticut College admitted male students, the faculty was approximately 75 percent female. To provide role models for male students, male professors were so actively pursued that by the mid 1980's the ratios were virtually reversed. Certainly no formerly male institution transformed its faculty in the opposite direction! On the other hand, Vassar actually had more male professors proportionally before coeducation and added more women faculty throughout the 1970s and 1980s. Now the faculty gender balance is approximately 50/50.

Admission materials had to be adjusted to reflect a coeducational campus, and new facilities were required to meet the changing needs of the student body, for women as well as men. On many of our campuses, for example, you will find excellent athletic facilities not only to meet the needs of strong male and female varsity and club teams, but also of fitness for all students.

Extracurricular and social activities are richer than ever, with the weekend exodus common to some of our campuses a thing of the far-distant past. Leadership is in most cases shared equally by women and men, as is classroom participation. No, the men have not taken over.

It's worth noting that none of our colleges has added sororities or fraternities. This may be why we have a less "cliquish" ethos that is "kinder, gentler" than other campuses. None of the colleges added football, either, despite some critics who claimed that a gender balance would be impossible without it. Our colleges made sports important for both sexes. These decisions about Greek organizations and sports have been critical perhaps to our distinctive culture. Coeducation for us means relationships between men and women not based on old stereotypes.

Lessons

To be perfectly clear, we believe that women's colleges contribute much to the wide range of choices that make U.S. higher education the envy of the world. We do claim, however, that our institutions offer an important alternative to women's colleges and also to other coeducational institutions without our distinctive values.

When people visit our campuses they feel the difference right away. We have a cooperative, collaborative culture that keeps the best values of the women's colleges and makes them available to both women and men. As one prospective student observed, "you have the best of both worlds here."

While many of the societal barriers women traditionally faced have been reduced, there are in many coeducational institutions the often subtle and not so subtle obstacles to women's full achievement. One dramatic obstacle is the often glaring absence of women in positions of authority. This is not a problem at our institutions. All of our colleges have women presidents in the year 2000. And on our campuses more women are senior faculty and upper-level administrators—and comprise a very strong presence on our trustee boards. Goucher College for example has a faculty where 60 percent are women. These women teach in all different disciplines, further breaking down the myths that women cannot succeed in fields such as science and math—and yet, at the same time, these women become mentors for young men while serving as mentors for women.

At President Studley's inauguration, President Judith Shapiro of Barnard said, Skidmore's history "as a women's college has been helpful to the achievement of true coeducation. Women's colleges are, after all, institutions with a history of gender equity on the faculty, of having both women and men in positions of administrative responsibilities, and on the Board of Trustees."

What is also different is that a particular kind of feminism is knit into the fabric of each of these six institutions—in the voices of those present on campus, in graduates around the world, and in the collective colleges' histories. Our successful graduates are predominantly female—and they are incredible role models for both genders in their contributions in every possible field. Many of them were pioneers and so teach our current students the most compelling aspects of risk-taking—lessons that make potential venture capitalists and dot com entrepreneurs sit up and take note.

Why would men choose colleges with these values? For the same reasons women do. They want an excellent faculty committed to teaching in a face-to-face learning community where students get individualized faculty attention. They value the same program strengths women value. They want a campus where they can have leadership opportunities. They like a campus that values equal opportunity for women and for men. They know that the world has changed and that they will undoubtedly be working in organizations with high-achieving women as well as men. They want to live in a world where men and women work shoulder to shoulder, neither gaining power at the expense of the other. They know that learning to respect each other will be a plus, on a par at least with computer skills and the ability to speak a foreign language.

As one young man, now an alumnus, wrote in the Vassar student newspaper, " . . . on a deeper level, it is not about men at Vassar anymore than it is about women at Vassar, or anywhere else. It is about individuals, about learning something of quality, about the person next to you . . . It's about reading the territory of fellow humans instead of the obsolete map of categories . . . What does it mean to talk about men at Vassar? Nothing. So relax . . ."

When a Wheaton College alumnus was interviewed for a job by a male interviewer, he was asked, "How will it be for you to have a woman supervisor?" He smiled and said that was no a problem because he went to Wheaton, where men quickly learned to respect women.

Our greatest contribution to gender equality may, in fact, be that for most of our students the "issue" of coeducation is no longer an issue at all. And, if we've been able to leave that behind, it's largely because our transitions were successful and we are busy fulfilling our mission: Educating a talented and independent group of students, men and women, who will take their mutual respect, confidence and strength with them into the world.

APPENDIX 2

List of Women's Colleges in Spring 2005 and Some Summary Characteristics

Table 1

Institution	Location
Agnes Scott College	Atlanta, Ga.
Alverno College	Milwaukee, Wis.
Barnard College	New York, N.Y.
Bay Path College	Longmeadow, Mass.
Bennett College	Greensboro, N.C.
Blue Mountain College	Blue Mountain, Miss.
Brenau University	Gainesville, Ga.
Bryn Mawr College	Bryn Mawr, Pa.
Carlow College	Pittsburgh, Pa.
Cedar Crest College	Allentown, Pa.
Chatham College	Pittsburgh, Pa.
College of New Rochelle (Arts & Sciences)	New Rochelle, N.Y.
College of Notre Dame	Baltimore, Md.
College of Saint Benedict/Saint John's	Saint Joseph, Minn.
College of Saint Elizabeth	Morristown, N.J.
College of Saint Mary	Omaha, Neb.
College of St. Catherine	St. Paul, Minn.
Columbia College	Columbia, S.C.
Converse College	Spartanburg, S.C.
Georgian Court College	Lakewood, N.J.
Hollins University	Roanoke, Va.
Judson College	Marion, Ala.
Lesley University[a]	Cambridge, Mass.
Lexington College	Chicago, Ill.

Mary Baldwin College	Staunton, Va.
Marymount College (Fordham Univ.)[b]	Bronx, N.Y.
Meredith College	Raleigh, N.C.
Midway College	Midway, Ky.
Mills College	Oakland, Calif.
Moore College of Art & Design	Philadelphia, Pa.
Mount Holyoke College	South Hadley, Mass.
Mount Mary College	Milwaukee, Wis.
Mount St. Mary's College	Los Angeles, Calif.
Peace College	Raleigh, N.C.
Pine Manor College	Chestnut Hill, Mass.
Randolph-Macon Woman's College	Lynchburg, Va.
Regis College	Weston, Mass.
Rosemont College	Rosemont, Pa.
Russell Sage College	Troy, N.Y.
St. Joseph College	West Hartford, Conn.
St. Mary-of-the-Woods College	Saint Mary-of-the-Woods, Ind.
Saint Mary's College	Notre Dame, Ind.
Salem College	Winston-Salem, N.C.
Scripps College	Claremont, Calif.
Simmons College	Boston, Mass.
Smith College	Northampton, Mass.
Spelman College	Atlanta, Ga.
Stephens College	Columbia, Mo.
Stern College (part of Yeshiva University)	New York, N.Y.
Sweet Briar College	Sweet Briar, Va
Trinity University	Washington, D.C.
University of Denver, Women's Weekend Coll.	Denver, Colo.
Ursuline College	Pepper Pike, Ohio
Wellesley College	Wellesley, Mass.
Wells College[a]	Aurora, N.Y.
Wesleyan College	Macon, Ga.
Wilson College	Chambersburg, Pa.

[a] Admitted men in the fall of 2005.

[b] Will close in June 2007.

Table 2

Institution	% of part-time students
St. Mary-in-the-Woods	72
College of Notre Dame	61
Cedar Crest	50
Wilson College	50
Mount Mary	48
Carlow	45
Trinity	45
College of St. Elizabeth	44
Chatham	42
Rosemont	40
Ursuline	40
Alverno	38
Midway	37
College of St. Catherine	35
Georgian Court	35
College of Saint Mary	33
Mary Baldwin College	30
Saint Joseph	29
Mount St. Mary	25
Regis	25
Blue Mountain	22
Columbia College	22
Meredith College	22
Salem	20
Stephens	20
Wesleyan	20

Sources: The list of women's colleges is based on www.univsource.com/womens.htm, eliminating those institutions that are not independent of the larger university. Part-time enrollment figures were obtained from www.usnews.com.

Contributors

Dorothy M. Brown is professor emerita of history and former provost of Georgetown University. She also served as interim president of the College of Notre Dame of Maryland.

Elizabeth A. Daniels, professor emerita of English on the Helen D. Lockwood Chair, has served Vassar College since 1948 as professor of English, dean of freshmen, dean of studies, and acting dean of the faculty. Vassar College historian since 1985, she was pivotally involved in Vassar's move to coeducation. A Victorian scholar, with a special interest in women, she has recently published an online Vassar College encyclopedia.

Frances D. Graham is the associate vice chancellor for student affairs at North Carolina Central University, Durham. Her doctorate is from University of Illinois at Urbana-Champaign where she was a student in the Educational Policy Studies Department. She has taught feminist studies at North Carolina State University and Duke University.

Clyde Griffen, professor emeritus of American history on the Lucy Maynard Salmon Chair, taught at Vassar for thirty-five years. He coauthored, with Sally Griffen, *Natives and Newcomers* (1978) in the Harvard Urban History Series and coedited, with Mark C. Carnes, *Meanings for Manhood* (1990). In recent years he has written about working-class suburbs in Dunedin, New Zealand, and he is collaborating with geographer Harvey K. Flad on a book about two centuries of landscape and social change in the Poughkeepsie, New York, urban region.

Leslie Miller-Bernal, professor of sociology, has been teaching at Wells College since 1975. Her two previous books, *Separate by Degree: Women Students' Experiences in Single-Sex and Coeducational College* (2000) and, with Susan L. Poulson, *Going Coed: Women's Experiences in Formerly Men's Colleges and Universities, 1950–2000*, address gender and higher education, particularly the differences between single-sex education and coeducation.

Prudence A. Moylan, a Mundelein College alumna (1963) and faculty member (1966–91), joined the history faculty at Loyola University Chicago in 1991. She is the coeditor of *Mundelein Voices: The Women's College Experience, 1930–1991* (2001). Her current research focuses on the history of women in peacemaking.

Sister Eileen O'Dea, SSND, is vice president for mission and former vice president of planning at the College of Notre Dame of Maryland in Baltimore. Her research interests are religious congregations of women involved in the education of girls and women on the secondary and collegiate levels.

Susan L. Poulson is professor of history at the University of Scranton, where she teaches the history of American women and twentieth-century American history. Her previous book, along with Leslie Miller-Bernal, *Going Coed: Women's Experiences in Formerly Men's Colleges and Universities, 1950–2000*, reviewed the transition to coeducation at men's colleges.

Alan R. Sadovnik is professor of education and sociology at Rutgers University, Newark, New Jersey. He received the Willard Waller Award in 1993 from the American Sociological Association's Sociology of Education Section for the outstanding article published in the field, and American Educational Studies Association Critics Choice Awards in 1995 for *Knowledge and Pedagogy*, and (with coeditor Susan Semel) in 2000 for *"Schools of Tomorrow," Schools of Today: What Happened to Progressive Education* and in 2002 for *Founding Mothers and Others: Women Educational Leaders during the Progressive Era*.

Claire L. Sahlin is an associate professor and the director of women's studies at Texas Women's University, where she teaches courses on feminist pedagogy, social ethics, and women's studies in religion. She is the author of *Birgitta of Sweden and the Voice of Prophecy* (2001), a study of the religious authority of a controversial, charismatic visionary of the fourteenth century. Her publications also include "Vital to the Mission and Key to Survival: Women's Studies at Women's Colleges" in the *NWSA Journal* (Summer 2005).

Susan F. Semel is professor of education at the City College of New York and the CUNY Graduate Center. Among her publications are *The Dalton School: The Transformation of a Progressive School* (1992) and, with co-editor Alan R. Sadovnik, *"Schools of Tomorrow," Schools of Today: What Happened to Progressive Education* (1999) and *Founding Mothers and Others: Women Educational Leaders during the Progressive Era* (2002).

Marianne Sheldon received her Ph.D. from the University of Michigan. She is currently associate provost for graduate studies and professor of history at Mills College, where she teaches history courses on American women, children and childhood, the American South, the American city, and history of immigration to the United States. She was teaching at Mills at the time of the coed strike in 1990.

Andrea Walton is associate professor at Indiana University, Blooming-ton, where she teaches in the History of Education and Higher Education and Student Affairs Programs. Her publications have focused on women's leadership in national organizations and on the contributions of women scholars, administrators, and donors to paradigm-setting academic insti-tutions. She is editor of *Women and Philanthropy in Education* (2005) and is completing a book on the history of women and institutional de-velopment at Barnard College and Columbia University

Index

Page references in *italics* indicate tables.